Cornell Studies in Classical Philology

EDITED BY

*Frederick M. Ahl, Kevin Clinton, John E. Coleman, N. Gregson Davis,
Judith R. Ginsburg, G. M. Kirkwood, Gordon R. Messing, Phillip Mitsis,
Alan J. Nussbaum, Pietro Pucci, Jeffrey S. Rusten,
Danuta R. Shanzer, Winthrop Wetherbee*

VOLUME LI

The Mask of Comedy:
Aristophanes and the Intertextual Parabasis
by Thomas K. Hubbard

A Poetics of Transformation:
Prudentius and Classical Mythology
by Martha A. Malamud

Epicurus' Ethical Theory:
The Pleasures of Invulnerability
by Phillip Mitsis

The Rhetoric of Imitation: Genre and Poetic Memory
in Virgil and Other Latin Poets
by Gian Biagio Conte, edited by Charles Segal

Seneca's *Hercules Furens:*
A Critical Text with Introduction and Commentary
by John G. Fitch

From Myth to Icon:
Reflections of Greek Ethical Doctrine in Literature and Art
by Helen F. North

Odysseus Polutropos:
Intertextual Readings in the *Odyssey* and the *Iliad*
by Pietro Pucci

THE TOWNSEND LECTURES

Artifices of Eternity: Horace's Fourth Book of Odes
by Michael C. J. Putnam

Socrates, Ironist and Moral Philosopher
by Gregory Vlastos

The Mask of Comedy

ARISTOPHANES AND THE
INTERTEXTUAL PARABASIS

Thomas K. Hubbard

Cornell University Press

Ithaca and London

First published 1991 by Cornell University Press.

International Standard Book Number 0-8014-2564-6
Library of Congress Catalog Card Number 91-11953
Printed in the United States of America
Librarians: Library of Congress cataloging information
appears on the last page of the book.

♾ The paper in this book meets the minimum requirements
of the American National Standard for Information Sciences—
Permanence of Paper for Printed Library Materials, ANSI Z39.48-1984.

Contents

Preface

Recent criticism of Greek drama has been stimulated by a renewed interest in the genre's social, religious, institutional, and educational context. Concern with the social function of drama ultimately goes back to the work of the Cambridge anthropologists, who early in this century undertook to view drama in terms of its ritual origins as a vehicle of social integration. Although this approach has long been out of favor, the influence of structural anthropology in recent decades has led to a broader interest in seeing literary forms as social constructs not limited to ritual, but socially determined both in their performative execution and in their underlying content. During the 1980s this hermeneutic program has been intensified by a resurgence of academic interest in Marxist literary theory, seeing literary works as reflections of social conflict and disequilibrium, particularly in the areas of race, gender, and class.

These various approaches offer much that is particularly helpful to the student of Attic Old Comedy—a socially engaged literary form if there ever was one. Over forty years ago Victor Ehrenberg wrote a "sociology of Old Attic Comedy" based on Aristophanes in a work that is still of great value not only to Aristophanists but to the social historian as well. But there are also dangers in this direction of emphasis. The extremes of the Cambridge anthropologists are by now familiar, but on some scholarly questions, such as the Old Comic parabasis, their false assumptions have continued to exert a lingering influence. The chief danger that sociological interpretations may face, however, is the temptation to view the literary work and literary taste within an overly rigid framework of social determination. Oral performance is sometimes treated as if it excluded textual sophistication and allusive depth, and the Dionysian context of dramatic performance is sometimes viewed as a guarantee of the drama's adherence to Athenian state ideology, as if such a monolithic entity had ever existed in fifth-century Athens. The age of Aristophanes was particularly one of accelerating intellectual and social fragmentation in which it was possible to give public expression to a wide range of attitudes. Although it is a matter of great interest to study the manifestation of these conflicts within Attic comedy, as anthropology and social history can help us do, it is a mistake to think that Aristophanes' work was strictly determined and regulated by social pressures or to suppose that he did not in fact have ample latitude as to which themes he would treat and how. As we know not only from Aristophanes' case, but even from as early a poet as Phemius in Book I of the *Odyssey,* poets did not always give the audience exactly what it wanted to hear.

My own approach to Aristophanes, therefore, insists on treating the poet not as a passive transmitter of social realia, but as a creative individual who is as much at war with his social environment as he is inevitably a part of it. Through his parabases Aristophanes invites us to see himself in this very way. Indeed, Greek tradition discussed its own poetry not primarily in terms of how it reflected the social situation of its time, but in terms of its being the work of a certain identifiable poet with a visible personality and audible poetic voice. Where necessary, poetic personalities would be invented to give the poetry an identity—Orpheus, Aesop, Homer, Theognis—or extensive fictional biographies would be invented to flesh out poetic figures whose private lives were otherwise little known—Sappho, Simonides, Euripides. That even dramatic poetry was popularly viewed as the reflection of a distinct ethical personality with individual concerns and idiosyncrasies is well attested by the presentation of Aeschylus and Euripides in the *Frogs* and of Agathon and Euripides in the *Thesmophoriazusae.* The idea of a distinct poetic personality has deep roots, going back to the traditions of early Greek monodic and even choral poetry, in which the first person can articulate a strong voice and persona that occupies a unique niche within the social environment.

Of course there are dangers in the biographical approach as well. The follies of the ancient *Vita* tradition are well known, and even what the poets themselves tell us cannot always be trusted. Indeed much of Aristophanes' comedy centers around popular misunderstandings of prominent intellectual figures such as Socrates or Euripides or even Aristophanes himself.

What is needed in criticism of an author like Aristophanes is clearly a refined synthesis of the social and biographical approaches that treats the work as a confrontation or nexus between the author and society, appropriately weighing various levels of social circumstance and individual poetic reformulation of those circumstances and suitably articulating the dynamic tension between social demands and authorial intentionality. Where much socially oriented criticism goes wrong is in failing to penetrate the poet's ironic stance toward his audience and social circumstances; where much biographically oriented criticism errs is in failing to appreciate that the poet's ironic self-image and dissonance with society are themselves part of a socially constructed role. The paradox of Aristophanes' comic art is its simultaneous announcement of its proud refusal to be subservient to its audience and its pursuit of that same audience's favor.

The present book is founded on the perception that the Old Comic parabasis provides the central point of access to the complex and manifold ironies of the comic poet's relation to his audience, to the social themes of his drama, and to society as a whole. Far from being a marginal digression or a vestigial relic of some long-forgotten ritual, as has often been assumed, the parabasis, I shall argue, is precisely the nexus between poet, chorus, dramatic characters, and polis that gives us critical insight into the drama's articulation of meaning. The parabasis both reveals and problematizes the identity of poet and chorus, both reflects and deconstructs the drama that surrounds it and the society that surrounds the drama. My interpretation of Aristophanes therefore begins by viewing each play through the prism of its parabasis, but moves to a broader understanding of both the play and the Aristophanic corpus from that starting point. The polymorphic rhetorical subterfuges and ambiguous character of Aristophanes' texts, particularly his parabatic texts, make it difficult for us to feel with certainty that we have recovered from them the historical Aristophanes or even the historical Athens, but we can with a fair degree of confidence succeed in reconstructing the complex and fascinating interaction between "Aristophanes" and "Athens."

In the course of my work on this book, I have over the last thirteen years accumulated many debts of gratitude. Chief among them is that for a fellowship from the National Endowment for the Humanities during 1987–88, as well as that for a partial leave from teaching during the spring semester of 1987, made possible by the Townsend Fund of the Department of Classics at Cornell University; it was this year-and-a-half period that afforded me the opportunity to write most of the book. In addition I was assisted by a research fellowship from the

University Research Institute of the University of Texas for summer 1989 when I undertook final work on the manuscript, and by travel grants awarded through the Faculty Research Committee of Skidmore College during 1982–83 when I was embarking on the first stages of the project. Acknowledgment is also to be made to the University of California Press for permission to reprint portions of my article "Parabatic Self-Criticism and the Two Versions of Aristophanes' *Clouds*" (originally published in *Classical Antiquity* 5 [1986]: 182–97) in chapter 5, and to the State University of New York Press for permission to reprint portions of my essay "Old Men in the Youthful Plays of Aristophanes" (originally appearing in T. M. Falkner & J. de Luce, eds., *Old Age in Greek and Latin Literature* [Albany, 1989], 90–113) in chapters 3, 4, and 6. All translations in this work are my own, unless otherwise footnoted.

I owe a primary personal debt to Jeffrey Henderson, *vir Aristophaneus,* for encouraging this project from its inception as an idea and for rendering valuable assistance at multiple stages since. Many other individuals have helped in various ways, both large and small, among whom I particularly thank Fred Ahl, Carl Anderson, David Armstrong, Tom Cole, David Dean-Jones, Greg Dobrov, Sir Kenneth Dover, Tom Falkner, Michael Gagarin, Karl Galinsky, Simon Goldhill, Deborah MacInnes, Tim Moore, Greg Nagy, Piero Pucci, Kenneth Reckford, Bernd Seidensticker, and Steve White. I am grateful also to the late Jack Winkler. I also thank Alan Nussbaum and Bernhard Kendler for ensuring the book's receipt of fair and prompt consideration by Cornell University Press and the Cornell Studies in Classical Philology series. Finally I express my gratitude to the Department of Classics at Cornell for providing the congenial atmosphere necessary to my writing the book during the period 1986–88 when it was my chief focus of attention. I will always regard this period as a pleasant interlude in my scholarly *Wanderjahre*. This book is in every sense a Cornell study, and I am very happy for it to be included in the department's distinguished monograph series.

Thomas K. Hubbard

Austin, Texas

Abbreviations

A&A	*Antike und Abendland*
AAntHung	*Acta Antiqua Hungarica*
AC	*L' Antiquité Classique*
AJP	*American Journal of Philology*
APF	*Archiv für Papyrusforschung*
ASNP	*Annali della Scuola Normale Superiore di Pisa, Classe di Lettere e Filosofia*
BSA	*Annual of the British School at Athens*
CA	*Classical Antiquity*
CJ	*Classical Journal*
CP	*Classical Philology*
CQ	*Classical Quarterly*
CR	*Classical Review*
G&R	*Greece and Rome*
GB	*Grazer Beiträge*
GRBS	*Greek, Roman and Byzantine Studies*
HCT	A. W. Gomme, A. Andrewes, and K. J. Dover, *A Historical Commentary on Thucydides* (Oxford, 1945–81)
HSCP	*Harvard Studies in Classical Philology*
ICS	*Illinois Classical Studies*
JHS	*Journal of Hellenic Studies*
LCM	*Liverpool Classical Monthly*
LÉC	*Les Études Classiques*
MH	*Museum Helveticum*
MLQ	*Modern Language Quarterly*
NJbPP	*Neue Jahrbücher für Philologie und Pädagogik*
PCA	*Proceedings of the Classical Association*
PCG	R. Kassel and C. Austin, *Poetae Comici Graeci* (Berlin, 1983–)

PP	*La Parola del Passato*
QS	*Quaderni di Storia*
QUCC	*Quaderni Urbinati di Cultura Classica*
RE	G. Wissowa, ed., *Paulys Real-Encyclopädie der classischen Alter-tumswissenschaft* (Stuttgart, 1893–)
RÉA	*Revue des Études Anciennes*
RÉG	*Revue des Études Grecques*
RFIC	*Rivista di Filologia e Istruzione Classica*
RhM	*Rheinisches Museum*
RPh	*Revue de Philologie*
SCO	*Studi Classici e Orientali*
SIFC	*Studi Italiani di Filologia Classica*
SO	*Symbolae Osloenses*
SPAW	*Sitzungsberichte der Preussischen Akademie der Wissenschaften*
TAPA	*Transactions of the American Philological Association*
UCPCP	*University of California Publications in Classical Philology*
WJA	*Würzburger Jahrbücher für die Altertumswissenschaft*
WS	*Wiener Studien*
YCS	*Yale Classical Studies*
ZPE	*Zeitschrift für Papyrologie und Epigraphik*

The Mask of Comedy

CHAPTER 1

Comedy and Self-Knowledge

The phenomenon of the self-referential parabasis is unique to Attic Old Comedy, although it has various analogues in the traditions of European comic drama: one need only examine the prologues of Plautus and Terence, Jonson or Dryden to find many of the same apologetic topoi and attitudes that appear in Aristophanes' parabases.[1] But a prologue is by its nature a different entity, in a sense standing outside of the dramatic enactment. What is distinctive about the parabasis is its simultaneous digressiveness and integration with the dra-

---

1. The relation of the Old Comic parabasis to the prologues of New Comedy is quite clear. The fragment *De tragoedia et comoedia*, usually attributed to Donatus, distinguishes four types of prologues in New Comedy: (1) συστατικός, in which the play or poet is praised, (2) ἀναφορικός, in which adversaries are maligned or the audience flattered, (3) ὑποθετικός, wherein the play's plot is expounded, and (4) μικτός, mixed. The third is a characteristic function of the prologue in Old Comedy; the first two types rather reflect normal parabatic functions. Among Plautus' and Terence's prologues we find the author's self-defense against his competitors, particularly in regard to charges of improper borrowing and contamination (Ter., *Andr.* 1–27; *Heauton.* 1–34; *Eun.* 1–45; *Phor.* 1–34; *Adel.* 1–25); his appeal to the audience for its attention after neglecting the play's first performance (Ter., *Hec.* 1–57; cf. Aristophanes, *Nub.* 518–62); his praise of influential patrons (Ter., *Adel.* 15–21; cf. *Nub.* 528–32), and of the audience's wisdom (Pl., *Cas.* 1–33; cf. *Nub.* 520–35) as well as criticism of the audience for lack of wisdom (Pl., *Poen.* 1–45; cf. *Nub.* 575–94, *Vesp.* 1009–50); promises of divine benefaction in return for the audience's favor (Pl., *Amph.* 1–85; cf. *Nub.* 1115–30, *Av.* 1058–1117); his refusal to employ stock comic topoi (Pl., *Capt.* 52–68; cf. *Nub.* 537–44); and his general satire of social malefactors (Pl., *Rud.* 1–30; compare the epirrhemes of any Aristophanic parabasis). On Aristophanes' influence with specific reference to the Terentian prologue, see Ehrman 1985, 370–76, Arnott 1985, 1–7. While classicizing poets such as Jonson or Dryden were to some extent influenced by both Greek and Roman models, direct Aristophanic influence seems particularly clear in the case of Jonson (on which, see Appendix 2).

matic events; as we shall see in the course of our investigation, the comic poet's personal presence is not only foregrounded in the parabasis but can be felt throughout an Aristophanic drama, often through identification with the play's protagonist.

The literary provenance of the parabatic form in Greek comedy will be examined in the next chapter. The present chapter explores the generalized phenomenon of self-referential humor from a theoretical perspective: I argue that the parabasis came to play such a pivotal role in Old Comedy not only due to specific literary influences on its evolution as a form, but also because it gives focus within the framework of comic drama to some of the most basic wellsprings of humor. Its motivation and nature can thus be explained in psychological terms as well as in purely formal ones.

Alazōn, Eirōn, and the Comic Man

The idea that Comedy and humor are basically functions of self-perception is one that recurs throughout the history of critical theory on the comic. It is in fact the central hinge of Plato's brief discussion of Comedy in the *Philebus*, in which Socrates defines the "laughable" (τὸ γελοῖον) as the opposite of the Delphic injunction "know thyself" (48C–D). Socrates illustrates this comic lack of self-knowledge with the character types of the man who supposes himself richer than he actually is, more beautiful than he is, or more virtuous than he is (48D–E). There are obvious parallels here with the character of the *alazōn* or "boaster," which Aristotle later discusses in *EN* 4.7.[2] The *Philebus* dis-

---

2. The character type of the *alazōn* was already well established long before Plato and Aristotle. Together with its derivatives, it is common as a term of abuse in Old Comedy and Tragedy (*Phil.* 49B–C). That Xenophon and Plato both depict Socrates 1492; *Pax* 1045, 1121; *Av.* 825, 983, 1016; *Ran.* 280, 909, 919; Cratinus, fr. 375 PCG; Eupolis, fr. 157.2 PCG). Xenophon, *Mem.* 1.7, records a Socratic conversation advising his followers against *alazoneia* in terms that, along with the related definition in *Cyr.* 2.2.11–13, foreshadow Plato's treatment of the comic man in the *Philebus*. Xenophon's Cyrus defines the *alazōn* as a man who pretends to be richer and more courageous than he actually is or who in some other way promises what he is not capable of doing (*Cyr.* 2.2.12); and Xenophon's Socrates elaborates that the *alazōn* who is found out is merely a comic butt whereas the *alazōn* who is not recognized for what he is and attains a position of power can lead to tragic results (*Mem.* 1.7.2–3), thus anticipating Plato's division between weak and strong men who lack self-knowledge as the figures respectively of Comedy and Tragedy (*Phil.* 49B–C). That Xenophon and Plato both depict Socrates discussing *alazoneia* suggests that *alazoneia* may indeed have been a matter of interest to the Socratic circle: such a topic does not seem unlikely, given Socrates' characteristic role as the *eirōn* and elenchus of the city's many impostors who presumed to know more than they did (on Socratic irony, see now Vlastos 1987, 79–96). Platonic usage does not treat

cussion goes on to distinguish between strong men who lack such self-knowledge and are properly the objects of fear, and weak men lacking self-knowledge, who are laughable (49B–C):

> *Socrates:* All men who mindlessly imagine this false opinion about themselves, like all men in general, must either be accompanied by strength and power or by the opposite.
> *Protarchus:* It is necessary.
> *Socrates:* Accordingly divide them in this way: you will rightly call "laughable" all such men who are weak and incapable of avenging themselves. But those who are capable of avenging themselves you will most correctly denominate by calling them "fearful," "strong," and "hateful." The folly of strong men is hateful and shameful, for both it and its images are harmful to those who are nearby; but weak folly has won the place and nature of the laughable among us.

Strong men who lack self-knowledge can cause harm to those near them, whether in real life or in artistic representation;[3] weak men cannot, however, and are thus legitimately objects of the spectator's derision (φθόνος), without any danger of negative consequences to the spectator.

Commentators have generally supposed Plato's statements about Comedy here to reflect fourth-century comedy.[4] The doctrine of the comic as a deficiency of self-knowledge has consequently received little attention in connection with Aristophanes and Old Comedy. But however much Middle Comedy may have been less topical than Old Comedy (and I think the difference has been greatly exaggerated) the basic character types were continuous; there is, for instance, much of the Old Comic Lysistrata in the Middle Comic Praxagora. Clearly what Plato implies about comic types is evident in Aristophanes: we see old men acting as if they were young, the humble acting as if powerful, the morally confused cloaking themselves in the mantle of wisdom and virtue. Indeed it seems to be the very essence of the Aristophanic hero

---

alazōn as a technical term, regarding it mostly as a general synonym for "liar" or "deceiver" (see *Gorg.* 525A2, *Charm.* 173C5, *Lysis* 218D2, *Euthd.* 283C8, *Rep.* 560C2, *Hip. Min.* 369E4, 371A3, D2), but there can be no question that Plato and his audience were familiar with the concept of *alazoneia* as elaborated in both Old Comedy and the Socratic conversation(s) of Xenophon.

3. That Plato is here speaking of real life as well as its representations in literature is clear from the wording of 49C (ἄνοια γὰρ ἡ μὲν τῶν ἰσχυρῶν ἐχθρά τε καὶ αἰσχρά· βλαβερὰ γάρ καὶ τοῖς πέλας αὐτή τε καὶ ὅσαι εἰκόνες αὐτῆς εἰσίν) and 50B (μὴ τοῖς δράμασι μόνον ἀλλὰ καὶ τῇ τοῦ βίου ξυμπάσῃ τραγῳδίᾳ καὶ κωμῳδίᾳ).

4. See Apelt 1912, 149–50; Hackforth 1972, 93. However, for Plato's interest in Aristophanes, see Cooper 1922, 37–39.

to transcend his low condition and act out a fantasy of being someone
greater than he is. On the other hand Old Comedy also shows us self-
ignorant men who are powerful and fear-inspiring in real life (for
example, Cleon, Lamachus, the Proboulos of the *Lysistrata*) reduced to
the role of weak, harmless, confused, and hence properly comic figures. In their onstage helplessness we can truly see them mocked and
taunted by representatives of the average spectator and his *phthonos*, as
Lamachus is by Dicaeopolis, Cleon by the Sausage seller, or Socrates by
Strepsiades. But the mocking characters also have their own forms of
self-ignorance that make them in turn a spectacle for the audience.[5] As
we shall see, the same is equally true, in a different way, of the chorus
and even of the poet himself as revealed in the parabasis.

Despite its relative neglect by modern critics the *Philebus* passage
was quite influential for Aristotle, who applies the division between
the self-ignorant man with power and the self-ignorant man without
power not to Tragedy and Comedy respectively, as Plato did, but
wholly to the tragic figure who, when powerful, evokes fear (compare
Plato's φοβερούς [*Philebus* 49B]) and, when bereft of power, evokes pity
(as opposed to Plato's comic *phthonos*).[6] But Aristotle is also influenced
by the *Philebus* in his definition of the "laughable" (τὸ γελοῖον)[7] and in
his identification of the primary comic character types.[8] As we have

5. Plato's discussion puts great emphasis on *phthonos* (not just "envy," but "malice")
as the dominant emotion of the comic spectator (see 48B, 49C–50A). *Phthonos* itself,
however, is not an attractive or praiseworthy emotion, and Plato associates it with the
"mixture of pain and pleasure" (48A, 49C, 50A—see Democritus, 68B88 D–K); on the
significance and centrality of *phthonos* here, see Milobenski 1964, 49–58. Indeed the
whole context of this discussion in the *Philebus* is devoted to proving that apparent
pleasures also involve pain and that pleasure cannot be the greatest good, as many men
assume. Inasmuch as the subject experiencing comic pleasure is unaware of the pain and
destructiveness involved, he too is self-ignorant, like the comic butt toward whose self-
ignorance he feels *phthonos*.
6. That Plato is hinting at a broader theory with application to both Tragedy and
Comedy is evident not only from the implied distinction between tragic and comic
figures in 49B–C but also from the explicit mention of Tragedy and Comedy in the
summarizing remarks of 50B. The influence of the *Philebus* passage on Aristotle's dramatic theory is explored in some detail by D. Armstrong, "Plato on the Tragic Flaw: The
Sources of Aristotle, *Poetics* 13" (unpublished essay). I believe the Platonic influence
helps us understand that Aristotle's famous definition of Tragedy means by φόβος more
than simply fear of external forces, as is usually assumed, but also fear of the tragic
character himself and his actions.
7. For Aristotle, as for Plato, the "laughable" is defined as a form of error and
ignorance (ἁμάρτημά τι καὶ αἶσχος [*Poet.* 1449a34–5]), distinguished from tragic *hamartia* by its connection with the "shameful" (αἶσχος) and by the important qualification that
it is "without pain or destruction" (ἀνώδυνον καὶ οὐ φθαρτικόν). This qualification is no
doubt connected with Aristotle's catharsis theory but may also be influenced by Plato's
idea of only weak and impotent men who are incapable of harming others being
"laughable."
8. That *alazōn* and *eirōn* were recognized by Aristotle as comic types is suggested by
their enumeration contiguous to the explicitly comic types of *EN* 4.8 (the *bomolochos* and

noted above, Plato's self-ignorant man, who supposes himself richer, more beautiful, or more virtuous than he actually is, is very much like Aristotle's *alazōn* or "boaster," who is "apt to claim the things that bring glory, when he does not have them, or to claim more of them than he has" (*EN* 4.7 1127a21–2). Yet Aristotle goes beyond Plato by opposing to the *alazōn* the figure of the *eirōn* or "ironic man," who pretends to less than he has. If irony takes the form of cynicism or ostentatious rejection of worldly wealth and values, Aristotle notes that it can itself become a form of boastfulness (1127b27–9). But irony can also be more virtuous if it is a mark of true modesty, as in the case of Socrates (1127b23–6).[9] Both *alazōn* and *eirōn* are characters who, in their different ways, present a public persona at radical variance from their true identities. Still, what for Plato was a purely negative phenomenon identified with lack of self-knowledge becomes something more complex and potentially more constructive in Aristotle; the figure of the *eirōn* offers a more positive alternative to the seemingly self-ignorant *alazōn* inasmuch as the *eirōn*, like Socrates, pretends to be ignorant though actually in a state of full intellectual cognizance.

Within a very different philosophical and aesthetic tradition, Hegel defines the comic in terms of a dialectic comparable to Aristotle's opposition of the *alazōn* and *eirōn*. For Hegel an event is comic when the agent pursues trivial aims in a serious manner, like the *alazōn*,[10] or serious aims in a trivial manner, like the *eirōn*.[11] Unlike Plato, however, Hegel insists on a certain self-consciousness of the comic character: to be comic rather than merely stupid he must be aware of the triviality of his aims or his manner, at once unable and unwilling to bring himself into a higher or more serious condition.[12] At the same time Hegel also

---

agroikos) with which they are also grouped in *EN* 2.7 and *Rhet.* 3.18; Aristotle's recognition is suggested also by their prominence in later tradition—not only Theophrastus' *Characters* (for the relation of which to Old Comedy, see Ussher 1977, 75–79), but also the *Tractatus Coislinianus*, which lists them along with the *bomolochos* as the primary comic character types. The term *alazōn* is frequently used in Comedy (see note 2 above) and is associated with laughter by Xenophon (*Mem.* 1.7.2, *Cyr.* 2.2.11). On these three types and their relevance to Old Comedy, see Cornford 1968, 119–21; Cooper 1922, 262–65; Janko 1984, 216–18.

9. On Aristotle's positive form of *eirōneia* and its relation to the Socratic model, see Gooch 1987, 95–104.

10. See the comparison of *alazoneia* to stylistic frigidity ("clothing small affairs with pomposity") in Demetrius, *Eloc.* 119.

11. Hegel 1920 IV, 303–4. Kierkegaard (1965, 265) defines irony in a similar way ("saying seriously what is facetious or saying facetiously what is serious"). In an earlier context (IV, 255–56), Hegel differentiates between Tragedy and Comedy on the basis that Tragedy resolves opposed powers externally and Comedy displays the contraries in a state of inner resolution within individual characters.

12. Hegel repeatedly emphasizes the importance of conscious intentionality in his definition of dramatic action (IV, 252) and of the comic (IV, 303); he also applies the

sees in comic characters an "imperturbable self-assurance which becomes all the more emphatic in proportion as they prove themselves incapable of carrying into effect that which they project";[13] one need think here only of Philocleon attempting to escape from his house or Strepsiades trying to master the subtleties of Socratic learning. Nevertheless it is difficult to reconcile this self-assurance of an unsuccessful character with self-knowledge in the Delphic sense Plato speaks of. What Hegel means by the comic character's self-awareness is rather a conscious self-satisfaction and refusal to behave other than he does. As such, Hegel sees in the comic character's self-consciousness a behavioral inelasticity that Bergson, like Plato, sees precisely as the sign of a mechanical lack of self-consciousness.[14]

The upshot of this theoretical ambivalence in Hegel's doctrine is that the comic character is in a sense both self-knowing and not so. He may appear self-knowing and be not truly so, similar to Plato's comic man or Aristotle's *alazōn*, or may appear to be self-ignorant though really being self-aware like the *eirōn*. In this sense Hegel sees the contraries in a state of inner resolution within the comic character.

We certainly find both types in Aristophanic comedy. Though most Aristophanic heroes are basically *alazōn*s who presume to a station higher than is properly theirs, they also have moments of *eirōneia;* one thinks, for instance, of Dicaeopolis pretending to be hoodwinked by the Megarian's disguised "piggies." At times a character's unabashed *alazoneia* may indeed be a necessary part of the act he puts on as an *eirōn,* as in the case of the Sausage seller who proudly boasts of his rascality and baseness only to be revealed at the end of the *Knights* as completely lacking in self-aggrandizing ambition and generally concerned with the good of the Demos; in fact the Demos himself turns out to have been playing the fool all along, actually quite aware of circumstances around him (see *Eq.* 1141–50). In the *Frogs* Dionysus, the god of dramatic illusion, alternates between *alazoneia* and *eirōneia,* first playing the role of a stronger god, Heracles, and later assuming the costume of his slave Xanthias.[15] This mutability of comic masks and personae is the very hallmark of Aristophanes' characters and

---

concept with specific reference to the comic self-awareness of characters in Aristophanes (IV, 328–29).

 13. Hegel 1920 IV, 329.

 14. See especially Bergson 1911, 16.

 15. This exchange of costumes is used by the anonymous Byzantine treatise *Peri Komoidias* (= XIb78–80 Koster) as an example of the comic effect produced by assimilation of characters from worse to better or from better to worse; although not using the terms *alazōn* and *eirōn,* the compiler, who draws heavily on the work of Tzetzes, is clearly referring to the same type of character transformation.

is what distinguishes their imaginative richness from the fixed one-dimensionality of Menander's type characters who are wholly *alazōn*s or *eirōn*s without qualification.

Nowhere are the postures of *alazoneia* and *eirōneia* more evident and nowhere is the question of self-knowledge more in the foreground than in the parabasis. The Birds' ornithocentric cosmogony (*Av.* 685–736) and the Old Men's reminiscences of erstwhile glory in the *Lysistrata* (*Lys.* 614–35) are among Aristophanes' masterpieces of *alazoneia* and false self-knowledge: the Old Men of the *Lysistrata* could not possibly be old enough to have participated in the events they describe, and the Birds are not at all aware of their divinity until persuaded of it a little earlier by Peisthetaerus. The boasting can also be tempered with elements of self-deprecatory irony: the Knights boast of their fathers but not as aristocrats. In the corresponding antepirrheme they devote similar praise to their horses and in *Eq.* 580 they beg the public's indulgence for their own soft manners. At times the parabasis can even provide a vehicle for introspection and self-recognition on the part of the chorus, as when the heretofore fearsome and swaggering old Acharnians come to perceive their actual weakness and helplessness in old age or when the still violent Wasps recognize opportunistic drones in their midst.

A more subtle interplay between *alazoneia* and *eirōneia*, as between self-knowledge and apparent self-ignorance, is evident in the poet's self-advertisements in the parabasis proper.[16] No Aristophanic character boasts more loudly than Aristophanes himself, whether in claiming responsibility for Cleon's downfall in the parabasis of the *Peace* or in claiming to be Athens' greatest national asset, known even to the Persian King, in the parabasis of the *Acharnians*. In the *Clouds* parabasis he boasts of not using theatrical devices he does in fact use in that very play, only there is a self-conscious irony behind the boasting: in the *Clouds* Aristophanes is actually highlighting his use of the much-deprecated comic topoi as a concession to popular taste, even while pretending not to use them. In the *Acharnians* his boast of world fame brings to our attention his lack of it, indeed, his relative obscurity behind the guise of his producer Callistratus; in the context of the *Acharnians* parabasis and its uninhibited bragging, the poet's pretense in his next parabasis (that of the *Knights*) to shyness and modest withdrawal from public attention can strike us only as consummate irony. Throughout his programmatic parabases Aristophanes treats serious

16. Dick (1974, 50) discusses the parabasis in these terms but is, I think, too one-dimensional in seeing the poet's and the chorus' stance strictly as one of *eirōneia*.

matters lightly, light matters seriously, and adopts a pose of profound self-ignorance when he is in fact profoundly aware of every nuance and wrinkle in his artfully modulated self-presentation.

Laughter as Self-Laughter

Classical theory on the nature of the comic emphasizes the psychology of the comic object, the person laughed at, as modern theory focuses on the comic subject, the person laughing. The subjective dimension of the comic process was certainly not unknown to the ancients, as is apparent from Plato's identification of *phthonos* as the spectator's dominant emotion, a combination of pleasure and pain (*Philebus* 48A–B, 50C–D). Although it is uncertain exactly how Aristotle applied this doctrine to Comedy, his catharsis theory also deals with the spectator's reaction to the dramatic spectacle.[17] The first subjective psychology of humor to be developed with any degree of complexity, however, is that of Thomas Hobbes who defines laughter in his *Essay on Human Nature* as "nothing but the sudden glory arising from sudden conception of some eminence in ourselves, by comparison with the infirmity of others, or with our own formerly."[18] Central to this definition is the matter of self-knowledge; only in this case it is a question of the spectator's self-knowledge rather than knowledge of a comic character. As in Plato's definition of laughter as *phthonos* or "malice," laughter can imply a consciousness of one's own superiority over a weak or stupid person. But Hobbes emphasizes that it can also imply consciousness of one's present superiority relative to one's own former state; an audience's appreciation of humor is thus a form of self-awareness, whether as a confident sense of superiority to others or as an introspective recognition of one's own conquered deficiencies.

The analogies between Hobbes's concept of laughter and that of Freudian psychoanalysis have been noted.[19] However, what Hobbes's insight perceives as conscious self-awareness becomes in psychoanaly-

---

17. The *Tractatus Coislinianus* speaks of a catharsis of "pleasure and laughter," but it is not clear why these emotions would need to be purged. Cooper (1922, 65–70) is more likely to be correct in seeing anger (*orgē*) and envy (*phthonos*) as the emotions purged by Comedy. The idea of "comic catharsis" bulks large in Reckford (1974, 41–69 and 1987, 53–69) who is doubtless right in applying the concept to Aristophanes in particular and to Comedy in general, though he means something rather different by it than Aristotle. See also Sutton 1980, 69–82. Olson (1968, 36) denies the relevance of catharsis to Comedy.

18. Hobbes 1839 III, 46.

19. See Kris 1952, 208; Bergler 1956, 4–5; Mauron 1964, 145–47.

sis just the opposite, an unconscious self-awareness; that is, an unconscious process wherein parts of the self and its infantile prehistory become identified with an object of derision. Freud's earliest work on the comic, *Wit and Its Relation to the Unconscious* (1906), presents the concept of "ideational mimicry": we laugh at the behavior of another by comparing it with what we would do in his place. Objects are comic if they expend more energy in physical motions than we would or less than we would in intellectual acts. In both cases laughter comes from a pleasurably conceived feeling of superiority. At the same time the feeling of superiority is accompanied by memory of an averted, superfluous anxiety over our own powers of mastery. On a level of mimetic projection, this infantile regression expresses the same tendency evident in child's play—namely, joyful repetition of an activity once perceived as dangerous but now functionally mastered and harmless.[20]

Whereas Freud's early theory of the comic was dominated by the concept of economy in psychic expenditure (i.e. laughter as a release of psychic energy dammed up in suppression or repression of some area which involves less effort in release than in continued blockage), his later essay "Humour" (1928) views the phenomenon in terms of intrapsychic dynamics (i.e. the relation between parts of the personality). In appreciating humor, not only do we recollect unconsciously our infantile anxieties of the past; we also on some level become aware of our infantile anxieties of the present. Freudians see the humorist's and the humor appreciator's attitude of superiority to the object of humor as a replication of the parental, authoritative superego in relation to the ego whose fears and concerns it dismisses as trivial and childlike.[21] By expelling these fears and concerns humor provides a means for the personality to assert its invulnerability to the real world and the real world's problems. Hence Freud's followers have found humor useful as a diagnostic tool in identifying areas of repressed anxiety[22] and have seen it even as a reaction to compulsive psychic masochism within the personality.[23]

Probably the most developed statement of this view is that of Freud's student Edmund Bergler. Bergler defines psychic masochism as the desire for rejection and defeat, with accompanying self-pity, and sees it as a fundamental fact of inner psychic life, with humor as a pseudo-

---

20. Freud 1938, 769–73; his remarks are extended and developed by Kris (1952, 209–11).

21. Freud 1928, 3–4.

22. See Brill 1940, 731–49; Zwerling 1955, 104–14.

23. See Winterstein 1934, 210–11; Dooley 1934, 50–57; Dooley 1941, 37–46; Brody 1950, 194; Bergler 1956, x–xii, 60–61.

aggressive alibi that attempts to deny and cover up this psychic masochism.[24] The butt of a joke is an artificially created masochistic surrogate, who is really a projection of the listener himself; the cruelty of the joke corresponds to the imagined cruelty of one's own parents and educators whose judgment is unconsciously enshrined in the superego. Most laughing matters thus involve outdistancing one's own psychic masochism by pointing to the comic butt and saying, "He is the masochistic one, not me." Having as the target of a joke an authority figure is particularly effective as a denial of psychic masochism, both as a mark of aggressiveness and as a denigration of the fear one formerly had in the face of the parental superego. An explicitly self-derisive joke functions as a preventive attack upon oneself to forestall the ridicule expected from others and particularly from the superego. Bergler builds on Freud's theory but invokes a much more complex model of intrapsychic relations; Freud localizes humor in the superego as an instrument for belittling the ego and its anxieties, but Bergler conceives it as the ego's instrument of self-defense against the superego, simultaneously denying and revealing the psychic masochism as itself an ego-response to the superego's unremitting inquisition.

I will not presume competence to judge the clinical validity of these competing intrapsychic models for the dynamics of the humor process. Yet it seems to me undeniable that humor appreciation as well as humor formation is based on some psychic identification between subject and object, however much the identification may be repressed on the conscious level. This psychological equivalence is readily apparent in Aristophanic comedy. Nowhere is this psychological doubling more evident than in the Sausage seller of the *Knights* who consciously professes to rival the Paphlagonian slave (= Cleon) in every form of baseness and projects his own image onto that of his comic target; the Sausage seller's mockery of the Paphlagon is in this way self-mockery, and his self-mockery is mockery of the Paphlagon. We can also see Aristophanes' protagonists mocking characters who represent former versions of themselves, as Dicaeopolis does when confronting the poor and helpless farmer, or as Strepsiades does when instructing his as-yet unenlightened creditors in the newly learned subtleties of his Socratic education.

But the most important psychological projections in Aristophanes are not those between characters so much as those of audience and author upon certain characters. Several main characters are emblematic of the common man though nevertheless funny to the common man in the audience; the audience could certainly identify itself with

24. Bergler 1956, x–xii, 46–47, 60–61, 75.

the sufferings as well as the foolishness of Demos, Strepsiades, Philocleon, Dicaeopolis, or of choruses such as the Acharnians and Wasps.
Aristophanes could equally project his own poetic personality onto
such of his characters as Dicaeopolis, the Sausage seller, Socrates,
Bdelycleon, Trygaeus, and still conceive them as funny and entertaining. As we shall see, the parabasis provides a focal point for the complex relations of identification and projection that occur between author, audience, and comic text. And as we shall also see, the parabasis
is a rich source of defensive mechanisms, anticipatory self-ridicule,
pseudo-aggressive transference, and conflict within the poet's personality.

Cognitive Theories

Another major tendency in comic theory has been to see the comic
effect in a conscious incongruity between expectation and fulfillment.
The process of "getting a joke" is a movement from anxious confusion
and incomprehension to a state of self-enlightenment and superior
understanding. As in Freud's theory, humor moves the individual from
a condition of tense maladjustment to adjustment, except that what
Freud sees as an unconscious and intrapsychic process rather operates
on a cognitive level in most incongruity theories. The prototype in this
tradition is Kant's famous dictum that laughter is "an affection arising
from the sudden transformation of a strained expectation into nothing."[25] Tension and energy built up in expecting a serious and anxiety-
producing event prove to be unnecessary when the actual event turns
out to be something trivial or unimportant and the accumulated but
unused emotional energy has nowhere to go except into a violent
physical explosion of hilarity. Though it may seem improbable in the
case of less anxiety-loaded expectations, the disappointment of a mere
intellectual anticipation will create momentary dislocation and disorientation which is itself anxiety-producing.

There are numerous variations on this formula, at times specifying
more precisely the kind of incongruity involved. Herbert Spencer
emphasizes the transfer of attention "from great things to small,"
which amounts to the same thing as Kant's reduction of an expectation
to "nothing," although perhaps different in degree of intensity.[26] Scho-

25. Kant 1951, 177–81. For a more modern formulation of this view, see Olson 1968,
15–16.
26. Spencer 1860, 400. There is a similar theory in Dessoir 1970, 173. Spencer's
theory adumbrated and influenced Freud's inasmuch as it emphasizes the transfer of
attention as taking place "unawares," suggesting an element of unconscious causality.

penhauer emphasizes the incongruity of the abstract concept and the perceptive apprehension of a real object, and A. W. von Schlegel sees the comic specifically in the conflict and incongruity between the sensual impulses and higher duties. Others see laughter more generally as a response to the suddenness of transformation from one frame of reference to another and the resulting shock on the unprepared emotions.[27] All these varieties of incongruity humor and absurd reduction are evident in Aristophanes, whether in the reduction of Socrates' grand speculative concepts about meteorological phenomena to an analogy with rumblings in Strepsiades' stomach (*Nub.* 383–87) or in the diminution of the gods to a level of thievish rascality in the *Peace* and *Birds* or in many other instances.

Incongruity theories are of interest to our present discussion because they again exhibit the dialectic of ignorance and knowledge, blindness and insight. Although the initial confusion and disorientation a witticism causes in the listener's mind is not necessarily a lack of self-knowledge, it may, as psychoanalysis has shown, reflect such a lack. In a sense all jokes are "on" the listener inasmuch as he is led to expect one thing, both intellectually and emotionally, but is given something else instead; after comprehending the joke the listener may feel a sense of embarrassment and awkwardness over his initial confusion.

Incongruity theories are primarily designed to explain the effect of brief witticisms or jokes, but they also have a broader dramatic application; among others, Northrop Frye has observed that every comic plot contains within itself a potential tragic plot, i.e. a set of negative expectations and fears which ultimately disappear.[28] As we have already noted, Aristophanic comedy is full of anxiety-producing objects of fear and loathing (Cleon, the war, sophists, and so on) translated into a comic context demanding an entirely different emotional response from the audience. The tension between these two response patterns, as between the literal and figural in language, is a rich and continuing source of comic effect. Nowhere is the tension between the conceptual dramatic world and the external "real" world more apparent than in the parabasis, which at the same time breaks dramatic illusion and prolongs the drama's illusions thereby putting the drama's spectators into a state of joyful disequilibrium and uncertainty.

27. Schopenhauer 1958 I, 59 and II, 91–101. Schlegel 1846, 149. Cf. Hazlitt 1903 VIII, 6–8; Koestler 1964, 59. Of course, the element of "suddenness" is already prominent in the theory of Kant and even of Hobbes.

28. Frye 1949, 65–66. For a more specific study of threatened death in Aristophanic comedy, see Penniston 1983, 15–86.

Spectator and Spectacle

The idea of the comic as a form of confusion is emphasized by Plato,
and by some later thinkers as well. In his essay "De l'essence du rire"
(1857), Baudelaire starts from the premise that laughter is the property of fools, not of wise men. Christ never laughed and laughter, like
pain, seems rather to be a consequence of Man's primordial fall from
grace.[29] Even when laughter comes from a feeling of superiority it is
really a sign of weakness and ignorance, since only fools regard themselves as superior to others; wise men like Socrates recognize their own
ignorance. On the other hand grotesque, violent, monkeylike laughter
in the spectator of a comic event can make the spectator himself a
spectacle for the entertainment of others. The laughing face is inherently an ugly, contorted face. Accordingly, though most laughing men
are completely unselfconscious in regard to their doubleness as spectator and spectacle, Baudelaire defines the artist as the man who is
completely aware of his doubleness.[30]

Baudelaire's doubling of the artistic persona into a seemingly mysti-
fied, unaware spectacle and a hyperconscious, self-knowing spectator
is fully consonant with Aristotle's theory of *alazoneia* and *eirōneia* and
with Hegel's theory of simultaneous self-knowledge and "imperturbable self-assurance" in a hopeless effort. It also foreshadows Freud's
perception of humor as a tension between two parts of the psyche and
is moreover clearly relevant to the dynamics of Aristophanic comedy.[31]
The choruses of Aristophanes' plays certainly fill both roles, bemusedly
watching the actors and at the same time themselves offering a colorful
comic spectacle. Even more fundamentally, the protagonists usually
appear as laughing spectators of Athenian society; Dicaeopolis sits on
the Pnyx awaiting the Assembly like a theater-goer; Demos sits as judge
and spectator of the contests between the Sausage seller and Paphlagonian, just as Philocleon sits as judge at the trial of Labes, and Strepsiades visits Socrates' workshop and witnesses the contest of the two
Discourses, even as Trygaeus visits Olympus and Dionysus visits Hades. There is no better example of this mixture of voyeurism and ex-
hibitionism, of spectator and spectacle, than Euripides' in-law dressed
up as a woman so that he can spy on the women at the Thesmophoria;

29. Baudelaire 1923, 371–74.
30. Baudelaire 1923, 395–96. On Baudelaire's essay as a reflection of the theoretical
tradition of romantic irony, see the penetrating discussion by de Man (1969, 191–209).
31. An application of Freud's theory to the psychic dynamics of the comic writer or
professional satirist appears in Bergler (1956, 161–67).

and even as he mocks the women and their deliberations, he becomes himself an object of mockery to us and to the women who discover his identity.

Almost every Aristophanic protagonist brings to the world of the comedy an observant pair of eyes and a sharp wit providing lenses through which the theatrical audience can view the same absurd world. But Aristophanes' spectator-protagonists are themselves comic spectacles as well—gross, self-indulgent, often foolish and conceited, with no apparent self-consciousness of their faults. This is equally true of the spectators in the audience for whom the protagonists stand as representatives. The vices ridiculed in Aristophanes' comedies and laughed at by the audience are in fact the vices of the audience, namely, support of Cleon, attachment to jury service, obsession with war and hatred for the Spartans, fondness for Euripides, and so on. The audience is itself represented mimetically in the comedies under various guises, now and then that of protagonist, of chorus, or of minor characters, and unawares laughs at itself as the spectacle upon the stage.

The spectators of the audience are explicitly made into a spectacle in one place—the parabasis. The poet's relationship to the audience is a subject of every parabasis in which the coryphaeus speaks on behalf of the poet. The audience is berated for its inconsistency, for its lack of loyalty and sophistication, or for its failure to give the poet his due; the audience may also be criticized for its political failures in the epirrhemes of the parabasis. In the act of transforming the audience-spectators into a comic spectacle, however, the poet reveals himself as a spectator of society and of his audience as well as a spectacle whose personal hopes, ambitions, feelings, and disappointments are witnessed and laughed at by the audience. The same is true of the comic chorus in the epirrhematic section of the parabasis. The parabasis thus serves as a crucial nexus-point for the multiplication of spectator-spectacle relationships among poet, audience, chorus, and (indirectly) comic characters.[32]

All are bonded together in the humor of the comic event, sharing in the fallibility, vulnerability, and imperfect self-knowledge characteristic of all mortals. To laugh is to be human, and it is equally human to be laughed at. By including himself in the spectacle along with the spectators of the audience, the comic poet makes himself part of the broader

32. Mauron (1964, 112) sees the personal story of the author and his self-realization in the parabasis as paradigmatic for the collective story of the audience that achieves a broader self-consciousness through the Old Comic theater. Mauron is certainly correct, but the mirroring relationships of self-ignorance and self-recognition go beyond the poet and the audience, in some cases to include chorus and comic characters.

community and thus makes his social criticism more palatable. His is not simply the laughter of an Olympian superior but of someone who both asserts his superiority and implicitly acknowledges it as a false pretension. The self-deconstructing parabasis is thus instrumental in implicating the poet himself in the human condition—not only a spectator but also a spectacle; not only *eirōn* but also *alazōn*; not only superego but also ego; not only the omniscient creator of comic discourse but himself, like all his creations, caught up seemingly unawares in the inescapable web of that discourse.

CHAPTER 2

The Intertextual Parabasis

Central to the self-cognitive processes of the comic imagination, as we have observed, is the choral parabasis of Old Comedy. This form is unique to Old Comedy and, because of its apparently digressive character, it has often been treated by critics as either a curiosity or an embarrassment. Gilbert Murray termed it "an unassimilated nugget of ritual embedded within the play," and Francis Cornford used similar language to describe it: "With its stiff canonical structure, it has all the air of a piece of ritual procedure awkwardly interrupting the course of the play."[1] The Cambridge anthropologists had special theoretical grounds for devotion to the search for elements of outmoded ritual, but their views on the Old Comic parabasis were already conventional before their time[2] and have had strong adherents in more recent times as well.[3] In his important 1971 monograph, G. M. Sifakis seriously challenged previous speculation concerning the parabasis as a ritual origin of Comedy, but even he did not question the related assumption that the parabasis was an irrelevant digression having no bearing on the dramatic plot and its themes.[4] Beginning with P. W. Harsh in 1934,

---

1. Murray 1964, 12; Cornford 1968, 93.

2. On the parabasis as the original element of Comedy, see Kolster 1829, 48–49; Koester 1835, 17–18; Hornung 1861, 23; Genz 1865, 6–11; Agthe 1866, 20; Poppelreuter 1893, 41; Radermacher 1954, 35.

3. See Herter 1947, 31–32; Kranz 1949, 1125; Ehrenberg 1962, 32; Seaford 1977, 85–86; Reckford 1987, 488.

4. This dogma on the parabasis goes back at least as far as Schlegel 1846, 151. Cf. Agthe 1866, 11; Zielinski 1885, 184–87; Pickard-Cambridge 1962, 199; Dearden 1976, 102; Sutton 1980, 2. This view has most recently and vigorously been reasserted by Heath (1987, 18–23, 43–44).

and in the last decade including Bowie, Harriott, and Reckford, some critics have been more willing to view the parabasis as an integral thematic unit within the play, but a more thorough and systematic examination of this problem and its implications is still needed.[5]

Lest the reader be in doubt about my own position on these issues, I wish to make it clear from the outset that I regard the parabasis not only as integral but as central to the drama's cognitive self-realization as both a literary and social event; it is therefore also central to our understanding and interpretation of each play. Moreover close examination of the extant parabases of Aristophanes together with the fragments of Old Comedy suggests that many received assumptions about the form's fossilized archaism are mistaken; I believe available evidence to reveal the parabasis rather as a very dynamic and flexible form of essentially literary origin, continually evolving and changing in both structure and content.

Parabatic Pieces

Before these questions can be treated in detail it will be useful to review briefly the constituent parts of the parabasis along with their various functions and interrelations. The term "parabasis" is derived from the verb *parabainein* ("to step forward"), used by Aristophanes himself in connection with this interlude specifically to describe the action of the chorus in turning around to face the audience instead of the stage, which the chorus watches during the episodes.[6] In dealing with the seven "canonical" parts of the parabasis, one must first observe with caution that only two of the extant plays of Aristophanes, *Knights* and *Wasps,* display all seven parts in their traditional form and function, and all others, including the substantial papyrus fragment from the parabasis of Eupolis' *Demoi* (fr. 99 PCG), deviate in one way or another from the ideal norms as they have been established by previous scholarship.

(i) *Kommation.* The term *kommation,* or "little coinage," is itself used by Eupolis (fr. 396 PCG) to designate the short song in lyric meter marking the departure of the actors and the beginning of the parabasis. Like

---

5. Harsh 1934, 183–89; Bowie 1982, 27–40; Harriott 1986, 21–34; Reckford 1987, passim. Even as early a critic as Koester (1835, 15–16) looked for ways that the parabasis is unified with the rest of the play, but unfortunately his inquiry was not pursued by his successors.

6. Cf. *Eq.* 508; *Pax* 735; *Thesm.* 785; and Plato, fr. 99 PCG. For explanation of the term, see Σ*Pax* 734b; and Kolster 1829, 6–7; Koester 1835, 3–4; Sifakis 1971b, 63–65.

the odes, the kommation seems to have been sung and danced by the
entire chorus, signalling a decisive break with the dramatic action,
since the chorus as a unit never intervenes in dialogue.[7] The function
of the kommation is essentially transitional and phatic, establishing
lines of communication: it often begins with a formulaic phrase like ἴθι
χαίρων . . . addressed to the exiting actors (*Eq.* 498, *Nub.* 510, *Vesp.*
1009, *Pax* 729) or with some other comment on the preceding dramatic
action, followed by a direct address to the spectators asking for their
attention to what follows (*Eq.* 503–6, *Vesp.* 1010–14; Cratinus, fr. 360
PCG; Eupolis, fr. 42 PCG; Pherecrates, fr. 84, 204 PCG). The kommation may seek to win the audience's favor by praising its *sophia* or
"cleverness" (Cratinus, fr. 360 PCG; Plato, fr. 96 PCG) or by praising it
ironically (*Eq.* 506–6, *Vesp.* 1010–14; Telecleides, fr. 4 PCG).[8] The
kommation may be used for altogether different purposes, as we see in
Av. 676–84, an ode to the nightingale, or its functions and formulae
may simply be assumed by the first few lines of the anapests (as in *Ach.*
626–27, *Pax* 729–33, *Av.* 685–88, *Thesm.* 785; Eupolis, fr. 42 PCG;
Pherecrates, fr. 204 PCG; Plato, fr. 96, 99 PCG). Significantly two of
these passages (*Ach.* 626–27 and *Pax* 729–33) allude to "stripping off"
of garments or paraphernalia, no doubt metaphorical for the dropping
of dramatic illusion and the poet's symbolic "unmasking" in the following anapests.[9]

(ii) *Anapests.* Aristophanes refers to the second major portion of the
parabasis simply as the "anapests" (*Ach.* 627, *Eq.* 504, *Av.* 684), although this passage sometimes employs a different long meter, as we
see in the *Clouds* parabasis and in numerous comic fragments.[10] Critics

---

7. Cf. Kock 1856, 13; Hornung 1861, 29–31; Agthe 1866, 42–43.

8. As we see from *Nub.* 518–35, the audience's *sophia* can also be a theme of the
anapests, since it is a matter central to the poet's relation with his audience. In this respect
the kommation is actually looking forward to the themes of the following anapests.

9. At the very least, however, the coryphaeus must remove his mask in speaking the
anapests (cf. Agthe 1866, 45, and Aristides 49.97 [Keil], who refers to those executing
the parabasis as πολλάκις ἀφελόντες τὸ προσωπεῖον). This is probably accompanied by
the whole chorus, although clearly not for performative reasons, since these two passages, simply anapestic lines and not actual kommatia, are not sung and danced. Indeed
the masks and costumes seem to have been put back on by the time of the epirrhematic
syzygy, which is delivered in the choral persona. *Lys.* 615 also refers to stripping, but in
this context it clearly is for performative reasons, since the old men and old women are
engaged in a fight; no anapestic dropping of persona is involved. Tomin (1987, 28–29)
argues on the basis of several Platonic passages that "stripping" was a common Socratic
metaphor to denote baring the soul for examination; if so, this could be the background
for Aristophanes' use of the metaphor in *Ach.* 626–27 and *Pax* 729–33, since the
parabasis is precisely such an act of soul-baring for both poet and chorus.

10. Cf. Aristophanes, fr. 58–59 PCG; Cratinus, fr. 153, 361 PCG; Eupolis, fr. 42
PCG; Pherecrates, fr. 204 PCG; Plato, fr. 96, 99 PCG (and perhaps 106 PCG); Adesp., fr.
53 K. Pherecrates, fr. 84 PCG refers to "anapests" though not actually in anapests. Often
meters were named by ancient metricians after the distinctive metrical form used by a

have therefore designated it also as the ἁπλοῦν or the "parabasis proper." To avoid confusion I shall refer to this section as the "anapests" even if it was actually composed in a different metrical form. The content of the anapests in the first five extant plays of Aristophanes is devoted to the poet's self-defense, whether in the first person[11] or third person;[12] self-praise of the poet's accomplishments is often connected with censure of his political and literary rivals.[13] All commentators agree that this long passage must have been spoken by the coryphaeus alone, and some have sought to explain the first person as the remnant of a time when the poet would have been coryphaeus.[14] However, one could just as well explain the first person as a mimetic act of representation in which the coryphaeus stands for the poet; indeed the earlier conventions of choral lyric, as reflected in the extant epinicia of Pindar and Bacchylides, show that even an entire chorus singing in performance can relay the first-person voice of the poet speaking in matters of literary self-defense.[15] Critics have tended to assume that poetic self-defense was the original and essential function of the anapests and that Aristophanes' use of the anapests for choral self-defense in persona, as we see in the *Birds* or *Thesmophoriazusae,* was a later development by which the poet tried to free himself from the undramatic form of the parabasis. But this may be a mistaken impression based on our possession of the first five parabases of Aristophanes (*Acharnians* through *Peace*) and his predilection for the apologetic form at this stage of his career. In fact *Ach.* 628–29 implies that his earlier plays did not feature such parabatic self-defense,[16] and the comic fragments strongly

---

poet in his personal parabatic apologies (e.g. "eupolidean," "cratineum," "platonic," or "pherecratean").

11. Cf. *Nub.* 518–62 (wholly in the first person) and *Pax* 754–74 (which toward the end of the anapests changes from third person to first person, like the pnigos of *Ach.* 659–64). For other instances of the poetic first person in the anapests, cf. Cratinus, fr. 251 PCG; Eupolis, fr. 89 PCG; Metagenes, fr. 15 PCG; Plato, fr. 106 PCG (if this is indeed parabatic). We also find the poetic first person in what appear to be epirrhematic passages; cf. Aristophanes, fr. 30–31 PCG; Eupolis, fr. 392 PCG; Plato, fr. 115 PCG. See the remarks of Perusino 1986, 18 n.2.

12. In addition to being Aristophanes' normal practice, clear third person references to the poet are found in Pherecrates, fr. 102 PCG and Adesp., fr. 53 K.

13. Aristophanes attacks Cleon in the anapests of *Acharnians, Wasps,* and *Peace,* and his comic competitors in *Knights, Clouds,* and *Peace.* Cf. Cratinus, fr. 213, 342, 346, 361a, 361c PCG; Eupolis, fr. 89, 132, 174 PCG; Philonides, fr. 5 PCG; Plato, fr. 184 PCG.

14. Cf. Koester 1835, 17–18; Genz 1865, 22–24; Agthe 1866, 44–45; Kranz 1949, 1125.

15. I categorically reject the recent speculation of Lefkowitz (1988, 1–11) that Pindar's odes were meant to be sung as monody; this is impossible, as I have shown in Hubbard 1987, 1–9. See also Burnett 1989, 283–93; Carey 1989, 545–65. On the general parallel between Pindar's and Aristophanes' modes of self-praise, see Harriott 1986, 59–60.

16. See Perusino (1986, 19) who notes that none of our many fragments from *Banqueters* and *Babylonians* seem to be parabatic at all.

suggest that the anapests were used almost as often for choral self-presentation as for the poet's self-defense.[17] Hence the content need not necessarily be different from that of the epirrhemes; like the epirrhemes, the anapests may also include elements of social satire or political advice to the city, as in *Ach.* 652–55, admonishing the Athenians not to accede to Spartan demands for Aegina.[18]

(iii) *Pnigos.* The *pnigos* or "choker," also called the *makron* or "long unit," derives its name from the perception of ancient scholars that it was sung ἀπνευστί, "without pausing for a breath."[19] Since it is usually composed in anapestic dimeters, some critics have assumed the pnigos to be merely a continuation of the preceding anapestic tetrameters and therefore spoken also by the coryphaeus.[20] It is clearly too long, however, to have been pronounced ἀπνευστί by one speaker alone and is consequently more likely to have been sung or chanted, but not danced, by the whole chorus.[21] Usually the pnigos serves to terminate the arguments of the anapests with a droll image wishing for the poet's favorable reception from his audience (*Eq.* 547–50, *Vesp.* 1051–59, *Pax* 765–74; Pherecrates, fr. 102 PCG),[22] or in the case of anapests delivered in the choral persona, the chorus' favorable reception from the audience (*Av.* 723–36; Cratinus, fr. 182 PCG). The emphasis and visual effectiveness of the passage would thus gain from the intervention of the full chorus, which at this point expresses its solidarity with the poet or coryphaeus; in this way, the chorus reinforces the call for social union in support of the poet/coryphaeus and in opposition to his enemies (see *Ach.* 659–64). As such the pnigos balances the kommation introducing the anapests, also sung by the whole chorus and concerned with attracting the audience's attention; it provides a transition from the anapests to the following choral ode by having the full chorus join the coryphaeus.[23]

17. Cf. Cratinus, fr. 105 PCG (the chorus of Malthakoi speaking in character about their flowery garlands); Eupolis, fr. 13 PCG (the chorus of Goats speaking about their food); Aristophanes, fr. 427–31 PCG (the ship chorus enumerating its cargo) in the *Holkades,* usually thought to be an early play; cf. Geissler 1925, 36–37, basing his conclusion on *Hyp. Pax* (= Test. iii PCG), which seems to group it together with *Acharnians* and *Knights* as a play attacking Cleon.

18. Cf. Eupolis, fr. 132, 174 PCG; Pherecrates, fr. 34, 52 PCG; Philonides, fr. 5 PCG; Plato, fr. 184 PCG; Telecleides, fr. 2 PCG.

19. Cf. Pollux 4.112, and Hephaestion 135 G.

20. Cf. Kock 1856, 16; Muff 1872, 90.

21. Pollux 4.112 says it was "sung." On the involvement of the entire chorus, cf. Koester 1835, 6; Hornung 1861, 36; Agthe 1866, 48–49, and my arguments concerning the pnigos of the *Knights* in Hubbard 1990, 115–18.

22. Even parabases without an actual pnigos have the anapests end with a similar appeal to the audience. Cf. *Nub.* 560–62. In this way the function of the pnigos is incorporated into the anapests, as that of the kommation sometimes is.

23. This argues against the contention of Sifakis (1971b, 60) in favor of the anapes-

(iv) + (vi) *Ode* and *Antode*. With a sense of social harmony established between poet, chorus, and audience at the end of the pnigos, the chorus typically turns to invocation of the gods in the lyric ode that follows. The request for audience favor is thus paralleled and reinforced by a prayer for divine assistance to the chorus, serving to confirm the role of the chorus, and ultimately of the poet, as agents of public benefaction in the city's cultic system. The divinities invoked will often have special relevance to the chorus' identity;[24] note the "Acharnian Muse" (*Ach.* 665–66), "Poseidon the horse-god" (*Eq.* 551–53), "Aether and Helios" (*Nub.* 570–74), "Muse of the thicket" (*Av.* 737), as well as the more generalized Muses and Graces of *Pax* 775–818 and *Ran.* 675, relevant to any chorus.[25] Not all parabasis odes, however, are hymns to gods; some simply continue the themes of the epirrhemes (see *Ach.* 692–702, *Vesp.* 1060–70, 1091–1101, *Lys.* 614–25, 636–47, 658–71, 682–95, *Ran.* 706–17; Eupolis, fr. 99.1–22 PCG), or combine the hymnic element with topical abuse (see *Pax* 775–818, *Ran.* 675–85). In some cases, as in the *Acharnians*, *Peace*, and *Frogs*, the ode begins as a hymn and the antode is more topical, though generally ode and antode are fairly unified in theme and content.

(v) + (vii) *Epirrheme* and *Antepirrheme*. The responsive epirrheme and antepirrheme are usually, although not always, written in trochaic tetrameters whose total number is a multiple of four.[26] The lines are probably spoken by the coryphaeus alone,[27] but the full chorus may accompany with some visible gestures or dance.[28] The coryphaeus

---

tic and epirrhematic parts of the parabasis being completely independent and self-contained. He may be right in declaring the two to be not mutually necessary in their origins, but the pnigos shows an attempt to integrate the more recently evolved anapests with the epirrhematic syzygy.

24. On the relevance of the chorus' identity to the divinities invoked and the way they are invoked, see Horn 1970, 16–19.

25. Compare also the lyric invocation of the Muse in Cratinus, fr. 237 PCG, probably from such a parabasis hymn.

26. One also finds some epirrhemes written in cretic-paeonic tetrameters: cf. *Ach.* 978–87, 990–99 (not a multiple of four); *Vesp.* 1275–91; fr. 112–13 PCG (from the *Farmers*); fr. 347–48 PCG (from the second *Thesmophoriazusae*); and Eupolis, fr. 173 (from the *Flatterers*). Eupolis, fr. 172 PCG (also from the *Flatterers*) is a 16-line epirrheme spoken in persona by the chorus in a choriambic meter, also used by Aristophanes, fr. 30–31 PCG (from the *Amphiaraus*).

27. Here I follow the view of Dover (1972, 50). Some older critics held different views: Agthe (1866, 56) and Muff (1872, 94–95) thought them to be delivered by the whole chorus; Hornung (1861, 40) by two semichoruses; Kock (1856, 19) by two members of the chorus other than the coryphaeus (cf. Arnoldt 1873, 142–44); Enger (1856, 119–20) by four members of each semichorus. Genz (1865, 26) is undecided between the views of Hornung and Kock. The insistence on different chorus members or semichoruses seems unnecessary, since the epirrhemes are no more antithetical than ode and antode, or strophe and antistrophe.

28. See Sifakis 1971b, 118 n.12.

typically speaks for the chorus in persona, with witty reflections on the chorus' identity and often unrecognized benefactions to the public.[29] This self-praise is usually combined with political advice or social satire directed against those whom the chorus perceives as its enemies— young orators (*Ach.*), current military leaders (*Eq.*), Cleon and Hyperbolus (*Nub.*), the opposing semichorus of old men or old women (*Lys.*);[30] the abuse may take the form of excluding from its ranks those who are unworthy—jurors who have never served in the military (*Vesp.*) or women who give birth to bad men (*Thesm.*). The coupling of choral self-praise with abuse of enemies thus makes the epirrhemes parallel to the similar dual function of the anapests on the poet's behalf.[31] The epirrhemes may be used, however, for a more positive form of political exhortation in cases when the usual epirrhematic functions of choral self-manifestation and social satire have been assumed by other passages, either in the parabasis or elsewhere, as in *Birds* or *Frogs*.[32] Sometimes also an epirrheme may be used for the poet's self-assertion, as is more usually expected in the anapests.[33] Finally we should note Aristophanes' tendency to coordinate the themes of epirrheme and antepirrheme very carefully; often the antepirrheme will use a humorous vignette or exemplum to give specific illustration to a general point made in the epirrheme, for instance, the bewildered Thucydides as a sample of old men victimized by young orators in the *Acharnians,* the horses' victory over the Corinthian crabs as a model of the Knights' military service, or the Clouds' whimsical revenge against Hyperbolus as an example of celestial punishment visited upon the Athenians for their erring ways.

The entire responsive unit formed by the odes and epirrhemes is referred to as an "epirrhematic syzygy." It thus counterbalances the non-responsive unit formed by kommation, anapests, and pnigos, effectively paralleling the concerns and enemies of the chorus with those

29. In addition to the familiar cases from Aristophanes' extant plays, cf. fr. 112–13, 319–20 PCG; Eupolis, fr. 172–73 PCG; Pherecrates, fr. 70 PCG.

30. Cf. fr. 424 PCG (from *Holkades*) on the young orators; Eupolis, fr. 99.23–34 PCG on an unnamed demagogue; Plato, fr. 115 PCG on Cleon.

31. For the coupling of praise and blame as interdependent poetic modalities in the Greek tradition, cf. Pindar, *N.*8.39, *P.*1.94–98, and the general discussions of Detienne (1967, 18–27) and Nagy (1979, 222–42).

32. In the *Birds,* the choral self-praise comes in the anapests, whereas in the *Frogs* it comes in the parodos, with the social satire coming in the parabasis odes.

33. This certainly happens in *Vesp.* 1284–91 (part of a second parabasis) and probably also occurs in fr. 30–31 PCG (from the *Amphiaraus*), fr. 347–48 PCG (from the second *Thesmophoriazusae*). Cf. Eupolis, fr. 392 PCG; Plato, fr. 106 (if this is parabatic at all), 115 PCG. It is conceivable, although I think less likely, that these fragments could derive from "anapestic" sections written in meters more usually associated with the epirrhemes.

of the poet; their opponents are indeed often revealed to be one and the same. The syzygy, or parts of a syzygy, can also be used by itself outside the framework of the main parabasis as a "second parabasis." Second parabases are usually not employed for choral self-praise so much as for topical satire on various personal targets, self-praise having already been accomplished in the main parabasis. There are occasions when they are addressed to the play's judges in the persona of the chorus, offering rewards or threatening punishment (see *Nub.* 1115–30, *Av.* 1102–17). They can also be used as celebrations of an achieved dramatic objective such as peace (*Ach.* 971–99, *Pax* 1127–90). Functionally the second parabasis is not much different from the non-parabatic choral odes.

Theories and Theses

As we have observed, many critics hold that the parabasis was the earliest ritual kernel from which Comedy arose or at least was a very early component of Comedy.[34] Their arguments are based on the perception of Comedy, like Tragedy, having its origins in nondramatic choral performances possibly connected with the phallic hymns mentioned by Aristotle,[35] and on the further inference that "such a rigid, awkward, and nondramatic form" as the parabasis could never have been invented by any comic poet and must be a predramatic remnant. The topical abuse of individuals in the epirrhemes combined with worship of the gods in the odes recalls the cultic aischrology integral to several well-known festivals[36] and has led some critics to consider the epirrhematic syzygy as the original kernel of the parabasis itself[37] as well as the source for the epirrhematic structure of the dramatic agon. The anapests are seen as the rhythm of the chorus' marching en-

34. See notes 1–3 of this chapter.
35. Aristotle, *Poet.* 1449a9. See Kolster 1829, 57; Koester 1835, 17–18; Hornung 1861, 23; Genz 1865, 16; Cornford 1968, 101–14; Pickard-Cambridge 1962, 133–47 (for a more skeptical view of the evidence on *phallophoroi*); Herter 1947, 17–18, 22–31; the last basing his arguments on the abundant iconographic evidence for early comic choruses. Even critics such as Cornford (1968, 6) and Giangrande (1963, 11–15) who think the mimetic, actor-centered element preceded the comic chorus still believe the chorus to have been very early. It is significant, although seldom noted, that the one phallic procession we find in extant comedy (Dicaeopolis' in *Ach.* 237–79) is led by actors and does not involve the chorus, which is in fact hostile to it.
36. For such *gephyrismos* rituals, see Burkert 1985, 104–5. Herter (1947, 28–29) denies these having been a major influence on the development of Comedy.
37. See Kolster 1829, 57; Koester 1835, 14; Hornung 1861, 23; Agthe 1866, 26–27; Reckford 1987, 488; and on different grounds, Sifakis 1971b, 68–69.

trance,[38] and some have therefore thought the parabasis first to have taken the place of the parodos, with the dramatic scenes following.

All of these theories about the parabasis and its connection with the early origins of Comedy are highly speculative, operating in a complete vacuum of empirical evidence. In fact, what evidence there is often runs contrary to the assumptions behind them. In the first place no comic fragment earlier than Cratinus can be demonstrated to have belonged to a parabasis;[39] though the number of fragments we possess from Magnes, Crates, Ecphantides, and other early poets is not large, it is large enough to make the absence of possible parabatic fragments striking. According to Platonius, many later plays of Old Comedy, such as Cratinus' *Odyssēs* and Aristophanes' *Aeolosicōn*, foreshadowed Middle Comedy in having no parabases or choral songs,[40] suggesting that the parabasis and even the choral songs were far from being canonical elements at any time. Aristotle tells us nothing about the parabasis, but he does say that Crates was the first poet to free Comedy from "the iambic form" and construct full plots (*Poet.* 1449b7–9). Other sources credit Cratinus with an influential role in introducing and refining the element of political invective in Comedy.[41] Although Aristotle must mean by "iambic form" something different from the exclusive use of iambic meters,[42] his remarks do suggest that Comedy underwent major changes and substantial development fairly late in its history.[43]

38. See Cornford 1968, 94; Trotzky 1926, 578–91; Herter 1947, 31–32; Seaford 1977, 85. Against this view, see the cogent remarks of Sifakis (1971b, 62) who distinguishes the anapestic tetrameter from the "marching anapests" sometimes found in tragic parodoi. And as Harsh (1934, 95) points out, the anapestic tetrameter has other functional associations in Comedy, such as its use in the agon.

39. Crates, fr. 28 PCG ("this is another solemn discourse for all the tragic poets"), assigned to a parabasis by Whittaker (1935, 188), seems more likely to be an anapestic line from an agon, perhaps a dismissive comment on the other speaker. The parabasis may be concerned with comic competitors but seldom deals with Tragedy.

40. Platonius, *De Diff. Com.* (= Test. I Koster) 22–31. Cratinus, fr. 153 PCG (from the *Odyssēs*) may be a parabatic line, but it could also come from an agon or prologue. For a defense of Platonius' credibility here (as against the doubts, for instance, of Bertan [1984, 171–78]), see Perusino 1986, 64, 71–72, 80–84, who believes that the parodos was the only true choral element in these plays (as later in the *Plutus*). Henderson (1990, 293 n.73) extends Platonius' statement to suggest a general lack of parabases, after the model of Epicharmus, in mythological burlesque comedies.

41. See chap. 4 n.34 below.

42. This term is generally taken in reference to Comedy's kinship with the tradition of iambic poetry represented by Archilochus and Hipponax (see bibliography in chap. 4 nn.27 and 28). But the term must refer to something more than merely a penchant for personal attack, since that tendency is said to have been developed by Cratinus, a poet later than Crates. "Iambic form" may have something to do with a loosely episodic plot structure comparable to what was found in the epodes of the iambographers.

43. On the pivotal roles of Crates and Cratinus in the formal development of Comedy, see the remarks of Händel (1963, 304–5).

There was likely far more difference between the form of Magnes' comedies and Aristophanes' than between the tragedies of Aeschylus and Euripides over the same time span. The parabasis was no doubt part of this innovation, whether in whole or in part; at least as we possess the form in Aristophanes and Eupolis, it is entirely noniambic and at the same time full of political invective, being therefore very much part of what Aristotle and others identify as new in Comedy. Moreover, the common characterization of the parabasis as a rigid, unchanging fossil is altogether false, as we have noted in our discussion of the various parabatic parts. Both the parabasis in general and its constituent elements were from the time of Cratinus undergoing constant change and experimentation in meter, form, and content. If the parabasis was a fossil, it was a very lively one.

The more specific arguments for the parabasis as a cultic remnant are also seriously flawed. The satirical abuse of members of the audience may bear some resemblance to cultic aischrology, but we do not find it in every parabasis and the parabasis is far from being the only place in Comedy where we do find it. What is most striking about the main parabases of Aristophanes' earliest plays (which supposedly contain the most archaic and formalized parabases) is precisely how little abuse of individuals by name they contain. There are a few favorite targets such as Cleon, Hyperbolus, or Theorus; but most of the epirrhematic abuse is directed against generic malefactors, such as young sycophants, generals who demand rewards for minimal effort, jurors who never earned their right to pay, or the Athenians in general. We find more personal satire in the second parabases and in some of the nonparabatic choral odes as well as in comic dialogue, though these prove nothing about the functional origins of the parabasis itself. Nor do the parabasis hymns indicate anything about the form's beginnings;[44] we often find prayers to the gods in other comic passages[45] as well as in the choral odes of Tragedy, which Fraenkel has convincingly argued were the real source of the parabasis hymns.[46]

On the question whether the epirrhematic syzygy of the parabasis was the source for the epirrhematic agon or vice versa, there is little to recommend the former view save the general presupposition about choral parts necessarily being older than actors' parts.[47] On the other

44. On this I share the skepticism of Horn (1970, 20–21).
45. For a complete listing of such prayers, see Horn 1970, 4–11.
46. Fraenkel 1962, 195. Cf. Händel 1963, 84.
47. This view has been championed by Körte 1921, 1250–51; Wilamowitz 1927, 14–15; Pickard-Cambridge 1962, 148 n.3; and most recently, Reckford 1987, 489–90. But as we have observed (above, n.35), the mimetic element in Comedy may have been as old as or older than the choral.

hand Sifakis has advanced powerful arguments for viewing the agon as the original element to which the epirrhematic form was indigenous and necessary, inasmuch as it represents a debate of two parties; the epirrhematic form is completely unnecessary to the parabasis, in which the antepirrheme is at most only a focussed development of the epirrheme, seldom antithetical.[48] Whereas *Lysistrata* features two antagonistic semichoruses arguing in the parabasis epirrhemes, there is no evidence that this was derived from earlier comic practice rather than being one of Aristophanes' many experiments in his middle phase;[49] the concept could have been inspired by the competing semichoruses sometimes involved in choral lyric, as in Alcman's *Partheneion*. Gelzer has argued that the similarities between the epirrhematic syzygy and agon are purely coincidental; he does not believe either of them to have influenced the development of the other.[50] Even he, however, admits that the pnigos attached to the end of the anapests was probably derived from the agon;[51] influence in this direction seems especially clear when we consider the one case of pnigos elements attached to parabatic epirrhemes, in the second parabasis of the *Peace* (*Pax* 1156–58, 1188–90). On this and other grounds the parabasis appears to be a later development. Even if we consider Comedy in the ritualistic terms of Cornford, the agon as struggle between New Year and Old Year, life and death, peace and war, young king and old king is fundamental and central to the very identity of Comedy, whereas the parabasis is far less obviously so.[52]

Finally the idea that the anapests of the parabasis embody the original entrance of the chorus may find some support in the inclusion within the parodos of the *Frogs* (*Ran.* 354–71) of a short anapestic section dealing with poetic themes and featuring other parabatic traits.[53] Nevertheless it must be noted that most parodoi in Aristophanes' extant plays are not in fact anapestic.[54] Even the *Frogs* parodos is clearly not a parabasis or epirrhematic: far from proving the parabasis

48. Sifakis 1971b, 54–55.

49. For the thesis that the semichoruses were a prominent feature of more archaic comedy, see Cornford 1968, 82, 97–98; Sifakis 1971b, 55; Seaford 1977, 86; Reckford 1987, 489–90.

50. Gelzer 1960, 209.

51. Gelzer 1960, 205.

52. See Cornford 1968, 5–13, 27–39.

53. See our discussion of this passage on pp. 203–5. On the archaizing character of the *Frogs* generally, see p. 201 below.

54. For a detailed survey of metrical patterns in the parodoi, see Zimmermann 1985 I, 34–140. Sodano (1961, 48–50) argues that Cratinus favored anapestic parodoi modelled on archaic tragedy.

to have originally come at the beginning of the play,[55] it may suggest that many of the themes and functions of the parabasis as developed by Cratinus, Eupolis, and Aristophanes were at one time handled by an extended parodos, ultimately truncated *pari passu* with the growth of a choral interlude in the middle of the play. Indeed, we have substantial papyrus remains of a similar parodos from Cratinus' *Ploutoi*,[56] treating parabatic themes but without parabatic structure, and we have testimonial evidence suggesting such a parodos in his *Dionysalexandros*[57] and in another unnamed play.[58] Given the natural potential for the parodos to act as an initial choral self-presentation, one can readily see it as a source of the move to poetic self-presentation as well inasmuch as the comic chorus appeals to the judges for victory, as in both the *Frogs* and the *Ploutoi*. These parallel themes at some point may have been transferred into a more formal anapestic and epirrhematic structure in the middle of the play where they could be treated at greater length. We cannot know whether this development was the work of Cratinus, a pacesetter and innovator in so many other respects, or of an earlier comic poet. But familiarity with the evidence for Old Comedy outside Aristophanes cannot help but leave one with the conviction that the genre had far more dynamism and structural experimentation than is acknowledged by critics of the "fossilized ritual" school.

My own perspective on the parabasis is conditioned by the view of it as fundamentally a product of self-conscious literary evolution with distinctly literary purposes. Even if it does in some way have a ritual antecedent, there is no question that as we know it from the extant plays of Aristophanes, the form is one with a literary history and literary significance in which any ritual origin has become obscured with time. My view of the form's literary function stems from its three essential characteristics, evident in all of Aristophanes' extant parabases, whatever their formal variations:

55. For strong arguments against the possibility of the parabasis in the form known from Aristophanes coming in the place of the parodos, see Harsh 1934, 191–95.

56. Fr. 171 PCG, on which see the detailed study of Sodano (1961, 37–47).

57. See the papyrus hypothesis (= Test. i.6–9 PCG), which tells us that the chorus speaks to the audience τινα π(ερὶ) τῶν ποιη (τῶν) after the initial scene in which Dionysus persuades Hermes to bring the three goddesses to him. This is much too early in the plot development to be a parabasis and must therefore be the parodos.

58. Cratinus, fr. 306 K (in anapests) addresses the audience and tells them to wash other poets out of their eyes after waking up in the morning. In quoting this fragment, Aristides 49.92 (Keil) makes it clear that the lines come from the play's beginning: ἐν ἀρχῇ τοῦ δράματος . . . ὡς προφήτης προαγορεύει τοιάδε. . . . I therefore disagree with Sifakis (1971b, 50) who assigns it to a parabasis. In spirit it is not unlike Dicaeopolis' deprecatory remarks about other poets at the beginning of the *Acharnians* (*Ach.* 1–16).

(a) The parabasis is *extradramatic*. It steps back from the play's plot without being totally removed from the play's thematics; in this respect it is not unlike the choral stasima of Tragedy, although it is certainly longer and more varied. In another important respect, however, the parabasis goes beyond ordinary choral odes in that it breaks "dramatic illusion"—i.e. it addresses the spectators directly and often speaks of theatrical or political events as if not part of a mimetic drama.[59] To the extent that the chorus may remove part of their costume during the anapests, as we can infer from *Ach.* 627 and *Pax* 729–32, this symbolic "unmasking" announces a breaking out of the mimetic structure of the dramatic event. Sifakis goes too far in trying to deny the Greeks any concept of dramatic illusion.[60] His premise is that Greek comic drama consisted of inherently disunified scenes written for instantaneous theatrical effect, and he thus concludes that the parabasis was merely one in a long series of such self-contained theatrical events. But this premise takes us back to a primitivist view of drama not unlike the one Sifakis elsewhere attacks. I would prefer to regard the whole point of the parabasis as its "otherness" and estrangement from the surrounding dramatic spectacle. Its independence from the drama is not to be regarded as an awkward embarrassment, but as an opportunity for mediating language which stands between the mimetic discourse of drama and the external world of signifieds (political and social reality), and thus helps the audience to connect the worlds of drama and reality. Inasmuch as the parabasis in Aristophanes functions as this extra-dramatic "other" discourse, its "otherness" presupposes the existence of developed mimetic drama which it can be "other" than, whether by difference or deferral. This function is hardly consistent with the view of the parabasis as the original kernel and nucleus of the dramatic; it is more accurately to be seen as a deconstruction of the dramatic.

(b) The parabasis is *self-critical*. As we have seen, the unifying charac-teristic of the two major parts of the parabasis is self-presentation, respectively of the poet and the chorus.[61] And as we saw in Chapter I, the issue of self-knowledge or its absence has been central to theories of the comic from antiquity to the present. We should therefore not be

59. On the concept of "dramatic illusion" in Aristophanes, see Stow 1936; Muecke 1977, 52–67; Chapman 1983, 1–23.

60. Sifakis 1971b, 7–14. His views are sharply criticized by Muecke (1977, 54–56), Bain (1977, 3–7), and Chapman (1983, 2–4), all of whom rightly point out that self-conscious play with dramatic forms and conventions is part of what gives Comedy its unpredictable spirit and humor.

61. On the concept of *Selbstdarstellung* as the fundamental characteristic of the parabasis, I am influenced by Händel 1963, 84.

surprised to find identities explored and problematized in the parabasis, which acts not only as a self-advertisement for poet and chorus,
but even as a form of self-satire. The chorus moves from its stationary
position as a spectator of the comic characters involved in various
debates and activities to become a central comic spectacle itself. Even in
self-defense the comic chorus occasionally reveals itself as weak, debili-
tated, and humorous: old Acharnians helpless as they are dragged into
court, young Knights defending their manhood while apologizing for
their curls and warm baths, wasp-tempered jurors wishing to purge
their own ranks of do-nothings and parasites. The creator of the comic
drama himself moves center stage for a while, as much a comic spectacle as any of his creations, whether in bragging of his fame while hiding
behind a producer (*Acharnians*), in pretending his shy and timorous
nature has held him back from open competition (*Knights*), or in be-
rating the public for failing to appreciate his cleverness (*Clouds* and
Wasps). As we shall see in the *Clouds,* the poet can even critique his own
theatrical practices in detail, under the guise of criticizing his competitors. The anapests create a comic persona for the poet himself,
which undergoes continuous modulation and revision from parabasis
to parabasis. For all the appearance of literary and political earnest-
ness, the comic poet remains a comic clown, the bald Aristophanes. But
to the extent that the poet and his chorus are revealed to be clowns in
the parabasis, they are synecdochic for the whole Athenian public,
which, even in the act of watching the comic spectacle, is itself *the*
comic spectacle—the ultimate target of satire in the anapests, the
epirrhemes, and in the play itself. Comedy is in its essence an act of
civic self-criticism, and the parabasis is Comedy's own pivotal moment
of self-criticism when the serious interests of poet, chorus, and audience are aligned, but all are at the same time allowed to take their
share in the city's ills and in the universal fact of human folly. For all
its seriousness of concern, the self-undercutting irony of the parabasis never allows the drama to sink into self-righteousness or didactic
preaching.

(c) The parabasis is *intertextual.* Every Aristophanic parabasis seems
to depend upon interaction with other texts for its full actualization of
meaning. It is in a sense internally cross-textual in its very arrangement
and composition as a sequenced pattern of correlated microtexts paralleling the self-manifestation of poet and chorus and their respective
relationships with the city, and in the process reconciling public favor
and invoking divine assistance for both. More broadly, we have seen
the parabasis serving as a critical nexus-point that ties together many

strands of textual cross-reference to tragic and lyric poets, to comic competitors, to the poet's own previous plays and career, and most significantly, to the surrounding drama itself.

At the same time that the parabasis stands apart and digresses from the dramatic plot it is also connected to the drama's themes, issues, and characters by many finely spun threads of language, imagery, political reference, and ideology. This connection becomes most evident in Aristophanes' later plays (*Birds* through *Frogs*) and is usually apparent for the epirrhematic portions, concerned as they are with the identity and social status of the chorus, which is obviously part of the drama. The public enemies whom the chorus attacks in the epirrhemes are always parallel to and in some cases identical with the implied enemies of the play as a whole.[62]

Despite the tendency of the connections to be less transparent, I would argue that even the poet's apologetic anapests gain added significance from being heard in dialogue with the surrounding dramatic events: Aristophanes' advocacy of free speech and self-defense against Cleon's charges of disloyalty (in *Acharnians*) resonate against the background of Dicaeopolis defending himself over the same issues. The vicissitude of public favor toward comic poets (decried in the *Knights* parabasis) is another form of the same mutability and fickleness the public displays toward political leaders—the subject of the play as a whole. The public's failure to appreciate Aristophanes' poetic *sophia* (criticized in the *Clouds* parabasis) instances the same intellectual rusticity and obtuseness which the common man Strepsiades reveals in grappling with Socratic *sophia*. The young Aristophanes' failure as a reformer (in the *Wasps* parabasis) is a paradigm for the young Bdelycleon's failure as a reformer of his father. Aristophanes' personal triumph over Cleon (proudly proclaimed on top of the demagogue's grave in the parabasis of *Peace*) is part and parcel of Trygaeus' general triumph over the forces of War and destruction. There is a certain sense in which the poet identifies himself with main characters in each of his first five extant plays; their ambitions and struggles against political or intellectual obstacles are those of the poet, and the poet's are theirs. In this sense many of Aristophanes' characters are metathe-

---

62. In addition to the many Aristophanic examples we shall be discussing in due course, this relevance is also apparent in some fragmentary plays. Plato, fr. 184 PCG, from the parabasis of the *Hyperbolus*, attacks, not surprisingly, Hyperbolus. The parabasis of Eupolis' *Demoi* (see fr. 99, 132 PCG) attacks present-day demagogues; it is of course their corruption and incompetence that form the background to the play's whole plot idea of resurrecting from the Underworld the statesmen of the past to help solve Athens' current problems.

atrical[63]—would-be dramatists staging and manipulating events as Aristophanes himself might. At the same time Aristophanes' early plays are revealed to be the drama of a heroic autobiographical fiction, a fantastic self-projection of the crusading young comic poet, alternately ironic and alazonic, confronting his public and combating the villains of his day. In the famous scene with the "feminine" Agathon (*Thesm.* 149–70),[64] Aristophanes quite explicitly formulates the idea of a dramatic poet being like his characters. And what we know of such plays as Cratinus' *Pytinē* and *Ploutoi* suggests that the idea of overt autobiographical drama was not unique to Aristophanes.[65] Indeed, it could go back to the earliest stages of Comedy if, as some speculate, the role of the first actor was once played by the poet.[66]

The anapestic parabases are the keyhole through which we see this underlying significance in the early plays of Aristophanes, which it will be the primary purpose of the next five chapters to unravel. As a second dimension of intertextuality, however, we must recognize that the parabases create this autobiographical fiction not only by relation to the texts of the surrounding drama but also by connection with the poet's preceding plays. Each anapestic parabasis encapsulates an overview of the poet's entire career and thus relates his intentions in the present play to those of earlier works and of his dramatic *oeuvre* as a whole. The primary concern here is frequently with the success or failure of previous works and the poet's often testy relation with his public, which he addresses in the parabasis. In the case of Aristophanes we are fortunate in possessing five firmly dated plays from five successive years (*Acharnians* through *Peace*, 425 to 421), and hence are in a good position to evaluate the poet's development and progression in his critical early period. Each parabasis comments on his previous plays and engages in an implicit dialogue with his previous parabases, often

63. For the term and concept of "metatheater," see Abel 1963, 60–61. The concept has received some currency in recent Plautine criticism (cf. Barchiesi 1970, 113–30, Slater 1985, 12–15), but has been relatively neglected in the study of Aristophanes (see, however, Kowzan 1983, 83–100).

64. Compare also the "lame beggar" Euripides in *Ach.* 410–13 and fr. 694 PCG. See Raines 1935, 202; Muecke 1977, 63.

65. As the plot summary given by $\Sigma Eq.$ 400a (= Test. ii PCG) shows, the *Pytinē* was quite unabashedly autobiographical, depicting Cratinus as married to Comedy, who wants a divorce (cf. fr. 194 PCG) because he has neglected her while devoting himself to the winebottle (cf. fr. 195–96, 199 PCG). Fr. 171 PCG (see n.56 above) suggests that Cratinus also made himself a character in the *Ploutoi.*

66. I question whether this continued to be the practice in Aristophanes' day (see chap. 3 n.16), but interesting arguments for it in connection with Comedy's iambographic origins have been made by Nagy (1979, 252). For the testimonial evidence, although of dubious value, see Perusino 1986, 37 n.3.

significantly repeating lines, images, poses, proclamations, and rebukes. Still, amid the repetitions and continuities, we are struck most
by the variety of the masks under which Aristophanes presents himself—boastful in *Acharnians,* diffident in *Knights,* ironically contemptuous in *Clouds,* angry in *Wasps,* exultant in *Peace.* Aristophanes' persona
is a moving target, never willing to be pinned down in one place or
typecast in one role.

The penchant of Aristophanes for self-citation and autoallusion
should not obscure the importance of his allusions to other poets. It has
been observed that parody of tragic and lyric poets frequently forms
the substructure of the parabasis odes.[67] Prayer formulae, like curse
formulae, naturally lend themselves to imitation.[68] Yet we should recognize that even Aristophanes' most personal statements about his
originality and unique service to the public interest actually form part
of a well-developed rhetoric of parabatic self-defense. The various
poses and masks of Aristophanes' persona are to a large degree conventional. As Plato shows (fr. 106 PCG) Aristophanes was not the only
poet to call attention to the plays he allowed others to produce, as he
does in *Knights, Clouds,* and *Wasps.*[69] Nor was he the first to give ironic
praise and at the same time make fun of the poets of older comedy, as
in the *Knights* parabasis; Cratinus, himself derided as an archaic poet in
this parabasis, does the same.[70] The rags of archaic choruses, alluded
to in the archaizing parodos of *Ran.* 405–7, were a stock joke.[71] The
Clouds parabasis was certainly not the first to rebuke the audience for
preferring other poets, or to assert the playwright's novelty and innovations, or to criticize his opponents for stealing material.[72] Attacks
and counterattacks on comic competitors were the stuff of parabatic
discourse.[73] Aristophanes' claim to have purified Comedy from farcical

67. Cf. Agthe 1866, 52–53; Fraenkel 1962, 205–15; Silk 1980, 143–44.
68. On prayer parody generally in Aristophanes, see Horn 1970, 38–57. For Aristophanes' parody of Eupolis' ὅστις . . . -formulae used in curses, see p. 86 below.
69. Plato's complaint about not winning when producing plays in his own name is
confirmed by the testimonium recorded as Aristophanes, fr. 590.44–51 PCG.
70. Cratinus, fr. 361a PCG, quotes a familiar song of Ecphantides (as Cratinus' songs
are quoted in *Eq.* 529–30). For other ironic criticisms of older comedy, cf. Callias, fr. 26
PCG, and Aristophanes, fr. 347 PCG (on Crates).
71. Cf. Aristophanes, fr. 264–65 PCG; Pherecrates, fr. 199 PCG.
72. For rebuke of the audience, see Eupolis, fr. 392 PCG, probably directed against
Aristophanes, and perhaps Adesp., fr. 47 K, although it is unclear whether those deceiving the public here are meant to be other poets or politicians. On the playwright's
novelty, see Cratinus, fr. 153 PCG; Metagenes, fr. 15 PCG; Pherecrates, fr. 84 PCG. On
stealing material, see Cratinus, fr. 213 PCG, and Eupolis, fr. 89 PCG, both directed
against Aristophanes over his alleged stealing from Eupolis in the *Knights;* Aristophanes,
fr. 58–59 PCG; Lysippus, fr. 4 PCG (a disclaimer).
73. In addition to the above, cf. Cratinus, fr. 342, 361c PCG; Adesp., fr. 46 K.

vulgarities like the starving Heracles (*Pax* 741–42; cf. *Vesp.* 60) repeats
a joke already made by Cratinus (fr. 346 PCG). His claim to have defeated Cleon with his comedy (*Vesp.* 1030–37, *Pax* 752–60) was shared
by Plato (fr. 115 PCG) who insists that he was the *first* to "make war" on
Cleon,[74] thus replying to Aristophanes' insistence in *Nub.* 551–59 that
Plato and others had merely followed his example of attacking Cleon
when they attacked Hyperbolus.

Our loss of most Old Comedy other than our eleven extant plays of
Aristophanes makes it difficult to appreciate the full extent of the
borrowings, parodies, claims, and counterclaims being made among
the various poets. But we can be sure that there was nothing less
original than the claim of comic originality. The parabasis is in its very
essence grounded in an atmosphere of developed agonistic competition and intense literary allusion, wherein the poets sought and created
for themselves visible public identities.[75] This environment is indeed
remote from Comedy's ritual origins in the countryside.

Intertextual Drama and Greek Intertextuality

The conspicuous intertextuality of the parabasis in Aristophanes
highlights a more far-reaching sense in which his plays as a whole can
be viewed as intertextual. We have noticed the frequent accusations the
comic poets level against one another of stealing jokes and plot material as well as their assertions about being the *first* to do something.
Almost as frequent are charges or self-defenses of repeating material
from a poet's own previous work.[76] All of this suggests a considerable
degree of borrowing and reworking on the part of the poets of Old
Comedy. Such reuse of material is quite well evidenced for New Comedy, but it may have its beginnings in Old Comedy.[77] Unlike Tragedy,
Comedy did not generally draw its material from the sphere of traditional myth; it depended more on the poet's own inventiveness, and

74. Plato's πόλεμον ἠράμην clearly seems meant to echo Aristophanes' πολεμεῖ
(*Vesp.* 1037) and πολεμίζων (*Pax* 759). On Aristophanes' extended use of military vocabulary and imagery here, especially in the *Peace* parabasis, see pp. 146–47 below.

75. This point, particularly as it relates to the apologetic anapests, is emphasized by
Sifakis (1971b, 61, 68–69). But it is also true of the choral self-presentation in the
epirrhemes, which is so often tied up with requests for the judges' favor (cf. *Nub.* 1115–
30; *Av.* 1102–17; *Eccl.* 1155–62) or in some other way proves the chorus' special merits as
against any other chorus (cf. *Eq.* 565–80; 595–610; *Nub.* 575–94; *Vesp.* 1071–90; *Av.*
753–68; 785–800; *Thesm.* 830–45; fr. 112–13 PCG).

76. See Adesp., fr. 46 K, and Aristophanes, fr. 590.6–9 PCG (as interpreted by
Luppe [1971, 97–99]).

77. See Perusino 1981, 407–13.

therefore the practice of poets imitating each other's ideas or reusing
their own should not surprise us. Inasmuch as their targets were the
same, their avenues of attack would inevitably be similar.

In addition to the outright rewriting of earlier plays, such as Aristophanes is known to have done with the *Clouds, Peace, Thesmophoriazusae,* and *Plutus,* he could also concentrate significant thematic and
imagistic allusions to an earlier play within a later work, which could
either capitalize on the previous drama's popularity or try to make
good its lack of success. Again we are greatly helped by possessing the
successive plays *Acharnians* through *Peace,* which allow us to grasp the
significance of the *Wasps* as a pastiche of themes from the *Knights* and
Clouds, and of the *Peace* as a continuation and sequel to the *Wasps.* Later
in Aristophanes' career we see the two women's plays of 411 closely
integrated, with *Thesmophoriazusae* picking up on many themes hinted
at but not yet fully developed in the *Lysistrata.* Later yet the *Ecclesiazusae*
gives us a nightmare inversion of the *Lysistrata.* The *Birds* gains new
meaning when viewed in the context of the recently revised *Clouds,*
which itself goes back for important elements to the model of Aristophanes' first play, *Banqueters.*[78] In turn the *Birds* inspires the idea of
overthrowing the Olympians by reinvigorating a primeval divinity in
the *Plutus.*[79] These "intra-intertextual" connections are often put into
focus by the parabases, and it will be a major goal of the following
chapters to elaborate their significance in detail.

No one can deny that Aristophanes' plays make reference to one
another in specific terms as well as with more general parallels. Aristophanes often gives the audience a hint about his next play, as in *Ach.*
300–301, in which the chorus promises to "cut Cleon to shreds for the
knights,"[80] or as in *Vesp.* 1448–49, in which Philocleon begins to tell the
Aesopic fable of the dung beetle and the eagle only to be cut off by his
son, leaving it to the next play to complete the story (= *Pax* 129–34).[81]
Similarly the conversation of the triremes in the antepirrheme of the
Knights' second parabasis (*Eq.* 1300–15) may be intended as a hint at
the ship chorus of the *Holkades,* if indeed that play was the one presented at the Lenaea of 423.[82] More often he will work clever allusions

---

78. See *Nub.* 528–33, which may imply that the debate of the two Discourses was
modelled on the debate of the two sons in *Banqueters.* See our discussion on pp. 92–93
below.

79. The *Plutus* also derives the motif of seeking a temple cure from the *Amphiaraus,*
dated the same year as the *Birds.*

80. On this passage and its relation especially to *Eq.* 314, see Pohlenz 1952, 103;
Sommerstein 1980, 169–70; Mastromarco 1988, 239–43.

81. See our discussion on p. 151 below. The fable, and thus the *Peace,* is also alluded
to retrospectively in *Lys.* 694–95, on which, see p. 194, below.

82. See p. 20 n.17 above, and chap. 6 n.14 below.

to his immediately preceding play into the prologue or parodos, as in *Ach.* 5–8 on Dicaeopolis' delight in seeing the knights make Cleon disgorge five talents, a detail usually taken as a figurative reference to the *Babylonians,* or in *Eq.* 19, deprecating the use of *skandix* (a herb with which the greengrocer's son Euripides is associated in *Ach.* 475–78), or in *Pax* 348–50, where the entering chorus identifies itself as a chorus of former jurors (i.e. the Wasps).[83] In the prologue reference can also be made to much earlier plays: for example, Lysistrata's comments on the women from Acharnae and Anagyros (*Lys.* 61–68),[84] or the insistence of Xanthias in *Vesp.* 61–63 that the present play is not going to exhibit the discomfiture of either Euripides, as in *Acharnians,* or Cleon, as in *Knights.* While this type of autoallusion may in itself seem slight and inconsequential, it shows Aristophanes' dramatic *oeuvre* as a mutually interconnected continuity in which the poet's relation to his other works was considered a fertile ground for comic inspiration.[85]

In discussing the phenomenon of autoreferential intertextuality in Aristophanes, we should bear in mind that it is a poetic practice having long roots in the history of Greek literature. Epic, lyric, and tragic poetry all offer significant examples of allusion from one text of the same author to another, both on the general thematic level and in specific verbal terms.

Scholars have long discussed cross-references between the *Iliad* and the *Odyssey* as significant moments highlighting the distinctive character of each text. Although some would deny the poems to be the work of the same author and others would argue for any apparent parallels being merely formulaic, it must be emphasized that the ancients considered the two poems to be the work of one man named Homer, and that a culture in which large sections of text were conventionally learned by memory would be particularly apt to register significant parallels and repetitions between the texts. Thus, as perceived by later Greek literary tradition, such parallels were indeed cases of autoreferential intertextuality.

The Homeric cross-references are both many and varied, but are usually assumed to be instances of the *Odyssey* (generally accepted as

83. See chap. 3 n.2, chap. 4 n.13, and pp. 151–52 below.
84. See p. 194 and n.104 below.
85. In this respect, as in so many others (see Appendix 2), Ben Jonson proves to be Aristophanes' most acute reader and imitator. Note the repeated allusions to the title of his play *The Devil Is an Ass* (1616) in his next play, produced after a ten-year absence from the public theater, *The Staple of News* (1626)—the Aesop's ass jokes in I.i.88–95; the devil jokes in I.Cho.26–55; the Devil Tavern in IV.i. The point of the intertextuality may be to remind the audience of Jonson's previous career as a poet for the public theater, seemingly forgotten during his period of court activity.

coming later) troping or reinterpreting familiar Iliadic passages. The *Odyssey*'s proem has been shown to respond in detail to the structure and themes of the *Iliad*'s proem, using the very fact of their parallelism to delineate and sharpen the *Odyssey*'s distinctive character.[86] Significant verbal and narrative parallels have also been demonstrated between the Circe episode and the ransoming of Hector's corpse in *Iliad* 24.[87] In a particularly illuminating article,[88] Walter Burkert has analyzed Demodocus' song of Ares and Aphrodite in *Od.* 8.266–366 as a conflation of motifs from the gods' feast in *Iliad* 1, the Deception of Zeus in *Iliad* 14, and the Theomachy of *Iliad* 20, thus importing into the *Odyssey* the Iliadic theme of the "easy-living gods" that is otherwise foreign to it, and situating within this contrastive Iliadic framework the *Odyssey*'s themes of marital fidelity and triumph through clever stratagem.

More recently Pucci has proposed an even more sophisticated model for understanding such references.[89] He cites the case of *Od.* 5.203–4 (Διογενὲς Λαερτιάδη, πολυμήχαν' Ὀδυσσεῦ,/οὕτω δὴ οἰκόνδε φίλην ἐς πατρίδα γαῖαν . . . = "Descendant of Zeus, son of Laertes, resourceful Odysseus, [are you ready to go now] back home to your dear fatherland?"), where Calypso warns Odysseus of troubles on his return to Ithaca, as a unique repetition of *Il.* 2.173–74, where Athena rebukes Odysseus for fleeing to the ships after Agamemnon's feigned abandonment of the war. Pucci sees knowledge of the parallel as enriching the meaning of the Odyssean text by implying that Calypso's remark is also, like Athena's, a rebuke based on superior divine knowledge of the future. Pucci notes further that both contexts stigmatize Odysseus' desire to return home as abandonment of a woman (Helen in *Il.* 2.176–78, Calypso herself in *Od.* 5.208–13); Odysseus' journey, the heroic theme of the *Odyssey*, is thus implicitly characterized as a rejection of his heroic mission in the *Iliad,* which Athena tells him is to stay. Going one step further, the Odyssean parallel serves also to rewrite the Iliadic passage and to give it new meaning as a reflection on the *Odyssey,* characterizing that epic's theme of heroic return as essentially unheroic in contrast with the *Iliad,* which compels the hero to stay and fight. Thus, for Pucci, the intertextuality functions in both directions, with each text acting as an "iridescent surface" disseminating new meanings in light of the other and implicitly differentiating itself and its standard of "heroism" from the other. In the case of texts whose very nature is to be continually repeated and reperformed and hence to resonate within

---

86. See Bassett 1923, 339–48; West 1988 I, 67–68; Cook 1990, 95–100.
87. See Beck 1965, 1–29 for the most comprehensive treatment of the question.
88. Burkert 1960, 130–44.
89. Pucci 1987, especially 33–43.

the full framework of epic tradition, the question of compositional priority becomes marginal.

It is difficult to appreciate the full extent of autoreferential intertextuality in the lyric tradition because there are so few classical lyric poets whose work survives in anything more than very fragmentary form. But the one lyric poet whose work is extant to an appreciable degree does afford a number of significant examples of cross-reference, ranging from the mere verbal tag to more substantive thematic reincarnations. The famous opening of Pindar's *O.*1 (Ἄριστον μὲν ὕδωρ, ὁ δὲ χρυσὸς αἰθόμενον πῦρ . . . = "Water is best, and gold like blazing fire . . .") is cited significantly in another ode written in the same year, *O.*3:

> εἰ δ᾽ ἀριστεύει μὲν ὕδωρ, κτεάνων δὲ χρυσὸς αἰδοιέστατος,
> νῦν δὲ πρὸς ἐσχατιὰν Θήρων ἀρεταῖσιν ἱκάνων ἅπτεται
> οἴκοθεν Ἡρακλέος σταλᾶν.

> If water is best, and gold the most honored of possessions,
> Theron now, reaching to the limit with his virtues, grasps
> The pillars of Heracles from his home.

> (*O.*3.42–44)

The insertion of the allusion into a condition grammatically marks its familiarity to the audience.[90] *O.*1 is particularly significant as the text chosen for citation here, since it was composed in 476 to celebrate the Olympian horse victory of Hieron, tyrant of Syracuse, and *O.*3 was written in the same year for the even more prestigious Olympian chariot victory of Theron, tyrant of Acragas, Hieron's in-law and occasional rival. The allusion thus serves to incorporate the splendid terms of praise accorded Hieron in *O.*1 within the praise of Theron, as if to imply everything said there of Hieron as also extending to Theron. But it does more; in the context of *O.*1, water and gold are presented as foils to victory in the Olympic games, as preeminent in its class as water and gold are in their respective categories (*O.*1.1–7). The tag "water and gold" accordingly implies the rest of the statement in *O.*1, suggesting Olympic victory to be the highest achievement a man can have. One could paraphrase the condition in this way: "if Olympic victory is indeed the highest mortal prosperity (as I have said before), then Theron reaches the limit of what a man can attain."

On still another level in both passages, water and gold symbol-

---

90. For such cases of "grammatical presupposition" as markers of either explicit or implied intertextuality, see Culler 1981, 111–14. On the rhetorical force of the particular grammatical form used here (an undeniable protasis coupled with a laudatory apodosis), see Bundy 1962 II, 54–59.

ize the power of poetic celebration as commissioned by the patron's wealth,[91] thereby adding the refinement that Theron reaches the limit not merely through Olympic victory but through Olympic victory as reflected in a commissioned epinician. Finally, it bears noting that the context in *O.*3 in fact replicates significant themes of *O.*1: immediately preceding these lines Theron has been praised for his excellence in Theoxenian hospitality (*O.*3.38–41), even as hospitality is a major theme of *O.*1, in which Hieron's positive hospitality is contrasted with Tantalus' violation of the rules of the feast.[92] And immediately after the passage, *O.*3 closes with a warning to Theron that one can go no further than the pillars of Heracles, and even that the poet himself can go no further (*O.*3.44–5). *O.*1 ends on the same note advising Hieron that no lot higher than the kingship exists for mortals, and no lot higher than being in the company of kings can exist for poets like himself (*O.*1.113–6).[93] *O.*3.42–4 thus serves to make *O.*3 resonate against the background of *O.*1, applying equally to both tyrants the same terms of both praise and admonition.[94]

Another significant case of evoking an ode by allusion to its proem is visible at the beginning of Pindar's *P.*6:

'Ακούσατ'· ἦ γὰρ ἑλικώπιδος 'Αφροδίτας ἄρουραν ἢ Χαρίτων
ἀναπολίζομεν, ὀμφαλὸν ἐριβρόμου
χθονὸς ἐς νάϊον προσοιχόμενοι·

Listen! For we again plow the field of rolling-eyed Aphrodite
And the Graces, approaching the sacred navel
Of the thundering earth.

(P.6.1–3)

As has been noted,[95] Aphrodite and the Graces had earlier been coupled by Pindar in the proem of *Paean* 6 as deities assisting his invocation to Delphi; as the verb ἀναπολίζομεν emphasizes, with its iterative ἀνα-prefix, the chorus now again needs their help in approaching

91. See my discussion in Hubbard 1985, 14–15.
92. For a more detailed discussion, see Hubbard 1985, 158.
93. On such limitation gnomes concluding Pindaric odes, with equal application to both poet and victor, see Hubbard 1985, 143–45.
94. That "water and gold" indeed function as an allusive tag evoking *O.*1 is confirmed by Bacchylides 3.85–90, in another ode for Hieron, which also includes a clear allusion to Pindar's *O.*2.83–88. Only here Bacchylides intentionally trifles with the idea of water and gold as preeminent by placing them as the second and third terms in a series, rather than first and second as in Pindar, and rejecting them in a priamel as inappropriate terms of comparison for human mortality, in contrast to Pindar's using them as positive terms of comparison for Olympic victory.
95. See Wilamowitz 1908, 345; Gentili 1988, 278 n.60.

Delphi, the scene of this Pythian athletic victory. Both texts thematize the act of approaching the sacred precinct (*P*.6.3; cf. *Paean* 6.5–9) and identify Delphi with its familiar epithet "navel of the earth" (*P*.6.2–3, *Paean* 6.17 χθονὸς ὀμφαλόν). Pindar's allusion to his previous evocation of these deities in approaching Delphi therefore constitutes an implied hypomnesis,[96] reminding not only Aphrodite and the Graces of their past association with the poet but also reminding Delphi of the poet's past services to it in *Paean* 6. As in the case of *O*.1 and *O*.3, the allusion serves to incorporate within the later text everything featured by the earlier text; the lengthy prayer to Delphi to receive the approaching Pindaric chorus with good favor in *Paean* 6.1–18 is thus by implication present at the opening of *P*.6, rendering further elaboration of that motif unnecessary. Pindar can rely on Delphi's favor now because he has beseeched and obtained it before with the help of Aphrodite and the Graces, symbols of the charm and beauty of the choral dance (see especially *Paean* 6.9, 15–18)[97] and, in the context of *P*.6, also fittingly symbols of the beauty of the young charioteer Thrasybulus.[98]

Still closer to Aristophanes we find autoreferential cross-reference at home in Greek tragedy. The verbal, thematic, imagistic, and structural links between plays of a connected trilogy are familiar to any student of Aeschylus. More significantly such links can from time to time be shown to exist between plays of the same author on related mythological themes, even when separated by many years, as is familiar from the case of Sophocles' *Oedipus Tyrannus* and *Oedipus at Colonus*.[99] There must also have been some such relation between Sophocles' *Ajax* and *Teucer*, given the prominence assigned Teucer in the second half of the *Ajax* and the particular emphasis placed on his fear of coming home to Telamon in Salamis (*Aj*. 1006–20). Equally the introduction of Ajax' young son Eurysaces as a mute personage (*Aj*. 574–77) does not seem to be motivated by internal considerations nearly so much as by allusion to Sophocles' *Eurysaces*. It is impossible to be sure whether these elements in the *Ajax* are allusions to the *Teucer* and *Eurysaces* as pre-

---

96. On the device of hypomnesis in archaic poetry, see Keyssner 1932, 134; Meyer 1933, 4–5.

97. For the general association of the Graces with choral dance in Pindar, see *O*.14.8–9; *N*.6.37–38; *I*.5.21–22; *I*.6.62–64. In the context of *Paean* 6, Aphrodite is also relevant in light of the juxtaposed young male chorus approaching Delphi, "bereft of the dance of men" (*Paean* 6.9), and the maiden chorus already celebrating Apollo inside the precinct (*Paean* 6.15–18).

98. It is conventional for a young *laudandus* to be addressed in terms of *eros*. Cf. *P*.10.55–60; *N*.8.1–8; and the discussions of Von der Mühll 1964, 168–72; Crotty 1982, 79, 101–2.

99. For the most complete study of the relations between these two plays, see Seidensticker 1972, 255–74.

vious plays or prospective devices foreshadowing future plans to treat
these tragic topics in the style of Aristophanes' forward-looking allusions in *Ach.* 300–301 or *Vesp.* 1448–49.

Entire dramatic scenes may be designed with an eye to such intertextual coordination. It has been argued that the Io scene in the *Prometheus Bound* is intimately connected with the motif of Io in Aeschylus'
Suppliants and acts to imply that trilogy's conception of Zeus as a
developed, compassionate god and a *telos* toward which the *Prometheia*
will move, even as Io did.[100] Similarly the burial scene at the end of
Aeschylus' *Seven Against Thebes,* which has seemed to many critics awkward and out of place, makes better sense if regarded as a device
coordinating the drama with Aeschylus' other trilogy on the Argive
war, in which we know that burial of the Argive dead was a major
issue.[101]

We therefore observe a well-developed tradition of self-referential
allusion in Greek literature from its very beginnings, taking the forms
of both specific verbal citation of prior works and more general thematic parallels of plot structure. As in other forms of intertextuality
these allusions function not merely as cross-references reminding us of
a previous text but as significant evocations incorporating and transforming the context and meaning of those prior texts; at the same time
they add a dimension of meaning to the alluding text, not present in
the words or motifs when taken in isolation.

Although the art of allusion in archaic Greek poetry has not been as
thoroughly studied as it has been for Roman and Hellenistic poetry
and although we are to some extent hampered by less complete remains, it can nevertheless be shown to have been practiced with great
sophistication and self-consciousness. Particularly in the form of auto-
referential intertextuality, allusion formed part of every Greek poet's
desire to present a distinct personal identity to his public, consisting
not of a single text's persona but of a reputation based on an entire career's *oeuvre* and bound together by multiple echoes and self-citations.
In this regard Aristophanes' self-presentation to his Athenian audience
is firmly grounded within the context of traditional Greek poetics.

100. See Murray 1958, 46–76. I persist in believing the *Prometheia* indeed to have
been a late work of Aeschylus.
101. On Aeschylus' *Eleusinioi* and its probable date in the late 470s, prior to the *Seven,*
see my discussion in Hubbard 1991, forthcoming.

CHAPTER 3

The Mask of Dicaeopolis

Few plays of Aristophanes make the connection between the poetic and political realms more evident than the *Acharnians,* in this respect rivalled perhaps only by the *Frogs.*

Spectator, Actor, Poet

At the opening of the drama we behold the farmer Dicaeopolis sitting alone before the deserted Pnyx, awaiting the entrance of the Prytanes and the start of the belated Assembly, even as the theatrical audience only seconds ago was waiting for the start of the present play. Like Dicaeopolis, many members of the audience were country folk and had no doubt been present in the theater since dawn (see v. 20).[1] This parallel between the political and theatrical is implied by the protagonist in his opening remarks: among the few pleasures he has enjoyed is the sight of the demagogue Cleon on the comic stage "disgorging" five talents (vv. 5–8).[2] But this delight has been dulled by the

1. On the audience's early morning arrival in the theater for extensive preliminary ceremonies, see Xenophon, *Oec.* 3.7.9; Athenaeus 11.464F; Aeschines 3.76; Demosthenes 21.74. Noting the lack of sufficient supernumeraries to constitute a credible assembly, MacDowell (1983, 147) observes that the theatrical audience itself is brought into the play as the assembly of the Pnyx, and Dicaeopolis acts as one of their number. On the physical analogy between the theater and Pnyx as the "public spaces" of Athenian cultural and political life, see Ober & Strauss 1990, 238, and the interesting essay of Kolb (1979, particularly 507–15), which derives the association from the theater's origins as a place of performance in the *agora.*

2. The surrounding context suggests that the event was primarily dramatic, although it may have had some historical basis too; it may in fact refer to Aristophanes' last

tedium of Theognis' tragedy, possibly presented on the same day (vv. 9–12),[3] even as his delight in the citharodist Dexitheus (vv. 13–14) last year is balanced this year by his boredom in waiting for Chaeris (vv. 15–16).

Nor is the vein of theatrical rivalry limited to this passage. Having witnessed the general Lamachus arming for battle while Dicaeopolis enjoys a feast, the chorus in the third stasimon wishes that their erstwhile choregus Antimachus,[4] himself called a "poet" (v. 1150), may be similarly deprived of a meal (vv. 1156–61); for Anti*machus*, like La*machus* (see vv. 595–619),[5] has deprived the chorus of their just due (vv. 1154–55), though enjoying the advantages of his exalted position. In the corresponding antistrophe they wish that in attempting to throw a stone at a street thug, Antimachus should actually pick up a fresh dog dropping and hit the comic poet Cratinus (vv. 1164–73).[6] Cratinus had already been ridiculed for his immorality in the first choral ode (vv. 848–53),[7] together with a list of other rogues and sycophants the

play, the *Babylonians*, which we know to have attacked Cleon (cf. Σ*Ach.* 378). Cf. Merry 1880, 3; Lübke 1883, 17–18; van Leeuwen 1901, 8–9; Rennie 1909, 86–88; Starkie 1909, 241–43; van Daele 1923 I, 12 n.1; Kraus 1985, 32–33. The Aristophanic *Vita* (XXVIII, 16–19 Koster) also seems to interpret this passage as an auto-referential allusion, although wrongly attributing it to the *Knights* (perhaps because *Eq.* 1147–50 seems to refer to the same event). The attempts of the scholia (Σ*Ach.* 6a) to reconstruct a historical basis for the allusion are neither consistent nor precise; for a discussion of the problems with their citation of Theopompus, see Connor 1968, 57 and Bugh 1988, 109–11. It seems quite unlikely that Cleon was actually convicted of taking a five talent bribe from the allies and was able to remain active in Athenian politics afterward; for a more likely source of the allusion, see chap. 4 n.54 below.

3. Comedies and tragedies would be produced on the same day during this period. See *Av.* 786–89, and Allen 1938, 40–42; Pickard-Cambridge 1962, 63. It may be that Aristophanes wishes to contrast the brilliance of his own effort with the dullness of the preceding tragedies. On Theognis' "frigidity," cf. vv. 139–40.

4. The scholia (Σ*Ach.* 1150a, c) speculate that Antimachus may have been responsible for a decree banning payment of choruses (unlikely) or restricting the freedom of Comedy (not what the chorus protests here). More likely he was just the choregus (either this year or last) for a competing comedy, perhaps Cratinus' *Cheimazomenoi*. Cf. van Leeuwen 1901, 184–85; Sommerstein 1980a, 212. It is improbable that Antimachus was a choregus for Aristophanes, as recently suggested by Halliwell (1980, 44–45); the choral first person can be generic, speaking for all comic choruses as well as for Aristophanes.

5. On the parallel between Antimachus and Lamachus, both in name and fate, see Moulton 1981, 22.

6. Note the skillful placement of Antimachus' name as the first word of the strophe (v. 1150) and Cratinus' as the last word of the antistrophe (v. 1173). The clear parallel between the two suggests some form of association.

7. A number of commentators regard this Cratinus as someone other than the comic poet. Cf. Mitchell 1835, 179; Halbertsma 1856, 64–65; Merry 1880, 52; Starkie 1909, 174–75; Rogers 1910, 130–31. But the later reference in v. 1173 seems more appropriate to the comic poet, and since Cratinus was competing in the comic contest at this festival (cf. *Hyp.* I), he would be the man the audience would tend to think of when

chorus wishes to be absent from Dicaeopolis' market. Clearly both Dicaeopolis and the chorus (and presumably Aristophanes) view the contemporary decline of dramatic poetry and music as part and parcel of the general deterioration of public life in contemporary Athens.

Given this connection, Dicaeopolis naturally serves as a positive foil who not only personifies the principles of the "Just City," but in many ways embodies the archetypal spirit of Comedy itself.[8] His outrageous fantasy of establishing a private peace with the Spartans, his successful defiance of the powers that be, and his unabashed and unreserved self-indulgence, all make Dicaeopolis the paradigmatic comic hero. It is in no small part the hero's nature and irrepressible appeal that make the *Acharnians* the play criticism most often cites as the ideal model against which all other Aristophanic plays are compared.[9] Dicaeopolis' self-assertion is unrestrained by social conventions, but at the same time is socially restorative in its capacity as a ritual sublimation; the hero en-acts the organic wellsprings of the Comic as a simultaneously individual and communal release, whether by his orchestration of the phallic procession (vv. 241–79)—from which, as Aristotle tells us, Comedy arose[10]—or with his riotous exit in the final *kōmos* (vv. 1198–1231).[11]

Dicaeopolis' self-conscious theatricality is most conspicuous in his insistence on donning tragic costume before addressing the hostile chorus of Acharnians. The point of this episode is surely not just to ridicule Euripides' predilection for ragged heroes but to comment on the interrelations of Tragedy and Comedy, and, more broadly, to ex-emplify the rhetorical nature of the dramatic spectacle in general.[12] Perhaps Comedy should appear to adopt the more serious guise of Tragedy when directly confronting the important political issues of the day. The gravity of the argument and its potential consequences are symbolized by Dicaeopolis' delivery of his speech with his head placed

---

hearing the name, rather than some obscure musician. The scholia's reference to a μελῶν ποιητής (cf. ΣAch. 849a, b) is nothing more than an inference from the text; for criticism of scholiastic assumptions on this issue, see Halliwell 1984, 88.

8. For the view that Dicaeopolis is a generic figure for Comedy, especially in his great *apologia* of vv. 496–507, see Dover 1963, 15; Edmunds 1980, 12; MacDowell 1983, 149.

9. Cf. Segal 1961, 217; Whitman 1964, 59–60; Sandbach 1977, 18–24; Torrance 1978, 42; Carrière 1979, 86.

10. Aristotle, *Poet.* 1449a9. See chap. 2 n.35 above.

11. On the final *kōmos* as one of the most important archetypal elements of comic structure, see Cornford 1968, 56–77.

12. On the paradigmatic rhetoricity of Dicaeopolis' speech here, see de Carli 1971, 37–38. On the general analogy between drama and rhetoric as forms allowing elite speakers to communicate with mass audiences, see Ober 1989, 152–55; Ober & Strauss 1990, 237–70; Redfield 1990, 319–21.

on the "chopping block" (vv. 353–57, 485–87).[13] It is not only Tragedy and Comedy that are being likened here, however; Dicaeopolis' speech in costume implies also that rhetoric is essentially dramatic and drama essentially rhetorical. As Aristotle emphasizes (see *Rhet.* I, 1356a4–13), the rhetorical art consists in the creation of an *ēthos* or persona for the speaker that arouses sympathy and even a sense of identification on the part of the audience. In the dramatic as well as the legal agon, the substance of the argument is not nearly so important as the apparent sincerity with which it is delivered. Dicaeopolis must therefore disguise himself as a creature even more miserable than he actually is: the beggar Telephus, who has been gravely wounded by war and now has the unpleasant task of appearing before a war-mad audience as the enemy's ally. And like Telephus, he must even resort to a desperate act of hostage taking before he can make the audience receptive.[14] In the end Dicaeopolis does win the sympathy of his audience (who are them-selves a rather pitiable lot, as we see in the parabasis) by convincing them that they are as much victims of the war profiteers as he is (vv. 607–17).

This self-conscious *eirōneia* applies not only to Dicaeopolis and the audience of Acharnians but also to Aristophanes and the real theatrical audience. It may be only through placing Tragedy, symbolized here by the Telephus figure, within the context of Comedy that a poet can safely address the contemporary political scene. The serious can be communicated only through the ridiculous, the higher through the lower mimetic. The techniques of Aristophanes and Euripides are similar in that both bring their heroes down to a level closer to that of the common man in the audience. Both poets also test the frontiers between Tragedy and Comedy, the one making his tragic heroes more comic, the other making his comic heroes more tragic (or paratragic).[15] In so doing, they attempt to make drama a closer reflection of the human condition in its variegated complexity.

13. Kannicht 1983, 252–55 observes that the image of speaking on the chopping block not only dramatizes Dicaeopolis' risk, but more broadly, Aristophanes' risk in speaking *dikaia* within the present political environment.

14. For the extended parody of Euripides' *Telephus* in this scene, see Starkie 1909, 248–51; Rostagni 1927, 312–30; Handley 1957, 22–25; Rau 1967, 19–42; and most recently, Foley 1988, 34–45 who shows its importance as a paradigm for the entire play. Telephus is not merely a tragic figure here, but a verbal and visual embodiment of Tragedy, as Dicaeopolis in his own persona is the incarnation of Comedy.

15. For Euripides' position as the preeminent experimenter with comic elements in Tragedy, see the detailed discussion of Seidensticker 1982, 89–241. The name Aristoph-anes often uses for his comedy, τρυγῳδία (see vv. 499–500), underlines its ambivalent status. It is like τραγῳδία, but operates on a lower level. On the word's origin as a comic deformation of "Tragedy," see Pickard-Cambridge 1962, 283–84; Ghiron-Bistagne 1973, 285–87; and on the paronomasia clearly apparent in *Ach.* 499–500, see Taplin 1983, 331–33.

It should therefore come as no surprise that Dicaeopolis is not only the spirit of Comedy in the abstract but is also, on a more specific level, the voice of the comic poet. Dicaeopolis progressively assumes the role of every person involved in the dramatic spectacle, first as a spectator (at the Pnyx), then as an actor (in Telephus' costume), and finally as the playwright. These multiple and overlapping levels of ironic discourse are all unfolded in the opening lines of Dicaeopolis' speech of defense, which is also a preliminary self-defense by the poet:[16]

> O spectators, do not begrudge me,
> If I am about to speak among the Athenians
> About the city, as a beggar, making Comedy.
> For even Comedy knows what is just.   500
> And Cleon will not slander me for
> Abusing the city with foreigners present.
> For we are by ourselves now, the contest is at the Lenaea,
> And foreigners are not yet present; neither tribute   505
> Nor the allies have come from the various cities,
> But we are by ourselves now, all winnowed out.
>
> (vv. 497–507)

We witness a skillful exploitation of ambiguities to effect a smooth transition from Dicaeopolis as a self-conscious actor in the play within the play to Dicaeopolis as a vehicle for the poet's voice from outside the play. The speaker first addresses the "spectators" (either the Acharnians, who are "spectators" in this context, or the real audience in the theater). In v. 499 he apologizes for his presumption in speaking about political affairs though appearing as a beggar (a disguise for both Dicaeopolis and Aristophanes) and making τρυγῳδίαν (either Dicaeopolis' mock τραγῳδία, or the comedy Aristophanes makes). The eloquent beggar is of course a fitting symbol for Comedy in general. Comedy knows τὸ δίκαιον (v. 500 "what is just"); this assertion reflects on *Dicaeo*polis and even more directly on the poet who repeatedly asserts his association with τὸ δίκαιον in his parabatic self-defense (see vv. 645, 655, 661).[17] V. 501 personalizes this general statement and

16. Some scholars have seen the identification between Dicaeopolis and Aristophanes as so close they have gone to the extreme of postulating that the role of the protagonist was acted by Aristophanes himself. Cf. Bailey 1936, 231–40; Lever 1956, 112. This view was foreshadowed by Briel (1887, 26), Müller-Strübing (1873, 607), and Schrader (1877, 396), all of whom, however, believed the chief actor to have been the producer Callistratus.

17. For the parallels between Dicaeopolis' speeches and the parabasis, cf. Rehdantz 1862, 7; Steinbrück 1865, 13–14; Harsh 1934, 188–93; Muecke 1977, 57; Landfester 1977, 43–44; Bowie 1982, 30; Perusino 1986, 25–30; Harriott 1986, 33–34; Reckford 1987, 188–90.

applies it to the present context. Vv. 502–7 support the gnome and self-application by allusion to the past example of Cleon's attack on the poet for "maligning" the city in the presence of foreigners. The point of this allusion must be the poet's intention to speak what he believes to be right even at the expense of incurring opposition from powerful enemies.

The poet defends himself against Cleon's charge only by evading it, playing on the ambiguity inherent in the delivery of these lines by Telephus/Dicaeopolis rather than by the poet himself. Dicaeopolis of course was not responsible for the *Babylonians* and therefore needs to assert only Cleon's inability to make such a charge now, since the present "play" is produced at the Lenaea and is consequently among fellow Athenians (such as the Acharnians). The interpenetration between dramatic fantasy and political reality is so well developed that we cannot at any moment assert with certainty which of the two realms is referred to.[18]

Nor is this passage the first in which Dicaeopolis takes on the poet's identity and refers to his struggle with Cleon. He also does so directly before the costume scene in vv. 377–84:

> And I myself know what I suffered from Cleon
> Because of last year's comedy:
> Dragging me into the Council-chamber,
> He slandered me and tongue-lashed me with lies,   380
> He roared like the Cycloborus and splattered me with his spray,
> So that I almost perished, soiled by his slime.
> Now then, first before I speak, allow
> Me to dress myself most wretchedly.

By this paradigm Dicaeopolis contrasts his own forthrightness with the hypocrisy of charming flatterers who manipulate the public (v. 374) by telling them only what they want to hear regardless of its rightness or

18. Σ*Ach.* 378 (and Σ*Vesp.* 1284) speak of a "lawsuit" Cleon brought against the poet; but it is quite clear that this is merely an inference from this text and from the parabasis. That the scholia did not have a historical source for information about the lawsuit is apparent from the discrepancy between Σ*Ach.* 378, identifying Aristophanes as the defendant, and Σ*Vesp.* 1284, identifying Callistratus as defendant. It is, however, not right to reject the historical reality of this conflict completely, as Lefkowitz (1981, 109) and Rosen (1983, 217 [= Rosen 1988, 63–64]) do. The insistent repetition of this allusion, in both Dicaeopolis' speeches *qua* comic poet and in the poet's parabatic self-defense, indicates that it must have had some basis in reality; cf. Foley 1988, 33 n.4. V. 379 (εἰσελκύσας γάρ μ' ἐς τὸ βουλευτήριον) certainly makes the event sound like a formal *eisaggelia,* although Aristophanes refers to it elsewhere merely as "slander" (v. 380 διέβαλλε, v. 502 διαβαλεῖ, v. 630 διαβαλλόμενος).

justice (vv. 372–73). By implication Cleon himself may be such a flat-
terer. In contrast Dicaeopolis (and the poet) will not hesitate to tell the
city when it has erred, even at the risk of being slandered before the
Council, as has occurred in regard to "last year's comedy." But this time,
he must take greater care and speak in disguise (vv. 383–84). The
following costume scene is thus clearly introduced as a metaphor for
the poet's technique of dramatic self-disguise.

But this act of concealment is always coupled with a comic impetus to
self-conscious deconcealment. The Acharnian spectators in the play
are to be deceived by the dramatic illusion, whereas all along the real
spectators in the audience are meant to see through the guise (vv. 440–
44):[19]

> "I must today seem a beggar,   440
> While being who I am, although not appearing so:"
> The audience must know me and who I am,
> While the choristers stand here like fools,
> So that I can mock them with my little phrases.

"Who I am" is not merely the disguised Telephus, nor only the disguised Dicaeopolis, but the dramatically disguised comic poet as well.
However, the spectators are perhaps not as omniscient as they might
suppose; though on the primary level recognizing the beggar as Telephus and Telephus as actually Dicaeopolis who on the secondary level
is identified with the comic poet, they could nevertheless miss a tertiary
level of dramatic disguise which they may not see through, inasmuch as
most of the original spectators did not know who the comic poet really
was, supposing the play to be the work of the producer Callistratus,
under whose name it was publicly announced at the opening ceremony.[20]

The Fame of the Unknown Poet

The play of identities climaxes in the parabasis, which is the play's
principal moment of extradramatic reflection; the comic poet, shad-
owy as he is, presumes to be world-famous, known even to the Persian
king (although his true identity might be known only to a few members
of the original audience). Here too the theme of costuming takes on a

---

19. For the topos of the omniscient audience, cf. *Ran.* 475, *Eccl.* 580–82; Plato, fr. 96
PCG; Ehrenberg 1962, 28–29.
20. On this question, see Appendix 1.

special significance as the chorus declares that it will approach the anapests ἀποδύντες (v. 627). The "undressing" must be metaphorical and not literal,[21] since the chorus, at least for this passage, drops its dramatic guise and addresses the audience on behalf of the "poet," who is, however, ironically lurking behind still another layer of mask and costume, Aristophanes dressed as Callistratus. The ultimate ambiguity of the parabasis' self-revelation is thus appropriately symbolized by the announced but actually unfulfilled undressing of the chorus.

> The man triumphs with his words, and persuades the people
> Concerning his peace-treaty. But let us advance to the anapests,
>> undressing.
> From the time when our teacher first stood over comic choruses,
> He has never before stepped forward to the audience, intending to
>> say how clever he is.
> But slandered by enemies among the swift-counselling Athenians,   630
> On grounds of laughing at our city and insulting the people,
> He asks now to reply to the counsel-changing Athenians.
> The poet says that he is worthy of many good things from you,
> Stopping you from being too deceived by foreign discourses,
> From taking pleasure in flattery, from being gape-citizens.   635
> The ambassadors from various cities were the first to deceive you
> And call you "violet-crowned;" and whenever anyone said this,
> You immediately sat on the tips of your buttocks because of the
>> crowns.
> If, in flattering you, someone had called you "shining Athens,"
> He would have won everything from the "shining," giving you the
>> praise of sardines.   640
> Doing this, the poet has become responsible to you for many good
>> things,
> Showing how the people of the allied cities are governed
>> "democratically."
> Therefore, they will come, bearing tribute to you from the various
>> cities,
> Desiring to see the best poet,
> Who among the Athenians took the risk of saying what is just.   645

21. See my remarks on p. 18 above. The discussion of Sifakis (1971b, 103–8), is inconclusive, foundering on his insistence that there is no such thing as "dramatic illusion." More cogent is Dale (1969, 289–90), who argues that vigorous dancing, such as would require undressing, was unlikely to take place in the anapests. Ketterer (1980, 219–21) argues that the chorus needed to be free to make vigorous gesticulations with the arms, but there is no reason to see a special need for such gesture here (as opposed to the parodos, for instance); in any event, the anapests were almost certainly spoken by the coryphaeus alone, not by the entire chorus. Cf. Muff 1872, 89–90; Arnoldt 1873, 140–41.

Fame concerning his daring has already reached so far that,
When the Great King tested the Spartan embassy,
He first asked them which side prevails with ships,
And then which side this poet rebukes;
For he said that these men have become much better,   650
And would triumph in war, possessing this counselor.
For this reason the Spartans offer you peace,
And demand the return of Aegina. They think not of that island,
But that they may take away this poet.
But may you never release him, since he will write comedy about
     what is just;   655
He says that he will teach you many good things, so that you can be
     happy,
Neither flattering you nor presenting bribes nor cheating you,
Nor committing all knavery nor sprinkling you with praise, but
     teaching the best.
     Let Cleon plot against these things,
     And contrive every plan against me.   660
     For the good and just will be
     Allied with me, and never shall I be found
     To be, like that man, a wretch and a bugger
       In matters of state.

(vv. 626–64)

The opening formula of vv. 626–27 takes the place of the kommation usually expected as a transition between the parabasis and the
preceding dialogue.[22] The tautometric repetition of καὶ τὸν δῆμον
("and the people") in vv. 626 and 631 points out a parallelism drawn
between Dicaeopolis, who at first antagonized the public by his criticism but has won them over, and the poet, who is also accused of giving
offense, but eventually justifies himself. This verbal parallelism effectively smooths the transition from the dramatic plot to the extradramatic parabasis. Vv. 628–29 seem to imply apologetically that this is the
first time the poet has used the parabasis as a vehicle for self-defense,
having done nothing to call attention to himself in the *Banqueters* and
Babylonians.[23] Despite the lack of precedent and the poet's youthful
reserve,[24] the circumstances of his present political situation require
him to come forward and defend himself against the slanders he
has received ἐν Ἀθηναίοις ταχυβούλοις (v. 630 "among the swift-

22. See pp. 17–18 above.
23. Cf. Harsh 1934, 191; Perusino 1986, 19. Again, see *Pax* 734–35 for a comparable
apologetic formula. For the rhetorical effect, see Rehdantz 1862, 7.
24. The parabasis of the *Knights* evokes the same tone of youthful modesty and
hesitation; see especially *Eq.* 545 and *Nub.* 530.

counselling Athenians"), so that he may regain the sympathy of the 'Αθηναίους μεταβούλους (v. 632 "the counsel-changing Athenians").[25] The poet's self-defense against Cleon's accusations forms the background for everything that follows, though Cleon is not mentioned by name until v. 659.

The self-defense is punctuated by parallel statements in v. 633 and 641, first that the poet is πολλῶν ἀγαθῶν ἄξιος ὑμῖν ("worthy of many good things from you") and then that he is πολλῶν ἀγαθῶν αἴτιος ὑμῖν ("responsible to you for many good things").[26] These statements structure a highly sophisticated argument through which the poet counters Cleon's charge of embarrassing the city in front of foreigners in the *Babylonians*, (1) by arguing in vv. 633–40 that he has in fact protected the city against foreigners and their flattery, and (2) by suggesting in vv. 641–58 that foreigners admire him for the frankness with which he speaks and at the same time see the self-critical freedom of speech available in a democratic society not as a weakness but as one of Athens' greatest strengths.

The first argument is intended as a demonstration of the poet's loyalty to the city. But the contrast of his own technique of sincere criticism with the hypocritical and insincere flattery of foreign ambassadors who have no real loyalty to Athens also serves as a potent refutation of Cleon's charge that the poet's criticism has harmed the city. Frank self-criticism, as provided by Comedy, is one of the best ways for the city to avoid being deceived by such flattery. The satirical impetus of the present play is intended to illustrate this principle. In the prologue, we have seen the Athenian leaders gulled and manipulated by foreigners, whether the Persian ambassador FalseArtabas or the Thracian king Sitalces, who presumes to love Athens so much that he writes "beautiful Athenians" on the walls (vv. 142–44).[27] Only the

25. Note the tautometric equivalence of the two phrases. The public may be swift in judging him, but correspondingly their judgments are mutable and may thus be reversed for the better. On the intended modulation, cf. Rehdantz 1862, 10–11; Steinbrück 1865, 14. Note also the echo of μεταπείθει (v. 626), of Dicaeopolis; on which, see Perusino 1986, 29 n.30.

26. Note again the significant metrical equivalence, supported by the parallel of ὁ ποιητής (v. 633) with ταῦτα ποιήσας (v. 641).

27. The mention of foreign flatterers and their hackneyed appellations of the city as ἰοστεφάνους 'Αθήνας or λιπαρὰς 'Αθήνας in vv. 636–40 is surely meant to recall this pompously verbalized infatuation with Athens; on the general connection of this passage with the prologue, see Rehdantz 1862, 11; Harsh 1934, 188; Bowie 1982, 30–31; Perusino 1986, 24 n.18. The flatterers of vv. 636–40 are described as ἀπὸ τῶν πόλεων and may also be a reference to ambassadors from the allies who appeared in the *Babylonians* (cf. Norwood 1930, 6–7; Forrest 1975a, 21; Welsh 1983, 141–42). But if such ambassadors did in fact appear in Aristophanes' previous play, the ambassadors of the *Acharnians* prologue would themselves constitute an auto-referential reminiscence of the

cantankerous ridicule of Dicaeopolis (who, as we have seen, is a surrogate for the comic poet) can unmask such impostors, even as later in the play he sees through the chicanery of the Megarian and Boeotian traders. Like the poet, Dicaeopolis perceives his own critical forthrightness as the very opposite of flattery (vv. 369–74).

By countering the vain sycophancy of such "foreign discourses," the poet claims that he prevents the Athenians from being χαυνοπολίτας (v. 635).[28] The prefix of this word is usually interpreted to mean "empty-headed" in the sense of overinflated self-satisfaction and idle acceptance of flattery. But the usage of the same prefix earlier in the term χαυνοπρώκτους (see vv. 104, 106 "gape-assed") is suggestive here of an added anal reference.[29] Even as the Persian king dismissed the Athenians as "Ionian pathics," so it is implied here that the Athenians allow themselves to be buggered by the wheedling of foreign orators whose florid epithets excite them to the point of sitting "on the tips of your buttocks" (v. 638). Cleon himself is the most servile pathic of all (v. 664 λακαταπύγων).

The poet does not engage in such perverted "love" for the Athenian populace. Instead he will tell them τὰ δίκαια (vv. 645, 655, 661 "what is just"), even if it is unpleasant, and even if it entails criticizing treatment of the allies in their presence (v. 642), as he did in the *Babylonians*.[30] The following argument is in many ways antithetical to the preceding one, in that the poet now emphasizes his positive reputation among foreigners rather than his antipathy toward them. Possibly he views art

---

Babylonians, particularly if Welsh (1983, 143–50) is correct in proposing that the chorus of Babylonians were refugees from Persian tyranny, on analogy with the younger Zopyrus [Hdt. 3.160], and thus that the play was full of Persian allusions.

28. Heath (1987, 22–23) is a bit oversubtle in contending that the parabasis is contradicted by the play itself, in which the Athenians are still shown as gullible. φησὶν . . . παύσας μὴ ἐξαπατᾶσθαι . . . is not a claim to have stopped the Athenians in the past (aorist tense), but to stop them from these actions with the satire of the present play (aorist aspect).

29. For the "empty-headed" interpretation, see Mitchell 1835, 137; Müller 1863, 118; Ribbeck 1864, 111; Sommerstein 1980a, 97. Rennie (1909, 186), Starkie (1909, 135), and van Daele (1923 I, 38) translate as "gobemouches," seeing herein an allusion to gaping with the mouth, and thus swallowing anything. For the anal interpretation, cf. Henderson 1975, 211. For the general comic abuse of the Athenian audience as pathics, see *Eq.* 1263, 1367, *Nub.* 1084–1104, *Pax* 11, and Henderson 1975, 209–11.

30. It is generally doubted today that the chorus of Babylonian slaves was meant as an allegory for the "enslaved" allies (cf. Norwood 1930, 1–5; Forrest 1975a, 19–20; Welsh 1983, 137–43), although they were certainly compared to the allies at one point in the play (fr. 71 PCG). *Ach.* 642–43 and *Pax* 759–60 make it clear that the *Babylonians* somehow criticized the condition of the allies; Forrest (1975a, 22–28) may be right in contending that the play was directed more against Cleon's extortion of the allies than against the Athenian empire *per se*, as is perhaps suggested by the extortion theme in fr. 75 PCG.

and poetry, and not domination through force and political power, as the realms proper for Athenian supremacy over the rest of Greece. This wish is expressed by the fantasy in vv. 643–45 for the allies to come from all parts of Greece bearing tribute to Athens because they desire to see the boldness and daring of this poet. News of his reputation reaches as far as the haughty king of Persia who, though once contemptuous of the Athenians (vv. 98–125), now taunts the Spartans with Athens' two greatest assets, possession of a strong fleet and the benefit of this poet's criticism (vv. 646–51). In contrast with the closed and landlocked nature of Spartan society, Athens was a cosmopolitan center thriving precisely in these two realms—trade and the free interchange of ideas.

By alluding to his association with Aegina in vv. 652–54, the poet implies his own cosmopolitanism.[31] Nevertheless, he insists on his loyalty to Athens by exhorting the Athenians not to let loose of him, however much the Spartans may want him (v. 655). Indeed, as an Athenian property owner on Aegina, he has a very tangible interest in Athens not surrendering the island out of an overhasty enthusiasm for peace. The poet thus refuses a private peace like Dicaeopolis'; he advises Athens to hold its ground and supports the king's prediction that the city will conquer in war (v. 651) if it follows his advice. Critical of the city's policies in the war, the poet nonetheless shows here that he is not a pacifist who advocates peace at any price;[32] nor does his critique of the city's policies indicate any disloyalty to Athens. He views his role not as revolutionary, but as didactic (v. 656 πολλὰ διδάξειν ἀγάθ’, v. 658 τὰ βέλτιστα διδάσκων; see v. 628 ὁ διδάσκαλος ἡμῶν).[33] The reasoned attitude of social responsibility the poet adopts in the parabasis serves as an antithetical check on the unrestrained self-indulgence of heroic fantasy embodied by his alter ego Dicaeopolis.

31. It seems that Aristophanes (or perhaps Callistratus; see Appendix 1) may have owned property on Aegina, whether as a cleruch (cf. ΣPlato, *Apol.* 19C) or as an ancestral inheritance, which could explain Cleon's supposed charge of *xenia*—cf. Σ*Ach.* 378, *Vita* XXVIII, 20–30 Koster. Cf. Schrader 1877, 389–94; van Leeuwen 1908, 40–42; Starkie 1909, xi–xii; Rogers 1910, viii–ix. Rodríguez Alfageme (1985, 63–65) has recently argued that τοῦτον τὸν ποιητὴν ἀφέλωνται (v. 654) is meant as an echo of Pericles' dictum τὴν Αἴγιναν ἀφελεῖν τὴν λήμην τοῦ Πειραιέως (Aristotle, *Rhet.* 1411a15–16). Even if so, this is not in itself sufficient to explain the allusion to Aegina in these lines.

32. It has been argued by Worthington (1987, 56–67) that Aristophanes did not support the unattractive Spartan peace proposals of 425, and by Sicking (1967, 115–24) that he did not necessarily support even the Peace of Nicias. As Heath (1987, 19) notes, telling the Athenians not to give up Aegina is as much as telling them *not* to accept Spartan peace terms. Similar caveats in regard to the *Lysistrata* have been advanced by Westlake (1980, 39–41), Erbse (1982, 101), and Heath (1987, 14–16). In general, see Newiger 1980, 236–37.

33. On this theme, see Perusino 1986, 31.

The closing pnigos appears to provide the first explicit allusion to Cleon and his machinations against the poet (vv. 659–60). Our initial inclination is to take the first person as a reference to the poet (who is clearly the subject of the preceding anapests though not formally the speaker), especially in light of his association with τὸ δίκαιον (vv. 645, 655; cf. vv. 661–62). Convention makes it equally possible, however, that the first person in this case is choral.[34] As the chorus associated its interests with Dicaeopolis at the opening of the parabasis, so here it sides with the poet in his struggle against Cleon.[35] The identity of the first person is highly problematic and unstable in this play: Aristophanes never really confronts Cleon directly but speaks through Dicaeopolis or the chorus, even as he produces the play only through the guise of Callistratus. It is significant that the poet's first person confrontation with Cleon, assuming this passage to be that, is mediated by the language of Euripidean parody,[36] parallel to Dicaeopolis' self-defense. The ambiguity of the first person here serves as an effective transition from the authorial anapests to the syzygy, which is more directly concerned with the chorus' identity and interests.

Young Men and Old Men

The following ode is also transitional, in that it invokes the "Acharnian Muse"—a Muse, and thus relevant to the poet, but Acharnian, and thus representative of the chorus:

Come hither, O flaming Muse,   665
    Intense Acharnian,
    Having the strength of fire.
Just as when from oak-wood coals

34. The poet is normally referred to in the third person in the parabasis proper, with the significant exception of the *Clouds* parabasis, where the first person may have something to do with the status of this parabasis as an addition to the play for its reading audience. However, the first person is used by other comic poets (see chap. 2 n.11 above), and Aristophanes does use it in other passages dealing with his relationship to Cleon (*Pax* 754–64, *Vesp.* 1284–91). These two passages may bear the same ambiguity as *Ach.* 659–64. Given Dicaeopolis' rather surprising first person statements in the persona of the poet, Aristophanes probably means to play with conventions here.

35. The chorus has already spoken in the poet's persona, again with reference to Cleon, in vv. 299–302. These lines seem to allude to the play Aristophanes was planning to produce the following year (*Knights*); see p. 34 above. As such, this passage complements those in which Dicaeopolis assumes the poet's persona to talk about last year's play (vv. 377–82, 502–7). A community of interest opposed to Cleon thus unites everyone: poet, protagonist, and chorus.

36. Vv. 659–62 are a close adaptation of Euripides, fr. 918 Nauck.

   A spark leaps up, aroused by a favoring breeze
   When the fish are ready,   670
   And others stir the Thasian pickle "of shining rim,"
   And others knead bread,
     Even so, come as a
     Rousing harmonious song of the country,
     Taking me as your fellow demesman.   675
We old men blame the city,
For not in a way worthy of those naval victories which we won
Are we fed by you in our old age, but we suffer terribly from you,
Who throw us old men into indictments
And allow us to be laughed at by young orators,   680
We, who are nothing, but dumb and exhausted,
For whom our staff is now our un-stumbling Poseidon.
Muttering with old age we stood at the voting table,
Seeing nothing but the fog of the trial.
The young man, hastening to speak against him,   685
Taking ahold of him with smooth round phrases, strikes him
   quickly,
And then dragging him up, questions him, setting up word-traps,
Tearing apart, mixing up, and stirring around the Old Tithonus.
He mumbles in his old age, and then goes off owing a fine,
Then whines and cries and says to his friends,   690
"I go off owing as a fine this money with which I should have
   bought my coffin."

   How is this right,
    To destroy at the water-clock
    A gray old man,
   Who has performed many tasks   695
    And wiped off much warm and manly sweat,
   A man good for the city at Marathon?
   When we were at Marathon, we pursued,
   But now we *are* pursued
    By evil men,   700
    And caught too.
   What will some Marpsias answer to this?
How is it right that a stooped man of Thucydides' age
Be destroyed by being tangled up with the "Scythian desert,"
The son of Cephisodemus, the blathering accuser?   705
Such that I pitied him and wiped away a tear, seeing
An elderly man pushed around by a bowman.
By Demeter, when that man was really Thucydides,
He would not easily have endured Achaea herself,
But would first have wrestled down ten Euathluses,   710
And yelling, would have shouted down 3,000 bowmen,

And would have outbowed the kinsmen of the accuser's father.
But since you don't allow old men to have any sleep,
Decree that lawsuits should be separate, so that
To an old man should be an old and toothless accuser,   715
And to young men a wide-assed and blathering son of Cleinias.
And for the future, you should banish, and if guilty, fine
An old man through an old man, a young man through a young man.

(vv. 665–718)

The epirrhematic syzygy sustains the litigation motif by applying it to the experience of the chorus.[37] Like the poet, the old men of the chorus complain that they are pursued by unjust accusations brought against them by the "young orators" (v. 680) currently in ascendancy at Athens. The "smooth, round phrases" (v. 686) against which the old men have to defend themselves are not unlike the fawning "foreign discourses" (v. 634) against which the poet had to contend, and the speed and facility of the young accusers (v. 686 ἐς τάχος) rival the speed and facility involved in the accusations against the poet (v. 630 διαβαλλόμενος . . . ἐν 'Αθηναίοις ταχυβούλοις). The anapests and the syzygy both show us the Athenian public victimized by fast-talking rhetoricians, first as χαυνοπολίτας (v. 635), then as men "muttering with old age . . . seeing nothing." In each case the accuser is character- ized by the imagery of anal homosexuality, whether in relation to the litigant Cleon (v. 664 λακαταπύγων) or in relation to the litigious Alcibiades (v. 716 εὐρύπρωκτος).

The syzygy also relates directly to the dramatic action. In the antode the Acharnians complain that even as they "pursued" the enemy at Marathon (v. 698 ἐδιώκομεν), so now they "are pursued" in their old age (v. 699 διωκόμεθα). This dramatic structure parallels the progres- sion in the character of the chorus which we see taking place within the play; reminiscent of their valorous past, they enter the drama in hot pursuit of anyone associated with the city's foreign enemies, only to be eventually brought around by Dicaeopolis into recognizing that they, like him, are victims exploited by the current Athenian power struc- ture. The antithesis not only embodies the contrast between the Achar- nians' past vigor and present decrepitude;[38] it also more broadly ex- presses a contrast between Athens' glorious past of united sacrifice

37. Rehdantz (1862, 8) and Harsh (1934, 188) also see the syzygy as forecasting the theme of sycophancy in the second half of the play (cf. vv. 725–26, 900–58).

38. That the Acharnians are represented as old and infirm may reflect the dimin- ished importance and vitality of the agrarian elements in Attic society of the late fifth century, on which see Ehrenberg 1962, 73–94. Dicaeopolis, of course, embodies the reinvigoration and reassertion of the agrarian party that could be brought by peace.

against the external enemy, symbolized by the victory at Marathon, and the city's present degeneration into self-destructive domestic infighting and litigiousness. In an inversion of the usual epic dichotomy between young warriors and old counselors, contemporary Athens contrasts the old warriors with young orators:[39] *erga* are abandoned in favor of *logoi*.

Dicaeopolis' conversion of the chorus helps them to comprehend their own situation better. They now understand that the present war, of which they were once enthusiastic supporters, is nothing like the noble war for freedom they fought many years ago and that the present generation of political leaders cannot compare with once towering figures like Thucydides, son of Melesias (vv. 708–12), who are now shoved aside. In a way the old rustic Dicaeopolis enacts the wish fulfillment of the chorus' desires. In his agon with the younger Lamachus (vv. 572–625) we have seen the old man triumph rhetorically. And in his private marketplace we see him set up an ideal state completely free of sycophants and their litigation (vv. 725–26, 836–59, 904–28).

Short of the realization of such a fantasy, the best hope the chorus can have is that young men will sue only other young men, and old men will be sued only by their peers (vv. 714–16). This closing wish returns us to the opening of the parabasis and the dispute between Cleon and the poet. Cleon is very likely the paradigm for the "young orators" criticized throughout the syzygy.[40] At the time of this play, Aristophanes was indisputably a very young man;[41] his implication may be that he can not only defend himself against Cleon but in fact he may be just the man to deal with Cleon and so protect the public as a whole. This promise is fulfilled in dramatic form by his next play, the *Knights*.

The Defeat of War

The brief second parabasis (vv. 971–99)[42] completes the integration of the chorus' sympathies with the undertakings of the protagonist and

39. See Pucci 1960, 27.

40. The phrase $\tau\alpha\rho\acute{\alpha}\tau\tau\omega\nu$ $\kappa\alpha\grave{\iota}$ $\kappa\upsilon\kappa\hat{\omega}\nu$ (v. 688) is explicitly used of Cleon in *Eq.* 692 and *Pax* 654; on the significance of these terms, cf. Newiger 1957, 27–30; Edmunds 1987b, 1–9.

41. Σ*Ran.* 504 informs us that Aristophanes was $\sigma\chi\epsilon\delta\grave{o}\nu$ $\mu\epsilon\iota\rho\alpha\kappa\acute{\iota}\sigma\kappa o\varsigma$ at the time that the *Banqueters* was produced, only two years earlier than the *Acharnians*. This also seems to be the implication of *Nub.* 530–31. For a review of the available information on Aristophanes' date of birth, see Kent 1905, 153–55.

42. Some commentators have denied that this syzygy constitutes a second parabasis: cf. Rennie 1909, 234; Sifakis 1971b, 35; Edmunds 1980, 20 n.62. But it is not mandatory for epirrhemes to consist of trochaic tetrameters (see chap. 2 n.26 above); the cretic tetrameters of vv. 979–87 and 991–99 clearly cannot be regarded as lyric meters.

is hence closely reflective of the dramatic context on an allegorical
level:

> O entire city, you have seen, you have seen the prudent,
>> most clever man,
> And the imported goods which he has to trade, after making
>> his peace;
> Some of them are useful in the house, others are good to eat
>> piping hot.
> All goods proceed to this man on their own.
> I will never receive War into my house,
> Nor will he ever sing the Harmodius-song sitting down   980
> Beside me, because he was born a drunken man.
> Revelling among those who possess all things good,
> He did all things bad, overturned, spilled out,
> And fought battles, and when I many times exhorted him,
> "Drink, lie down, receive this toast,"   985
> He all the more burned up the vine-props in his fire,
> And by force poured the wine out of the vines.
>
> He has flown to his feast and has great thoughts,
> And has thrown out these feathers before his door as a mark
>> of his life.
> O Peace, sister of fair Cypris and the dear Graces,
> You have escaped our notice, though possessing such a fair face.   990
> How could some Love, like the one painted with a crown of flowers,
> Take you and me, and bring us together?
> Or perhaps you have considered me too much an old man?
> But taking you, I expect that I could still engage you thrice.
> First, I would plant a long row of grapevines,   995
> Then beside this row, young suckers of figs,
> And third a row of cultivated vines—this old man, indeed!—
> And around the entire spot in a circle, olive trees,
> So that you and I can be anointed from them at the new-moon
>> festivals.

This syzygy immediately follows the two market scenes in which Dicaeopolis trades with the Megarian and the Boeotian respectively and
refuses to do business with Lamachus. After the dismissal of Lamachus'
servant, the chorus comments on Dicaeopolis' cleverness and prosperity in obtaining merchandise, "some . . . useful in the house" (v. 974,
referring to the Megarians' daughters) and "others . . . good to eat
piping hot" (v. 975, referring to the Boeotian's Copaic eels). But in the
epirrheme they express the wish that the riotous feaster Polemos stay
away from Dicaeopolis' banquet. War is an unwelcome intruder into

the private life of men and Lamachus, the play's dramatic personification of War, is such an intruder in the present context.

The separation of war from the simple joys of domestic life is dramatized by Lamachus' exclusion from the marketplace and even more
vividly by the following confrontations between the general and Dicaeopolis; they are juxtaposed, first with Lamachus being brought his
armor and Dicaeopolis being served his dinner (vv. 1071–1142), and
subsequently with Lamachus howling in pain from his battle wounds
and Dicaeopolis howling in ecstasy at the hands of two hetaerae (vv.
1190–1227). The political debate of the first confrontation between
Lamachus and Dicaeopolis directly before the main parabasis (vv. 572–
625) is now translated into sensual and appetitive terms, of food and
sex respectively, the same two aspects of fertility provided by Diallage
in the antepirrheme (vv. 995–99 on the agricultural bounty provided
by Peace and vv. 989–94 on Peace as an object of the old men's sexual
desire);[43] they were represented earlier by the merchandise of the
Boeotian (Copaic eels) and the Megarian (his daughters and their
χοῖρος). On the other hand it is an appropriate irony that the farmers'
vine props (v. 986 χάρακας) which the drunken Polemos heaps on the
fire serve as the comic instrument of Lamachus' wounding in battle (v.
1178 τέτρωται χάρακι): the perversion of the vine props into palisades
and the consequent destruction of Athens' agricultural fertility can
result only in pain and deprivation for those responsible.

The self-conscious theatricality of Dicaeopolis and his undertaking is
quite fittingly reasserted at the close of the play, as Dicaeopolis' drinking contest, itself a parody of the city's Anthesteria festival, becomes
metaphorical for the dramatic contest (vv. 1224–34).[44] The κριτάς (v.
1224) to whom the hero is carried surely stand for the "judges" of the
dramatic agon. And Dicaeopolis' victory over Lamachus with the echoing τήνελλα καλλίνικος (vv. 1227, 1228, 1231, 1233) is surely meant to
presage the poet's dramatic victory.

Throughout the *Acharnians*, we have watched the dramatic and civic
realms interpenetrate: the theater of Dionysus becomes the Pnyx,
where phony ambassadors and dishonest politicians stage for the public what is in turn merely another level of theatrical illusion. The hero
Dicaeopolis discusses important civic issues of war and peace, but can
safely do so only in dramatic guise, appearing both as the Euripidean
tragic hero Telephus and speaking in the persona of the comic poet.

---

43. Peace would bring the old men, so pathetic in the syzygy of the first parabasis, a
sort of sexual rejuvenation. Cf. v. 993 ἢ πάνυ γερόντιον ἴσως νενόμικάς με σύ.
    44. See Rennie 1909, 267; Cassio 1985, 143.

Nothing can offer a more bewildering illustration of dramatic illusion than the spectacle of a beggar who is really the disguised Mysian king Telephus who is really the Euripidean character "Telephus" as acted by the comic character "Dicaeopolis," who clearly speaks for the comic poet, known to most of the play's audience as Callistratus, who is however really fronting for the little known Aristophanes. Reality becomes visible only through a complex series of mimetic mirrors, each putting its own distorting twist on the image. The blurred lines between the historical and dramatic realms, between signifiers and signifieds, are not meant to be disambiguated; they are meaningful precisely in their overlap and indeterminacy. Cleon's "lawsuit" (or whatever it was) against the comic poet was a historical, civic event, but is here transformed into a dramatic event through its appropriation by the character Dicaeopolis who speaks of it as a lawsuit against himself; even in the parabasis, the lawsuit assumes the theoretical status of a dramatic issue (it was, after all, a lawsuit about drama), but it is framed in the syzygy as one of many unnecessary and destructive lawsuits now plaguing the city. Attacks on Comedy are themselves bound to become absorbed and reinterpreted as the material of Comedy, which is what makes Comedy ultimately undefeatable, as Syracosius was to learn a decade later, when ridiculed by Aristophanes as a "bird" (*Av.* 1297), the very year after he successfully proposed a decree restricting comic license. Those who attack the stage are those who belatedly learn that the world is merely a stage.

CHAPTER 4

Aristophanes and the Poetry of Hate

As we have seen, the *Acharnians* is in many ways constituted as a complex play on identities, with Aristophanes speaking through Callistratus, who speaks through Dicaeopolis, who in turn assumes the guise of Telephus dressed as a beggar. In the parabasis of the *Knights* (vv. 512–19) Aristophanes announces through the Knights his decision to come forward and produce his own plays without the aid of an intermediary like Callistratus.[1] It is no accident that the *Knights* is the play with which the young Aristophanes introduces himself directly to the Athenian public. More clearly than the *Acharnians* or *Babylonians*, this play is an *ad hominem* statement about the current leadership of Athens. We see none of the caution and defensiveness the *Acharnians* exhibited, still conscious of Cleon's recent accusations. It is rather as if Aristophanes had now decided to take off his training gear and fight Cleon man-to-man in a naked contest of wills. No play of Aristophanes displays such a singularity of purpose or so obsessively reiterates the same structural pattern of one-on-one confrontation between a pair of diehard antagonists: in the *Knights'* figural allegory of the Paphlagon's struggle with the upstart Sausage seller we must see nothing less than Aristophanes' fantastic projection of his own verbal combat with Cleon.

---

1. Aristophanes felt the issue of his having once used a producer to be significant enough to return to it several years later in the revised *Clouds* (vv. 530–33) and in *Vesp.* 1018–22. As we argue in Appendix 1, some members of the audience would have known all along that Aristophanes, and not Callistratus, was the true author of the earlier plays; but this is the first play in which he officially acknowledges his identity to the general public and assumes full responsibility for the play's success or failure.

Poetic Daring

The Knights open the parabasis by accenting the poet's courage; he alone of the comic poets is worthy of having them as a chorus, "because he hates the same men we do and dares (τολμᾷ) to say just things (τὰ δίκαια) and nobly moves against (γενναίως πρὸς . . . χωρεῖ) the Typhoon and hurricane (i.e. Cleon)."[2] Aristophanes' verbal daring is not only assimilated to the Knights' own military valor, but is identified with their political sentiments and innate nobility (γενναίως). This passage recapitulates the poet's self-defense in the parabasis of the *Acharnians* (*Ach.* 644–45), where we are told he is the best poet because he "took the risk (παρεκινδύνευσ᾿) of saying just things (τὰ δίκαια) among the Athenians," analogous to Dicaeopolis who risked his neck on the chopping block.[3] His "fame for daring (τόλμης)" reached even the king of Persia who praised the value of the poet's critical advice. The claim of poetic courage in the *Knights* is repeated and magnified in the parabasis of the *Wasps* (*Vesp.* 1029–31): "when he first began to train choruses, he did not set upon ordinary men, / but he laid his hand upon the greatest, having a wrath of Heracles, / straight from the start boldly (θρασέως) standing against the jag-toothed hound itself (Cleon). . . ." Even after Cleon's death, Aristophanes repeats virtually the same description in the *Peace* (*Pax* 752–58) and reminds us of his fearless confrontation with the monster (*Pax* 759–60). Several years later in the parabasis of the revised *Clouds*, Aristophanes declares ironically that he "struck Cleon in the stomach, when he was greatest, / but did not dare (κοὐκ ἐτόλμησ᾿) to jump on him again once he was down" (*Nub.* 549–50). As we shall see in the next chapter, this parabasis consistently states the opposite of what Aristophanes actually does, and his real meaning is that he did indeed dare to jump on Cleon again once dead, not only in the *Peace*, but also in the parabasis of the second *Clouds* itself (*Nub.* 575–94). Thus every full parabasis we have from Aristophanes' early period makes some reference to the poet's boldness and daring, particularly in regard to Cleon.

The idea of a poet running risks and acting courageously when

---

2. *Eq.* 511–12. The image of Cleon as a storm must reflect his windy (i.e. verbal) nature, as well as his disruptiveness to the city. On the application of storm imagery to the Paphlagon throughout the *Knights*, see Taillardat 1962, 180–84; Whitman 1964, 90–91; Edmunds 1987b, 6–16.

3. For the theme of the poet's "risk" in writing Comedy, see also *Vesp.* 1021 κινδυνεύων καθ᾿ ἑαυτόν; the theme is continued by the Pindaric chariot of song metaphor in *Vesp.* 1022, 1050. The idea of poetic "risk" had a special resonance for Old Comedy, since the poets in fact were liable to legal prosecution for slander; see Henderson 1990, 287–90.

taking a public stand for or against something was certainly not new
with Aristophanes. As we have noted, Pindar's choral lyric also features
the poet engaged with his subject matter in what appears to be at once a
very personal and a very public way. In praising the victor against all
envious opposition, the poet himself faces danger: "Many things have
been said in many ways, but there is every risk (κίνδυνος) for a man
discovering new things to make test against the touchstone. Words are
a delicious sauce for the envious; they always fasten onto the good and
do not contend with the inferior" (N.8.20–2).[4] The poet stakes his
credibility in praising the athlete against cavil and detraction. Courage
is an essential attribute: "May I be a fitting inventor of words to lead the
story's way in the chariot of the Muses; may daring (τόλμα) and far-
spreading might come along with me" (O.9.80–3).

In O.13.11–13, Pindar prefaces his praise of Corinth in this way: "I
have noble things to relate and straight daring (τόλμα εὐθεῖα) arouses
me to speak. It is impossible to conceal inborn character;" but, as
he shows in the line immediately preceding this passage, warning
against "Hybris (Arrogance), the bold-mouthed (θρασύμυθον) mother
of Koros (Surfeit)," the poet is equally aware of the dangers of too
much boldness in speech.[5] This dialectic between verbal boldness and
restraint is made clearer by N.7.50–3: "It is bold (θρασύ) for me to
speak the princely road of words which runs from their home through
their brilliant virtues. But pause is sweet in every work. Even honey
and the delightful flowers of Aphrodite can bring surfeit (κόρον)."[6]
Both passages imply that a poet's boldness can reach too far by saying
too much and must therefore be balanced by a sense of temperance
and self-control.

Pindaric statements reflect the inherently ambivalent status of boldness and daring as ethical concepts in Greek thought. In the maxim of
the Parian sophist Euenus, "having daring (τόλμαν) in addition to
wisdom is beneficial, but without wisdom it is harmful and brings
misery" (fr. 4 W).[7] Similarly Plato, *Laches* 197A–B distinguishes between true courage (ἀνδρεία) based on consciousness of future perils
and mere fearlessness (θρασύτης καὶ τόλμη καὶ τὸ ἄφοβον), which

4. Some critics (such as Köhnken [1971, 31]) see the "new things" described in this
passage as the poet's mythological innovations; others (such as Miller [1982, 111–15])
see it as praise of the athletic victor. On poetic *tolma* and *kindunos* generally in Pindar, see
Gundert 1935, 69, and Bundy 1962 I, 29–32.

5. On the tension involved in this passage, see my remarks in Hubbard 1986b, 37–
38.

6. See Hubbard 1985, 13–14 and 1986c, 66–67.

7. Euenus' principal concern with rhetoric (cf. Plato, *Phaedr.* 267A) makes it possible that this fragment also refers to language.

even children and animals can possess. Applied to the verbal realm, *tolmē* and *thrasos* have negative connotations in Greek poetry as often as they have positive ones:[8] "boldness" is often insolence. Although extolling his own *tolmē* in the parabases, Aristophanes' usage can also pair the term with "shameless" (*anaischuntos,* see *Pax* 182, *Thesm.* 702, *Ran.* 465) and "loathsome" (*miaros,* see *Ach.* 557–58, *Vesp.* 342–43, *Pax* 182–83, 362, *Ran.* 465–66, *Plut.* 472).[9]

"Boldness" and "daring" are often terms of abuse in Aristophanes, and it comes as no surprise that they are used in the *Knights* in invective addressed to the Sausage seller (*Eq.* 181, 429) or to Paphlagon (*Eq.* 304, 331, 693). At the same time the Sausage seller makes a virtue of the insults by praying to his patron spirits to "give me now boldness (θράσος) and a resourceful tongue and shameless (ἀναιδῆ) voice" (*Eq.* 637–38); his lack of restraint and inhibition in addressing the Athenian council is precisely what gives him power and effectiveness as an orator against Cleon. Verbal daring is a central characteristic of many Aristophanic heroes; we have seen Dicaeopolis boldly speaking the unspeakable in defiance of consensus and political authority (*Ach.* 311–12, 488–89, 558, 563, 578), and later we shall see Bdelycleon accused of the same (*Vesp.* 342–45). Even the less creditable are noted for their rhetorical audacity: Strepsiades (*Nub.* 444–45), Euripides (*Thesm.* 888, 1109, *Ran.* 950–51, 1326), and Euripides' kinsman (*Thesm.* 520–26).

Our conclusion from all of this must be that in praising himself for "daring to say just things" Aristophanes calls attention to an important quality he shares with many of his characters. But we must also conclude from Aristophanes' characters and from the poetic conventions of "bold speech" that this rhetorical exuberance, even in the pursuit of what may appear to be laudable motives, involves the speaker in moral ambiguity and social conflict. I would argue that the *Knights* is in large part intended as an exploration of the complex issues posed by Aristophanes' rhetorical engagement and emerging public identity: speaking frankly and forcefully concerning the issues of the moment may inevitably render the speaker "shameless" and "loathsome."

---

8. Cf. Archilochus 96.4 W; Aeschylus, *Sept.* 612, *Supp.* 203, *Ag.* 1399; Bacchylides 13.199; Sophocles, *Phil.* 380, 1307, fr. 724 Radt; Euripides, *Hec.* 1286, *Phoen.* 716, *Or.* 607, fr. 3 Nauck. There is a tendency to distinguish θράσος (with negative connotations) from its cognate θάρσος (with positive connotations); cf. Chantraine 1968–, II, 424. But the two terms interpenetrate to a considerable degree. On the ambiguity of *tolmē* as an ethical concept in Greek tragedy, see Zawadzka 1964, 44–55 and in general, see Carter 1986, 11–15.

9. For these collocations of terms throughout Greek literature, see Parker 1983, 5 n.15.

The Powers of Comic Language

From the very opening of the play, the issues of rhetorical engagement and linguistic efficacy are highlighted. The manuscripts tell us that the two slaves who appear onstage represent the generals Demosthenes and Nicias:[10]

> Slave #1 (Demosthenes): Iattataiax for my grief! Iattatai!
>   May the gods grievously destroy the new-bought grief
>   Paphlagon, with his own plots!
>   From the time that he got into this house,
>   He brings thrashings to the other servants.   5
> Slave #2 (Nicias): Most grievously indeed may the gods first destroy
>   this man of the Paphlagonians
>   With his own slanders. #1: How are you, grief-stricken one?
> #2: Full of grief, just like you. #1: Come here, so that
>   We can wail together a melody of Olympus.
> #1 and #2: Mumu mumu mumu mumu mumu mumu.   10
> #1: But why do we moan? Isn't it better for the two of us
>   To seek some salvation than to keep bawling?
> #2: What salvation could there be? #1: You say. #2: No, you tell
>   me.
>   I don't want to fight over it. #1: By Apollo, I won't.
> #2: But take heart and speak, and then I'll speak to you.   15
> #1: "Couldn't you somehow say for me what I ought to say?"
> #2: But the courage isn't in me. How could I
>   Ever say it in clever Euripidean fashion like you?
> #1: Don't, don't, don't throw chervil over me.
>   But find some jig away from the despot.   20
> #2: Say "let's go," putting it together thus.
> #1: And indeed I say, let's go! #2: Now say
>   "Off" after "let's go." #1: Off! #2: Very well.
>   Now, just as when peeling, first gently say
>   "Let's go," then "off," and then speed up.   25
> #1: Let's go—off—let's go—off—let's go off!
> #2: Isn't it sweet? #1: By Zeus! Except that my skin
>   Fears this eagle. #2: Why so?
> #1: Because when you peel, the skin goes away.
> #2: Then, since the two of us are here, it is best   30

10. Dover (1959, 198–99) argues for the identifications in the *sigla* being only Alexandrian conjectures. The identifications, however, have more recently been defended on particular grounds by Sommerstein (1980b, 46–47) and Kraus (1985, 115–19). Given the allegorical nature of the characters in this play (i.e. Paphlagon is like Cleon, but is not Cleon), it would be incorrect to say either that the slaves are Nicias and Demosthenes or that they are not.

> To go and fall before the image of one of the gods.
> #1: What image? Do you believe that the gods are real?
> #2: I do. #1: Using what evidence?
> #2: That I am hated by the gods. Isn't that likely?
> #1: You win me over. But we must look in another direction.   35
>   Do you want me to tell the plot to the spectators?
> #2: We'll be no worse for it. But let us ask one thing of them—
>   To make it clear to us by their faces,
>   If they delight in the words and plot.

(vv. 1–39)

The chatter might be easily dismissed as inconsequential avoidance of the issue at hand, but this linguistic evasion is the very point of the scene.[11] The slaves' lamentation starts out on the level of inarticulate speech (v. 1 Ἰατταταιάξ) and repetition of each other's language (v. 1 κακῶν . . . , v. 2 κακῶς . . . κακὸν . . . , v. 6 κάκιστα . . . , v. 7 κακόδαιμον . . . , v. 8 κακῶς),[12] regressing to undifferentiated sobs shared by the two slaves (v. 10 μυμῦ μυμῦ μυμῦ . . .). The first slave then proposes that they seek a solution to their problem (vv. 11–12), but each slave asks the other to speak first (vv. 13–20). The second slave protests his lack of the courage (v. 17 τὸ θρέττε) and verbal facility (vv. 17–18 πῶς . . . εἴποιμι . . . κομψευριπικῶς;), thereby introducing the theme of verbal courage we have noted above. The Euripidean quotation (v. 16 = *Hipp.* 345) and the allusion to speaking in "clever Euripidean fashion" (v. 18) turn our attention to the dramatic sphere as a paradigm of verbal dexterity, but the first slave rejects Euripides (v. 19 μὴ διασκανδικίσῃς)[13] as a solution, in favor of Comedy (v. 20 τιν' ἀπόκινον). The comic jig is literally a "movement away" (ἀπό-κινον) from the Paphlagon and stands figuratively as an announcement of the present play, further expounded (in vv. 36–37) as a political statement designed to move the public away from Cleon.

The ἀπόκινον initiates a long series of comic word plays that exploit the tension between literal and figural. The cowardice of the generals is

11. For an acute analysis of this scene and the importance of language generally in the *Knights,* see Littlefield 1968, 6–7.

12. On the acoustic and rhetorical structure of this repetition, see François 1977, 12–13.

13. This metaphor not only entails the usual allusion to Euripides' mother as a green grocer (cf. *Thesm.* 387, 456; *Ran.* 840; *Vita Eur.* 113–14); it moreover seems to be an auto-reference to Aristophanes' own satire of Euripides on this point in last year's comedy, in which Dicaeopolis specifically asks him for some *skandix* (*Ach.* 475–78). Ruck (1975, 16–19) argues that *skandix* was a psychotropic aphrodisiac, and thus relates this metaphor to the masturbatory double entendres in αὐτομολῶμεν (*Eq.* 21–26) and δέρμα δεφόμενος (*Eq.* 24–29).

suggested not only by their initial reluctance to speak, but literally by their repetition of αὐτό and μόλωμεν (= αὐτομολῶμεν "let's go off!," also a masturbatory double-entendre). At the same time we see developed a series of allusions to Cleon's profession as a leather merchant, also exploiting the sexual undercurrent: δεφόμενος (v. 24), δέρματι (v. 27), τὸ δέρμα δεφομένων (v. 29). Interlocking with this imagery is the reference in v. 28 to Cleon as τουτονὶ τὸν οἰωνόν a bird of prey (= v. 197 βυρσαίετος ἀγχυλοχήλης; see vv. 203–5) tearing off the hides of his victims and by implication plundering the state with his sharp talons. He is equally an οἰωνός in the sense of being a bird of omen, a purveyor of oracles. Vv. 30–34 extend the power of language to the point of proving the existence of the gods: there must be gods, the second slave reasons, because he is "hated by the gods" (v. 34 θεοῖσιν ἐχθρός). The figural expression θεοῖσιν ἐχθρός is interpreted literally and infused with metaphysical significance. The slave compellingly proposes, not supplication of the gods themselves, but one of the *images* of the gods (v. 31), that is, an artistic representation. In some cases art is more potent than reality.

Building up to the slave's exposition of the dramatic situation, this passage is one of the most densely packed metaphorical sequences in Aristophanes, exploiting the literal meanings of common figures of speech in characteristic comic style. Tropologically this introductory sequence prefigures the play's own self-realization; as expounded by the first slave (vv. 40–72), the whole play operates as an allegory which similarly exploits figural and literal meanings (master Demos = the people [*dēmos*], Paphlagon = Cleon, slaves = generals).[14] The movement from inarticulate speech to linguistic pyrotechnics puts the slaves on the path to resolving their problem; but the path is completed only through enactment of the play itself, which is the ultimate paradigm of linguistic and rhetorical cleverness. It is the power of language,[15] and more specifically, the metaphorical language of this very dramatic event, with its frame of reference constantly shifting between domestic

14. On the play's multifaceted manipulation of allegorical symbols and levels, see Newiger 1957, 11–23. Vv. 228–33 on the refusal of the mask makers to produce a portrait mask of Cleon have often been taken literally or as an indication that Aristophanes himself shrank from a direct attack on Cleon here; for other views, cf. Landfester 1967, 14–15; Kraus 1985, 128. But Aristophanes' meaning is surely that he need not rely on literal representation of political figures in this play, but trusts in the public's ability to interpret his characters allegorically (vv. 232–33 "he will be recognized anyway, since the audience is smart").

15. On the magical efficacy of language as a general theme in Aristophanes, see Moutsopoulos 1964, 216–19 and Walsh 1984, 85–97. Walsh associates it specifically with the influence of Gorgias. On the traditional background of the concept in early Greek poetics, see Laín Entralgo 1970.

allegory and political reality, that will defeat Paphlagon/Cleon. After putting their situation into a dramatic context in vv. 40–72 the first slave, inspired by the wine of Dionysus (vv. 85–100), conceives the idea of stealing the Paphlagon's oracles, his special claim to knowledge of a uniquely powerful and visionary verbal form that can foresee and thus control the future. In possession of the Paphlagon's most closely guarded oracle, the slaves learn the identity of his successor and proceed to put the play's plot into action by unleashing against the Paphlagon his ultimate rival and counterpart, the Sausage seller. The dramatic role of the Sausage seller hero, who orchestrates the linguistic and rhetorical assault on the Paphlagon, figures the political role of the dramatist, who perceives his own verbal activity (= the play) as the means for ridding the city of Cleon.

Thus the Sausage seller is at once a manipulator of symbols and a symbol himself, one created by the dramatist and at the same time representative of the dramatist. Like the other petty merchants who preceded him in positions of political authority (vv. 128–43) the Sausage seller is a figure who emerges from nowhere (v. 158 "today nobody, tomorrow a man of great stature"); in a theatrical demonstration of the common man's ascent we see the Sausage seller climb on top of his humble vendor's table to survey the Mediterranean empire the generals promise him (vv. 168–93).[16] His qualifications for leadership are none other than his unpleasant voice, low birth, and marketplace origins (v. 218). His claim is to surpass the Paphlagon in "shamelessness" (ἀναιδεία, vv. 277, 409–14; see vv. 322–25, 1206), "boldness" (θράσος, vv. 328–32), "ability to do and say all" (πανουργία, vv. 331, 683–85, 949–50), "trickery" (κοβαλικεύματα, v. 332; see δόλοι ποικίλοι, v. 686), "knavery" (πονηρία, vv. 333–37), and "flattering words" (ῥήματα αἱμύλα, v. 687). Unencumbered by considerations of morality or good taste, the Sausage seller and Paphlagon compete in the art of aggressive verbal self-assertion. Each of the two slaves quarrels out of a desire to have the other speak first (vv. 13–20), and the two demagogues quarrel because each is eager to speak first (vv. 335–50).

The Sausage seller's rhetoric (which is the rhetoric of Comedy) reduces the affairs of the *polis* to the level of food and sex, raw physical drives seemingly without higher purpose. We have seen the *Acharnians* depreciate the Athenian public as passive victims of sodomy; assuming power, the Sausage seller boasts of his relationship to the "city of Openmouthed citizens" (v. 1263, κεχηναίων). Earlier he openly boasted of his own self-prostitution (vv. 167, 423–28, 483–84, 721, 1241–42) and

---

16. On the folkloric element in this scene, see Williams 1964, 52–60.

began his speech to the assembly with a visible gesture of the posterior (vv. 638–42). The Paphlagon is much less open in matters of sexuality and seldom boasts about it.[17] His chief claim of benefit to Demos is rather to have "stopped the perverts" (vv. 876–77 τοὺς βινουμένους); the Sausage seller answers this moralistic claim (vv. 878–80) by asserting that the Paphlagon's only aim was to suppress his own competitors in politics and sex. The same sexual practices that the Sausage seller openly boasted about become insults when associated with the more self-conscious Paphlagon (cunnilinctus, v. 352; passive anal sex, vv. 78, 364, 375–81; fellatio, v. 1010). Paphlagon's claim to be a devoted "lover of the Demos" are portrayed by the Sausage seller as mere pretexts for his sodomy and rape of the people (vv. 732–40, 1340–44).[18] The Sausage seller's complete openness and lack of inhibition in both language and behavior are contrasted with the Paphlagon's pretension and hypocrisy. It should not escape us that the Sausage seller is in his very nature a purveyor of phallic material.[19] He is thus not unlike the spirit of Comedy itself, emerging from the rural *phallika* and, without shame, using sex both to abuse and amuse.

But the sausage is of course also a symbol of food, the play's other major pattern of imagery characterizing the political process.[20] And again the Sausage seller's rhetoric, not Paphlagon's, plays the leading role here. The Paphlagon is repeatedly accused of stealing food for his own benefit (vv. 51–60, 103, 280–83, 381–84, 824–27, 1025–34). In imitation of Cleon's stolen "barley-cake" at Pylos (vv. 51–60) the Sausage seller claims for himself a comparable ability to steal the delicacies of others for the sake of the Demos (see vv. 742–45, 778, 1192–1204) and demonstrates his potential in this regard even in his childhood by pilfering the butchers' meat and hiding it in his crotch (vv. 417–26). The two rival demagogues compete in their ability to devour food (vv. 351–62, 698–701) and, as in sexual matters, the Sausage seller freely admits to the most disgusting appetites (vv. 356–58, 413–16). The

---

17. Where Paphlagon does refer to sex he always couches it in ambiguous terms (cf. vv. 363, 719–20) whose meaning is made sexually explicit only by the Sausage seller's rejoinder. In both cases Paphlagon's claim is to pederastic control over the public; as Henderson (1975, 209, 215) points out, the active and dominant role in such relationships involves no disgrace. On the relative mildness of Paphlagon's obscenities, see also Henderson 1975, 69.

18. On the motif of Paphlagon as *erastēs* of the Demos, see Landfester 1967, 50–55, 58–59, and Henderson 1975, 68. Connor (1971, 99–108) associates this with stock phrases from Cleon's rhetoric.

19. For the phallus as "sausage," cf. Hipponax 84.17 W. In this play, it is highlighted by the Sausage seller's meat = phallus equation in vv. 423–28 and 483–84.

20. The dominance of food imagery has been well noted by Newiger (1957, 24), Whitman (1964, 92–95), Littlefield (1968, 13), and Reckford (1987, 115, 127).

Paphlagon's excessive gluttony on the other hand results in wishes that he should regurgitate his food (vv. 402–4) or choke on it (vv. 927–40); in both cases, the food stands for financial gain through political manipulation such as bribery and lawsuits.

The demagogues claim to feed the people at the very time when they feed *off* the people. The Paphlagon "feeds" Demos with jury pay (vv. 256, 904–5, 1359–60; cf. 1089), and Demos is imagined as sitting on the Pnyx chewing dried figs (v. 755).[21] Indeed the emblem on Demos' seal ring is none other than "beef fat" (v. 954 δημοῦ βοείου).[22] But the Paphlagon's claim to know what the Demos likes to eat is countered by the Sausage seller's assertion that the Paphlagon holds Demos in a state of infantile dependency like a nurse and gulps down most of the food himself (vv. 715–18). The idea that Athens' political discourse has been debased to the level of merely satisfying the public's appetite is strikingly expressed in the Sausage seller's speech to the assembly, concerning itself with no greater political problem than the price of sardines (vv. 644–82). The two demagogues even hold contests over their respective abilities to produce tantalizing food for Demos (vv. 1100–1106, 1166–1223). The Sausage seller wins by virtue of being able to prove that he alone has held nothing back in his food hamper (vv. 1211–23).

The Sausage seller's profession is by its nature one of feeding the public, an apt metaphor for political leadership and rhetoric, as is made clear by the slave who recruits him: "Do the same things which you do now. Stir up affairs and stuff them into skins, and always go after the people/Demos, sweetening them with culinary turns of phrase" (vv. 213–16). We are not surprised at the displaced Paphlagon assuming the profession of a sausage seller at the end of the play (vv. 1397–1401). In a significant interlude the demagogues' apparent manipulation of Demos is revealed to be *his* manipulation of *them:* he allows them to steal food in order to fatten them up for eventual sacrifice and eating (vv. 1125–40).

The Sausage seller recognizes his status as an instrument manipulated by other interests (= the two slaves, the Knights, Demos), whereas the Paphlagon is under the delusion that all is within his control and

21. Here again we see the food imagery interacting with the sexual, inasmuch as "dried figs" can be equated with the phallus and/or testes (cf. *Ach.* 801–2, *Pax* 1349–50, and in general, the discussion of Buchheit 1960, 200–29; I do not agree with the insistence of Henderson [1975, 118] that they can only refer to the vulva). Again Demos is characterized as a habitual passive partner in homosexual acts committed with Paphlagon.

22. Of course the image implies that the public is itself eaten and consumed by its leaders, as well as being merely a personification of food.

will remain so. For all his vulgarity and elemental brutishness, the Sausage seller paradoxically serves to advance the interests of the most elite and discriminating classes of society in their assault on the demagogic Cleon/Paphlagon.[23] Neither the Knights nor the two slaves symbolizing the generals can overthrow Cleon/Paphlagon on their own; they can do so only by using a lower class person who in every way mirrors and exceeds the Paphlagon's own uncouthness. For most of the play the Sausage seller is precisely such a copycat persona, not a character with a strong, independent personality or even a name of his own.[24] Some critics have been troubled by his apparent change of character at the end of the play,[25] but we should perhaps see the emergence of Agoracritus the selfless benefactor and reformer as his true self-revelation, in contrast to the role he had to play in order to win the public's confidence. At the end Agoracritus returns merely to his initial posture when we first meet him, a disinterested private individual without any personal ambition whose words and actions in vying with Paphlagon are those logically required by his temporary dramatic role as would-be demagogue. With all its emphasis on unrestrained self-expression and sensual self-indulgence, this dramatic role is nothing less than the paradigmatic function of Comedy itself. Athens cannot rid itself of Cleon through serious political debate but only by reducing issues to the gross physical terms of Comedy and its invective; the Knights can displace the Paphlagon only by an unholy alliance with what appears to be a lower class rogue who is in many ways the polar opposite of their values and background.

We have shown how the hero of the *Acharnians* also functioned as an embodiment of Comedy itself, and how he exhibited the necessary interdependence of serious issues, expressed by the speech on the chopping block, with a ridiculous form of communication. But where Dicaeopolis was a comic hero in his very essence from beginning to end, the Sausage seller's comic identity is more problematic, framed as a matter of role-playing. Dicaeopolis' private peace is an act of shameless self-indulgence whose consequences are presented onstage in his enjoyment of bountiful food, drink, and women when the play ends; he is unwilling to share the fruits of his peace, contemptuously dis-

23. Reckford (1987, 114) sees the union of the Knights and Sausage seller as symbolic of the creative synergism between the highest and lowest parts of human nature, or man's spiritual and instinctual self. For more on this dialectic as it applies to Aristophanes' aesthetics of Comedy, see pp. 140–48 below.

24. See the perceptive remarks of Albini 1965, 22–24.

25. For a review of the controversy and a sensible approach to the problem, see Landfester 1967, 83–91. I am not convinced by the recent thesis of Brock (1986, 15–27) that we are dealing with a double plot.

missing a suffering farmer (*Ach.* 1018–36) while trading a drop of the peace libation to a bridesmaid totally out of voyeuristic caprice (*Ach.* 1059–68).[26] The Sausage seller's shamelessness and self-indulgence, though equally extravagant, are purely verbal constructs useful in his debate with the Paphlagon. The Sausage seller is not motivated by selfish desires either when we first meet him or after the defeat of his enemy at the end; his refusal to exploit his newfound power gives him an ultimately altruistic character altogether lacking in Dicaeopolis. This shift in the comic hero's persona may be connected with the change in the author's relation to the play: Aristophanes presented the *Acharnians* under the cover of Callistratus and could through this device afford a certain measure of *alazoneia* in his protagonist as well as in his own parabatic persona, while in producing the *Knights* under his own name, Aristophanes felt the need to reassure the audience of his personal modesty and temperate character, which would use comic vulgarity only when needed.

Moral Ambiguities of the Blame Poet

The Sausage seller's function as a dramatic and metadramatic persona can be illuminated further by consideration of the iambographic tradition.[27] In the character of the iambic poet we also see a persona that is at once individual, dramatic, and generic.[28] In the passage in which he connects Comedy with iambic poetry (*Poet.* 1448b24–25) Aristotle calls those poets engaging in "blame" (ψόγος) and imitating "baser men" (οἱ φαῦλοι) "the more worthless" poets (οἱ εὐτελέστεροι) as contrasted with serious poets who write on exalted themes such as those of Tragedy and Epic. The underlying concept here is that what a poet says about others somehow mirrors his own tastes and preoccupations. This general equivalence between a poet's subject and his life is certainly prominent in the ancient traditions concerning our best pre-

26. Dicaeopolis' "selfishness," particularly in the scene with the farmer, has been a matter of discomfort to some critics; cf. Strauss 1966, 71–76; Dover 1972, 88; Newiger 1980, 223; Bowie 1982, 39–40. However, MacDowell (1983, 159–60) argues in favor of the farmer (*Ach.* 1028 Dercetes of Phyle) being a figure with some political significance, like Lamachus, and thus properly excluded from Dicaeopolis' marketplace. See also Sutton 1980, 19–20.

27. On the close relation of the iambic tradition to Comedy, cf. West 1974, 33–37; Henderson 1975, 17–29; Rosen 1983, passim; Kraus 1985, 17–21.

28. On the conventional iambic persona with particular reference to Archilochus, see Dover 1964, 199–212; Seidensticker 1978, 5–22; Nagy 1979, 243–52; Miralles & Portulas 1983, 11–60.

served iambographer, Archilochus, who, while attacking his putative enemies in the most caustic and astringent terms, speaks quite without shame of his own cowardice in war (fr. 5 W), sexual impotence (fr. 252 W), or descent from a slave mother (fr. 295[a] W).[29]

Nagy has shown that the morally ambiguous archetype of the "blame poet" extends beyond iambic poetry to include such figures as Aesop in the moralist tradition and Thersites in the epic tradition, whose very name means "bold (*thrasus*) in speech."[30] Personal invective, particularly if addressed to social superiors, has the traditional effect of casting doubt on the character of the attacker, who appears to be motivated by envy and *Schadenfreude*. Aristophanes' Sausage seller must be perceived as one more figure within this traditional context; the ridicule of Cleon requires an opponent whose boldness, shamelessness, and moral ugliness are commensurate with the object, although at the conclusion of the play we see that this persona serves an *ad hoc* function and should not be confused with the individual Agoracritus.

The moral ambiguities of being publicly identified as a "blame poet" concerned Aristophanes himself, as is clear from the parabasis:

> Fare thee well! May you succeed
> After my wish, and may Zeus of the marketplace
> Protect you. When you have won,   500
> May you come back to us again,
> Decked out with crowns.
> But all of you out there apply your minds
>   To our anapests,
> All of you trying on your own   505
>   Every kind of Muse.
> If any of the old comic producers compelled us
> To come forward and speak these lines to the theater,
> He would not have gained this lightly. But now the poet is worthy,
> Because he hates the same men we do, and dares to say just things,   510
> And nobly moves against the Typhoon and hurricane.
> He says that many of you come to him and wonder,
> Asking why he didn't long ago ask for a chorus on his own.
> He asked us to speak to you about this. For the man says
> That he has not passed his time this way from folly, but considering   515
> Comic production to be the most difficult of all labors—
> Indeed, out of many trying it, the art favors few.

29. On Archilochus' and Hipponax' ambiguous reputations in the testimonia, see Rosen 1983, 35–47 (= Rosen 1988, 12–16).

30. Nagy 1979, 258–64, 279–308. On the etymology of Thersites' name, see Redard 1949, 194, 257–58 n.3.

He long ago saw that you are seasonal in your nature,
And betrayed former poets along with old age.
He knew what Magnes suffered along with falling gray hair,   520
Magnes, who raised the most victory-trophies of all competing
        choruses,
Sending out to you all manner of voices—twanging, flapping,
Lydianizing, gall-fly buzzing, coloring himself frog-green,
He did not suffice, but finishing in old age, no longer young,
He was thrown out by you, an old man, because he lost his jest.   525
Then he remembered Cratinus, who once overflowing with praise
Streamed through the flat plains; sweeping from their station
Oaks and plane-trees and uprooted enemies, he carried them off.
One could not sing anything at a symposium save "Fig-slippered
        Doro"
And "Builders of Handy Songs." Thus did he flourish.   530
But now you have no pity, as you see him muttering,
With amber studs falling out of his lyre and the tune undone,
The strings gaping loose. But though an old man, he runs around
Like Connas, wearing a dry crown and sorely thirsting for drink.
For his past victories, he ought to drink in the Prytaneum,   535
And not mutter, but be a spectator, sitting in splendor beside
        Dionysus.
What spite and maltreatment Crates has endured from you,
Crates, who sent you off after feasting you at small expense,
Kneading most urbane insights from his most cabbage-dry mouth.
This man only sufficed, sometimes failing, sometimes not.   540
Fearing these things has our poet delayed, biding his time. In
        addition, he has said
One should first become a rower before taking hand to the rudder,
And then move to the prow and stare into the winds,
And only then be captain for oneself. For all these things,
Because he has acted modestly and has not fooled around,
        heedlessly jumping in,
Raise up a wave of applause for him, at eleven oars convey   545
        A good Lenaean noise,
        So the poet can leave
            Faring well after his wish,
        Brilliant with a gleaming forehead.   550
                                         (vv. 498–550)

The coryphaeus steps forward to praise the poet's boldness in attacking
Cleon and also responds to those who have asked why Aristophanes
has not previously ventured to produce comedies in his own name.
Comedy is a "most difficult" (χαλεπώτατον) art, as evidenced by the
few poets who have been successful in it (v. 517) and by the forever

mutable nature of the public's taste (v. 518). These assertions are fleshed out with the examples of three comic predecessors who enjoyed the public's favor at one time and eventually lost it. Magnes won more victories than any rival and introduced many theatrical innovations, possibly including the use of animal choruses.[31] As soon as old age approached, however, he lost his ability to "jest" (σκώπτειν) and was "thrown out" (vv. 520–25). At the opposite extreme from Magnes' rather coarse and primitive antics are the "urbane ideas" (ἀστειοτάτας ἐπινοίας) of Crates[32] who at best received only a mediocre response from the public, "sometimes failing, sometimes not" (vv. 537–40). But the high point of Aristophanes' description of his predecessors is the vivid portrait of the senescent Cratinus (vv. 526–36) who, although still living, is enumerated between the dead Magnes and Crates, with the implication that he is equally a has-been.[33]

Cratinus is generally credited with being the seminal figure who turned Old Comedy in the direction of personal attacks and ad hominem invective against contemporaries;[34] as the preeminent "blame poet" in the comic tradition, he is appropriately described as at one time flattening everything in his path like a flooding river.[35] Once so caustic and pitiless in his treatment of others, Cratinus is now a helpless

31. See Sifakis (1971b, 73–85), who traces the use of theriomorphic choruses back to the earliest stages of Comedy. Spyropoulos 1975, 247–74, however, denies Magnes' use of such choruses and merely sees the participles of vv. 522–23 as general illustrations of comic buffoonery.

32. On Crates' noninvective character, see Aristotle, *Poet.* 1449b7–9 τῶν δὲ ᾿Αθήνησιν Κράτης πρῶτος ἦρξεν ἀφέμενος τῆς ἰαμβικῆς ἰδέας καθόλου ποιεῖν λόγους καὶ μύθους. As such he is a foil to Cratinus who is said to have emphasized the ad hominem satire characteristic of iambic poetry (see n.34 below).

33. On the order of presentation, see the remarks of Sommerstein 1981, 171; Harriott 1986, 23.

34. See Athenaeus 268d; Platonius, *De Diff. Char.* (= Test. xvii PCG); Poppelreuter 1893, 28–32; Norwood 1931, 141–44; Pieters 1946, 51–131; Schwarze 1971, 5–90; Mattingly 1977, 239–45; Rosen 1983, 145–60 (= Rosen 1988, 37–49). Cratinus' astringent satire may also be the point of his epithet "bull-devouring" (ταυροφάγος) in *Ran.* 357.

35. The imagery of vv. 526–28 seems to be primarily Homeric in inspiration (cf. *Il.* 5.87–92, 16.384–92, and especially 11.492–5), although the application of the river image to poetry is Pindaric (*N.*7.12, 62, *I.*7.19, fr. 334a.3 S.-M.). Cratinus, fr. 198 PCG (from the *Pytinē*) apparently responds to this passage. The chief Homeric models are similes describing a raging warrior and emphasize his activity as a form of uncontrolled violence; later applications of the river image to poetry (Callimachus, *Hymn* 2.108–9; Horace, *Sat.* 1.4.11, 1.7.26–27, 1.10.36–37, 50–51, 62–63, *C.* 4.2.5–8) refer to poetic inspiration that has run out of control and lacks discrimination. The same implication may be present in Aristophanes' reference to Cratinus. We should perhaps note the use of the imperfect verb ἔρρει (v. 527 "used to flow") as also possibly the present of ἔρρω ("goes to perdition," cf. *Pax* 500, *Lys.* 1240, *Plut.* 604), aptly descriptive of Cratinus' present condition.

old man in need of the audience's pity (and manifestly without it). His lyre is in disrepair and Cratinus himself is given over to drink. The picture of Cratinus is not unlike Pindar's famous description of "reproachful Archilochus in his poverty fattening himself on heavy-worded hate" (*P*.2.54–56); it also resembles the familiar stories of *Vita* tradition concerning the violent and disgusting deaths of other literary misanthropes, often at the hands of a vengeful public, as in the case of Thersites beaten to death by Achilles, Aesop thrown off a cliff after being falsely accused of theft, Heraclitus packing himself in dung as a cure for dropsy only to be eaten by dogs, and Euripides torn apart by Macedonian hunting dogs or Orpheus by Thracian Bacchants.[36]

Although Aristophanes complains of the treatment accorded his predecessors, we should not make the mistake of regarding his sympathy as sincere. The portrait of Cratinus as a drooling and incompetent old man in the grip of advanced senility was hardly flattering or true. If Cratinus was turning toward alcoholism and allowing his lyre to fall apart,[37] that is, declining in musical and poetic ability, this was not the fault of the theatrical public. When Aristophanes presumes to commiserate and wish for better treatment (vv. 535–36), he only calls further attention to Cratinus' descent into drink (v. 535 πίνειν ἐν τῷ πρυτανείῳ, v. 536 παρὰ τῷ Διονύσῳ). By wishing Cratinus a prosperous retirement, Aristophanes is also implying that the not-yet-retired Cratinus (who was competing against this play) ought to be retired, himself becoming a member of the audience (v. 536 θεᾶσθαι) rather than a competitor. Cratinus certainly did not feel that Aristophanes was paying him a compliment; the *Pytinē*, presented in the following year, not only defended its poet against the charge of alcoholism, but attacked Aristophanes in turn.[38]

In the same way Crates is praised on the surface for his polish and refinement, yet his supposed lack of popularity emanates not so much

---

36. For Thersites: *Aethiopis*, fr. 1 (= Proclus, *Chrest.*). Aesop: *Vitae* G, W (Perry), and the discussion of Nagy (1979, 279–88). Heraclitus: 22A1a D.-K. (= Suidas). Euripides: *Vita Eur.* 122–23, and the discussion of Lefkowitz 1981, 76–78. Orpheus: Ovid, *Metam.* 11.1–66.

37. For the interpretation of the image, see Perusino 1982b, 151–58. I do not believe, however, that we are to understand Cratinus himself as a lyre, as she and most other commentators on the passage do, but as the owner of such a lyre, which mirrors his own dissolution.

38. Cratinus charged Aristophanes with plagiarizing from Eupolis (fr. 213 PCG) and with imitating Euripides at the same time he criticized the tragic poet (fr. 342 PCG, plausibly assigned to the *Pytinē* by Runkel). Pieters (1946, 151–52) thinks Aristophanes and Eupolis may have been presented as dramatic characters in the *Pytinē*. The last laugh was indeed Cratinus', inasmuch as the *Pytinē* won the first prize in the Dionysia, as opposed to the *Clouds'* humiliating third place.

from the public's lack of taste as from his own lack of comic inspiration; his "most cabbage-dry" (κραμβοτάτου) mouth is an uninspired mouth,[39] and the "small expense" with which he feeds the public may reflect small effort.[40] Similarly Magnes' fall from favor is traced directly to his loss of the ability to "jest."[41] Thus clearly what begins as a comment on the theatrical public for shifting tastes is ironically subverted into a subtle criticism of Aristophanes' predecessors masked as praise and sympathy. Against this background Aristophanes holds himself to a higher standard and insists on learning the art thoroughly, in metaphorical terms taking every position on the boat (vv. 541–44) before exposing himself fully to the hazards of public favor and posthumous reputation.[42] In this most immodest and invective-filled play, the poet goes out of his way to emphasize his own personal modesty and restraint (v. 545 σωφρονικῶς κοὐκ ἀνοήτως), thereby hoping to avoid the *invidia* and suspicion that eventually beset any unabashed blame poet. This persona is reinforced in the parabasis by a satirical technique of ironic sympathy dissociated from the open hostility and animus characteristic of this play and of the genre as a whole.

At the end of the parabasis the chorus addresses the audience directly and asks them to reward the poet's modesty with "Lenaean

39. The presence of two superlatives in one line (v. 539 κραμβοτάτου, ἀστειοτάτας) is rather striking and may be stylistic parody of Crates. Our fragments of Crates are too few to draw any positive conclusions, but at least two of them (fr. 2 K γλυκύτατον δ', ὦ Ζεῦ, βασιλείου μύρου; fr. 40 K πάνυ γάρ ἐστιν ὡρικώτατα τὰ τιτθί' . . .) feature notable exclamatory superlatives. For the most recent and thorough discussion of κραμβοτάτου (and the ambiguity of Aristophanes' attitude toward Crates generally), see Bonanno (1972, 36–39), who follows the scholia in connecting it with cabbage (κράμβη) as an antidote for intoxication and thus sees Crates as antithetical to the overinspired Cratinus.

40. The term δαπάνη usually has connotations of large expenditure and even extravagance; the reference here to σμικρᾶς δαπάνης thus contains an oxymoronic tension within itself, implying Crates' expenditure as less than it should be. On the imagery here of "feeding" as parallel to the politicians' feeding of Demos in the play, see Reckford 1987, 127.

41. The passive expression τοῦ σκώπτειν ἀπελείφθη, parallel to the passive ἐξεβλήθη at the beginning of the line, creates an impression of helplessness on Magnes' part. In a comic poet, though, such helplessness can come only from a decline in imagination.

42. Mastromarco (1979, 172–73) and Halliwell (1980, 39) independently revive the theory first proposed by Leo (1878, 401 n.2; cf. Hiller 1887, 365–67) of *Vesp.* 1018–19 as referring to an earlier stage in Aristophanes' career when he helped other comic poets write their plays. Mastromarco and Halliwell conclude that the three positions on the ship described in *Eq.* 541–44 refer to three stages of the poet's career: (1) prior to *Banqueters,* helping other poets write their plays, (2) from *Banqueters* to *Acharnians,* writing his own plays but having them produced by someone else, and (3) starting with *Knights,* both writing and producing his own plays. But MacDowell (1982, 22–23) is probably right in doubting whether such a first stage ever existed; the progression of *Eq.* 541–44 can just as well be a general reference to the poet's assumption of progressively greater responsibility for the details of production. See Appendix 1.

applause" (vv. 545–47). This exhortation provides a positive counter-point to the audience address that opened the anapests in the komma-tion (vv. 503–6), reminding the public of its fickle tastes and fore-shadowing the remarks of the following parabasis ("all of you, trying on your own every kind of Muse"). The parallels between the komma-tion and pnigos reach further: framing the audience-addresses are farewells to the Sausage seller (vv. 418–502) and poet (vv. 548–50). The verbal and imagistic correspondences are close (v. 498 ἴθι χαίρων = v. 548 ἀπίῃ χαίρων; vv. 498–99 πράξειας κατὰ νοῦν τὸν ἐμόν = v. 549 κατὰ νοῦν πράξας; v. 502 στεφάνοις κατάπαστος = v. 550 φαιδρὸς λάμποντι μετώπῳ). In both passages the chorus effectively wishes for its friend's victory in the respective arenas of assembly and theater and puts its personal support fully behind his effort.[43] Aristophanes draws attention to the Sausage seller's status as a double for himself in pas-sages framing the very parabasis in which he ironically distances him-self from the Sausage seller's unrestrained style.

Indeed, there is quite a lot in this parabasis which suggests the situation of the *Knights* as a whole. Some critics have pointed out that the poet's competition for public favor corresponds with the rivalry of the politicians for the affection of Demos and that in both cases the public's loyalties are transitory and evanescent.[44] The mobility and inconstancy of public opinion had already been a theme in the *Achar-nians* (see *Ach.* 626, 632 "counsel-changing Athenians"). In the *Knights* we can appreciate the series of three comic poets successively favored and despised by the public (Magnes, Cratinus, and Crates, with Aris-tophanes as the implied fourth) as directly complementing the succes-sion of demagogues whom the public elevates and eventually rejects (vv. 128–43: the hemp seller, sheep seller, leather seller Paphlagon, and finally, the Sausage seller). It should come as no surprise that we find the poets characterized by the same imagery of food and drink as the politicians. The drunken Cratinus is always "thirsty" (v. 534), like the voracious demagogues (see vv. 351–62, 698–701), and is treated by Aristophanes as a candidate for drink at public expense in the pry-taneum (v. 535; see vv. 280–83, of Paphlagon). On the other side Crates is described as "feasting" the public (v. 538) and "kneading" his ideas for them as if preparing a cake (v. 539); we have noted above

43. In vv. 500–502 the Sausage seller is asked to return to the Knights after his victory; in v. 546 the Knights raise eleven oars to support the coryphaeus' demand for applause in honor of the poet (see my interpretation of this passage in Hubbard 1990, 115–18).

44. Harriott 1986, 21. On the parallel between the Sausage seller and Aristophanes generally, see Solomos 1974, 99–101.

several passages in which the public is thus pampered by the politicians (see especially v. 54, for the "kneading" metaphor). Here again we find the public allowing its artistic judgment, like its political judgment, to be perverted by short-term and selfish considerations, instead of being governed by mature and disinterested reflection.

In this environment of popular vicissitude Aristophanes is at first reluctant to enter the fray of poetic competition, just as the Sausage seller was initially reluctant to leave his humble and obscure status for a political career (vv. 150–241). The Sausage seller even tries to run away at first sight of the Paphlagon until he is persuaded to face him by the timely intervention of the Knights, who lead the attack (vv. 242–77). Aristophanes was also encouraged by powerful and influential backers during the early stages of his struggle against Cleon (perhaps alluded to in vv. 512–13, and perhaps including some of the knights),[45] but eventually felt able to stand on his own, just as the Sausage seller comes to depend on the Knights less and less as the play progresses.

The final reflection of the parabasis concerning Aristophanes' conviction that a poet must learn the trade thoroughly before commencing full-scale competition also provides a lesson germane to the political sphere: politicians should not presume to lead the state unless they have gained long experience in all the particulars of statecraft. This insight could not be more relevant than in the environment of "new politicians" such as Cleon, who have risen out of nowhere into positions of dominance.

Apology of the Upper Class

The necessity of establishing one's credentials by a long record of service to the state is further expounded by the epirrhematic syzygy:

> Horse-lord Poseidon, whom
> The thunder and neigh
> Of brass-rattling horses pleases,
> And dark-rammed swift
>   Pay-bearing triremes,   555
> And the contest of young men
> Both shining and lamenting fortune
>   In their chariots.
> Come hither to your chorus, O golden-trident god,

45. On Aristophanes' relation to such patrons, see Halliwell 1980, 42–43. Croiset (1909, 70–73) and Sartori (1957, 73) suppose Aristophanes to have had support and encouragement from the knights themselves, on which relationship, see also Robert 1967, 164.

> O god invoked at Sunium, ruling over dolphins, 560
> > O Geraistian son of Cronus,
> > And of all the other gods
> > Dearest to Phormio and the Athenians
> > > In present affairs.
> We wish to eulogize our fathers, because 565
> They were men worthy of this land and of Athena's robe,
> Who in battles both on land and sea
> Always glorified this city, winning everywhere.
> Never did anyone of them count the enemy whom he saw,
> But his spirit was straight on guard like Amynias. 570
> If they should anywhere fall on their shoulder in some battle,
> They would have wiped it off and denied having fallen,
> And would wrestle again. And no general of those before today
> Would have ever asked Cleainetus for free meals;
> But now, if they don't get honored seating and free meals, 575
> They say they won't fight. But we think it right
> Nobly to defend our city and native gods for free.
> In addition, we ask nothing more than only this:
> If peace ever comes and we cease from our travails,
> Do not begrudge us our long hair and bath-scrapers. 580

> > O Pallas the city-holder,
> > Ruling over the most holy
> > Of all lands
> > And the most excellent
> > > In war, poets, and power, 585
> > Come hither, taking with you
> > Victory, our fellow-worker
> > > In armies and battles,
> > Who is also a friend of choral affairs
> > And sides with us against our enemies. 590
> > > Now show yourself here,
> > > Since to these men
> > You should provide victory with every device,
> > > If ever before, then even now.
> We wish to praise what we know of our horses. 595
> They are worthy to be eulogized. Indeed, many things
> They have endured with us, both attacks and battles.
> But we do not wonder so much at their feats on land,
> As when they manfully jumped aboard the cavalry-ships,
> Having bought themselves drinking cups, some even onion and
> > garlic. 600
> Then taking the oars like we men do,
> They started to row and bellowed forth, "Horsey-go, who rows?
> We must stroke faster. What are we doing? Aren't you moving,
> > S-brand?"

> They jumped out at Corinth. Then, the younger ones
> Dug out beds with their tools and went after straw.   605
> They ate little crabs instead of Persian grass,
> If one should come ashore or even if they had to hunt them in the
>   depths.
> And so, Theorus related that the Corinthian crab said,
> "It's terrible, O Poseidon, if I can flee the Knights
> Neither in the depths nor on land nor at sea."   610
>   (vv. 551–610)

As we have seen before, the ode serves a transitional function, invoking
Poseidon as the god both of seamanship (and thus the poet's activity, metaphorically described in nautical terms by vv. 542–46) and of
horsemanship (the Knights' natural realm of action).[46] As such the
interests of poet and chorus are united under the god's patronage; the
Knights' chariot contests in which some win and some fail (vv. 556–58)
are not unlike the dramatic contest described in the anapests above.
More broadly the interests of chorus and poet are also united with
those of the whole city, as represented by Poseidon's association with
Athens' naval success (vv. 554–55, 562–64).

In the epirrheme the Knights praise their fathers for military self-
sacrifice on both land (v. 567 $\pi\epsilon\zeta\alpha\hat{\imath}\varsigma$ $\mu\acute{\alpha}\chi\alpha\iota\sigma\iota\nu$) and sea ($\nu\alpha\nu\phi\acute{\alpha}\rho\kappa\tau\varphi$
$\sigma\tau\rho\alpha\tau\hat{\varphi}$) and find in this heritage the model for their own selfless
dedication to the defense of the state (vv. 576–80). The young Knights'
respect for their elders shows a traditionalism and reverence quite
antithetical to the popular *Zeitgeist* described in the anapests, always in
quest of new leaders, new models, and new entertainments, and de-
spising the old guides of the past. We are here reminded of the *Acharnians* parabasis, where the old demesmen feel mistreated by the young
demagogues but are defended by the young Aristophanes.[47] Indeed,
the selflessness of the Knights and their fathers is contrasted quite
explicitly with the venality and greed of the present leadership (including Cleon, evoked by the allusion to his father Cleainetus in v. 574).[48]
As throughout the play, food (v. 574 $\sigma\acute{\iota}\tau\eta\sigma\iota\nu$; v. 575 $\tau\grave{\alpha}$ $\sigma\iota\tau\acute{\iota}\alpha$) provides
the dominant image reflecting the excessive appetites of the present-

---

46. The fusion of the two domains is expressed theatrically by the spectacle of the
mounted Knights holding "oars" (cf. v. 546, and my interpretation in Hubbard 1990,
115–18).

47. The theme of generational conflict is also explored dramatically in the next two
plays of Aristophanes (*Clouds* and *Wasps;* cf. Whitman 1964, 119) and, as we shall see in
our interpretation of the *Wasps,* can stand for the poet's relationship to his public. See
also Hubbard 1989, 90–113.

48. The allusion to $\pi\rho o\epsilon\delta\rho\acute{\iota}\alpha$ in v. 575 also points to Cleon/Paphlagon, who brags of
his $\pi\rho o\epsilon\delta\rho\acute{\iota}\alpha$ in v. 702.

day generals. Despite Paphlagon/Cleon's claims to military greatness based on his victory at Pylos (vv. 54–57, 702, 742–43), it becomes apparent from the contrast with the Knights which of them was really protecting Athens.

The antode is addressed to Athena, Poseidon's mythological counterpart as Athens' defender.[49] It corresponds to the ode in its dual emphasis on the god's patronage of the poetic sphere (vv. 583–84 ποιηταῖς) as well as the martial area (v. 583 πολέμῳ). Athena is asked to bring with her Nike who is also relevant in both domains (v. 587 ἐν στρατιαῖς τε καὶ μάχαις; v. 589 χορικῶν ἑταίρα).[50] The prayer to Athena concludes with a hypomnesis begging her to appear and provide victory "to these men" (v. 591 τοῖς ἀνδράσι τοῖσδε); the vague and ambiguous expression can refer either to Athens' army, those with aristocratic sympathies like the knights, the dramatic chorus, or the Sausage seller and other characters (including the chorus in its dramatic role) fighting the Paphlagon. The "enemies" (v. 590 τοῖς ἐχθροῖσι) equally combine Athens' foreign enemies, radical democrats, the competing playwrights, and Paphlagon/Cleon.[51] We see in this parabasis a complex fusion between the historical, political, performative, and dramatic dimensions.

Just as the antode corresponded directly to the ode, we also see a close relation between the antepirrheme and epirrheme (note the parallel εὐλογῆσαι βουλόμεσθα in v. 565 and βουλόμεσθ᾽ ἐπαινέσαι in v. 595, and in the next lines, τῆσδε τῆς γῆς ἄξιοι and ἄξιοι . . . εὐλογεῖσθαι). In many ways, however, the antepirrheme stands as a comic inversion of the serious themes treated in the epirrheme; here the Knights are not praising their noble forebears for service on land and sea (v. 567), but their horses (vv. 598–600). Of course the Knights' praise of both their fathers and their horses is by transference an act of self-praise, though one offered with a degree of modesty and humorous self-deprecation guaranteed to reconcile the otherwise suspicious and antiaristocratic audience.[52]

49. Neil (1901, 88) emphasizes Poseidon's identity as a god with aristocratic associations, especially horsemanship, as opposed to Athena's more democratic character; cf. *Av.* 1565–71, and Ehrenberg 1962, 265. But Edmunds (1987b, 40–44) acutely notes the merging of both gods' political identities in the present context.

50. One should note the humorous play on the two senses of ἑταίρα as "comrade" and "courtesan" (cf. *Pax* 440, *Thesm.* 346, *Plut.* 149) of the young Knights.

51. On the various ambiguities of this passage, see Kock 1882, 108; Neil 1901, 89; Sartori 1957, 76; Sommerstein 1981, 176; Zimmermann 1985 II, 207; Reckford 1987, 391.

52. Edmunds (1987a, 253–56 [= Edmunds 1987b, 39–41]) has acutely emphasized the role of the entire syzygy in reconciling the interests of the upper class Knights with those of the general public who formed Athens' naval force; even as the poet represented

As Cleon was attacked indirectly through the allusion to his father Cleainetus in the epirrheme (v. 574), so he is now attacked through his associate Theorus (v. 608) who perceives that the "Corinthian crabs" (i.e. corrupt politicians who greedily grab everything with their claws)[53] cannot escape from the Knights anywhere on land or sea. As in the epirrheme and antode the Knights' courage is at once counterposed to foreign enemies (the Corinthians) and domestic enemies (Theorus and other crablike politicians). The droll imagery helps soften and modulate the blistering criticism of Cleon lurking beneath the surface of this parabasis (and surrounding it in the play as a whole); a similar modulation of tone is introduced with the final couplet of the epirrheme (vv. 579–80), in which the Knights beg the public's tolerance for their long hair and hot baths.

The Knights' self-defense against charges of effeminacy and cowardice is probably intended as a response to Cleon's denunciation of the knights for *leipostratia* a few years earlier (alluded to by Theopompus, *FGrH* 115F93).[54] Cleon's charges were echoed by the comic poets, especially Eupolis, whose fragments are full of insinuations that the upper class youth were luxuriant effeminates who failed to do their share in the war effort.[55] Such criticism of the "cowardly" knights may

himself to be an "oarsman" (v. 542), the Knights and their horses go to sea in vv. 598–99 and claim descent from common soldiers and sailors in vv. 565–68. Bugh (1988, 66–67) notes that the expansion of the cavalry from 300 to 1,000 during the Periclean period in fact made it a somewhat less elite organization in terms of its members' class background.

53. The greed and avarice of Corinthians was proverbial. Our interpretation of the crab image is reinforced by the image of Paphlagon as an ἀγκυλοχήλης eagle in vv. 197–98, grasping game in his claws. Commentators seem not to have understood the significance of the crab image: Σ*Eq.* 608a ineptly associates it with Theorus' reputed fondness for eating fish, as one of a series of speculations, and Neil (1901, 91) follows Kock (1882, 109–10) in seeing *karkinos* as a nickname for Corinthians in general; Ruck (1975, 57 n.123) applies it specifically to Corinthian prostitutes. No parallels are adduced to support any of these identifications. Halliwell (1982, 153) sees in the speaking crab parody of a familiar skolion (fr. 892 PMG), but this alone does not explain why the crab image seemed appropriate to Aristophanes here.

54. For the same idea, see Kraus 1985, 138. On this event and its probable date (c. 427), cf. Gilbert 1877, 139; *HCT* II, 289–90; Connor 1968, 50–53; Bugh 1988, 111–13. Fornara (1973, 24) is probably correct in supposing that Cleon attacked the Knights not with a formal prosecution, but by proposing to withdraw the state's usual provision of an equipment loan for new recruits (with Σ*Eq.* 226a misinterpreting Theopompus' κατάστάσει as πολιτείᾳ). This equipment money may have some relation to the five talents which the *Babylonians* showed the Knights forcing Cleon to give up; see chap. 3 n.2 above.

55. Eupolis, fr. 293 PCG (from the *Philoi*, datable to the early 420s, as is clear from the allusion to Aspasia in fr. 294 PCG; cf. Geissler 1925, 34–35; Edmonds 1957 I, 407) seems to allude to the Knights' unearned equipment money. The *Taxiarchoi* featured a lazy and effeminate Dionysus being drilled for military service by the admiral Phormio (d. 428): cf. fr. 268.50–55, 269–72, 274–76 PCG, and the discussions of Wilamowitz

very well have been the inspiration behind Aristophanes' choice of the
Knights as the chorus of this play, for we see their martial courage
defended not only in this syzygy, but also in their aggressive cavalry
attacks on Paphlagon (vv. 247–54, 453–56).[56] If the knights were an
object of ridicule by other comic poets in the wake of Cleon's denunciation, their appropriateness as comic antagonists to Cleon becomes
obvious, and we can see the real meaning behind the statement at the
opening of the anapests that they would speak on behalf of no other
comic poet (vv. 507–9).

Aristophanes and Eupolis

The influence of Eupolis may also be reflected in parts of the second
parabasis:

"What is fairer for those beginning
Or ending a song"   1265
Than for the riders of horses to sing
   Nothing against Lysistratus,
And not aggrieve the homeless Thumantis
   With willing heart?
O dear Apollo, this man is always poor,   1270
   And with warm tears
Clutches your quiver at divine Pytho,
   Asking not to be so grievously poor.

There is no envy in abusing the base,
But it does honor to good men, if anyone reasons well.   1275
I would not have mentioned a good man dear to me,
If that man himself were better known, who ought to have a bad
   reputation.
Now there is no one who doesn't know Arignotus,
If he knows the color white or the high C-scale.
He has a brother, not at all kin in his manners,   1280
The low Ariphrades. But this lowness he desires.
He is not only low, for then I wouldn't have noticed him,
Nor even extremely low, but he has discovered something further.

1880, 66–67; Norwood 1931, 197–98; Wilson 1974, 250–52; Handley 1982, 24–25. But
Eupolis' most thorough treatment of the theme was his *Astrateutoi/Androgynoi* (see especially fr. 35, 37, 46 PCG).

   56. One can imagine that these passages were accompanied by vivid stage action on
the part of the chorus, especially in the parodos. Sifakis (1971b, 99) holds such stage
action to be also taking place in the background of the parabasis syzygy, thus providing a
visual component to the verbal description of the Knights' valor.

He soils his tongue with filthy pleasures,
Licking the most loathsome dew in brothel-houses,   1285
Sliming his beard and stirring up the hearths,
Acting like Polymnestus and staying with Oeonichus.
"Whoever, then, does not utterly hate such a man,
He will never drink from the same cup as we."

    Often I have communed   1290
    With my night-time thoughts
    And wondered where Cleonymus
      Is able to eat at small expense.
    For they say that he, snatching
      The food of rich men,   1295
    Would never depart from the meal-tub.
      But they would beseech him all the same,
    "By your knees, O lord, go,
      Depart and spare the table."
They say that the triremes came together for a parley,   1300
And one of them, who was oldest, said:
"Maidens, don't you inquire about these affairs in the city?
They say that someone demands 100 of us against Carthage,
A villainous man, a sharp-tongued citizen named Hyperbolus."
To them this seemed terrible and intolerable,   1305
And one of them, who had never come near men, said:
"Heaven forbid! He will never rule me, but if I must,
I will grow old here, rotting away with woodworms."
"Nor will he rule Ship-phante, daughter of Ship-so—no indeed, O
    gods,
If I am built of pine and wood.   1310
If these proposals please the Athenians, then I think
We ought to sail to the Theseum or the Dread Goddesses and sit
    there.
He won't laugh at the city, commanding us!
But let him sail away to hell, if he wants,
Launching with him the wood-tubs on which he used to sell lamps." 1315
                                          (vv. 1264–1315)

Vv. 1264–66 insert us into a context of literary parody; the scholia
identify the lines as a distortion of Pindar (fr. 89a S.-M.) transferred
from a high-flown praise of Leto and Artemis to ridicule of the miserable Lysistratus and Thumantis.[57] But the Pindaric formula is here
used as a priamel rejecting these two as a theme in favor of abusing even baser men, such as the young sophist and sexual deviant

____

57. Σ*Eq.* 1264b. On the dynamics of the Pindaric parody here, see Wilamowitz 1919,
54–56, and Fraenkel 1962, 204–6.

Ariphrades.[58] Not only does Ariphrades' rather peculiar use of his tongue (vv. 1284–87)[59] remind us of Paphlagon/Cleon's active tongue (vv. 352, 378, 1034; cf. vv. 637, 837 of the Sausage seller), but his degrading desire to gratify common prostitutes this way reflects the extremes to which Athens' political leaders have gone to abase themselves before the petty appetites of the populace.

The scholia tell us that the final couplet of this epirrheme is the work of Eupolis[60] and that it motivated some Alexandrian scholars to identify the whole second parabasis as the fruit of Eupolis' collaboration with Aristophanes; indeed, we find a similar (although not identical) formula at the end of the epirrheme in a parabasis from Eupolis' *Demoi* (dated to 412/1), which has led most recent scholars to regard the whole story as a case of scholiastic confusion.[61] Yet the parallel between the *Demoi* couplet and *Eq.* 1288–89 is not close enough to motivate even a confused Alexandrian to assign this parabasis to Eupolis. Critics have not observed that the same type of formula also occurs in *Nub.* 560 ($\ddot{o}\sigma\tau\iota\varsigma$ $o\mathring{\upsilon}\nu$ $\tauo\acute{\upsilon}\tauo\iota\sigma\iota$ $\gamma\epsilon\lambda\hat{q}$, $\tauo\hat{\iota}\varsigma$ $\mathring{\epsilon}\muo\hat{\iota}\varsigma$ $\mu\grave{\eta}$ $\chi\alpha\iota\rho\acute{\epsilon}\tau\omega$) in a parabatic context clearly parodying Eupolis.[62] What has also escaped notice is the proliferation of otiose $\ddot{o}\sigma\tau\iota\varsigma$ clauses in the *Knights* epirrheme in what seems to be deliberate mannerism and parody (v. 1275 $\ddot{o}\sigma\tau\iota\varsigma$ $\epsilon\mathring{\upsilon}$ $\lambda o\gamma\acute{\iota}\zeta\epsilon\tau\alpha\iota$, v. 1278 $\ddot{o}\sigma\tau\iota\varsigma$ $o\mathring{\upsilon}\kappa$ $\mathring{\epsilon}\pi\acute{\iota}\sigma\tau\alpha\tau\alpha\iota$, v. 1279 $\ddot{o}\sigma\tau\iota\varsigma$ $\mathring{\eta}$ $\tau\grave{o}$ $\lambda\epsilon\upsilon\kappa\grave{o}\nu$ $o\mathring{\iota}\delta\epsilon\nu$ . . .). I would thus argue that we should take the scholia seriously

58. On Ariphrades' identity as a pupil of Anaxagoras and a progressive thinker with many "new ideas," see Degani 1960, 196–202, 210–17. Aristotle, *Poet.* 1458b31–32 suggests the possibility of his also having been a comic poet, hence a rival of Aristophanes (cf. Sommerstein 1977b, 276); if so, the second parabasis would be just as much a literary polemic as the first. Ostwald (1986, 269–70) associates Ariphrades' $\gamma\lambda\omega\tau\tauo\pi o\iota\epsilon\hat{\iota}\nu$ with his reputation as a public speaker.

59. That cunnilinctus was not anything inherently disgraceful for the Greeks is argued by Henderson 1975, 52–53. The really humiliating aspect of Ariphrades' behavior is his repeated performance of this act with common prostitutes, who should be gratifying him orally.

60. This is surely the correct interpretation of $\Sigma Eq.$ 1291, not that Eupolis' contribution begins at this point in the parabasis, as has been demonstrated by Pohlenz 1912, 316–17.

61. Eupolis, fr. 99.33–34 PCG $\ddot{o}\sigma\tau\iota\varsigma$ $o\mathring{\upsilon}\nu$ $\ddot{\alpha}\rho\chi\epsilon\iota\nu$ $\tauo\iotao\acute{\upsilon}\tauo\upsilon\varsigma$ $\ddot{\alpha}\nu\delta\rho\alpha\varsigma$ $\alpha[\acute{\iota}\rho\epsilon\hat{\iota}\tau\alpha\iota$ $\pio\tau\epsilon/$ $\mu\acute{\eta}\tau\epsilon$ $\pi\rho\acute{o}\beta\alpha\tau$' $\alpha\mathring{\upsilon}\tau\hat{\wp}$ $\tau\epsilon\kappa\nuo\hat{\iota}\tauo$ $\mu\acute{\eta}\tau\epsilon$ $\gamma\hat{\eta}$ $\kappa[\alpha\rho\pi\grave{o}\nu$ $\phi\acute{\epsilon}\rho o\iota$, as compared to *Eq.* 1288–89 $\ddot{o}\sigma\tau\iota\varsigma$ $o\mathring{\upsilon}\nu$ $\tauo\iotao\hat{\upsilon}\tauo\nu$ $\ddot{\alpha}\nu\delta\rho\alpha$ $\mu\grave{\eta}$ $\sigma\phi\acute{o}\delta\rho\alpha$ $\beta\delta\epsilon\lambda\acute{\upsilon}\tau\tau\epsilon\tau\alpha\iota,/o\mathring{\upsilon}$ $\pio\tau$' $\mathring{\epsilon}\kappa$ $\tau\alpha\mathring{\upsilon}\tauo\hat{\upsilon}$ $\mu\epsilon\theta$' $\mathring{\eta}\mu\hat{\omega}\nu$ $\pi\acute{\iota}\epsilon\tau\alpha\iota$ $\pio\tau\eta\rho\acute{\iota}o\upsilon$. The theory of the scholia somehow mistaking this passage for the source of *Eq.* 1288–89 was first advanced by Pohlenz (1912, 316–17), who did not, however, totally deny Eupolis' collaboration in the *Knights*, merely that it could be localized to this parabasis; the theory has been extended to a complete denial of Eupolis' influence by Landfester (1967, 79–82), followed by Schwinge (1975b, 177) and Kraus (1985, 159–60). Also cf. Sommerstein 1980b, 51–53.

62. See our discussion on pp. 104–5 below. Not only is the *Clouds* parabasis written in the "eupolidean" meter; this line also terminates a passage specifically criticizing Eupolis and others for copying the *Knights*.

here, at least to the extent of recognizing this curse formula to be a stylistic habit of Eupolis and perhaps lifted verbatim from an earlier play.[63] This would also explain Cratinus' charge the following year that Aristophanes was guilty of saying τὰ Εὐπόλιδος (fr. 213 PCG), and Eupolis' ironic claim several years later (fr. 89 PCG, from the *Baptae*) that he "co-authored" the *Knights* and "gave it as a gift" to Aristophanes.[64] One can imagine Eupolis' unhappiness over seeing his words repeated, particularly in application to someone as disgusting as Ariphrades. By quoting Eupolis here, Aristophanes manages to place the most savage invective of the play onto another poet's shoulders, thereby avoiding the opprobrium he might otherwise have to bear as a "blame poet" in this unabashedly blame-filled epirrheme (see vv. 1274–77).

The antode parallels the ode in its parody of high-flown lyric used to lampoon a poor rascal (here, the hungry Cleonymus). The antepirrheme turns its attention to a more serious nuisance, the demagogue Hyperbolus who, like Cleon, is characterized as an upstart from the mercantile class (v. 1315) and the advocate of an unnecessary expansion of the war (v. 1303). The dialogue of the personified ships who refuse service responds antiphonally with the personified horses who gladly go to sea in the antepirrheme of the first parabasis.[65] Whereas the Knights willingly undertook service on missions truly beneficial to Athens, through the persona of the triremes they imply their unwillingness to serve on wasteful and unnecessary attempts to expand Athens' mercantile empire. This assertion of courage coupled with discretion stands as their final reply to the charges of *astrateia* and cowardice made by Cleon and some comic poets.[66] In certain cases refusal to serve may be the courageous act.

---

63. The idea of a verbatim quote here at the end of the epirrheme is corroborated by the verbatim quote from Pindar at the beginning; we seem also to be dealing with a parodic quote in vv. 1290–91 at the beginning of the next epirrheme, as is suggested by Wilamowitz (1919, 56). Sommerstein (1980, 51–53) has correctly interpreted ΣEq. 1225a to mean that v. 1225 is a verbatim repetition of a line from Eupolis' *Helots* (also confirmed by the wording of Eupolis, fr. 89 PCG). Given our paltry remains, we cannot know how many more such borrowings from Eupolis there were in this play unrecognized by the scholia.

64. The scholia interpreted this statement literally and thus assigned a whole section of the play to Eupolis on the basis of vv. 1288–89. But Eupolis' real meaning is probably that Aristophanes had used so many phrases and ideas from Eupolis' previous plays that he deserved to claim coauthorship. That he in turn parodied the *Knights* in his *Marikas* (cf. *Nub.* 551–55) and possibly in other plays (cf. Aristophanes, fr. 58 PCG, from the *Anagyros*) also suggests that something in the *Knights* made it an appropriate target for him.

65. On the parallel between these two parabases, see Pohlenz 1952, 121–22.

66. Eupolis, fr. 376 PCG, generally assigned to *Astrateutoi/Androgynoi*, although the citation in *Et. Magn.* 174.50 is corrupt, and fr. 353 PCG may suggest Aristophanes'

Thus the defeat of comic scapegoats like Ariphrades and Hyperbolus coincides with the Knights' (and Aristophanes') inversion of a major poetic rival. It moreover coincides with the expulsion of the play's principal scapegoat in the immediately preceding scene.[67] Liberated of these parasites, the public (= Demos) is symbolically born anew and no longer appears as a dependent old man but as a vigorous youth.[68] Even so Aristophanes himself hopes to purge and reinvigorate the Athenian public through his self-conscious use of comic language and theatrical metaphor in the ritual context of the Dionysian festival.

---

finding precedent for his personification of the ships in Eupolis; however, our lack of context makes it impossible to interpret these fragments with any certainty. This passage may also be meant to look forward to the ship chorus of Aristophanes' *Holkades*, on which, see p. 34 above.

67. On this ritual structure in the *Knights*, see Cornford 1968, 33. It has recently been applied to the play in a different way, however, by Bennett and Tyrrell (1990, 235–54).

68. The rejuvenation of a play's hero is in one way or another a feature of many Aristophanic comedies: *Plutus, Wasps, Clouds, Peace, Amphiaraus, Gēras.* See Cornford 1968, 42–45; Auger 1979, 76–78; Carrière 1979, 90–91.

CHAPTER 5

Misunderstood Intellectuals
and Misunderstood Poets

In many respects the *Clouds* is the most troubled and self-questioning of Aristophanes' plays. Critics have often commented upon its atypical plot structure and lack of a sympathetic comic hero.[1] One is also struck by the absence of the "happy ending" and communal festivity which we usually find at the conclusion of a comedy;[2] instead we have an ending that is violent, discordant, unforeseen, and far more at home in Tragedy than in Comedy. Perhaps the most controversial aspect of the play, however, is its portrait of Socrates and the exact nature both of Aristophanes' attitude toward the philosopher and of his intentions in making such a portrayal. Traditionally critics have seen the Socratic figure in this play as bearing little resemblance to the historical Socrates; they see instead a composite caricature of contemporary sophists, rhetoricians, and intellectual hucksters in general, designed to amuse by conforming with the anti-intellectual prejudices of Aristophanes' lowbrow audience.[3] Some, however, have pointed out the younger Socrates' interest in natural philosophy and his sometime study under Anaxagoras (which we know from Plato, *Phaedo* 96A–D, and Xenophon, *Mem.* 4.7.2–8). Although we are still dealing with a comic caricature, the Socratic figure in this play may have a stronger footing in reality than many modern readers suspect.[4] Some have even

1. See Whitman 1964, 136–37; Henderson 1975, 70; Torrance 1978, 48–50.
2. Cf. Cornford 1968, 56–57; Frye 1957, 163–64; Whitman 1964, 120–22.
3. See, for example, Grote 1862 VI, 136–38; Bertram 1865, 8–24; Pucci 1960, 120; Dover 1968, lii–liii.
4. For various aspects of the Aristophanic Socrates that may reflect the historical figure, cf. Taylor 1911 I, 129–77; Phillipson 1932, 30–38; Murray 1964, 92–94; Schmid 1948, 209–28; Erbse 1954, 386–87; Turato 1972, 79; Havelock 1972, 1–18; Nussbaum 1980, 71–74.

argued that Socrates himself is not so much an object of criticism in this play as is the ignorant misunderstanding of Socrates by people like Strepsiades.[5] It may be that inasmuch as the "hero" of the *Clouds* is unattractive, his chief antagonist gains in sympathy.

This ambivalence in our reaction to both protagonist and antagonist is paralleled by a similar ambivalence in the nature of the chorus. As critical commentary has long noted, the Clouds seem to shift their allegiance near the end of the play, particularly after the second parabasis, and adopt a highly traditional and moralistic posture seemingly contrary to their previous identification with Socrates and the New Learning.[6] As Segal demonstrates,[7] the ambivalence is not only a matter of temporal development, but is adumbrated throughout the course of the play: they appear as fertility spirits associated with the rustic interests of characters like Strepsiades (vv. 1115–30; cf. vv. 275–90), in addition to acting as enthusiastic patronesses of Socratic education and its airy intellectual nebulosities (vv. 359–63, 412–77, 510–17, 700–706, 804–13, 949–60, 1024–35). They are even associated with the traditional Olympian religion in conspicuous passages like the parodos (vv. 275–90, 298–313) and parabasis (vv. 563–68, 595–626). As Socrates explains, the Clouds can assume any shape which mirrors the follies of human imagination (vv. 346–55), but in a figural rather than a mimetic way.[8] Like the Clouds, Aristophanes deliberately plays with his audience and leaves it open to them to project their own sympathies into the drama and its characters, but at the same time deconstructs those projections through a complex rhetoric of ambiguity and irony.

5. Cf. Murray 1964, 95–99; Erbse 1954, 385–420; Erbse 1982, 106–16; Strauss 1966, 46; de Carli 1971, 9–10; Tomin 1987, 26–31. Heath (1987, 9–12) has recently argued on the basis of the Platonic evidence that Aristophanes was not really hostile to Socrates and that his caricature in the *Clouds* was never meant to be taken seriously.

6. Cf. Newiger 1957, 68–69; Pucci 1960, 41–42; and Whitman 1964, 129; Whitman believes that the shift is the result of incomplete revision. A change in the chorus' attitude is fairly common in Aristophanes, as in the *Acharnians, Wasps,* or *Birds.* But the change of attitude usually occurs before the parabasis, not as late as it does in this play. This postponement of the chorus' development may be related to the diptych structure of the *Clouds* (noted by Mazon [1904, 63]): the development is a feature of the later Pheidippides plot, rather than the earlier Strepsiades plot.

7. Segal 1969, 143–61.

8. This passage does not refer to a simple process of imitation in which signifier replaces signified (e.g. a cloud shaped like Cleonymus standing for Cleonymus), but a more complex process of metonymic figuration in which signifier replaces signifier (e.g. a cloud shaped like a deer, standing metaphorically for the concept "cowardice," also represented by the coward Cleonymus). Ambrosino (1983, 17–20) observes that the Clouds speak here through a semiotic code which must be interpreted by someone initiated into their mysteries, like Socrates. The uninitiated may read the code differently, as the figural code of Aristophanic drama is read differently by different subjects.

Highbrows, Lowbrows, and the Two Versions of the *Clouds*

The problems of this play are further complicated by our possession of it, not in the original version performed at the City Dionysia of 423, but in a second edition, probably written in the period 419–417,[9] apparently never performed, and in the view of some never completed. As we know from the parabases of this play and of the *Wasps* (*Vesp.* 1016, 1037–50), Aristophanes was, or at least pretends to have been, deeply disturbed by the third-place showing of the original play in the dramatic competition (also attested by *Hyp.* II [Dover]). This was his first last-place finish, and was particularly discouraging for a play which he regarded as one of his most sophisticated and ambitious. His attempt to revise and rehabilitate the play a few years later is therefore not surprising. That the parabasis proper is unique to the second version of the play vv. 523–26 make clear. But beyond this, critics are not at all agreed concerning what changes were made in the second version or what Aristophanes' purposes were in making those changes.

Given the uncertainty over the value or meaning of the external evidence and the wide range of scholarly opinion about the extent of a rewriting,[10] it seems best to rely on the poet's own statements about the play. Commentators have always read the parabasis as a defense of the poet's *sophia* and a criticism of his rivals for reliance on cheap theatrical sensationalism. But clearly it also implies something about the particulars of his own practice:

> ὦ θεώμενοι κατερῶ πρὸς ὑμᾶς ἐλευθέρως
> τἀληθῆ νὴ τὸν Διόνυσον τὸν ἐκθρέψαντά με.
> οὕτω νικήσαιμί τ' ἐγὼ καὶ νομιζοίμην σοφός,   520

9. Cf. Emonds (1941, 290) and Dover (1968, lxxx), who dates it to the period 420–417, on the basis of the allusions to Hyperbolus in vv. 551–59. The *terminus post quem* is probably at least a year later, since if Eupolis' *Marikas* (firmly dated to the Lenaea of 421) was the first to ridicule Hyperbolus and was followed by Hermippus (who did not compete in the Dionysia of 421, as we know from the third hypothesis to the *Peace*, but in the Lenaea of 420 or later), and he was in turn followed by others (such as Plato whom we know to have written a *Hyperbolus*, presumably for the Dionysia of 420 or later), the probability is that this passage can be written no earlier than 419. Bianchetti (1979, 238–39) believes vv. 549–52 imply the ostracism of Hyperbolus (in the spring of 417) and therefore dates the play more precisely to the Dionysia of 417; this thesis about the implication of vv. 549–52 is probably correct (and also gives more point to vv. 623–26), although we need not fix the play to the Dionysia, since it seems not to have been performed. We should certainly reject the testimony of Hypothesis II (Dover), dating the second *Clouds* to the archonship of Ameinias (422); on the provenance and unreliability of this hypothesis, see Gröbl 1889/90, 26–32.

10. I have presented elsewhere a full review of the evidence offered by Hypothesis I (Dover) and the fragments of the first *Clouds*, as well as the entire scholarly debate over the play's revision (or lack thereof). See Hubbard 1986a, 183–85.

ὡς ὑμᾶς ἡγούμενος εἶναι θεατὰς δεξιοὺς
καὶ ταύτην σοφώτατ' ἔχειν τῶν ἐμῶν κωμῳδιῶν,
πρώτους ἠξίωσ' ἀναγεῦσ' ὑμᾶς, ἣ παρέσχε μοι
ἔργον πλεῖστον· εἶτ' ἀνεχώρουν ὑπ' ἀνδρῶν φορτικῶν
ἡττηθεὶς οὐκ ἄξιος ὤν· ταῦτ' οὖν ὑμῖν μέμφομαι   525
τοῖς σοφοῖς, ὧν οὕνεκ' ἐγὼ ταῦτ' ἐπραγματευόμην.
ἀλλ' οὐδ' ὣς ὑμῶν ποθ' ἑκὼν προδώσω τοὺς δεξιούς.
ἐξ ὅτου γὰρ ἐνθάδ' ὑπ' ἀνδρῶν, οἷς ἡδὺ καὶ λέγειν,
ὁ σώφρων τε χὼ καταπύγων ἄριστ' ἠκουσάτην,
κἀγώ, παρθένος γὰρ ἔτ' ἦν, κοὐκ ἐξῆν πώ μοι τεκεῖν,   530
ἐξέθηκα, παῖς δ' ἑτέρα τις λαβοῦσ' ἀνείλετο,
ὑμεῖς δ' ἐξεθρέψατε γενναίως κἀπαιδεύσατε·
ἐκ τούτου μοι πιστὰ παρ' ὑμῖν γνώμης ἔσθ' ὅρκια.
νῦν οὖν Ἠλέκτραν κατ' ἐκείνην ἥδ' ἡ κωμῳδία
ζητοῦσ' ἦλθ', ἤν που 'πιτύχῃ θεαταῖς οὕτω σοφοῖς·   535
γνώσεται γάρ, ἤνπερ ἴδῃ, τἀδελφοῦ τὸν βόστρυχον.

O spectators, I shall freely speak the truth to you,
By Dionysus who has reared me.
May I win victory and be thought clever,   520
Since I hold you to be sharp-witted spectators
And this to be the cleverest of my comedies.
I thought you worthy first to taste this work, which gave me
The most labor; but then I withdrew, unworthily vanquished
By vulgar men. For this, I blame you the clever,   525
For whom I was undertaking this toil.
But even so, I shall never willingly betray the sharp-witted among
       you.
From the time when Mr. Chaste and Mr. Lewd heard the best
       compliments
From men, to whom it was pleasant to speak,
And when I, still a virgin, unable to give birth,   530
Exposed my child, and another woman took it up,
You nobly reared and schooled it.
From this time, I have trusty pledges of your good judgment.
But now, this comedy comes searching, in the manner of Electra,
If she shall anywhere meet with spectators so clever.   535
For she will recognize the lock of her brother, if she sees it.
                                                        (vv. 518–36)

Readers have often been confused over which edition of the play is
referred to at each point of the parabasis. The most straightforward
approach is to take present and future verbs generally in reference to
the present revision and past verbs generally in reference to the origi-

nal version. Under this reading, vv. 518–36 make good sense. No one will deny that vv. 520–26 refer to the first *Clouds*, since the play's defeat is explicitly alluded to. We note the past tenses of ἠξίωσε (v. 523 "thought worthy"), παρέσχε (v. 523 "gave"), ἀνεχώρουν (v. 524 "withdrew"), and ἐπραγματευόμην (v. 526 "was undertaking toil"); the present μέμφομαι (v. 525 "I blame") refers to the rebuke for his past defeat which he is presently making in this very parabasis. With the emphatic adversative ἀλλ' ("But") and the future vaunt of v. 527 (οὐδ' . . . προδώσω = "I shall never betray"), however, we are clearly shifting to a discussion of the present version of the play.[11] The statement about retaining loyalty to the sophisticates among his audience despite the defeat is explained (note the expository γάρ) by the following allusion to Aristophanes' first play, the *Banqueters,* in contrast a play well received by Aristophanes' patrons (vv. 528–31)[12] and by the audience as a whole (v. 532); the earlier play is again denoted by past tenses (ἠκουσάτην, ἦν, ἐξῆν, ἐξέθηκα, ἀνείλετο, ἐξεθρέψατε, κἀπαιδεύσατε). This digression is closed in ring form with ἐκ τούτου . . . (v. 533 "from this time . . ."), resuming ἐξ ὅτου of v. 528 ("from the time"). There is also a return to primary tenses: we note μοι . . . ἐσθ' (v. 533 "I have"), γνώσεται (v. 536 "she will recognize"), the vivid future conditions expressed by the subjunctives (v. 535 'πιτύχη = "meet," v. 536 ἴδη = "sees") and ἦλθ' (v. 535 "comes") which, although aorist, is clearly atemporal in this context.[13] The reference to the present edition of the play is further emphasized by the νῦν οὖν ("but now") of v. 534. We should perhaps also notice the contrast between ἥδ' ἡ κωμῳδία (v. 534 "this comedy," with the prospective demonstrative) and ταύτην . . . τῶν ἐμῶν κωμῳδιῶν in v. 522 ("this . . . of my comedies," with the retrospective demonstrative).

The allusion to the *Banqueters* may be more than a mere illustration of the audience's erstwhile favor. Critics have noted before that there is a parallelism between the debate of the modest and prodigal sons in that play (v. 529 ὁ σώφρων τε χὠ καταπύγων = "Mr. Chaste and Mr. Lewd") and the debate of the two Discourses here in the *Clouds.*[14] Our

11. Such future vaunts concerning poetic activity should be interpreted as virtual presents; see Bundy 1962 I, 21, and Slater 1969, 86–94.

12. Halliwell (1980, 42–43) is surely right in referring these verses to the backing of the *Banqueters* by influential patrons such as Callistratus, although the *sophoi* being addressed in the passage as a whole are clearly a somewhat larger group.

13. ἦλθον often has no real temporal value, merely designating a state of arrival. This is particularly true when it is used as an auxiliary verb with an emphatic participle like ζητοῦσ' (on which use, see Goodwin 1890, 354). That it is not a true past here is quite clear from its connection with a subjunctive condition.

14. Fr. 206 PCG in particular seems to indicate there being a formal debate between the two sons; for a reconstruction of the general context and the *Banqueters'* contrast

analysis of the verb tenses above suggests that this relevance of the *Banqueters* is a characteristic principally of the second version of the play (hence its enclosure as a digression within vv. 527–36); since the debate is also one of the sections designated by Hypothesis I (Dover) as substantially new (unless we interpret ὅπου ὁ δίκαιος λόγος πρὸς τὸν ἄδικον λαλεῖ ["where the Just Discourse chatters with the Unjust"] to refer only to the *proagon* in vv. 889–948), it seems probable that the appearance of the two Discourses is entirely an innovation of the second edition.[15] Evidence does not allow us to speculate on what may have occupied its place in the original;[16] perhaps Socrates' initial exam-

---

between the new and old education, see Croiset 1909, 30–35, and Cassio 1977, 26–31. On the parallelism between the two debates, cf. Süvern 1836, 35–39; Koechly 1859, 418–19; Kock 1894, 36–37; Witten 1877, 6–7; Heidhues 1897, 5; Russo 1962, 30–31; Montuori 1966, 159 n.30.

15. Erbse (1954, 395–99), Newiger (1957, 144–50), and Pucci (1960, 5–12) argue that the theme of the two Discourses was implied throughout the play (cf. vv. 99, 112–15, 244–45, 657, 883–85, 1336–41, 1437–39) and thus that the debate must have been integral to the first version. But it is possible that many of these passages may have been added too; as Hypothesis I (Dover) states, "some things have been removed, other things have been woven in"; cf. Gelzer 1960, 150. Dover (1968, xc–xciii) argues that a debate between the two Discourses was in some form part of the first *Clouds*, on the basis of Σ*Nub.* 889, which states that the two Discourses were brought onto stage ἐν πλεκτοῖς οἰκίσκοις . . . δίκην ὀρνίθων διαμαχόμενοι; since we can find nothing in the text of the present play to support such a staging (indeed, Fabrini [1975, 13] demonstrates they are always referred to as human in form), Dover infers that this must have been a reference either to the production or to the language of the first version and that the tradition about such a performance was falsely attributed to the second *Clouds* by the scholia. But this staging may be nothing more than scholiastic speculation, perhaps based on analogy with a staged debate in some other comedy (see, for instance, fr. 446 PCG, from *Holkades*, τί δὲ τὸν ὀρνίθειον οἰκίσκον φέρεις;) or, less probably, on a fourth-century reperformance of the *Clouds* (for iconographic evidence suggesting such a reperformance of *Thesmophoriazusae*, see Taplin 1987, 98–100). On the unreliability of ancient commentators in matters of staging and performance, see the prudent remarks of Henderson (1987, lxviii). I am very unconvinced by Taplin (1987, 95–96) when he suggests that the Getty vase showing two ithyphallic birds and a flute player (82.AE63) depicts this debate of the two Discourses. There are no cages on the vase, which could easily depict one of dozens of late fifth-century comedies, if it depicts a comedy at all. The scholium here does not say the two Discourses were costumed as fighting cocks, but that they were brought onstage "in cages, fighting *like* birds."

16. Bücheler (1861, 672) speculates that there was a scene in which Socrates himself proceeded to instruct Pheidippides; Koechly (1859, 425–26) rather thinks Socrates continued to instruct Strepsiades and Strepsiades in turn instructed Pheidippides. Teuffel (1852, 342–43) notes the presence of Chaerephon in the *dramatis personae* and supposes Chaerephon may have assisted Socrates in Pheidippides' instruction; in what is perhaps the most detailed attempt at reconstruction, Russo (1962, 160–68) argues in favor of Chaerephon doing so alone. But it is difficult to see how Chaerephon's presence as a character in the first play could explain his inclusion in the *dramatis personae* of the second play, since the manuscript traditions seem to have been separate. It is much more likely that the scholiast who compiled the *dramatis personae* either mistook one of the students for Chaerephon or based the *dramatis personae* on a separately circulating commentary that at some point mentioned Chaerephon. Further scenes of philosophical instruction would seem too repetitive at this point of the play. Gelzer (1960, 141–48) is

ination and acceptance of Pheidippides (vv. 866–67) were continued
and the boy was somehow persuaded of the usefulness of Socratic
education. The following second parabasis (now vv. 1115–30), during
which the formal education of Pheidippides takes place offstage,[17] may
have served the same function in the original version.

Sophia is a dominant theme throughout this parabasis. The poet
should be considered *sophos* (v. 520) and this the most *sophos* of his comedies (v. 522). Later on, he defines his *sophia* as consisting in continual
experimentation with new forms (v. 547 "But I am clever [σοφίζομαι],
always bringing in new forms . . . all sharp-witted [δεξίας]"). The poet
addresses his work to spectators who are equally *sophoi* (vv. 526, 535)[18]
and *dexioi* (vv. 521, 527). Whether these terms are meant to designate a
select elite among the audience or are intended as flattery of the
audience in general is not clear. The agreement of the adjectives with
the second person plural pronoun in vv. 521 and 525–26 seems to
indicate a reference to the entire audience, and the partitive genitive in
v. 527 and the hypothetical condition of v. 535 seem to designate a
more select group.[19] The poet may wish to gain the audience's sympathy by playing on the ambiguity, first appealing to every spectator, then
progressively limiting his attention to the truly *sophoi*—i.e. those who
are clever enough to understand and appreciate his own *sophia*. This
gradual movement encourages every member of the audience to regard himself as *sophos* and to live up to that identification through taste
for Aristophanes' intellectual brand of Comedy. Every spectator is
flattered by being invited to consider himself part of an elite.[20]

---

probably correct in analyzing vv. 365–477 as the remnants of what was a full epirrhematic agon in the first version and thus in concluding the play's original debate to have come
before the parabasis rather than in its present position.

17. In the present version, vv. 1105–12 make it clear Pheidippides is accompanied
into the school by the Lesser Discourse (or according to the MSS, by Socrates, although
the MSS' *nota personae* is probably just an inference from the scene following the second
parabasis). Parabases are often used by Aristophanes to cover offstage action: for instance, Dicaeopolis sets up his *agora* and word of it reaches other cities (*Ach.* 626–718),
the Paphlagonian and Sausage seller argue their case before the Council (*Eq.* 498–610),
Trygaeus flies back to earth (*Pax* 729–818), Peisthetaerus and Euelpides enter the
Hoopoe's house and are transformed into birds (*Av.* 676–800), Dionysus and Xanthias
enter the house of Hades and Persephone (*Ran.* 675–737). Cf. Todd 1915, 59–64.

18. The *sophia* theme has been adumbrated already in the first version; compare the
address ὦ σοφώτατοι θεαταί in v. 575, opening the epirrheme (from the first version: see
n.47 below). See also *Vesp.* 1048–49 and pp. 116–18 below.

19. Of course, the phrase τοῖς σοφοῖς in v. 526 is already ambiguous, being open to
interpretation either as an appositive to ὑμῖν (in which case all of the audience are *sophoi*)
or as an attributive adjective (in which case the general class designated by ὑμῖν is limited
here to those members who are *sophoi*). Cf. *Vesp.* 1048 ὑμῖν τοῖς μὴ γνοῦσιν, antithetically
juxtaposed to the select σοφοῖς in the next line.

20. In an interesting study of the class dynamics of Attic oratory, Ober (1989, 224–

In the context of this play the theme of *sophia* has further implications. It is surely no accident that the word is used in the very last line of the kommation leading up to the parabasis (v. 517) in reference to the Socratic education Strepsiades is undertaking. Indeed, *sophos, dexios,* and their derivatives are used throughout the play in reference to Socrates and the New Education (see vv. 94, 148, 205, 331, 489, 491, 757, 841, 852, 1399) or to the two Discourses he keeps in his school (see vv. 895, 898, 925, 956, 1024, 1057, 1111).[21] Clearly the parabasis draws both a parallel and a contrast between the *sophia* offered by Socrates and other sophists and the *sophia* of Aristophanes. Socrates and Aristophanes are both educators of the Athenian public, although each exercises his didactic leadership in a different way.[22] And both are misunderstood by the general public: Aristophanes' *sophia* is not appreciated, as evidenced by the humiliating defeat of the first *Clouds,* and Socrates' *sophia* is commonly confused with that of the rhetoricians, sophists, and natural philosophers by unenlightened burghers like Strepsiades.[23] The two therefore maintain the pretense of directing their attention to a more select audience: Socrates' "initiates" (vv. 140–43, 254–62), or in Aristophanes' case, the *sophoi* among his audience (vv. 527, 535).[24] But Aristophanes differs from Socrates in that there is a moral dimension to his *sophia;* his comedy is not only *sophos* but also *sōphrōn* (vv. 529, 537),[25] and not only "clever" but also "prudent." On

---

25) observes the parallel tendency for elite orators to flatter their mass audience by pretending they are all liturgy-paying men of substance on a level with the speaker.

21. These words are used more often in the *Clouds* than in any other play of Aristophanes, and not only in reference to Socrates and his followers. Euripides is *sophos* in vv. 1370, 1378, Prodicus in 361; Strepsiades also aspires to be *sophos* (cf. vv. 412, 418, 428, 764, 773, 1202, 1207, 1309), as Pheidippides does in v. 1111. On the parallel between Aristophanic and Socratic *sophia,* cf. Gomme 1975, 96–97.

22. For the poet as *didaskalos,* cf. *Ach.* 628, *Pax* 738, *Av.* 912, and fr. 348.3 PCG. See our discussion of the *Acharnians* parabasis on p. 52 above. The parallelism between Aristophanes' and Socrates' teaching is emphasized by the similar iambo-choriambic rhythms used in the kommation and parabasis hymns (prefatory to the poet's *didaxis*) and the later systems (vv. 700–706, 804–10, 949–58, 1024–33) that exhort and encourage the characters engaged in Socratic education. Cf. Spatz 1972, 70–75.

23. Also, note that Socrates' impatience with Strepsiades' jesting (vv. 296–97 "Won't you stop joking and making poetry [ποιήσεις] like these comedians [τρυγοδαίμονες]? But speak piously!") parallels Aristophanes' pretended rejection of the cheap theatrical tricks practiced by other comic poets to appeal to popular tastes.

24. Reckford (1987, 397) sees the defeat of the *Clouds* as critical in shaping Aristophanes' consciousness of a split between the *sophoi* and the not *sophoi* in his audience; but I suspect the idea was important even in the first version of the play (with Strepsiades representing the ignorant public), just as it is in the *Knights* (with ignorant Demos) and *Acharnians* (see p. 47 above).

25. There is no etymological connection between the words, but one cannot deny the soundplay.

the other hand Socratic education, at least as presented in this play, seems to be a godless mechanism completely devoid of moral considerations or concern with traditional values. The use of *sophos* and its derivatives in regard to both forms of education plays upon the word's inherent ambiguity in Greek of this period, designating at once "cleverness" in the narrow sense of technical skill in a specific field and "worldly knowledge" in the broader, political sense of knowing how to deal with people and society.[26] Socrates and his followers are undeniably clever, but they lack the ethos of social responsibility which Aristophanes sets up as the goal of his poetic skill.

Aristophanes defines the nature of his poetic *sophia* in the verses which follow, but relies principally on negative illustrations.

> ὡς δὲ σώφρων ἐστὶ φύσει σκέψασθ'· ἥτις πρῶτα μὲν
> οὐδὲν ἦλθε ῥαψαμένη σκυτίον καθειμένον
> ἐρυθρόν, ἐξ ἄκρου παχύ, τοῖς παιδίοις ἵν' ᾖ γέλως·
> οὐδ' ἔσκωψε τοὺς φαλακρούς, οὐδὲ κόρδαχ' εἵλκυσεν,   540
> οὐδὲ πρεσβύτης ὁ λέγων τἄπη τῇ βακτηρίᾳ
> τύπτει τὸν παρόντ' ἀφανίζων πονηρὰ σκώμματα,
> οὐδ' εἰσῇξε δᾷδας ἔχουσ', οὐδ' ἰοὺ ἰοὺ βοᾷ,
> ἀλλ' αὑτῇ καὶ τοῖς ἔπεσιν πιστεύουσ' ἐλήλυθεν.

See how chaste she is by birth and origin: she did not first
Come in stitched with a leather phallus, hanging down,
Red, thick at the end, a source of laughter to boys.
Nor did she mock bald men, nor did she drag out the *kordax*,   540
Nor did an old man strike a bystander with his staff,
Concealing his bad jokes,
Nor did she burst in with torches, nor did she cry "Alas! Alas!,"
But she has come, trusting in herself and her words.

(vv. 537–44)

On first reading, under the influence of the present ἐστί (v. 537 "is") and perfect ἐλήλυθεν (v. 544 "has come"), and also noting the indisputable present reference of the framing vv. 534–36 and 545–46, we are inclined to take these statements as general denials that the poet uses cheap theatrical tricks, applying to the present version of the play as much as to the earlier one. As such, this passage would exhibit the same irony that we find in similar pronouncements of stylistic discrimination

---

26. Though less common in Aristophanes, this latter sense is frequent in Tragedy and high lyric, as in later philosophy. For an explicit contrast of the word's two senses, cf. Euripides, *Bacch.* 395 τὸ σοφὸν δ' οὐ σοφία.

(e.g. *Vesp.* 54–66, *Pax* 739–51, *Ran.* 1–20), which may be contradicted by the poet's own practice. But if Aristophanes really wanted to make a general denial of these practices valid for all time, he would have used present or perfect verbs throughout vv. 537–44. On a more precise reading, we can see that the poet was very deliberate in choosing to use aorist verb tenses in the relative clause (v. 538 ἦλθε, v. 540 ἔσκωψεν, v. 540 εἵλκυσεν, v. 543 εἰσῆξε)[27] and that the πρῶτα μὲν . . . ("first . . .") may be meant as temporal rather than merely rhetorical,[28] with the μέν being *solitarium*.[29] Understood in this way, the negative statements of vv. 537–43 refer exclusively to the first version of the *Clouds*, but the present ἐστί (v. 537) and perfect ἐλήλυθεν (v. 544) frame these specific assertions with general statements that include both versions and imply the enduring quality of the play. In other words, because the first

27. The present verbs τύπτει (v. 542) and βοᾷ (v. 543) that appear in this series are clearly historical presents, as is usually the case with presents embedded within a narrative series of aorists. On this phenomenon, see Schwyzer-Debrunner (1966 II, 271), who note its use to express the vivid dramatic presence of past actions. It should also be noted here that the aorist of τύπτω is extremely rare in Attic, and the poet may have had no choice but to use a historical present; the βοᾷ in v. 543 is very closely connected with the preceding εἰσῆξε (cf. vv. 1490–98 and our discussion below) and could easily take its temporal value from the earlier verb. This explanation is clearly preferable to any of the alternatives: that the aorists are all virtual presents, or that the two present verbs refer to the present play and the four aorist verbs refer to the earlier version, or that Aristophanes is sloppy and his verb tenses are fundamentally without meaning.

28. If this sentence were taken in isolation we might very well be tempted to take the πρῶτα μὲν . . . as a rhetorical emphasis, complemented by the following series of οὐδές. But in a context where the poet is talking about two different temporal levels (as he clearly is from v. 518 onward), it is difficult to think the temporal application would not be in his mind, particularly since it has already been adumbrated with πρώτους in v. 523, which as we have observed above, must refer to the audience of the first *Clouds* (strangely enough, this line has also been misinterpreted: Göttling [1856, 19] refers it to the second *Clouds'* reading audience, and Enger [1853, 16–18] imagines a reference to the production of the second *Clouds* before an audience at the rural Dionysia in the Piraeus; it remains unclear how either of these audiences can be called "first"). An apt parallel for both the temporal πρῶτα and μὲν-*solitarium* is provided by the πρῶτον μὲν . . . of *Pax* 739, in a similar parabatic context dealing with past stylistic practices (and again reinforced by πρῶτος in *Pax* 742); note also the aorist verbs.

29. It is difficult to understand why the leather phallus in vv. 538–59 should be an object of overwhelming rhetorical emphasis (as we would be compelled to construe it if we took πρῶτα μὲν οὐδὲν . . . in antithesis to οὐδ' . . . οὐδὲ . . . οὐδ' . . . οὐδ' . . .); Aristophanes does not use μέν elsewhere in responsion with οὐδέ, and several examples (*Nub.* 545–51, 1401–3, *Vesp.* 1104–6, *Av.* 555–59, *Plut.* 149–52) seem to indicate that even when the two particles appear in successive clauses, they are not related. Denniston (1934, 191) observes that when the two particles are connected (in other authors), it is generally to contrast a positive assertion with a negative one, not to parallel two negative clauses (as we would have here). πρῶτα is better taken as temporal, and the μέν as *solitarium*, with the implied δέ being the second version of the *Clouds;* on μὲν-*solitarium* as a means of implying an unexpressed antithetical term, see Denniston 1934, 380.

version did not use cheap tricks in its performance, the *Clouds* is a good play "by birth and origin" (φύσει),[30] even if its revised version has gone astray by including such tricks.

The text thus manipulates its audience by appealing to more than one level of understanding and by employing more than one level of irony. The poet is not only making stylistic pronouncements he fails to observe in his own practice; he is also reminding us, or at least the *sophoi* among us, that he did not in fact use these tricks "the first time," albeit he clearly does utilize every single one of them in the present version of the play. Even the scholia noted that the torches and "*ἰοὺ ἰού*" of v. 543 evoke the conflagration at the play's conclusion, especially vv. 1490–8.[31] And as we know from Hypothesis I (Dover), this section, "where the residence of Socrates is burned down," is one of those identified as substantially new in the second edition.[32] It should also be noted that "*ἰοὺ ἰού*" are the words with which the play opens. A leather phallus, like the one described in vv. 538–39, was almost certainly a part of Strepsiades' attire, probably displayed in such passages as vv. 196–97, 653–54, and 734[33]—all passages that critics on independent grounds have believed to show traces of revision.[34] The derision of

30. φύσις clearly bears this precise sense of "birth and origin" in *Av.* 691 and *Ran.* 1183; even in its more general sense of "nature," the Greek concept always refers to a quality present from birth and never to something acquired later. In this context the ἐστί is a present of general truth, illustrated by specific examples in the past (the aorists and historical presents of vv. 538–43); an exact analogue to this usage is provided a few lines above with the present ἔσθ' of v. 533, giving the general conclusion to the specific past events related by the aorists of vv. 528–32. Similarly the perfect ἐλήλυθεν of v. 544 relates the past events (or nonevents) of vv. 537–43 to the play's enduring quality as a literary achievement; that a perfect may be used of an old dramatic work (and not a present performance) is clearly illustrated by the πάλαι πεποίηχ' of v. 556, referring to Phrynichus' play. We sometimes find the perfect ἐλήλυθε being used in a manner approaching the aorist in sense; cf. *Nub.* 238–39, *Vesp.* 636–37.

31. Σ*Nub.* 543a. The scholium goes on to elaborate: ἐν δὲ ταῖς πρώταις Νεφέλαις τοῦτο οὐ πεποίηκεν. ποιεῖ δὲ αὐτὸ μετὰ λόγου, οὗτοι δὲ ἀκαίρως. The implication is clearly that the first version did not have a conflagration scene. The next sentence is probably a palliative interpretation, i.e. although Aristophanes makes use of such a scene in the second *Clouds*, he does it with more restraint than his rivals (= οὗτοι).

32. The majority of commentators agree the element of burning, at the very least, was new. A small minority (cf. Koechly 1859, 429; Solomos 1974, 122) believe that the change in the exodos is simply one of abbreviation; but what they see as elliptical in the present account would have been communicated in large part by the stage action (cf. Kopff 1977, 113–22).

33. On the phallic references in these passages, see Henderson (1975, 116, 220) and particularly Stone (1981, 75–80), who argues for the display of the phallus and agrees with our interpretation of all the parabatic remarks here as ironic, as does Fisher (1984, 155–56). On the phallus generally as a part of Aristophanic costume, see Catteruccia 1961, 8–9.

34. Almost all analyticist critics regard the bed scene (vv. 694–745) as a contamination of the play's two versions, with the κόρεις-motif (vv. 694–730 or parts thereof)

bald men mentioned in v. 540 may not be a reference to Aristophanes himself, as is often assumed, but to Socrates, whose baldness seems to be alluded to in vv. 146–47 and 171–73 and who may have been represented by a portrait mask.[35] The *kordax* of v. 540 may have been used in lively dances like those of Strepsiades in vv. 439–56 or 1201–13. And the old man striking an opponent with his cane in order to make up for his bad jokes (vv. 541–42) can be none other than Strepsiades chasing off the second creditor with a κέντρον in vv. 1296–1302 after his wretchedly ignorant travesty of Socratic *sophia.*

Past commentators have sometimes recognized these parallels, but have either dismissed them or misinterpreted their significance. Convinced that Aristophanes could not possibly be critical of his own practices, some critics have attempted to deny them one by one and have looked for distant allusions to other comic poets instead.[36] Other scholars have admitted the validity of the parallels but, in keeping with the theory of incomplete revision, have argued that these were all things that Aristophanes intended to change in the second edition but never quite came around to.[37] Still others believe Aristophanes to be not so much denying his use of these theatrical tricks as asserting his use of them with greater restraint than his competitors.[38] It nevertheless seems curious that Aristophanes would enumerate as examples of lowbrow humor things he so visibly does in this very play; if his intention were merely to criticize his rivals, he surely could have chosen

----

belonging to one version (usually identified as the revision; cf. Fritzsche 1849–52, III, 3–4; Teuffel 1852, 325–29; Kock 1894, 51–52; Koechly 1859, 425; Naber 1883, 320; however, Beer [1884, 130–31] took the opposite view) and the πέος-motif (vv. 731–39) to the other. But the two are not necessarily in contradiction; as Heidhues (1897, 25) observes, the bugs may be imagined as bothering Strepsiades' genital area (cf. v. 713). It is true that the scene would seem entirely complete without vv. 731–39, but this would rather seem to suggest that the κόρεις-motif stood alone in the original play and the πέος-motif is a conscious (and well placed) development of it in the play's revision. On vv. 195–99, cf. Koechly 1859, 423; Naber 1883, 317. And on vv. 636–93, cf. Koechly 1859, 424; Bücheler 1861, 672; Schwandke 1898, 155–56.

35. This association with Aristophanes' own baldness originates with ΣNub. 540a. V. 540 seems to imply more than just a passing allusion to baldness but, like the rest of vv. 537–43, probably refers to a stage prop (i.e. the portrait mask of a bald character). Given the reference to not being a "long-hair" in v. 545, we cannot rule out a secondary reference to the poet's own baldness, but it is secondary. On the question of Socrates' portrait mask, see Dover 1967, 26–28.

36. For a more detailed discussion of their arguments, see my earlier remarks in Hubbard 1986a, 190–91.

37. Cf. Hermann 1799, xxvii–xxix; Koechly 1859, 421–22; Montuori 1966, 162; Dearden 1976, 112.

38. Cf. Süvern 1836, 115; Kock 1894, 125; Witten 1877, 7–8; Heidhues 1897, 7. This interpretation reads into the text, ignoring the clear statement in vv. 537–43 that he did *not* do these things.

examples of their theatricality not having such close parallels to his own work.

Clearly we must admit that vv. 537–44 do indeed constitute an act of self-criticism, even if veiled as a criticism of the poet's rivals. The self-criticism is moreover not merely the usual programmatic irony of pretending not to do things he often does; it is very specific and distinctive in its focus upon aspects of the present play. This can be illustrated by contrast with the other major passages of stylistic criticism in Aristophanes.[39] In priamel form *Vesp.* 58–63 eschews a number of comic topoi, such as the pair of slaves throwing nuts at the spectators, the gluttonous Heracles, and the ridiculing of Euripides or Cleon; although some of these may have parallels in the earlier or later plays of Aristophanes, none is really central to the *Wasps* itself.[40] In *Pax* 739–51, another context of parabatic self-praise, the poet lauds himself for being the first to rid the stage of characters in rags (v. 740), the "kneading Heracles" (v. 741), and slave beatings (vv. 742–47); although the characters in rags may have some reference to Dicaeopolis in the *Acharnians*,[41] none of these motifs appears in the *Peace*.[42] *Ran.* 1–20 opens the play with a dialogue in which Dionysus urges the slave Xanthias to avoid certain vulgar and low-comic terms such as πιέζομαι,

39. For the topical nature of such stylistic criticism in Aristophanes, cf. Emerson 1889, 273–78; Murphy 1972, 170–74; and for its self-contradiction by the poet's practice in general, see Solomos 1974, 157–59; Dobrov 1988a, 18–26.

40. Cleon is to some extent attacked in the *Wasps* (cf. Edmunds 1987b, 51–57), but the expression οὐδ' . . . αὖθις τὸν αὐτὸν ἄνδρα μυττωτεύσομεν (vv. 62–63) seems only to promise that he will not be made a major character in the drama, as he was in the *Babylonians* and *Knights* (for the metaphor, compare especially *Eq.* 372 περικόμματ' ἔκ σου σκευάσω). οὐδ' αὖθις ἀνασελγαινόμενος Εὐριπίδης (v. 61) seems to point back to the *Acharnians* (cf. Σ*Vesp.* 61c and van Leeuwen 1909, 16). The burlesque Heracles (v. 60) was of course a stock figure of Comedy, but we may also be meant to think of his appearance in the *Centaur* (426 BC); cf. fr. 300 PCG, Wilamowitz 1870, 14–16 (interpreting Σ*Vesp.* 60); Solomos 1974, 158. Aristophanes certainly uses this figure later in *Av.* 1574–1693, *Ran.* 549–78, and in the *Aeolosicon* (fr. 11 PCG). *Pax* 960–67 shows Aristophanes also not to be above having slaves throw food to the audience.

41. It should be noted, however, that Dicaeopolis' appearance in the rags of Telephus is intended as a self-conscious parody of Euripides' stylistic predilection for heroes in rags and is not designed as a satire on poor people, which seems to be what is abjured here; the parody in the *Acharnians* is thus quite in keeping with the programmatic thrust of Aristophanes' explicit criticism in this passage.

42. The verb μάττω is used in *Pax* 14 to refer to the activity of the two slaves, but they are not Heracles; nor is there a scene of real slave beating either here or in any earlier play of Aristophanes (although Murphy [1972, 174] suggests that this may allude to the opening of the *Knights*, in which the two slaves come onstage after having been beaten by their master; see also *Nub.* 58, where Strepsiades at least threatens to strike his slave). The scholia (Σ*Pax* 740a, b, 741b, c, e) may be right in seeing this passage as a genuine criticism of Eupolis and other comic poets; Russo (1962, 215–16) believes Aristophanes is taking credit for humane treatment of his slave characters who appear differently in each play and are not mere stereotypes.

θλίβομαι, and χεζητιᾷς; the humor derives from the terms themselves being used in this passage even as their use is deprecated, but they are not specifically used later in the play.[43]

The allusive focus of the *Clouds* passage sets it apart from all of these. Vv. 537–44 list the kind of cheap theatrical tricks the poet shunned in the first version of the *Clouds* (πρῶτα), but felt compelled to include in the second edition in order to make his formerly unsuccessful play more appealing to the coarse humorous tastes of his mass audience and judges. Of course this attempt at popularization required a debasement of the presumably high artistic standards of the original play, vaunted in vv. 522–24. Aristophanes is uncomfortable with this admission and thus obscures it even while making it; by shifting back and forth between references to each version of the *Clouds* and never making altogether explicit which version is under discussion at any given point, the dramatist plays with the audience, winking at its more perceptive members while deliberately confusing the majority. The transitional ambiguity of v. 537 ὡς δὲ σώφρων ἐστὶ φύσει σκέψασθ’ ("See how chaste she is by birth and origin . . .") must be understood within this framework. As we have noted above, this line strictly refers to the first version of the *Clouds*, its form by birth and origin, described in the following verses; on another level the present tense of ἐστὶ appears to suggest that this line continues vv. 534–36 and their reference to the present version of the play. Although the detailed enumeration following σκέψασθ’ is past, the statements are all negative (things the original *Clouds* did not do) and are consequently just as much reflections on what the present play is doing. The first version, though, is truly σώφρων, the revision only ironically so. We may be meant to see the two brothers of the *Banqueters* not only as parallels for the two Discourses but indeed as figurations of the two versions of the *Clouds* itself, one σώφρων, chastely observing high artistic and moral standards, relying on "herself and her words" (v. 544), the other καταπύγων, self-consciously abandoning principles in pursuit of short-term theatrical gains.

Aristophanes' assertion of stylistic discrimination is thus couched in sufficiently ambivalent terms to sound like a praise of both editions,

---

43. See Stanford 1963, 70–71; Werner 1969, 18–19, 22; Murphy 1972, 170; Higgins 1977, 62. However, *Ran.* 479–91 shows Dionysus defiling himself in fear (cf. *Ran.* 479 ἐγκέχοδα). The terms are occasionally used in other plays: Σ*Ran.* 3 cites the use of θλίβομαι in the second version of the *Thesmophoriazusae* (= fr. 340.2 PCG); see also *Vesp.* 1289. The excretory image of χεζητιᾷς is certainly common enough (in addition to *Ran.* 479–91, cf. *Nub.* 295, 1384–90, *Av.* 790–92, *Eccl.* 311–71). The passage does not say Aristophanes would never use such stock comic utterances, merely that Dionysus forbids their use here; like *Vesp.* 58–63, the passage functions as a prefatory priamel.

even though strictly referring only to the first, and correspondingly his *sotto voce* confession of stylistic debasement is made to sound like a criticism of poets other than himself. Similarly Aristophanes masked his criticism of the audience for its failure to appreciate the *sophia* of the first *Clouds* in vv. 518–36 as an ironic praise of the audience's *sophia*. As we have noted, it is never altogether clear whether the second person plural addressed throughout this passage refers to the entire audience or only the select portion of the audience capable of understanding the poet's true meaning. The text operates on two levels, inviting the masses to think that they are all complimented as *sophoi* and *dexioi*, but at the same time written with the intention of actually limiting the compliment to those who have always understood and appreciated the poet's subtlety.[44] By calling himself *sophos* (vv. 520, 522, 547–48) and flattering the audience with this epithet (vv. 521, 525–26, 535), Aristophanes engenders a sense of rhetorical identification and sympathy. In the final analysis, however, this identification is just as specious as the delusory hope of *sophia* which the genuinely *sophos* Socrates engenders in the vainly ambitious Strepsiades. As we have seen, both Socrates and Aristophanes must for their livelihood play upon the ignorance and vanity of their respective audiences.

One can readily understand Aristophanes' reasons for adopting this ironic mode of expression. He could hardly hope to gain the audience's sympathy by telling them outright that they were fools for having given the first *Clouds* a third prize and that he has now debased the play to conform better with their lowbrow tastes. On the other hand the poet could not maintain self-respect among his more perceptive fans without apologizing in some way for what he has done. This ironic structure is also evident in vv. 545–62:

κἀγὼ μὲν τοιοῦτος ἀνὴρ ὢν ποιητὴς οὐ κομῶ,   545
οὐδ' ὑμᾶς ζητῶ 'ξαπατᾶν δὶς καὶ τρὶς ταῦτ' εἰσάγων,
ἀλλ' ἀεὶ καινὰς ἰδέας ἐσφέρων σοφίζομαι,
οὐδὲν ἀλλήλαισιν ὁμοίας καὶ πάσας δεξιάς·
ὃς μέγιστον ὄντα Κλέων' ἔπαισ' ἐς τὴν γαστέρα,
κοὐκ ἐτόλμησ' αὖθις ἐπεμπηδῆσ' αὐτῷ κειμένῳ.   550
οὗτοι δ', ὡς ἅπαξ παρέδωκεν λαβὴν Ὑπέρβολος,
τοῦτον δείλαιον κολετρῶσ' ἀεὶ καὶ τὴν μητέρα.
Εὔπολις μὲν τὸν Μαρικᾶν πρώτιστον παρείλκυσεν
ἐκστρέψας τοὺς ἡμετέρους Ἱππέας κακὸς κακῶς,

---

44. Even the genuinely *sophoi* are treated with irony, as in the promise of v. 527 never to betray the wiser members of the audience; the play's revision, with its less sophisticated brand of humor, does in a sense betray them, even as they betrayed the poet by failing to secure the success of the first *Clouds*.

προσθεὶς αὐτῷ γραῦν μεθύσην τοῦ κόρδακος οὕνεχ᾽, ἣν   555
Φρύνιχος πάλαι πεποίηχ᾽, ἣν τὸ κῆτος ἤσθιεν.
εἶθ᾽ Ἕρμιππος αὖθις ἐποίησεν εἰς Ὑπέρβολον,
ἄλλοι τ᾽ ἤδη πάντες ἐρείδουσιν εἰς Ὑπέρβολον,
τὰς εἰκοὺς τῶν ἐγχέλεων τὰς ἐμὰς μιμούμενοι.
ὅστις οὖν τούτοισι γελᾷ, τοῖς ἐμοῖς μὴ χαιρέτω·   560
ἢν δ᾽ ἐμοὶ καὶ τοῖσιν ἐμοῖς εὐφραίνησθ᾽ εὑρήμασιν,
ἐς τὰς ὥρας τὰς ἑτέρας εὖ φρονεῖν δοκήσετε.

And although such a poet, I am not a long-hair,   545
Nor do I seek to deceive you leading in the same things twice and
    thrice,
But I am clever, always bringing in new forms,
In no way like each other, and all sharp-witted.
Although I socked Cleon in the paunch when he was greatest,
I did not dare kick him again when down.   550
But once Hyperbolus gave them a handle, these men
Always drill on the poor wretch and his mother.
Eupolis first dragged in his *Marikas*,
A bad man badly twisting around our *Knights*,
Adding a drunken crone for the dance,   555
Whom Phrynichus had created long ago—she whom the beast ate.
Then Hermippus again made for Hyperbolus,
And now all the others press Hyperbolus,
Copying my image of the eels.
Whoever laughs at these, let him not favor mine;   560
But if you delight in me and my inventions,
In another time you will seem to think well.

Aristophanes pursues the theme of his originality as a poet by claiming not to repeat himself or borrow material from other poets, but always to use καινὰς ἰδέας (v. 547 "new forms") and εὑρήμασιν (v. 561 "inventions"). The primary verb tenses in vv. 545–48 and 560–62 clearly indicate a reference to the second edition; but as in vv. 527–36, these enclose an illustrative passage in past verb tenses with reference to previous plays. On one level Aristophanes is here apologizing for his use of the theatrical tricks enumerated in vv. 537–43 by explaining that he does not want to repeat the same old play but will add something new. The statement about not being a "long-hair" (v. 545 οὐ κομῶ) is another way of saying he does not mean to be too discriminating or aristocratic in his rewriting and will not disdain the tastes of his broader theatrical audience.[45] On another level we see Aristophanes as again

---

45. For long hair as a feature of young aristocrats, cf. *Eq.* 580, 1121–22; Dover 1978, 78–79; Donlan 1980, 161–62; Ostwald 1986, 235; Bugh 1988, 118–19. Compare the

ironic, since he does in fact repeat himself and his "new" additions are for the most part old and traditional comic topoi such as those listed in vv. 537–43.

In asserting his novelty, Aristophanes first presents the paradigmatic example of his own restraint in not repeating his attacks on Cleon (vv. 549–50) as other poets do in continually attacking Hyperbolus (vv. 550–59). But any student of Aristophanes knows that Cleon was in fact attacked in every play Aristophanes wrote during the period 426–421 BC. The claim about not continuing to attack Cleon when he is down is clearly belied by the *Peace,* which, even though performed after Cleon's death,[46] repeats almost verbatim a passage of invective from the *Wasps* (*Vesp.* 1030–37 = *Pax* 752–59). Indeed in this later revision the *Clouds* itself retains an attack upon Cleon in the epirrheme of this very parabasis (vv. 581–94).[47] As for Hyperbolus, it is difficult to take seriously Aristophanes' criticism of other poets for continuing to attack him, when Aristophanes himself does so no fewer than three times in this play (vv. 623–26, 874–76, 1063–66); all three of these allusions are located in sections of the play we know from the hypothesis to have been revised in the second edition—respectively, the parabasis,[48] the scene building up to the debate of the two Discourses,[49] and the debate itself. Indeed, in the parabasis of the *Thesmophoriazusae* (*Thesm.* 839–45), Aristophanes attacks Hyperbolus "and his mother" even long after his ostracism. And it seems significant that Aristophanes criticizes Eu-

---

poet's disclaimer of any interest in pederasty in *Vesp.* 1024–25 and *Pax* 762–63 (see chap. 7 n.33 below). On these passages as Aristophanes' self-dissociation from an overly close identification with the class interests and mannerisms of the knights, see Robert (1967, 161–62), who views the *Clouds* generally as a more democratic counterpoint to the aristocratic sympathies of the *Knights.*

46. The *Peace* was performed at the City Dionysia of 421; Cleon's death is firmly dated to the battle near Amphipolis in the late summer of 422 (cf. Thuc. 5.10.9).

47. Vv. 591–94 in particular speak of Cleon in the future tense, with the clear implication of his still being alive. The consensus of scholarly opinion has thus been that this epirrheme dates to the play's original version; however, Hermann (1799, xxii), Koechly (1859, 427), and Kock (1894, 32–33) believe the epirrheme to be an early revision only one year later than the original. The retention of this epirrheme, particularly after Cleon's death, need not be written off as an accident or sign of incomplete revision; the decision to retain such a passage from the play's original is every bit as deliberate as the decision to write something new.

48. Scholarly consensus is that the antepirrheme must be dated to the same layer of composition as the epirrheme; but Witten (1877, 11–12) is probably correct in assigning it to the revision, since Meton's calendar reform is not likely to have been fully implemented earlier than 422 (cf. *Pax* 414–15) and Hyperbolus' prominence in the Assembly materialized only after Cleon's death (cf. *Pax* 679–92).

49. If the debate was entirely new, there must have been some modifications in the preceding scene, certainly including vv. 882–88 (where the two Discourses are mentioned) and possibly also encompassing vv. 872–76.

polis for imitating his work (vv. 553–55, 559) in a parabasis that is itself written in the "eupolidean" meter.[50] Especially ironic is his criticism of Eupolis for imitating the *Knights,* since Cratinus had earlier censured the *Knights* for plagiarizing from Eupolis (fr. 213 PCG, from the *Pytinē,* which defeated the first *Clouds*).[51] Indeed the whole idea of attacking Socrates in the *Clouds* may have been taken from other comic poets, especially Eupolis.[52]

Our conclusion must again be to attribute to Aristophanes the use of the parabasis to imply that he is not doing what he in fact does; but by bringing these matters up at all, he subliminally calls attention to the fact that he is doing it. The issue of novelty and repetition is a particularly sensitive one for this play: not only does the debate of the two Discourses repeat the debate between the virtuous and prodigal sons in the *Banqueters,* as we have seen from vv. 528–33, but the whole play is of course a reworking of the earlier version performed in 423 BC. Aristophanes tries to head off criticism of the second *Clouds* for lack of originality by preempting the charge. The text proclaims its own originality, but in the very act of doing so implicitly acknowledges its antecedents.

The eupolidean parabasis proper of the *Clouds* constitutes an implicit apologia for the poet's reworking of the play, suggesting a great deal about the specific aims and objects of that revision. Our examination of vv. 537–44 allows us to conclude that the general intention of Aristophanes' revision was to broaden the play's humorous and theatrical appeal;[53] he must have planned to accomplish this through the use

50. The irony is also noted by Fisher (1984, 156) and Perusino (1986, 18–19). Σ*Nub.* 520 tells us this meter was not used in the first *Clouds.* The one other context where it is attested for Aristophanes (fr. 58, 59 PCG) is from the parabasis of the *Anagyros,* also criticizing Eupolis for plagiarism; on these fragments, see Hofmann 1970, 6–7. The *Anagyros* probably dates to the same general period as the second *Clouds;* cf. Geissler 1925, 50.

51. As we have noted on pp. 85–87 above, Cratinus' charge has some justification. Eupolis himself entered the controversy with his statement that he had practically coauthored the *Knights* (fr. 89 PCG, from the *Baptae,* of the same general date as the second *Clouds,* although we cannot be sure which was prior). Aristophanes also seems to be criticizing his rivals for rehashing material (whether his or theirs) in fr. 590.5–10, 67–68 PCG, again of approximately the same date; cf. Hofmann 1970, 3–10; Luppe 1971, 97–99, 108.

52. The theme of Socrates' poverty seems to have been commonplace in the comic poets, especially Eupolis (cf. fr. 386, 388 PCG τὸν πτωχὸν ἀδολέσχην). Σ*Nub.* 179e cites Socrates' cloak stealing as parallel to Eupolis, fr. 395 PCG. And Lucian, *Pisc.* 25 names Eupolis and Aristophanes as the two principal caricaturists of Socrates. Also, cf. Telecleides, fr. 41, 42 PCG; Ameipsias' *Connus* (produced at the same festival as the first *Clouds*) centered on Socrates and his music teacher (cf. fr. 9 K).

53. A similar thesis is advanced, although without detailed arguments, by de Carli (1971, 25).

of lively action and such conventional stage devices as torches, phallus, cane, and portrait mask where these were eschewed in the first version of the *Clouds*.[54] This information reinforces the impression of detailed attention having been devoted to revising the exodos, the scene of Strepsiades' first entry into the Phrontisterion, and the bed scene in vv. 694–745. Noting that almost all the cheap comic devices listed in vv. 537–43 are connected with the behavior of Strepsiades and that Aristophanes' defeat with the first *Clouds* gave him a status of unappreciated and ridiculed *sophia* similar to Socrates', we may be justified in speculating that one of the overall intentions of the play's revision was to make Strepsiades even more boorish and lowbrow as a paradigm for the Athenian public and to shape Socrates into a somewhat more sympathetic character in contrast, in some sense paradigmatic for the poet.[55] In addition, the allusion to the debate of the *Banqueters* in vv. 528–33 may hint at the debate of the two Discourses being an innovation of the second edition, but this is less certain.

Cloudy Ambiguities

The same kind of ambivalence and irony characteristic of the poet's self-manifestation in the parabasis proper is also evident in the choric self-manifestation of the epirrhematic syzygy. We see the two-sided identity of the Clouds already in the ode:

> First I summon to the chorus
>   Great Zeus, lofty-ruling
>   Tyrant of the gods,   565
> And the mighty keeper of the trident,
>   Fierce upheaver
>   Of land and salty sea,

54. This puts in doubt the thesis that the second version of the *Clouds* was merely the version intended for publication (cf. Dover 1968, xcviii; Boruchowitsch 1973, 95). Fabrini (1975, 1–16) has presented strong arguments for our present text being in fact fully ready for theatrical performance.

55. Because of the stress which Plato gives the *Clouds* and its negative impact (*Ap.* 18B, 19C, *Phaedo* 69D, passages surely referring to the play presented in the theater), Solomos (1974, 153–54) also argues that the play's first version presented a much more caustic and unattractive picture of Socrates. Howald (1922, 31–33) maintained the opposite thesis, based on his view that the fight between Strepsiades and Pheidippides was unique to the second version. However, Gelzer (1960, 148–51), who also believes the Pheidippides plot belongs to the second version, uses this and the novelty of the two Discourses to argue that the second version downplays the role of Socrates generally, and is thus less a personal attack on him than the original.

> And our father of great name,
>   Holiest Aether, life-nourisher of all,   570
> And the horse-guiding Sun,
>   Who holds down the plain of the earth
>   With brilliant rays,
>   A great spirit among gods and men.
>   (vv. 563–74)

The ode opens with invocations to Zeus (vv. 563–65) and Poseidon (vv. 566–68), the two most powerful Olympian gods.[56] In the second half of the ode, they shift away from the traditional religion to the more elemental deities, Aether (vv. 569–70) and Helios (vv. 571–74). This shift is underscored by a significant variation of meter in the third colon: embedded within a generally iambo-choriambic context, Aether is announced with a sequence of lyric dactyls evocative of the Clouds' entry in the dactylic parodos, during which they are invoked by Socrates as companions of Aether (v. 265; cf. v. 285).[57] This metrical echo of the Clouds' entrance is appropriate in that Aether is here specifically identified as ἡμέτερον πατέρ' (v. 569 "our father"). In the corresponding colon of the antode, Athena is supplicated as ἡμετέρα θεός (v. 601 "our goddess," same metrical position).[58] Although not a new god, Athena is the daughter of Metis and is therefore identified with the realms of intellect and craftsmanship; she stands as a more constructive and socially responsible (v. 602 πολιοῦχος = "city-holder") counterpart to the pseudointellectual insubstantiality of Aether and the other Socratic abstractions.

The Clouds' duality as representatives of both the new intellectual order and traditional religion is further expressed in the epirrheme:

> O cleverest spectators, hold your attention here.   575
> Having been wronged, we blame you face-to-face:
> Although of all the gods we help the city most,
> To us alone of the gods you neither sacrifice nor pour libations—

56. The *Clouds'* association with the traditional religion was already evident in the parodos (cf. vv. 302–13) and is reaffirmed in their final address to Strepsiades at the end of the play (cf. v. 1461 ὅπως ἂν εἰδῇ τοὺς θεοὺς δεδοικέναι).

57. On the significance of this metrical shift, cf. Fraenkel 1962, 196–98. We have already noted the didactic function of the iambo-choriambic meter in this play (see n.22 above). I cannot agree with Scodel (1987, 335) that Zeus and Poseidon are, like Aether and Helios, primarily nature gods, but she is right in noting the shift from ode (concerned with more universal gods) to antode (giving gods very specific cult settings). This is parallel to the usual focussing movement that takes place from epirrheme to antepirrheme.

58. Note the tautometric responsion of Αἰθέρα (v. 570) with αἴγιδος (v. 602).

We, who watch over you. For if there is some expedition
With no reason, then we either thunder or drizzle rain.   580
When you elected as general the Paphlagonian tanner,
Hated to the gods, we knitted our brows
And did terrible things, while thunder and lightning broke out,
The Moon left her course, and the Sun,
Immediately pulling his wick back into himself,   585
Said that he would not appear if Cleon were general.
But all the same you elected this man. They say that ill counsel
Belongs to this city; however, these errors of yours
The gods will turn to the better.
How this will be of benefit, we shall easily instruct: 590
Convicting of bribery and theft that sea-hawk Cleon
And gagging his neck in wood,
It will again be like the good old days for you and the city's affairs
Will turn out for the best, even if you erred before.

                                                        (vv. 575–94)

They are here identified as gods not traditionally worshipped at Athens (vv. 576–79); yet their agency seems to be linked with that of the
other gods (vv. 584–89; cf. 608–26) and their practice of sending
omens through lightning and thunder (vv. 579–83) is typical of the
divine powers we usually associate with Zeus. Though new divinities
linked with Socratic relativism in their fluid intangibility, the Clouds
also exhibit a brand of social conservatism that makes them look very
traditional. New politicians like Cleon and Hyperbolus, who is attacked
in the antepirrheme, are just as much signs of Athenian impiety and
decadence as the new philosophers. Both groups are perceived by
Comedy as advocates of radical change, the leveling of society's established laws, conventions, and hierarchies in favor of apparent intellectual and moral anarchy. This casual disregard for custom is vividly
expressed in the antepirrheme by the metaphor of the calendar which
has fallen out of synch with the gods' expectations. The Clouds see it as
their function to call attention to such contemporary social malefactors
as these, even as they change their shape to mock rascals like the thief
Simon, the coward Cleonymus, or the effeminate Cleisthenes (vv. 346–
55).

   This figural and satirical function is of course also that of the poet.[59]
Like the Clouds, Aristophanes combines poetic novelty with traditional
prejudice: in the preceding section, he simultaneously boasts of his

---

59. On the parallelism of the Clouds' polymorphous mockery of social pests with
Comedy's, cf. Pucci 1960, 33; Reckford 1967, 223.

"new forms" and *sotto voce* admits the necessity of using all the old comic tricks. Aristophanes is a young poet (the original *Clouds* was his fifth or sixth dramatic production and only the second under his own name), one of the subtle-speaking Euripidaristophanizers lampooned by the older Cratinus (fr. 342 PCG) for simultaneously ridiculing and imitating Euripides' new style of poetry (see ΣPlato, *Ap.* 19C). Despite the poet's youth, stylistic experimentation, and intellectual modernity, Aristophanes' comedy embodies the conventional bourgeois values, prejudices, and suspicions to which it must appeal in order to be "funny" and win the prize of popular favor. The Clouds' paradoxical iconoclasm and traditionalism, imaged also in the confrontation of the two Discourses, foregrounds a fundamental contradiction in the poet's own personality, torn between the inherited ethos of loyal patriotism and his own modernist upbringing influenced by contemporary sophistic ideas.[60]

Thus there is an important sense in which the Clouds become emblematic of the *Clouds*. The Clouds allege that they have not received a just valuation at the hands of the spectators (vv. 575–79); this is the same allegation that we have seen the poet himself make in regard to the original *Clouds* (vv. 518–26). Even the specific formula of address used in the epirrheme (v. 575 ὦ σοφώτατοι θεαταί = "O most clever spectators") cannot help but remind us of the theme of *sophia* that bulks so large in the parabasis proper. The Clouds cite their warnings against Cleon as the prime example of their service to the Athenians (vv. 581–84); clearly Aristophanes himself could make the same boast, as in fact he does in the parabasis of the *Wasps* (*Vesp.* 1029–37) and *Peace* (*Pax* 751–60). The Clouds see it as their role to teach the audience (v. 590 διδάξομεν = "we shall instruct"), even as the comic poet is conventionally a *didaskalos*.[61]

What is especially interesting about this allegorical interpretation of the epirrheme is that it involves a new meaning (that the Clouds' lack of esteem is symbolic of the first *Clouds*' poor showing) which is assigned to a passage derived from the older version of the play.[62] The poet's decision to retain an old passage in the midst of new passages is just as deliberate and meaningful as the decision to add or delete. Aristophanes saw that the Clouds' accusation of ingratitude on the part of the Athenians gained a new and added significance in the wake of the

60. Cf. Pucci 1960, 30–31, 118–19.
61. The Clouds also encourage teaching; cf. vv. 457–77, 794–96, 804–13. For the poet as *didaskalos*, see n.22 above.
62. See n.47 above.

Clouds' defeat. This new significance is enhanced by the antepirrheme, which was probably unique to the second edition.[63]

> When we were prepared to start our path here,
> The Moon, meeting us, told us first to say
> "Hello!" to the Athenians and their allies.
> Then she said she was angry for faring ill from you,   610
> Although herself helping you all not in words but conspicuously:
> First, you save not less than a drachma a month for torches,
> So that all of you, going out at evening, can say,
> "Slave, don't buy a torch, since the light of the Moon is so clear."
> And in other respects she says that she does you well,   615
> But that you don't reckon the days rightly, mixing them up and
>   down.
> So, she says, the gods threaten her every time
> They are cheated of a feast and go home
> Not getting a festival by the reckoning of the days.
> When it is right to sacrifice, you judge and torture,   620
> And often when we gods are keeping a fast,
> Mourning either Memnon or Sarpedon,
> You make libations and laugh. Because of this, Hyperbolus,
> Allotted the priestly office this year, lost his crown
> By our doing; and so, he will better know   625
> How it is right to reckon the days of his life by the Moon.
>
>   (vv. 607–26)

As usual the antepirrheme provides a more individualized illustration of the collective assertions made in the epirrheme. The Moon complains that she has not received due regard from the Athenians for her beneficence. More specifically their dereliction consists in false reckoning, a calendar out of synch with the Moon's own. We need not suppose that Aristophanes was seriously interested in reform of the Athenian calendar here. Clearly the import of the passage is again metaphorical: men are out of step with the divine will in favoring impostors like Cleon and Hyperbolus, not to mention Socrates and the philosophers, as in failing to appreciate the merits of Aristophanes' comedy. The idea of false reckoning and a bogus calendar also reflects Strepsiades' debts, paid according to the monthly calendar (see vv. 16–17, 1178–1200); indeed, Strepsiades' first idea for evading his debts, curiously praised by Socrates, is to hire a Thessalian witch and lure the moon out of the sky (vv. 749–56). Strepsiades' pecuniary dishonesty, for which he seeks the aid of Socratic relativism, is not unlike the thievery and corruption of Athens' leaders (vv. 591, 1065–66), some of whom, like Hyperbolus,

---

63. Cf. Witten 1877, 11–12.

were also educated by Socrates (v. 876), who is himself a cloak thief (vv. 177–79, 497–500). The breakdown of the relation between men and gods signalled by the whole syzygy is part of a broader breakdown of moral reckoning and social responsibility.

Socrates and Aristophanes

Throughout the play Socrates has been connected with this social and moral disintegration, whether in his skywalking indifference to practical human affairs or in his active debunking of belief in the Olympian gods. Any number of ethical criticisms can be made against the Socrates of this play. He is not sufficiently selective about the students to whom he reveals what are potentially very dangerous and subversive doctrines,[64] a carelessness we see in his unhesitant acceptance of the obviously unprepared Strepsiades as an initiate ready to hear the most radical cosmological and theological axioms. He can also be faulted for relativism (the rejection of all established *nomoi* in favor of the demands of each man's nature) and solipsism (as in the scene of Strepsiades' forced self-contemplation under the bedcovers, vv. 694–745).[65] Perhaps the most dangerous aspect of this Socrates is his total lack of a constructive program to replace the traditional beliefs he criticizes.[66] His only divinities are Chaos, Clouds, and Tongue: void, delusion, and language. More than any other contemporary author Aristophanes reveals in the personality of his Socrates that "infinite absolute negativity" which Kierkegaard perceived as the essence of Socratic irony.[67] Socrates' true purposes may be misunderstood and misinterpreted by common men like Strepsiades, but his lack of a clear and positive program is in large part to blame.

Of course, the comic poet himself is guilty of many of the same vices for which Socrates is condemned in this play. Poets are lumped together with sophists, physicians, astronomers, soothsayers, and all the other "do-nothing" intellectual quacks who are nurtured by the Clouds (vv. 331–34).[68] Like the Clouds themselves, poets are mutable creatures without fixed allegiances or programs who use the powers of

64. Cf. Strauss 1966, 22; Nussbaum 1980, 81.
65. Cf. Havelock 1972, 11–12.
66. Again, cf. Nussbaum 1980, 81.
67. Kierkegaard 1965, 181. It is no surprise that Kierkegaard saw Aristophanes' as the most accurate portrayal of Socrates.
68. For the association of poetry with aerial flight and the Clouds, see also *Pax* 827–37, *Av.* 1373–1409; Ambrosino (1983, 15–23) sees the Clouds preeminently as goddesses of language. On the general association of poets and other intellectuals with air, see also Gelzer 1956, 79–87; Pucci 1960, 113.

mimetic illusion to engage and mirror men's fantasies and follies. Comedy mocks and criticizes many things but does not presume to offer a realistic alternative. And like the Socratic Lesser Discourse, Comedy allows men to fulfill, if only vicariously, the appetitive impulses of their *physis* uninhibited by the bonds and constraints of society's *nomoi*.[69] The nature and purpose of comic fantasy, however, are not understood by all; like Socrates, Aristophanes lacks as sensitive and subtle an audience as he would desire. Comic fantasy is not merely a self-indulgent transgression of social norms like the immoralism of the Lesser Discourse; it also has the ultimate goal of reintegrating and renewing social cohesion even as it momentarily challenges society's authority structures.[70] Paradoxically Comedy defends social tradition in reality by the very act of exceeding it in fantasy.

This reestablishment of order never really occurs in the *Clouds*. There is no hero's triumph, no feast of reconciliation, nor even a positive hero with whom we can identify. Strepsiades is shown up as a fool and he wreaks vengeance on Socrates for what is really the result of his own greed and lack of principle; by burning down the Phrontisterion, Strepsiades does not reestablish *nomos* and order, as he thinks, only again violates it.[71] Socrates sees his entire educational mission go up in flames, properly resented by the public whose values it threatens.[72] The play ends without a sense of fulfillment or satisfying resolution for any of the parties involved. This all-around frustration of ambition may be one of the chief reasons why the *Clouds* ultimately failed, in both the first version and the second edition, which was never produced. The vigorous affirmation of life which we expect in a comedy is here submerged in the ironic gloom of intellectual despair, whether of the disappointed poet or his negative alter ego, the ill-tempered philosopher. By questioning the position of the intellectual within society, Aristophanes also questions the status of his own art; in this play more than anywhere, we see the poet doubting the value and efficacy of Comedy itself.

69. On the *nomos/physis* polarity in this play, cf. Heinimann 1945, 131; Whitman 1964, 130–32; Nussbaum 1980, 52–63; Ostwald 1986, 262–66. For the equal applicability of the same dialectic to Aristophanes' own practice as a comic poet, cf. Whitman 1964, 132; Strauss 1966, 32–33; Pucci 1960, 30–31; Sutton 1980, 10. In many ways the unrestrained hedonism of the Lesser Discourse bears greater affinity with the spirit of Comedy than it does to Socratic asceticism.

70. On the "cathartic" function of Comedy as a constructive periodic release of the individual's antisocial impulses, cf. *Tract. Coisl.* 3; Iamblichus, *De Myst.* 1.11; Cooper 1922, 82–86; Reckford 1974, 41–69; Sutton 1980, 69–82.

71. Cf. Nussbaum 1980, 78–79.

72. Many commentators have seen herein an allusion to the Crotoniates' incineration of the Pythagoreans' meetinghouse. Cf. Taylor 1911 I, 173–74.

CHAPTER 6

A Quarrel with the Jury

The defeat of the first *Clouds* was a profound disappointment to the young Aristophanes, as seen not only in his extensive rewriting of the play and his artfully manipulative self-defense in the new parabasis but also in the reproach he addresses to his audience in the parabasis of the play presented the year after the defeat. In both parabases (*Nub.* 546–48, *Vesp.* 1044, 1052–53) Aristophanes declares the *Clouds* to be an attempt to elaborate "new ideas"; its failure understandably provoked the author's critical revaluation of his developing aims and methods as a comic poet. Aristophanes reacted to his disappointment at the Dionysia of 423 not by giving up or withdrawing, but by redoubling his efforts and presenting two plays at the Lenaea of 422: the *Wasps* and, under the cover of his sometime producer Philonides, the *Proagon*.[1]

1. Hyp. I.33–34 (MacDowell) merely records the *Proagon* as the work of Philonides; but we have no other references to such a play by Philonides, although possessing a number of fragments and testimonia for a play of the same name by Aristophanes (cf. fr. 477–86 PCG). The picture is clouded further by the testimony of the hypothesis concerning the *Wasps'* production διὰ Φιλωνίδου (I.32). Some scholars assume confusion and delete διὰ Φιλωνίδου (cf. Ranke 1846, 229; Petersen 1862, 664–65; Briel 1887, 49–56); but Gröbl (1889/90, 58–59) deletes Φιλωνίδης as the subject of ἐνίκα πρῶτος . . . Προάγωνι and Leo (1878, 403–4) emends to give the *Wasps* the first prize rather than the *Proagon*. These changes, however, are all unnecessary. I believe Geissler (1925, 38–39) has explained the crux correctly by arguing that a poet could not present two plays simultaneously during the scaled-back dramatic festivals of this period (with only three comedies), and thus that Aristophanes had to present the *Proagon* through a producer, keeping his identity as the real author secret, and at the same time making himself publicly known as the author of the *Wasps*, even if it was also directed by Philonides. The real authorship of the *Proagon* would become known by the time of its publication, although Aristotle, when compiling the *didascaliae,* may not have recognized it to be the *Proagon* referred to here. On Aristophanes as the true author of the *Proagon,* see also Teuffel 1852, 352; Zelle 1892, 21; Russo 1962, 191–92; Solomos 1974, 127.

Although from different perspectives, the subject matter of both plays responded to Aristophanes' experience with the defeat of the *Clouds:* the *Proagon* (= the ceremony before the dramatic competition) was a play about poets, featuring Euripides as a main character,[2] and the *Wasps* is a play about irresponsible judges and the sting they inflict. As such the *Wasps* is conceived not only as a satire on the abuses inherent in the Athenian jury system but also as a figural comment on political manipulation of the dramatic juries. In the figures of the young Bdely-cleon (Cleon-hater) and his father Philocleon (Cleon-lover) we are surely meant to see the confrontation between the crusading young comic poet and the obstinate, incorrigible Athenian public he attempts to reform with only limited success.[3]

The Poet's Apology

The failure of the *Clouds,* only a year after Aristophanes' self-presentation to the public in the *Knights,* realized his worst fears about the vicissitude and instability of popular favor adumbrated in the *Knights* parabasis (*Eq.* 507–50). He thus approaches his audience in the *Wasps* parabasis with some wariness:

> Now go wherever you wish, faring well! And as for you,
> O countless multitudes,   1010
> Take care now that the things about to be said well
>   Not fall to the ground lightly.
>   It is the mark of dumb spectators to let this happen,
>   Not of spectators like you.
> Now then, people, keep your minds tuned in, if in fact you like
>   something pure.   1015
> For the poet now wishes to blame the spectators.
> He says that he is mistreated, although having done them many
>   good turns before—
> Some not openly, but secretly assisting other poets,
> Imitating the prophetic plan of Eurycles

2. See Σ*Vesp.* 61c.

3. Bdelycleon's identification with the comic poet is made explicit by vv. 650–51, which serve as an apologetic preamble to his debate with Philocleon: "Curing an ancient disease inbred in the city is difficult and the mark of a clever judgment greater than one finds among comic poets." This statement recalls the similar remarks made about Comedy by Dicaeopolis (*Ach.* 377–84, 496–508). On the identification, see also the remarks of Russo 1962, 194; Paduano 1974, 71; and Reckford 1977, 296–97, 301–2, 310 (= Reckford 1987, 254–55, 273–75).

And pouring forth much comedy after entering into the stomachs
    of others.   1020
After this, he openly ran the risk by himself,
Harnessing the mouths not of other men's Muses, but of his own.
Being raised up to great height and honored like no one among
    you ever before,
He did not turn out haughty nor puff up his pride,
Nor raise a ruckus and make passes at the boys in the gym. Not
    even if any lover   1025
Asked him to make fun of a hated boy-love
Did he ever obey, as he says, but he kept fitting thoughts in mind,
Lest he make bawds out of the Muses which he employs.
Nor, when he first began to train choruses, did he set upon
    ordinary men, as he says,
But he laid his hand upon the greatest, having a wrath of Heracles,   1030
Straight from the start boldly standing against the jag-toothed
    hound itself,
From whose eyes the most dreadful rays of Cynna flashed,
And around whose head a hundred heads of wailing flatterers
    licked
In a circle, while the hound itself had the voice of a death-bearing
    mountain torrent,
The odor of a seal, the unwashed balls of Lamia, the asshole of a
    camel.   1035
Seeing such a monster, he says that he did not take bribes in fear,
But still even now makes war on your behalf. And he says that after
    this,
Last year, he laid his hand upon the chills and fevers,
Who throttled their fathers at night and choked their grandfathers,
And lurked behind the beds of every private citizen   1040
With counter-oaths, summonses, and depositions gathered
    together,
So that many leap up in fear and run to the polemarch.
Finding such a guardian and purifier of this land,
You betrayed him last year, as he sowed the newest ideas,
Which you made fruitless by not judging clearly.   1045
And yet, making many and many libations, he swears by Dionysus
That you have never heard better comic verse than this.
This is on the spot shameful to you who don't understand,
But the poet has been thought nothing worse by the wise,
If in passing his opponents he crashed his purpose.   1050
      But for the rest, good men,
      Love and cherish more
      Those poets trying
      To say and invent something new.

Preserve those poets' thoughts   1055
And throw them into chests with citrons.
And if you do this, through the whole year
Your cloaks
Will smell of cleverness.

(vv. 1009–59)

The kommation appeals to the audience with studied ambiguity, addressing them with the not very honorific formula "O countless multitudes" (v. 1010 ὦ μυριάδες ἀναρίθμητοι), and warning them not to let the poet's words "fall to the ground" through their inattention.[4] The poet's care in speaking (vv. 1011–12 . . . εὖ λεγέσθαι) should be complemented by equal care on the part of those hearing (v. 1013 . . . εὐλαβεῖσθε); lack of receptivity to his words is the mark of "dumb spectators" (v. 1013), but the poet hastens to reassure the audience that he does not think they are such (v. 1014 "not of spectators like you"). This statement functions as a rhetorical protreptic encouraging the audience to behave in a manner worthy of its putative intelligence. Nevertheless it is clear that the poet himself is not so sure of his audience; otherwise he would not need to warn them. The multitudes who are uncountable may also be unfathomable and unpredictable in other respects.

At the end of the parabasis, however, Aristophanes qualifies his image of the audience by distinguishing them into two parts, the ignorant (v. 1048 μὲν . . . τοῖς μὴ γνοῦσιν) and the wise (v. 1049 δὲ . . . τοῖσι σοφοῖς). Even if his work has not been appreciated by the audience as a whole, the poet claims not to have lost credit among the intellectual elite because of the *Clouds'* defeat: we see here the genesis of the appeal to the *sophoi* among the audience which plays such a large part in structuring the rhetoric of the new *Clouds'* parabasis. Yet Aristophanes is not satisfied with entertaining merely the *sophoi*, and in the concluding pnigos turns again to the broader public (v. 1052 ὦ δαιμόνιοι), exhorting them to treasure the thoughts of innovative poets like himself and to benefit from the "cleverness" so acquired (v. 1059 δεξιότητος, the last word of the parabasis). Those who do so will become *sophoi* even if they were not in the past. As the chorus goes on to promise in the epirrheme, they will teach the members of the audience who were "museless before" (v. 1074).[5]

____

4. The phrase μυριάδες ἀναρίθμητοι occurs in Plato, *Theaet.* 175A, and *Leg.* VII, 804E, in reference to races of men who are unfathomable and remote either in time or place. The formula may have a poetic origin.

5. The phrase κἂν ἄμουσος ᾦ τὸ πρίν is a quotation from Euripides' *Stheneboea* (=

The hint of good-natured condescension to the audience has already been seen in the slave Xanthias' introduction of the plot:

> Come now, I will tell the story to the spectators,
> First giving them this small preface: 55
> Expect nothing too grand from us,
> Nor in turn jokes stolen from Megara.
> For we don't have two slaves
> Tossing the spectators nuts from a basket,
> Nor Heracles cheated out of his dinner,   60
> Nor Euripides again lewdly mocked;
> Not even if Cleon has by luck shined brightly,
> Will we again chop the same man into mincemeat.
> But we do have a little fable with a message—
> Not more clever than you yourselves,   65
> And yet wiser than commonplace comedy.
>   (vv. 54–66)

Aristophanes does not propose anything grand in this play (v. 56), such as his attacks on Euripides in the *Acharnians* (v. 61) or on Cleon in the *Knights* (vv. 62–63)[6] or, by implication, his attack on Socrates and the New Learning in the *Clouds*. On the other hand he will not debase himself to the level of merely borrowing from Megarian farce (v. 57), pandering to the audience with slaves passing out nuts (vv. 58–59) or with Heracles cheated out of a meal (v. 60).[7] Aristophanes wishes to present something "wiser than commonplace comedy" (v. 66 κωμῳδίας δὲ φορτικῆς σοφώτερον) but not more clever than the audience (v. 65 ὑμῶν μὲν αὐτῶν οὐχὶ δεξιώτερον). Like the revised version of the *Clouds*, the *Wasps* identifies itself as a concession to public taste without being a total concession.

---

fr. 663 Nauck), as we are informed by ΣVesp. 1074. The tragic quotation itself evokes the idea of literary education and learning. Philocleon's statement in v. 989 about not knowing "how to play the cithara" as an excuse for his antisocial behavior (cf. Bdely-cleon's defense of Labes in vv. 959–61) also implies that the Athenian public, for whom Philocleon is a figure, lacks musical and artistic sophistication, and that this lack is directly connected with its poor political judgment.

6. The αὖθις in vv. 61 and 63 suggests that these things have appeared in previous plays; μυττωτεύσομεν (v. 63) also clearly alludes to the *Knights* (cf. *Eq.* 372, where the Sausage seller threatens Paphlagon περικόμματ' ἔκ σου σκευάσω; also, cf. *Eq.* 771). See chap. 5 n.40 above. For such ad hominem attacks as what Aristophanes means by λίαν μέγα, cf. Paduano 1974, 16.

7. Again, see Paduano 1974, 16–17, and Murphy 1972, 173, for the identification of these two elements with the low-comic farce of Megara. However, a drunken Heracles may have appeared in Aristophanes' *Centaur;* see chap. 5 n.40 above. Russo (1962, 193) thinks we have an allusion here to farcical elements in the plays which defeated the *Clouds*.

In the parabasis the *Clouds'* defeat is attributed to the public's "not judging purely" (v. 1045 τοῦ μὴ γνῶναι καθαρῶς), that is, not giving the play a fair critical reception but being misled by inappropriate criteria. Two lines earlier the poet presented himself as a "purifier" of the state (v. 1043 καθαρτήν) in his struggle against Cleon and the sycophants,[8] who are presented as filthy monsters (v. 1035 "having the odor of a seal, the unwashed balls of Lamia, the asshole of a camel") and diseases (v. 1038 "chills and fevers"). At the beginning of the anapests the poet presented his remarks as "something pure" (v. 1015 καθαρόν τι) but seemed uncertain whether the public really wanted to hear them.[9] The poet implies that the purity of his own standards is not matched by his audience, which is contaminated by contact with the diseased Cleon, even as Philocleon is infected with his Cleon-inspired mania.[10]

Aristophanes defends himself by devoting the bulk of the parabasis to a synopsis of his career and services on behalf of the public. The audience is faulted for not seeing the *Clouds* as part of a continuous pattern of public-spirited activity. Aristophanes began his career by writing plays for production by other poets, benefiting the city through his mantic powers (v. 1019) without any personal gain or glory.[11] With the *Knights* he began to produce plays on his own (vv. 1021–22), attacking not private men, but no one less than the terrifying monster Cleon (vv. 1029–36); the image of Cleon alludes not only to the *Knights* in general[12] but more specifically functions as an intertextual echo of the *Knights* parabasis, which introduces Aristophanes to the public as the man who dares to attack the great "Typhon" (*Eq.* 511 τὸν τυφῶ).[13]

---

8. Commentators (e.g. Merry 1893 II, 74; Starkie 1897, 319; MacDowell 1971, 268; Sommerstein 1983, 218–19) have noted that the epithets ἀλεξίκακον and καθαρτήν are traditionally associated with Heracles and therefore recall the poet's self-characterization as a Heracles in his anger against Cleon (v. 1030).

9. The force of the εἴπερ clause calls the matter into question. The notion of "purity" implied in καθαρόν τι combines frankness (characteristic of the present parabasis) with artistic integrity (characteristic of the first *Clouds*).

10. I am not entirely persuaded by the underlying thesis of Reckford 1977, 285–86 (= Reckford 1987, 272–73) that Aristophanes' remarks here adumbrate Aristotle's catharsis theory of drama, but he is right to point out the thematic relation of terms for "purity" in this parabasis.

11. The allusion to secret plays presented under another poet's mask has a special point in this play, since Aristophanes is now doing exactly the same thing with the *Proagon* (presumably unbeknownst to the public).

12. *Eq.* 1017 describes Cleon in the same terms as a "jag-toothed hound" (κύνα καρχαρόδοντα; cf. *Vesp.* 1031), and *Eq.* 137 describes his voice as that of the torrent Cycloborus (cf. *Vesp.* 1034).

13. On the relation of *Vesp.* 1029–36 to Hesiod's description of the Typhon (*Th.* 824–30), see Merry 1893 II, 72; Starkie 1897, 314; MacDowell 1971, 266. Edmunds (1987b, 56) thinks the allusion is rather to Cleon as Cerberus (*Eq.* 1030). It clearly combines elements of both.

Although pleased with his first prize and the public honor it conferred (vv. 1023–24), the poet did not abuse his position for private gain or to pursue private animosities (vv. 1024–28).

Last year (v. 1038 πέρυσιν), the year after the *Knights*, Aristophanes presented a play attacking sycophants (the "chills" and "fevers" of vv. 1037–42); these are young men who, like Cleon, use the legal system out of corrupt motives, harassing private citizens through malicious prosecution. It is uncertain whether this passage alludes to Strepsiades' and Pheidippides' misuse of legal argument in the *Clouds* or to some lost play which Aristophanes could have produced at the Lenaea of 423.[14] On balance I incline to believe that the reference to the *Clouds* in vv. 1044–45 as last year's comedy (v. 1044 πέρυσιν) would be too confusing and abrupt if it were not the same as the play referred to as last year's comedy in vv. 1037–43. Although the imagery of vv. 1038–42 is not specific to the *Clouds* as we know it, except for the motif of parricide in v. 1039, we must remember that we do not possess the *Clouds* presented in 423 and that the revisions resulting in the extant play may have been quite substantial;[15] if pressed, the image of Cleon in vv. 1029–36 is not in every respect specific to the *Knights*, though clearly Aristophanes is referring to the *Knights* in that passage. Wilamowitz may be right in saying that vv. 1037–43 are an intentionally slanted reinterpretation of the *Clouds*, attempting to align Aristophanes' attack on rhetoric and the New Learning with his earlier attack on Cleon and the sycophants.[16] Whatever the exact reference of these lines, however, Aristophanes manifestly presents his comedy as a form of public service and claims that the *Clouds* deserves better recognition if viewed within this context.

14. In favor of the *Clouds*, see Σ*Vesp.* 1038c; Ehrhardt 1890, 14–15; van Leeuwen 1893, 115–16; Merry 1893 II, 73; Wilamowitz 1935 I, 295–96; Strauss 1966, 127. In favor of some other play (usually identified as either *Holkades* or *Farmers*), see Meineke 1839 II, 1113–18; Zelle 1892, 24–25; Starkie 1897, 316–17; Platnauer 1949, 7; MacDowell 1971, 267; Sommerstein 1977b, 271–72; Perusino 1986, 52 n.53. There is no conclusive independent evidence dating any lost play of Aristophanes to the Lenaea of 423, but see p. 34 above. We should certainly reject the idea of Boruchowitsch (1973, 93–95) that this passage refers to the *Wasps* itself and is part of a later parabasis added to the published version of the play; but he is right to note the relevance of the legal theme to the *Wasps* (see below).

15. Given the propensity to parabatic cross-referencing sometimes apparent in Aristophanes, it is possible for the sycophants to have figured prominently in the play's original parabasis.

16. Cleon's alignment with the objects of attack in the *Clouds* is already implied by his presence in the epirrheme of the parabasis (*Nub.* 581–94), which was certainly part of the first version; see chap. 5 n.47 above. For Aristophanes' connection of the sycophants with intellectuals like Gorgias and Socrates, cf. *Av.* 1694–1705, and the corresponding strophe (*Av.* 1553–64).

What critics have usually neglected is the relevance of both the attack on Cleon and the sycophant passage to the *Wasps* itself.[17] The sycophants, with their "counter-oaths, summonses, and depositions" (v. 1041), are precisely the people who exploit for gain the jury system depicted in this play. No sycophant manipulates the system more effectively than Cleon, who was known as the jurors' chief patron and protector, having raised their pay to three obols a day.[18] Although Cleon is not the chief focus of the *Wasps*, as Xanthias has told us (in vv. 62–63), his presence behind events is never forgotten, whether he is praised as the jurors' watchful guardian (vv. 242, 596–97) or cursed as the biggest thief who steals from them (vv. 758–59). Later in the play Bdelycleon imagines Cleon as a paradigmatic *bon vivant* (vv. 1219–20), and the poet assures us in the second parabasis that his enmity toward Cleon has not been forgotten (vv. 1284–91). The "hundred heads of flatterers" who lick the Cleon monster like Medusa's hair (v. 1033) are as present in this play as their master (vv. 42–45, 683);[19] Cleon's "unwashed balls of Lamia" and "asshole of a camel" (v. 1035 Λαμίας ὄρχεις ἀπλύτους, πρωκτὸν δὲ καμήλου) remind us of Philocleon who boasts of Cleon as his patron (vv. 596–98), and is thus called by his son an "asshole beyond all washing" (v. 604 πρωκτὸς λουτροῦ περιγιγνόμενος). Κλέων is clearly the Κύων who threatens to bite if not fed a portion of everyone's food (vv. 970–72), and prosecutes Labes for not sharing the Sicilian cheese. The "jag-toothed hound" (v. 1031 τῷ καρχαρόδοντι) is therefore not only the κύνα καρχαρόδοντα of *Eq.* 1017, but also the malicious dog who has just been defeated in the scene immediately before the parabasis. The overall effect of the parabasis is to situate the *Wasps'* ambitions of social and political reform within the framework of Aristophanes' previous plays. The poet has long been working toward the same goals.

Significantly the description of the loathsome Cleon-monster in vv. 1030–35 is framed by the poet's protestations that he will not be bribed or bought off, either to attack someone (vv. 1025–28) or to call off his attacks on Cleon (vv. 1036–37). This purity of behavior, surely part of what the poet means by calling his discourse καθαρόν τι (in v. 1015), contrasts visibly with the massive bribery and corruption Bdelycleon attributes to the city's leaders, presumably including Cleon (vv. 669–77, 692–94). Aristophanes' insistence that he "still even now makes war on your behalf" (v. 1037) echoes the politicians who declare that they will never betray the people but always fight on its behalf (vv. 593, 666–

17. See however Harsh 1934, 187, and Boruchowitsch 1973, 93–95.
18. See *Eq.* 799–800 and Σ*Vesp.* 88.
19. On the connection between v. 1033 and the κόραξ/κόλαξ joke of vv. 42–45, see Paduano 1974, 64.

67), even while they solicit bribes from the allied cities. In an elegantly rhetorical presentation the parabasis juxtaposes the poet's sincerity with the evident insincerity of the political leaders whom the play attacks.

Workers and Drones

The contrast between industrious service to the state and idle self-aggrandizement on the part of the state's leaders is elaborated further in the epirrhematic syzygy of the parabasis:

<pre>
We were once long ago valiant in the chorus,   1060
Valiant in battle,
And the most valiant men especially in this thing here.
These things were before, before, and now
    Are gone, and whiter than a swan
    Do these hairs bloom.   1065
But even from these remains we must
Hold onto youthful strength, as I think
That my old age is stronger than the curls
    And fashion and wide-assedness of many young men.   1070
If someone like you, O spectators, looks at my nature
And seeing me wasped-through around the middle, then wonders
What the point of our sting is,
I shall easily teach him, "even if he be museless before."
We, who possess this rump,   1075
Are the only truly native earth-born Attic men,
A most manly race and the race helping this city most
In battle, when the barbarian came,
Filling the whole city with smoke and setting it ablaze,
Wishing by force to drive us out of our hives.   1080
Immediately running out "with spear and shield"
We did battle with them, having taken a swig of acrid spirit(s),
Standing man to man, biting our lip in anger.
One couldn't see the sky for all the arrows.
But all the same, with the gods, we pushed forward till evening, 1085
For an owl flew through our host before doing battle.
And then we pursued them, harpooning them in the trousers,
And they fled, stung in their jaws and brows,
So that everywhere among the barbarians, even now,
Nothing is called more manly than an Attic wasp.   1090

    I was terrible then, such as not to fear anything,
    And I threw down
    The enemy, sailing there in the triremes.
</pre>

> We did not then have any thought
>   Of how we should deliver a good speech   1095
>   Or denounce someone,
> But of who would be the best oarsman.
> Thus, having taken many cities of the Medes,
> We are most responsible for the receipt of the tribute,   1100
>   Which the younger men steal.
> Examining us from many places and in every way, you will find us
> Most like wasps in our habit and life.
> First, no animal, when angered, is more
> Sharp-tempered or difficult than us.   1105
> And then, we devise all other things most like wasps.
> For gathering together in swarms just as into hives,
> Some of us judge where the archon is, others in the court of the
>   Eleven,
> And some in the Odeon, so thickly packed against the walls,
> Bending to the ground, hardly moving,   1110
> Just like grub-worms in their cells.
> In the rest of our life we are most inventive,
> For we sting every man and provide a livelihood.
> But there are drones sitting among us
> Not having a sting, who wait for the offspring of our tribute   1115
> And eat it up, not going through any of the toil.
> This is most painful to us, if someone who was never a soldier
> Slurps down our pay, never in service of this country
> Taking ahold of an oar, a spear, or a blister.
> But in short, it seems to me that from now, those of the citizens   1120
> Who don't have a sting shouldn't take three obols.

$$\text{(vv. 1060–1121)}$$

In keeping with its frequent transitional function, the ode begins by
paralleling the Wasps' valor as a chorus (v. 1060 ἄλκιμοι μὲν ἐν χοροῖς)
with their erstwhile military valor (v. 1061 ἄλκιμοι δ' ἐν μάχαις). They
view dramatic activity as a means of defending the city, not unlike their
courageous self-sacrifice in war (elaborated in vv. 1077–90). But they
were "the most valiant men especially in this thing here" (v. 1062 καὶ
κατ' αὐτὸ τοῦτο μόνον ἄνδρες ἀλκιμώτατοι), by which they refer to
their phalli, now things of the past (vv. 1063–64). The place of their
once vigorous phalli is now taken by their wasp stings, described at
length in the epirrheme as the essence of their manliness (v. 1077
ἀνδρικώτατον γένος, v. 1090 μηδὲν Ἀττικοῦ καλεῖσθαι σφηκὸς ἀνδρικώτερον).[20] Similarly Philocleon's juridical resolve is expressed in

20. For the equation of the Wasps' stings with surrogate phalli, and the general idea
of their aggressive nature compensating for erotic frustration, see Reckford 1987, 236–
38. It should be noted also that φύσιν in v. 1071, referring on the primary level to the

terms of phallic potency, which he loses at the moment that he begins to doubt the system (vv. 713–14).[21] Although old, the Wasps are hearty and fearless souls who defended Athens against the overwhelming might of the Persians (vv. 1077–90), again like Philocleon who fought at Marathon (v. 711). Whereas the jurors' waspish irascibility and hard-spirited nature has been censured throughout the play, it is here made a matter of self-praise (vv. 1082–83, 1104–5), even as the poet's "wrath of Heracles" is praiseworthy.[22] The Wasps' sturdy masculinity, accented by the final word of the epirrheme (v. 1090 ἀνδρικώτερον), over-shadows even in old age the frail effeminacy of modern youth, with their curls, postures, and sodomy, vividly portrayed at the end of the ode (vv. 1067–70).

As is customary, the antode and antepirrheme become more specific in their application of the contrast. Here the young men are not just silly but a positive threat to the political order and stability created through the sacrifices and labor of the Marathon and Salamis genera-tions.[23] While the old Wasps were concerned with defeating the Per-sians by hard rowing at sea (vv. 1091–97), the younger generation practices oratory (v. 1095), sycophancy (v. 1096), and theft of the tribute made possible by their fathers (vv. 1098–1101); the charge that the allies' tribute is being embezzled by Athens' present political leader-ship rather than given to the public is of course the very heart of Bdelycleon's argument in his debate with his father (vv. 655–718). The Wasps take their jury duty as seriously as they take their long past mili-ary accomplishments (vv. 1106–11), but complain of drones among them who earn the money without ever having served in the military and suffered hardship (vv. 1114–21). These unworthy jurors resemble the unwarlike and larcenous young demagogues attacked in both the ode and antode, and thus exemplify on one more level the idea that rewards are not going to those who have truly deserved them.

In many ways the chorus of Wasps reminds us of the old Acharnians who also claimed to be valiant Marathon veterans (*Ach.* 692–700), now

---

Wasps' form and appearance, is also a term used with specific application to the genitals (see Nicander, fr. 107.3 [Schneider], and Henderson 1975, 5). On the possible connec-tion of ithyphallic choruses with early Dionysian cult and the phallic rites from which Comedy arose, see Herter 1947, 17–18.

21. For "sword" (ξίφος) jokes as double entendres, see *Lys.* 155–56, 632, and Hen-derson 1975, 122.

22. On the theme of "anger" (*orgē*), see the discussions of Whitman 1964, 147; Konstan 1985, 32–33.

23. The Wasps' hostility to the younger generation reflects the conventional conflict between νεώτεροι and πρεσβύτεροι attested so often in Greek politics and political theory; on which, see Roussel 1951, 204–14; Forrest 1975b, 37–52; Reinhold 1976, 29–38; Carter 1986, 119–25; Ostwald 1986, 229–36, all focussing on this period.

suffering mistreatment by the young orators and sycophants (*Ach.* 676–91). But the Wasps are themselves a part of the legal system responsible for the Acharnians' problems; despite having been persuaded by Bdelycleon of their leaders' corruption, even as the Acharnians were persuaded by Dicaeopolis, the Wasps do not abandon their identity as jurymen. Albeit the Acharnians, so fearsome at the moment of their entrance, are progressively softened by Dicaeopolis' rhetoric and ultimately revealed to be helpless old men in the parabasis syzygy, the Wasps, if anything, gain in resiliency. They enter in the parodos as slow old men, dependent on young boys for guidance (vv. 230–72)[24] and unable to rescue their imprisoned companion; but in the parabasis they appear spirited and vigorous. Accordingly the Wasps' development is not unlike Philocleon's. Although they are defeated by Bdelycleon's arguments on a rational level, the Wasps' nature (v. 1071 φύσιν) is intractable and emerges proudly triumphant.

Father and Son

The Wasps of course are not alone in showing the ultimate incorrigibility of human nature. The entire confrontation between Bdelycleon and Philocleon can be interpreted in terms of the sophistic opposition between *nomos* and *physis,* with the enlightened modern son representing the demands of society and convention, his recalcitrant father exhibiting the uncontained and antisocial urges of self-indulgence.[25] But this dichotomy conceals a self-destructive ambivalence in the personality of both characters: in different forms, both father and son pursue ultimately selfish ends under the guise of upholding law and social order. As he reveals in the debate with his son (vv. 548–630), Philocleon uses the legal structure of the courts to flatter himself with a sense of self-importance and power, whether over once great men now reduced to begging for mercy (vv. 548–602) or over his own family for whom he provides a meager but welcome financial supplement (vv. 605–18). Bdelycleon presumes to free his father from dependence on the socially corrupt jury system,

24. On the ways in which this dependence foreshadows the relationship of Philocleon and Bdelycleon, see Paduano 1974, 207–8, and Long 1976, 19.
25. The opposition is explicit in vv. 1457–61, as the chorus reflects on Bdelycleon's attempt to reeducate his father: "Departing from the nature (φύσεως) / which one has is difficult. / And yet many do this; / being exposed to the opinions of others, / they change their habits (τρόπους)." For the issue of *nomos* and *physis* in reference to Philocleon, see Whitman 1964, 145, and Henderson 1975, 78–82. On the problem in sophistic thought of this period generally, see the treatments of Heinimann 1945; Pohlenz 1953, 418–38; Guthrie 1969 III, 55–134; Kerferd 1981, 111–30; Ostwald 1986, 247–73.

but substitutes for it a domestic autarky and retreat from political life which is in its own way anti-democratic and antisocial,[26] and designed clearly to keep the old man under his son's firm control. The elegant society into which Bdelycleon tries to introduce his father is itself an environment of hedonistic self-indulgence, full of wine, prostitutes, and empty talk, rather than a paradigm of social order. Philocleon's riotous and unrestrained behavior only externalizes the implications of his son's destruction of juridical social controls. In different ways and on different levels Bdelycleon and Philocleon have similar motives. And, despite their excesses, both characters have our sympathy.

Indeed, one of the most distinctive features of the *Wasps* is the presence in it of two sympathetic protagonists with mutually opposed visions. The *Acharnians, Knights, Peace,* and most of Aristophanes' other plays feature a single protagonist, sometimes with accomplices, who somehow overturns the usual order through conflict with an antagonist, often representative of political authority. The *Clouds* introduced a radical innovation into this traditional formula by lacking a sympathetic "comic hero" altogether: we expect Strepsiades to be another Dicaeopolis but he turns out to be merely a boor and a fool, even more noisome than his intellectual antagonist Socrates. As we have pointed out, there is a sense in which Strepsiades represents the ignorance of the general public, misunderstanding and abusing intellectuals like Socrates, and by implication the poet. But the implications were only nettlesome to the play's audience, and the *Clouds* was rejected by the dramatic judges with a third-place rating.[27] In the *Wasps* Aristophanes corrects his mistake by presenting two contrasting but sympathetic characters, one a crafty and stubborn old trickster representing the common man of Athens (and thus Aristophanes' audience), the other an iconoclast with social and intellectual pretensions representing the Athenian elite (including the poet himself). It is impossible to say which of the two is primary or deserves to be called the "comic hero"; Bdelycleon is the protagonist formally manipulating the action of the plot and trying to realize social reform, but Philocleon is the one who truly succeeds in fantastic transcendence of the social order.[28] Bdelycleon appears to be as much a straight man to his father's comedy

26. See Konstan 1985, 41–42. On Bdelycleon as a paradigm of upper class *apragmosynē* and retreat from politics, see Carter 1986, 63.

27. Paduano (1974, 42) sees the *Clouds'* lack of a sympathetic hero and immediately apparent political message as the chief problems leading to its defeat.

28. Critics usually stress the centrality of Philocleon as the imaginative, antinomian "comic hero": see Whitman 1964, 149–62; Strauss 1966, 125–26; Dover 1972, 125–27. Paduano (1974, 28–35) rightly sees the identity of the protagonist as more ambiguous and problematic.

as Socrates was to Strepsiades, Paphlagon to the Sausage seller, or
Lamachus to Dicaeopolis.

Intertextual Drama: The *Wasps* as *Knights* Plot and *Clouds* Plot

Just as the *Wasps* features two protagonists moving in opposite directions, it has been noted that the play is composed of two fundamentally
separate dramatic plots, Bdelycleon's successful effort to keep his father away from the juries before the parabasis, and his totally unsuccessful attempt to integrate his father into polite society after the
parabasis.[29] The two plots are clearly connected, yet each is capable of
standing on its own as a comedy with its own triumphant hero and its
own set of moral lessons. I would submit that the reason for the *Wasps'*
rather atypical diptych structure is Aristophanes' desire to recapitulate
and reflect his whole dramatic career within the scope of this play. The
half of the play leading up to the parabasis is political in nature and
borrows motifs from Aristophanes' earlier political plays, *Babylonians*,
Acharnians, and particularly *Knights*. Here we see the young reformer
Bdelycleon succeed in his explicitly political program, like Aristophanes, his alter ego, who won dramatic victories with his political plays.
The half of the play after the parabasis, on the other hand, is devoted
not so much to the political reform of Philocleon as to his social and
cultural education; the scenes of geriatric pedagogy and the ultimately
antisocial misuse of new learning evoke the social and intellectual
critique in Aristophanes' most subtle play, the *Clouds*. And like the
Clouds, Bdelycleon's attempt to reeducate his father is a total failure. As
the *Knights* and the *Clouds* both treated serious political and social
issues dramatically through situations of domestic conflict, so does the
Wasps, and with analogous results. Hence the parabasis dividing these
two sections recapitulates the poet's past career not only as an apologetic self-defense, but also as a hermeneutic key to the structure of the
Wasps, which is itself a recapitulation of the poet's past career; the
parabatic focus on the successful *Knights* and unsuccessful *Clouds* is no
accident.

The first half of the *Wasps* is a veritable cento of ideas and motifs
from the *Knights*. From the beginning we are reminded of the *Knights*,

---

29. For various attempts to criticize or justify the play's diptych structure, see Kolster
1829, 5; Wilamowitz 1935 I, 298; Vaio 1971, 335–51; MacDowell 1971, 6–7; Schwinge
1975a, 41–43; Landfester 1977, 146–47; Lenz 1980, 16; Heath 1987, 48–49. Relying on
a favored technique of nineteenth-century scholarship, Stanger (1870, 48–58) attributes
the second half to an imperfectly constructed revision of the play.

as we witness two slaves complaining of their wearisome task in language reminiscent of Nicias and Demosthenes and fearing further beatings (*Vesp.* 3).[30] As in the *Knights* their situation is doubly difficult in that they have to deal with both an old and somewhat senile master (Philocleon), like Demos a representative of Marathon-era Athens, and a younger master who effectively manages the household (Bdelycleon), like Paphlagon a modern man of affairs. The *Wasps* prologue centers on the slaves' interpretation of dreams corresponding to the *Knights* prologue which was based on the discovery and interpretation of the Paphlagon's oracle. The chorus of Wasps, as we have suggested, is in many ways like the Acharnians, but it is significant that the Paphlagon, when first beset by the hostile chorus of Knights, invokes as his natural allies the jurymen of Athens (*Eq.* 255–57 "Old men of the juries, clansmen of the Three Obols, / Whom I foster by thundering both just and unjust charges, / Come to my rescue, for I am thrashed about by conspirators!"). Throughout the play, in fact, Paphlagon identifies himself as the patron and protector of jurors (*Eq.* 50–51, 797–800, 1019; cf. vv. 897–98, 1316–17, 1356–60). Despite the old jurymen never coming to Paphlagon's aid in the *Knights,* we can see whence Aristophanes derived his idea for another comic chorus antithetical to the young Knights; in the *Wasps* the scene is inverted as an anti-Cleon figure is nearly overwhelmed by a chorus of ardent Cleon supporters (*Vesp.* 242 "Cleon our guardian").

The influence of the *Knights* is most evident in the debate between Philocleon and Bdelycleon over the virtues of jury service. Philocleon argues that jury service is a form of rule as powerful as any monarchy (*Vesp.* 548–51), since the humble jurors are flattered, begged, and favored by all the rich and prominent defendants who appear before them. He can boast that the great Cleon is the jurors' servant, shooing flies away, even as Theorus polishes their shoes (*Vesp.* 596–600). The image is taken directly from *Knights* 58–60, in which the servant Paphlagon is described as gaining Demos' favor obsequiously by shooing away orators with a leather fan while his master dines. Despite his trade as a leather merchant, however, Paphlagon conspicuously does not provide Demos with a pair of shoes (*Eq.* 868–77). Philocleon delights in speakers who promise "never to betray the masses and always to fight on their behalf," even if they are cowards like Cleonymus (*Vesp.* 592–93

---

30. The repetition of *kakon* in *Vesp.* 1 (ὦ κακόδαιμον Ξανθία) and *Vesp.* 3 (κακὸν ἄρα ταῖς πλευραῖς τι προυφείλεις μέγα) recalls its prominent reiteration in *Eq.* 1–8 (also with the appellation ὦ κακόδαιμον and feared beatings in the future). On the general parallel between the two prologues, see Strauss 1966, 112–14; Paduano 1974, 9–10; Reckford 1987, 221–22.

οὐχὶ προδώσειν ἡμᾶς φασιν, περὶ τοῦ πλήθους δὲ μαχεῖσθαι; cf. 666–67, 1036–37); the cant again comes from Paphlagon's rhetoric in the *Knights* (see *Eq.* 767 περί σου μάχομαι μόνος, addressed to Demos, and *Eq.* 1038 περὶ τοῦ δήμου . . . μαχεῖται, in Paphlagon's oracle about himself as a lion fighting gnats) and resembles the repeated and hypocritical assertions about being a "lover of the Demos" (*Eq.* 732, 769–918, 1340–44).[31] Philocleon and his fellow jurors insist that anyone proposing a law in the assembly also propose to release the jurors after judging one case in a day (*Vesp.* 594–95); this was another of Paphlagon's tricks for gaining the public's favor (*Eq.* 50–51).

In response to his father's blind trust in Cleon's political leadership Bdelycleon contends that the jurors' fancied "monarchy" (*Vesp.* 549 βασιλεία) is really "slavery" (*Vesp.* 682 δουλεία), since the politicians take in far more revenue in bribes and corruption than the jurors ever see in pay (*Vesp.* 655–712). Throughout the *Knights* Paphlagon/Cleon is accused of soliciting bribes, particularly from the allied cities (*Eq.* 326–27, 361, 402–4, 438–39, 465–67, 801–2, 832–35, 930–33, 994–96, 1082–83); compare Bdelycleon's indictment of bribes solicited from the allies by politicians' threats in *Vesp.* 669–77,[32] and his attack on bribes extorted from individual defendants in the courts (*Vesp.* 691–95; cf. *Eq.* 63–70). Paphlagon's rapaciousness is often characterized as outright theft (*Eq.* 52–57, 137, 248, 258–60, 280–83, 296, 391–94, 444, 742–45, 824–27, 1025–26, 1145–50, 1252). Out of all the empire's wealth, amounting to some 2000 talents in tribute a year (*Vesp.* 656–60), the jurors receive only 150 talents in pay (*Vesp.* 661–63), and Bdelycleon implies that the rest has disappeared into the politicians' pockets:[33]

> So consider that, when it's possible for you and all these men to be
>   rich,
> You are somehow kept enclosed by the self-styled democrats—
> You, who ruling over most cities from Pontus to Sardinia,   700
> Do not enjoy anything except this small bit which you earn. And
>   this bit by bit
> They dribble into you like oil with a piece of wool, for the sake of
>   living.
> They want you to be poor, for the reason I will say to you:

31. See p. 68 above.

32. On the relation of this passage to charges in the *Knights*, cf. Edmunds 1987b, 54 n.16.

33. Although Bdelycleon never explicitly makes this charge, the whole structure of his argument seems designed to create this impression; the section on bribery and corruption (*Vesp.* 666–95) is surrounded on each side by his arithmetic calculations (*Vesp.* 655–63, 698–712), allowing the audience to infer what is responsible for the discrepancy in the figures.

So that you may recognize your tamer, and then wildly leap upon
    them,
Whenever he hisses and sics you against one of his enemies.   705
(Vesp. 698–705)

The idea that political leaders like Cleon keep the public impoverished
in order to manipulate it better, all the while enriching themselves, is
clearly derived from the Sausage seller's critique of Paphlagon in the
Knights:

S. S.:   How very much you have regarded the Demos as yours.
Paph.:   I understand him and what kind of morsels he is fed upon.
S. S.:   And then, just like wet-nurses, you feed him badly:
    For chewing the food, you put a little bit into his mouth,
    And yourself gulp down thrice as much.
(Eq. 714–18)

Paph.:   So that he can rule over all the Greeks. For it is among the oracles
    That this man must at some time be a judge in Arcadia for five
        obols a day,
    If he waits for it. But in every way I will nurture and serve him,
    Discovering both fairly and nefariously whence he will have his
        three obols.
S. S.:   Not envisioning that he should rule Arcadia, by Zeus, but that
    You should rather plunder and take bribes from the cities, while
        the Demos
    Through the mist and war cannot see what evil you do,
    But gapes after you out of need, want, and pay.
    If this man ever comes back to his field and spends his time in
        peace
    And takes heart after eating grits and coming face-to-face with
        the olive-press,
    He will recognize from what benefits you deprived him with your
        wages,
    Then he will come back to you as a sharp countryman, tracking
        down a voting-pebble against you.
    Recognizing this, you deceive him and sell dreams about him.
(Eq. 797–809)

Demos: Alas, how full of many good things his basket is!
    What a big piece of cake he put away for himself!
    He gave me this little bit, cutting it off.
S. S.:   Indeed, he did such things to you even before:
    He handed down to you a small portion of what he took,
    And saved the greatest part for himself.
(Eq. 1218–23)

As Bdelycleon goes on to point out, even the politicians' promises of free barley distributions always turn out to be less substantial than imagined (*Vesp.* 715–18); again, the same charge has been adumbrated in the *Knights* (*Eq.* 1100–1103).

In contrast with the miserly stipend and nurture which the jurors receive from the politicians, Bdelycleon promises to provide his father with every sensual indulgence—food, drink, whores, elegant clothing (*Vesp.* 719–24, 736–40, 1003–6; cf. 341)—and he proceeds to do so in the following scenes, to the extent of setting up a private court in his household so that Philocleon can judge cases in total comfort. Once more Bdelycleon's rhetoric and practice imitate the rhetoric and practice of the Sausage seller, who wins the Council over to his side by pledging cheap sardines with free coriander and leeks (*Eq.* 642–82) even as he wins his final victory over Paphlagon in the contest for Demos' favor by bringing more and better food (*Eq.* 1152–1223). The idea of letting Philocleon judge cases in greater comfort, with fire, soup, and pisspot ready at hand (*Vesp.* 805–14), reminds us of the Sausage seller's attention to providing Demos with a cushion to sit on (*Eq.* 781–85), as well as good shoes and a warm tunic to wear (*Eq.* 868–86).[34]

The trial of the dog Labes over which Philocleon presides is an allegorical representation of Cleon's charges against the general Laches for an offense committed during his command in Sicily (already alluded to in *Vesp.* 240–44 as the trial to which the Wasps are hastening).[35] This scene too draws imagery and motifs from the *Knights*. Cleon is infamous for fabricating false and malicious charges on the basis of which he can prosecute political rivals (*Eq.* 45, 63–64, 261–65, 278–79, 306–7, 475–87, 710), and we thus have no trouble seeing Κλέων behind the Cydathenian Κύων who accuses Labes. However, the dog's real complaint is not that Labes stole the Sicilian cheese but that he refused to share the fruits of his theft and devoured it alone (*Vesp.* 914–16, 922–25); we are reminded of Paphlagon's offer to share his Potidaean bribe with the Sausage seller in return for silence (*Eq.* 438–40). Indeed the idea for Labes' theft of cheese from the kitchen and for

34. This is also echoed in Bdelycleon's giving his father a new cloak and slippers in *Vesp.* 1122–73, with one significant difference: they were basic necessities of which Demos had been deprived in the *Knights*, whereas Philocleon's new cloak and slippers are imported luxury items designed to enhance his social prestige. The parallel shows Bdelycleon's motives as less creditable than the Sausage seller's.

35. As seen by ΣVesp. 288. For the most recent and complete treatment of the historical background here, see Mastromarco (1974, 44–64, 85–96), who argues (not altogether convincingly) for this section of the play being added at the last minute to allude to the trial taking place soon before the Lenaea of 422.

Cleon's characterization as a dog comes from the rival dog oracles presented in the *Knights:*

Paph.:   "Son of Erechtheus, consider the path of words which
          Apollo   1015
       Shouted out to you from his shrine through the priceless
          tripods.
       He bid you to preserve the sacred jag-toothed hound,
       Who will provide pay to you, gaping before you and
          barking terribly
       On your behalf. If you don't do this, he will be destroyed,
       For many daws in hatred croak against him."   1020
Demos: By Demeter, I don't know what these words mean.
       What does Erechtheus have to do with daws and a hound?
Paph.:   I am the hound. For I howl on your behalf.
       And Phoebus told you to preserve me, your hound.
S. S.:   The oracle doesn't mean this, but this dog here   1025
       Eats up oracles just like your porridge.
       I possess the correct oracle concerning this dog.
Demos: Tell it now. But I will first pick up a stone,
       So that the oracle about the dog cannot bite me.
S. S.:   "Son of Erechtheus, consider the slave-dealing hound
          Cerberus,   1030
       Who, fawning on you with his tail, when you dine, waits
       And eats up your dish, whenever you gape in another
          direction.
       Wandering into the kitchen at night, doglike, he will
          escape your notice
       Licking clean all the plates and islands."

(Eq. 1015–34)

Cleon is himself guilty of the kind of theft he here accuses Labes of committing. The theft of Sicilian cheese in fact reminds us of Paphlagon's stealing the Pylian barley cake (*Eq.* 52–57, 742–43, 1166–67, 1200–1201),[36] thus taking credit for what others had accomplished; even so the Cydathenian dog merely sits at home claiming a part of any food which others bring into the house (*Vesp.* 970–72) but never actively going out and protecting the household, like Labes (*Vesp.* 957–58, 968–69).

Critics have recognized the trial of Labes as an exemplary instance of

---

36. We should also mention the "Boeotian cheese" he accuses the Sausage seller of making (*Eq.* 479–80).

Aristophanic "metatheater," or play within the play.[37] Inasmuch as we have seen an identification between Bdelycleon and the poet built up throughout the *Wasps,* we should find in Bdelycleon's stage management of this mock trial a reflection on the nature and function of Aristophanes' own dramatic art. We are struck by the equation between the legal and dramatic agons as two kinds of spectacle presented for the entertainment and enjoyment of the audience;[38] affairs of state and judgments of guilt or innocence are apparently taken no more seriously than a day at the theater, and conversely, political comedy is every bit as serious and important as other public affairs.

What is unique about this play within the play is that the audience itself (Philocleon) becomes part of the play,[39] and it is really the complex relation between author, audience, and spectacle that is problematized. The actual trial is trivial, even ludicrous: of the two dogs, Labes cannot speak and has his defense delivered by Bdelycleon who also testifies for the mute Cheesegrater. More important is the reaction of Philocleon whose response to the spectacle is just as carefully manipulated and stage-managed by Bdelycleon. Some critics have regarded the net effect of the whole metatheatrical event, and by extension of Aristophanic comedy in general, as therapeutic or even cathartic,[40] but as we see after the parabasis, Bdelycleon's tricking his father into acquittal of Labes does not really purge or cure Philocleon of his destructive tendencies. What the play within the play and its aftermath do show is that Aristophanes viewed his drama as a way of making the audience imagine familiar events in new and unfamiliar ways. Like the poet, Bdelycleon exercises total power over the presentation of the material and ultimately forces his father to experience something which Philocleon would never allow himself to experience in normal everyday life, acquittal of a defendant. The power of Comedy is the

37. See Russo 1962, 199; Dracoulides 1967, 107–10; Paduano 1974, 183; Reckford 1977, 296.

38. As Reckford (1987, 246–47) notes, the idea of trials as a form of entertainment is already implicit in the earlier debate between Philocleon and his son; the pleasures of watching great men tell jokes or fables, of witnessing melodramatic scenes with begging families, and of listening to Oeagrus deliver a speech from the *Niobe* are all dramatic pleasures, and it is these which Philocleon praises as among the chief rewards of being a juror. On the general parallel between forensic rhetoric and theater, see Ober 1989, 153–55.

39. See Schwinge 1975a, 36–37, on the paratragic nature of Philocleon's language and behavior in vv. 995–1002, as he recognizes his "*hamartia*" in acquitting Labes.

40. See especially Dracoulides 1967, 112–16, and Reckford 1977, 296–97. The play's later metatheatrical episode (in vv. 1122–1248; see p. 134 below) is certainly not cathartic in nature. Nor does the trial of Labes really provide Philocleon with a safety valve for his destructive and aggressive urges, since he is not in fact allowed to convict the defendant.

power to manipulate public imagination into new modes of perception and, it is hoped, new modes of judgment.

This is a power fraught with potential for misunderstanding and abuse. Like Bdelycleon spinning his blindfolded father around and taking him to the wrong voting urn, the poet can intentionally confuse issues and drag his audience into false conclusions.[41] In the preceding debate between father and son Bdelycleon succeeded not by making rational and judicious arguments, but by carefully noting down each of his opponent's points, all matters of appetite and prejudice, and by responding with arguments of the same character: far from ruling over and exploiting the rich, the jurors are themselves enslaved and exploited by corrupt leaders enriched at the public's expense. The argument is highly demagogic and misleading, implying as it does that the difference between the city's total foreign revenue and the jurors' stipend disappears into the politicians' pockets and is not expended on Athens' many public works and military obligations. More irresponsible yet is the implication that all of Athens' revenue could go to support the jurors (vv. 706–12); such a proposal out-Cleons Cleon as effectively as anything the Sausage seller offers in the *Knights*. It should not surprise us that the chorus, when they first hear of Bdelycleon's attempts to restrain his father, call him a "Demologocleon" (v. 342),[42] and later accuse him of tyrannical ambitions (vv. 463–76; cf. v. 487). But of course, Bdelycleon's demagogic reasoning is never meant to be taken seriously; his argument is a characteristic comic argument, founded, like Aristophanes' social satire, on a careful study of popular attitudes and prejudices turned around to his own use. Bdelycleon's words and actions, like the Sausage seller's earlier, illustrate the truism of Comedy necessarily becoming like the very thing it attacks. The danger herein is that Comedy may become too much like the thing attacked, and risk misunderstanding or misapplication on the part of its public; the result may be that the public merely applies its old prejudices in new ways.

This misapplication of new learning is already to be seen in the first half of the play. After Bdelycleon's victory in the debate Philocleon's reaction is not to give up serving on juries, but to transfer his aggressive

41. On the implications of Bdelycleon's sophistry and deceptive tactics in dealing with his father, see Reckford 1977, 293–96 (= Reckford 1987, 253–55).

42. The epithet δημολογικός is pejorative (cf. Plato, *Soph.* 268B), referring as it does to superficial rhetorical persuasiveness before the mob in contrast with the true statesman (the πολιτικός). The name "Demologocleon" reflects on the demagogic qualities of both Bdelycleon and Cleon (cf. Starkie 1897, 185; Sommerstein 1983, 177; Edmunds 1987b, 54) and implies a certain parallelism between the two, despite their supposed enmity.

instincts elsewhere and threaten Cleon with conviction for embezzle-
ment (vv. 752–59).[43] Rather than being reformed he simply converts
his animus to a new target. After Labes' trial Philocleon uses the same
argument with which Bdelycleon defended Labes to justify his own
equally antisocial behavior in always condemning defendants (v. 989 "I
don't know how to play the cithara," in other words, I am too ignorant
and uneducated to act otherwise; cf. v. 959, where the same line is used
of Labes).[44] This tendency to learn the wrong lessons is displayed on a
large scale in the part of the play following the parabasis.

Bdelycleon's attempt to train his father in the ways of fitting into
polite society is itself metatheatrical in nature; the essential preliminary
is dressing Philocleon in a new costume composed of a luxurious
Persian cloak and Laconian slippers (vv. 1122–73).[45] After equipping
the old man with this new external identity, Bdelycleon trains him to
tell stories and sing songs in proper symposiastic style by asking Philocleon to imagine himself reclining on a couch at an elegant banquet,
gazing at the ceiling, listening to a flute-girl, and surrounded by urbane
guests such as Theorus, Aeschines, Phanus, and Cleon (vv. 1208–22).
Bdelycleon in turn plays the role of each guest, offering to Philocleon
the first line of a *skolion* (a drinking-song) which he is to take up and
complete; each of Philocleon's responses is funny, but also insulting to
his imagined interlocutor. This technique of teaching by putting the
student into an imagined dramatic situation reminds us not only of the
Labes trial but of the schema we have seen Socrates use in the *Clouds;*
after robbing Strepsiades of cloak and slippers, thus putting him into
appropriate philosophical costume, Socrates places him into a flea-
ridden bed and asks him to imagine himself involved in various legal
problems and to think of an appropriate escape in each case (*Nub.* 735–
90). Strepsiades' answers are all ludicrous: hiring a Thessalian witch to
draw the moon down so that the end of the month will never come and
debts will never be due, or using a mirror to melt the wax on the court
clerk's tablet, or hanging himself. Like Bdelycleon's instruction of Philocleon, Socrates' teaching is meant to make his pupil seem "clever in
society" (*Nub.* 649 κομψὸν ἐν ξυνουσίᾳ). Socrates and Bdelycleon exhibit the same insistence that their pupil persevere despite his obvious
discomfort; *Vesp.* 1166 repeats *Nub.* 698 verbatim. But Strepsiades'
foolery often excites his teacher's impatience and disgust: Socrates
frequently belabors him with paired epithets, such as "unlearned and
barbaric" (*Nub.* 492 ἀμαθὴς καὶ βαρβαρός), "rustic and unlearning"

43. See Starkie 1897, 271–72; MacDowell 1971, 235; Paduano 1974, 195.
44. See Paduano 1974, 149–52.
45. On this scene as a "psychodrama" within the play, see Dracoulides 1967, 110–12.

(*Nub.* 646 ἄγροικος καὶ δυσμαθής), "rustic and dumb" (*Nub.* 655 ἀγρεῖος καὶ σκαιός), and finally, after Strepsiades' proposal to evade a lawsuit by suicide, "most forgetful and dumb" (*Nub.* 790 ἐπιλησμότατον καὶ σκαιότατον).[46] These exclamations of pedagogical despair are echoed by Bdelycleon's "dumb and untaught" (*Vesp.* 1183 ὦ σκαιὲ κἀπαίδευτε).

Like Strepsiades and Pheidippides misusing the lessons learned from Socrates, Philocleon puts his newly acquired knowledge to a very different use from the one his son intended. After the second parabasis we hear from the slave Xanthias that Philocleon has insulted the guests and behaved riotously at the urbane symposium to which Bdelycleon brought him and is now drunkenly assaulting people on the street (*Vesp.* 1299–1325). As he appears onstage we see one of his victims threatening to bring him to court for the injuries inflicted, but Philocleon, once the archjuror and hanging judge, has been so thoroughly persuaded by his son's arguments against the juries that he now professes contempt for the whole legal system (*Vesp.* 1335–41) and chases his accuser off-stage;[47] he later threatens his son with a story about the old man Ephudion defeating the younger Ascondas in a boxing match at Olympia (*Vesp.* 1382–86), which had of course been suggested to him by Bdelycleon as a paradigmatic story for polite company (*Vesp.* 1190–94). Similarly Philocleon chases off the bread seller and Chaerephon with Aesopic stories and allusions to the poets (*Vesp.* 1399–1414) and drives away another accuser with Aesopic and Sybaritic fables (*Vesp.* 1427–28), as suggested to him earlier by Bdelycleon (*Vesp.* 1258–61). Philocleon's evasion of his two accusers clearly reminds us of the final scenes of the *Clouds*, when Strepsiades evades his two creditors, both of whom also threaten legal action, by replying to them with irrelevant travesty of Socratic learning and logic (*Nub.* 1214–1302). Philocleon's use of his son's teachings to justify beating his son undoubtedly evokes Pheidippides' use against his father of the unjust logic his father was so eager for him to learn (*Nub.* 1321–1475);[48] the father-beating of the *Clouds* becomes son-beating in the *Wasps,* but that son-beating is really a form of father-beating, inasmuch as the rejuvenated Philocleon treats Bdelycleon as his older and more responsible relative (see *Vesp.* 1352–65).[49]

46. Compare also *Nub.* 628–29 (οὐκ εἶδον οὕτως ἄνδρ' ἄγροικον οὐδένα/οὐδ' ἄπορον οὐδὲ σκαιὸν οὐδ' ἐπιλήσμονα), where all these terms are combined.

47. On the stage action here, cf. MacDowell 1971, 311; Sommerstein 1983, 135.

48. The whole idea of a better-educated son teaching his father, on which the *Wasps* is based, originates in this scene. See Wolfring 1979, 21–22.

49. This idea is supported by the convincing reassignment of vv. 1364–65 to Philocleon, proposed by Rusten (1977, 157–59).

Needless to say, Bdelycleon has no one but himself to blame for the total failure of his educational enterprise. By denying the system of Athenian jurisprudence and by putting nothing positive in its place except hedonistic self-indulgence at home and in the symposium, Bdelycleon has disrupted the very fabric holding society together and restraining human relations from degeneration into a state of uninhibited anomie. Bdelycleon's ambitions for social advancement are ultimately as amoral as the compulsive jury obsession and corrupt political manipulations from which he has rescued his father. His concern with modern habits and social fashion puts him in the same class with the young men ridiculed by the chorus in the parabasis, with their "curls/and fashion and wide-assedness" (vv. 1069–70). Bdelycleon, who was once the "Cleon hater," now places Cleon and Theorus among the bon vivants of polite society (vv. 1219–40) and in vv. 1224–26 himself plays the role of Cleon;[50] indeed, it is Philocleon, the former "Cleon lover," who sasses Cleon and Theorus with his witty *skolia* and is upbraided by his son for doing so. At the end of the scene Philocleon very soberly and prudently warns his son that drinking is a great evil, giving rise to violence and costs (vv. 1252–55). But Bdelycleon, once the influence of restraint and moderation, now proposes carefree symposiastic indulgence and advises his father to dismiss any problems with a witty story (vv. 1252, 1256–61); naturally the results of his advice turn out to be disastrous. At the moment when the great metatheatrical manipulator considers himself most fully in control of his father he has actually lost control, the way Strepsiades, the Twister, loses his son at the very moment when he thinks he has won everything. By the end of the play Bdelycleon appears helpless and irrelevant, watching his father dance wildly out of control.

The *Clouds* and the *Wasps* both end with the hero's failure,[51] and it is perhaps no surprise that the plays themselves were relative failures with the public.[52] Neither play is able to articulate a positive vision of the world as it ought to be, in the sense that the *Acharnians, Knights,* and

50. See especially v. 1224 καὶ δὴ γάρ εἰμ' ἐγὼ Κλέων. Associating with Cleon and his circle makes Bdelycleon himself look merely like another ambitious *nouveau riche:* cf. Wilamowitz 1935 I, 311–12; Whitman 1964, 146; Strauss 1966, 129; Vaio 1971, 337; Konstan 1985, 43. It may just be that Bdelycleon is trying to be funny here, although he always plays the straight man elsewhere.

51. This was particularly true of the first version of the *Clouds*, which lacked the present exodos with the burning of the Phrontisterion; at least in the later version of the play, Strepsiades is successful in avenging himself on intellectuals.

52. As the hypothesis tells us (Hyp. I, 33 [MacDowell]), the *Wasps* finished second. Public dislike of the ending with the dancing sons of Carcinus may even be alluded to in the parabasis of the *Peace* (*Pax* 781–95); see Nicole 1884, 163–67.

some of Aristophanes' later plays do. As long as Bdelycleon and Aristophanes were attacking the politicians, they were successful, in however limited a way. When Bdelycleon and Aristophanes attempt to change the nature of the public itself either by reeducating Philocleon in social manners or by poking fun at popular misunderstanding of the intellectuals in the *Clouds,* they are doomed to failure, since human nature cannot be changed. Bdelycleon's fall stems from a hybristic overconfidence in his ability to effect social reform, moving his father from democratic engagement to a life of self-contained *apragmosynē*; it is precisely when Bdelycleon assumes his ability to control his father totally that he himself becomes like the tyrannical, manipulative politicians he had formerly criticized but later presumes to fraternize with. And as the poet now recognizes, the public is its own master and cannot be controlled by him any more than by the politicians. By projecting his own experience onto his main character Aristophanes clarifies both the potential and the limitations of the comic art.

Despite Bdelycleon's failure, the chorus pays him a retrospective tribute in its final ode (vv. 1450–73). The strophe reflects on the option Philocleon now has of living a comfortable and luxurious life, though his inborn nature may resist making such a change. The antistrophe praises Bdelycleon for his "filial devotion and wisdom" (v. 1465), his kindness (v. 1467), and his desire to "adorn the one begetting him with more seemly affairs" (vv. 1472–73). On another level the chorus' praise of Bdelycleon is certainly a praise of the poet[53] who is to be appreciated for his sincerity and devotion to the welfare of his elders, although only partially successful in his attempts to reform the Athenian public. We cannot help being reminded here of the chorus' last words in the anapests of the parabasis: "the poet has been thought nothing worse by the wise, / If in passing his opponents he crashed his purpose" (vv. 1049–50).

Aristophanes is also very much present in the play's second parabasis:

> I have often thought myself   1265
>   To be born clever and
>   Never dumb,
> But Amynias son of Boaster,
>   Descended from the sons of Hairbun, is even more so:
> This is the man whom I once saw
>   Dining with Leogoras
>   Instead of on an apple and pomegranate.

53. See Russo 1962, 194.

> For he's as hungry as Antiphon.   1270
> But he went to Pharsalus as an ambassador;
>   There he was alone with
>   Only the Penestae of Thessaly,
>   Himself a poor man (*penestēs*)
>   Less than no one.
> O fortunate Automenes, how we marvel at your fortune!   1275
> You have begotten sons most skilled in craft—
> First the man dear to all and wisest,
> The citharaodist, whom Charm follows;
> And then another, the actor, awfully skillful;
> And then Ariphrades, by far the most clever-spirited of all,   1280
> Whom his father swore learned from no one
> How to do things with his tongue, every time he visits brothels.
>   [lacuna]
> There are certain men who said that I came to a peace-treaty
> After Cleon attacked me and stirred me up   1285
> And grated me with abuse. And back then, when I was being
>   skinned alive,
> The spectators outside laughed at me crying out,
> Having no care about me, only wanting to know
> If I would send out a little joke when pressed.
> Seeing this, I played the monkey for a while,   1290
> And now the prop deceives the vine!
>   (vv. 1265–91)

As we have seen, the second part of the *Wasps* tends to be dominated by
themes and motifs from the *Clouds* and not from the *Knights*. The
second parabasis runs counter to this trend by very clearly evoking the
Knights, and particularly the second parabasis of the *Knights*. Amynias,
the voracious pauper who dines with rich men, cannot but remind us
of Cleonymus, satirized in the antode of the *Knights'* second parabasis
for exactly the same thing (*Eq.* 1290–99). The ode may also reflect on
the incongruity of Philocleon's going off to a banquet among social
superiors, an incongruity that becomes more evident from its tragicomic consequences after this parabasis. Like the corresponding part
of the *Knights'* second parabasis (*Eq.* 1274–89), the epirrheme focuses
on the sons of Automenes, particularly Ariphrades, the man who
gratifies prostitutes with his tongue.

Although the antode is missing, the antepirrheme does something
uncommon in Aristophanes' syzygies: speaking in the persona of the
poet, such as we sometimes see in the anapests of the main parabasis.[54]

---

54. While the poet's first person is uncommon in epirrhemes, it does occur: see
chap. 2 n.33 above.

Aristophanes asserts that despite the politician's attacks, he has not made any sort of truce with Cleon. This passage must allude to the misconception entertained by some on the basis of the *Clouds*, supposing that Aristophanes had dropped Cleon as a target.[55] The poet vigorously asserts himself, even in an unconventional way, to assure his public that he will still be attacking Cleon in his comedy, as he has done in the *Knights* and to some extent here in the *Wasps*, no matter how painful the consequences.[56] In choosing Cleon and the sophist Ariphrades as his two principal targets in this parabasis, the poet shows the audience that the attack on the New Learning in the *Clouds* was not inconsistent with his opposition to the New Politicians in the *Knights*. However, by evoking the *Knights* in the *Clouds* half of the *Wasps* even as the *Clouds* plot is on the verge of collapsing around him, the poet effectively signals that he will continue in the future with what he is successful at, namely, political comedy. Not surprisingly this is what we see the following year in the *Peace*, which indeed makes good Aristophanes' promise to continue attacking Cleon no matter what.

55. Cf. Müller-Strübing 1873, 608–9; Starkie 1897, 379; MacDowell 1971, 299; Sommerstein 1983, 233–34; Edmunds 1987b, 57.

56. Edmunds (1987b, 56–57) sees a close relation between ἔτι καὶ νυνί in v. 1037 of the first parabasis and εἶτα νῦν (v. 1291) here, representing Aristophanes' continued battle against Cleon. Van der Valk (1967, 128–29) regards the verbs of vv. 1285–89 as having erotic undertones, suggesting the poet's homosexual rape by Cleon. This conforms well with the active homosexual imagery used to characterize Paphlagon in the *Knights* (see p. 68 above) and provides an appropriate counterpoint to Ariphrades' act in the epirrheme.

CHAPTER 7

The Flight of the Dung Beetle

With the death of Cleon near Amphipolis in the summer of 422 and the ensuing prospects for a peace accord, Aristophanes abandons the self-questioning and alienated pose of the *Clouds* and the *Wasps* to reaffirm his solidarity with the Athenian public in a collective celebration of peace and the *Peace*.

High and Low

More than any other Aristophanic hero, Trygaeus embodies the average Athenian[1] and at the same time the spirit of Comedy itself. His very name implies the sort of small farmer we have seen before in Dicaeopolis or Strepsiades (note the play on the verb $\tau\rho\upsilon\gamma\hat{\alpha}\nu$ = "to harvest fruit" in vv. 913, 1337–38); more importantly it echoes the special term with which Aristophanes designates his comedy, *trygoidia*.[2] As we have remarked, *trygoidia* is modelled on *tragoidia*;[3] that is, Comedy expresses itself through the conventions and commonplaces of Tragedy in a necessary symbiosis of the higher and lower mimetic. What more fitting symbol of this aesthetic paradox could be invented than Trygaeus' soaring flight to Olympus on the back of a lowly dung beetle? The heroic Pegasus of Euripides' *Bellerophon* is here transformed into a much earthier and more appropriately comic steed.[4] But

1. See Whitman 1964, 105–6.
2. On the ambiguity of Trygaeus' name, see Strauss 1966, 139.
3. See chap. 3 n.15 above.
4. Vv. 135–36 and 146–48 refer quite explicitly to this undertaking as "tragic" in nature, and as Σ*Pax* 154 tells us, vv. 154–55, invoking Pegasus, are a direct parody of

we would do well to remember that Bellerophon failed in his attempt to scale heaven, whereas Aristophanes' hero succeeds, at least partially, in his ascent and quest:[5] the low, animalistic, and disgusting aspects of human experience are revealed as integrally necessary to the highest acts of human creativity and achievement.

In a moment of extradramatic interplay one of the slaves in the prologue imagines two spectators conversing about the significance of the beetle, with one of the pair, a foreigner, speculating on its being a symbol for Cleon, who also eats excrement (vv. 43–46).[6] What is most worthy of note here is that on the surface this interpretation is quite wrong. Cleon is hardly the vehicle for flying to heaven and obtaining Peace; we are told on the contrary of his being deep down in the Underworld (vv. 649–56), a ghost who should not be awakened or conjured up again. In this play Cleon's significance is precisely his absence. But in another sense the Ionian man of vv. 45–48 may be right without realizing it; although the dung beetle does not represent Cleon *tout court,* the topos "Cleon" is certainly part of the repulsive, dirty, invective, low-comic world the dung beetle embodies.[7] Cleon may be dead, but as the parabasis reveals (vv. 752–59), "Cleon" will always remain alive in Aristophanic comedy. Much as Aristophanes presumes to direct his comic efforts toward higher political and intellectual aims, his comedy can succeed only by employing tricks and devices of the gutter, the Cleon jokes being among them. We have seen the poet reflect on this paradox in both the *Clouds* and *Wasps.* It is here expressed through the vivid theatrical spectacle of the dung beetle's flight, with the crane wildly swinging Trygaeus between heaven and

---

Euripides' *Bellerophon* (fr. 307 Nauck). On the Euripidean parody generally in this passage, see Rohdewald 1854, 19; Rau 1967, 89–97; Harvey 1971, 362–64; Cassio 1985, 51–52.

5. Aristophanes may intend us to understand that Trygaeus never reaches heaven in anything other than his imagination: he does not meet the gods except Hermes (their usual messenger to men) and War (long active on Earth); he is joined by a chorus of earthlings who arrive without transport and manages to walk back home without his dung beetle. ἐνθάδ' of v. 314 suggests ironically that the scene is still somewhere near Athens. Nevertheless a vivid imagination is enough, at least in this comedy, to win back Peace.

6. Although much neglected, this passage is extremely important for students of ancient literary criticism. It proves that ancient audiences were expected to interpret Comedy, and by extension we can infer other forms of drama, in symbolic and allegorical terms; I do not agree with Reckford 1987, 10–11, that the joke criticizes all such attempts to look for symbolic meaning. On the concept of *ainos* as an animal fable with a coded message that can be either understood or misunderstood, and the related semantics of the verb *ainissomai* (used here in v. 47), see Nagy 1979, 237–41.

7. On Paphlagon/Cleon's reduction of political affairs in the *Knights* to the purely physical level of eating, defecation, and sex, see our remarks on pp. 67–69 above.

earth (vv. 80, 152 μετέωρος),[8] as the wavering beetle aims his nose one instant at Zeus, the next instant at the alleyway latrines of the Piraeus; in parallel fashion Trygaeus' high-flown Euripidean lyric (vv. 154–56) quickly degenerates into scatological doggerel (vv. 157–72), as all attempts at stylistic transcendence fall to the ground.

Much emphasis is placed on the danger and risk involved in Trygaeus' lofty enterprise (vv. 146–48, 169–76). Aside from the physical danger of Trygaeus' flight, the framework of tragic allusion to Bellerophon and Prometheus characterizes his challenge to the gods as an act of metaphysical risk as well.[9] He refers to his undertaking as a "new deed of daring" (v. 94 τόλμημα νέον), and upon arriving on Olympus, he is himself addressed by Hermes as "you disgusting, daring, and shameless man, / loathsome, all-loathsome, and most loathsome, / . . . most loathsome of loathsome men" (vv. 182–84 ὦ βδελυρὲ καὶ τολμηρὲ κἀναίσχυντε σὺ / καὶ μιαρὲ καὶ παμμίαρε καὶ μιαρώτατε, / . . . ὦ μιαρῶν μιαρώτατε). Indeed, Trygaeus makes his objectionable smell and appearance a matter of pride, answering Hermes' questions about his name and origins with the repeated epithet "most loathsome" (vv. 185–87 μιαρώτατος). The connection of daring with shamelessness and loathsomeness reminds us of the Sausage seller's boldness in doing or saying anything in the *Knights*.[10] We have seen that the Sausage seller, like Trygaeus, is an emblematic figure of Comedy, with its generic lack of scruple, inhibition, and restraint. Like the *Knights*,

8. The epithet μετέωρος ("mid-air") reminds us of Socrates in the *Clouds*, who was also suspended by a crane in the prologue in order to investigate τὰ μετέωρα πράγματα (*Nub.* 228). Drawing on Diogenes of Apollonia, Socrates elaborates a doctrine of earthly gravity impeding the heavenward ascent of thought (*Nub.* 225–34), not unlike the dialectical tension of the dung beetle's flight; compare also the image of the lizard in the rafters, which defecates on Socrates' forehead as he looks up at the moon (*Nub.* 169–74).

9. Trygaeus uses his knowledge of a conspiracy by the Sun and Moon against the Olympian gods in order to win Hermes' compliance with his wish to retrieve Peace (vv. 403–15); this may be meant as an allusion to Prometheus' secret concerning the destiny of Zeus, which ultimately wins his release (for Aristophanic travesty of the *Prometheia*, cf. *Av.* 686–87, 1494–1552, and the prudent remarks of Rau [1967, 175–77], as against the more tenuous speculations of Herington [1963, 236–43]). Cf. Albini 1971, 24. Sicking (1967, 119) correctly emphasizes the aggression and *hybris* involved in Trygaeus' invasion of Olympus and wish to confront Zeus. This is particularly clear from the parallel with Euripides' Bellerophon, for whose explicit impiety and contempt toward the gods, see fr. 286, 292 Nauck. Those who criticize the *Peace* for lack of conflict and dramatic tension (cf. Murray 1964, 62; Whitman 1964, 104; Russo 1962, 213–14; Gelzer 1970, 1454; Henderson 1975, 62; *contra*, see Landfester 1977, 161–62, 187, and Cassio 1985, 35) do not give sufficient attention to the revolutionary nature of Trygaeus' actions; the plot of the *Peace*, though not as complex as that of the *Clouds* or the *Wasps*, is no less dramatic than that of the *Birds*, and in many ways served as a model for that play (on which, see van der Valk 1981–82, 105–6).

10. See pp. 61–63 above, on the semantics of "boldness" and "daring" in Aristophanes. On the parallel of Trygaeus and the Sausage seller in this regard, see Whitman 1964, 107.

Peace reflects the irony of high ambition necessarily coupled with the lowest possible origins and standards and dramatizes the paradox that tranquility can be obtained only through effrontery and presumption.

The term *miaros,* with which Trygaeus is characterized, not only refers to general repulsiveness, but also has specific associations with ritual defilement and pollution.[11] His contact with dung, the basest form of earth, makes him impure in the context of intercourse with the gods. Trygaeus' prayer for silence and ritual purity at the beginning of his flight is from the start undercut by the irony of its own impossibility:

> It is fit to speak propitiously and not mutter
> Anything trifling and common, but cry to the gods.
> Tell men to be silent,
> To wall up with new bricks
> The latrines and alleys,
> > And lock up their assholes.
>
> > > (vv. 96–101)

Of course, men can never wall up the latrines and lock tight their assholes, as we see in vv. 164–69, for this is contrary to human nature. Nor is it the dung beetle's nature to hold itself aloof from dung. All the same, despite the *hybris* and seeming vanity of his efforts, Trygaeus apparently succeeds in arriving on Olympus, precisely through the impurity and defilement represented by the dung beetle. True ritual purity is almost a contradiction in terms, since sacrificial ritual is based on a collective sharing of defilement,[12] as we see also with Trygaeus' slaves in their preparation of the dedicatory "cakes" and their manipulation of impure matter.[13] Similarly the ritual of comic drama involves the audience collectively sharing in a form of defilement that consists in the low and obscene matters presented onstage,[14] though

11. On the semantics of the adjective, see Parker 1983, 3–5.

12. For animal sacrifice as an act of collective aggression and sharing of bloodguilt, see the fundamental work of Burkert 1983, 1–12, 35–48. In Aristophanes' time Orphic and Pythagorean doctrine clearly articulated the internal contradictions and ironies inherent in traditional ritual practice.

13. Aristophanes may be thinking here of the handling of putrefied pig remains brought out of the sacred chasm by specially purified women (*Antlētriai*) at the Thesmophoria festival; note the jokes on ἀντλία in vv. 17–18. Strict purity must be observed before handling the most impure matter, representing subterranean death and decay but also bearing agricultural fertility. On the significance of this ritual, see Deubner 1932, 40–44, 50–51; Parke 1977, 83–84; Simon 1983, 19–22; Burkert 1985, 242–45.

14. The connection between low comedy and ritual defilement is established here by the term φλαῦρον (v. 96), which Trygaeus uses in his call for ritual purity; the word is more applicable to the aesthetic propriety or taste of comic utterances (cf. *Nub.* 834, *Lys.* 1041, 1045) than to ritual propriety per se.

the poet in the parabasis presumes to maintain strict standards of aesthetic purity.

Aristophanes insists on the artistry and *technē* involved even in this low mimetic presentation. Not just any excrement will do for Trygaeus' dung beetle; as the slave explains to us (vv. 22–28), this beetle is far more discriminating than an ordinary pig or dog and insists on high-grade dung carefully kneaded and fashioned like a pastry cake. In heaven it will feed on nothing less than Ganymede's "ambrosia" (= excrement, v. 724). With this sustenance the dung beetle need not return to earth. The pairing of the beetle with Ganymede again illustrates the beauty and the beast theme, the mutual dependence of corporal messiness and aesthetic sublimity within the world of comic drama. It moreover signals a broader transformation that takes place at this point in the play, immediately before the parabasis—the movement from scatological interests, such as the dung beetle and his food, to sexual ones, not only Ganymede but Opora and Theoria as well.[15] Freud has identified the transition from the anal-erotic to the Oedipal as a crucial stage in infantile development, but the Greeks were more likely to think in terms of masculine development from passive, pathic sexuality to active, genital sexuality. Ganymede is thus an appropriate mediating figure between the dung beetle on one side and Opora and Theoria on the other. Projected in aesthetic terms this evolution moves from elements of low, farcical, popular comedy to the higher social integration represented by comic marriage, feasting, and celebration. The dung beetle in fact is no longer needed in the second half of the *Peace* and can quite well stay with the gods (vv. 720–26). Along with the beetle Aristophanes can also leave behind all the shit jokes, Cleon jokes and other comic dross.

Cheap Humor and Heroic Humor

The dialectic between the low comic and high comic is also central to the parabasis:

15. Immediately after the dismissal of the dung beetle in vv. 720–24 Trygaeus turns to Opora and Theoria, telling them that "many men await you with great desire, standing erect (ἐστυκότες)" (vv. 727–28), as the chorus (= "many men") move into place for the parabasis in v. 729. Similarly Trygaeus looks back in vv. 865–67, observing that with his dung beetle he has made it possible for all the Greeks safely "to screw and sleep"; his remark is followed by Theoria's presentation to the Council with a long string of bawdy metaphors and jokes (vv. 868–909). On the general dominance of heterosexual imagery in the play's second half, as opposed to the scatological and pathic imagery in the first half, cf. Henderson 1975, 63–65; Moulton 1981, 89–90.

Now go and farewell! Let us give these tools and costumes
To the servants to keep, since many thieves are wont   730
To poke around the stage and do mischief.
Now guard these things manfully! And let us speak to the audience
The path of words which we have and as much as our mind holds.
It is fit that the ushers should beat him, if any comic poet
Praises himself, stepping forward in the anapests.   735
But, O daughter of Zeus, if it is right to honor anyone,
Who has become the best and most famous comic producer among
        men,
Our producer says that he is worthy of great praise.
First, he alone of men stopped his rivals
From always making jokes about rags and warring with lice,   740
And he first drove out with dishonor those kneading
And starving Heracleses, and freed the slaves
Who escape and deceive and get beaten up on purpose,
Whom other poets always brought out crying, on account of this,
So that a fellow slave, mocking his blows, could then ask,   745
"Wretch, what has your hide suffered? Has the whip attacked
Your ribs with a numerous army and cut trees on your back?"
Taking away such faults and cheap humor and ignoble clowning,
He made a great poetic craft for us and raised a tower, constructing
        it
With great words and ideas and jokes not of the common
        marketplace,   750
Not ridiculing private mannikins and women,
But having a wrath of Heracles, he set his hand upon the greatest,
Marching across the malodorous hides and muddy-minded threats.
And first, of all men I do battle with the jag-toothed hound itself,
From whose eyes the most dreadful rays of Cynna flashed,   755
And around whose head a hundred heads of wailing flatterers
        licked
In a circle, while the hound itself had the voice of a death-bearing
        mountain torrent,
The odor of a seal, the unwashed balls of Lamia, the asshole of a
        camel.
Seeing such a monster, I was not afraid, but making war on behalf
        of you
And the islands I always held out. For which it is now right   760
That you remember and repay me with your favor.
For even before, faring as I wished, I did not go around the gyms
And make attempts on the boys, but picked up my clothing and
        straightway retreated,
Vexing little, delighting much, and offering all that is needed.
        For this, it is fitting   765
        That both men and boys be with me;

> And we exhort all bald-headed men
> To join in our hope for victory.
> For when I am a winner, everyone
> At the table and parties will say,   770
> "Bring sweetmeats to the bald man,
> Give sweetmeats to the bald man,
> And do not take them away from a man having a face
>   Like the noblest of poets."

(vv. 729–74)

The coryphaeus claims that this poet is to be honored above all others for having freed Comedy from "cheap humor" (v. 748 φόρτον) and "ignoble clowning" (v. 748 βωμολοχεύματ' ἀγεννῆ),[16] such as is derived at the expense of ragged and starving characters or maltreated slaves. As we have noticed from analyzing similar passages in the *Clouds* and *Wasps*, Aristophanes is himself just as guilty of using such well-worn comic topoi as any of his rivals, although he may be technically correct in saying that he has avoided the particular things listed here.[17] The self-undercutting irony of this passage is in fact set up by the patently ironic vv. 734–35, when it is proclaimed that any poet who makes a parabasis (παραβάς) praising himself ought to be beaten up by the ushers; Aristophanes does indeed praise himself in this parabasis, not only through the mouthpiece of the coryphaeus, but even breaking into the first person in vv. 754–74.

Aristophanes' professed aim in rejecting the trivial and farcical devices of his competitors is to redirect his attention toward greater objects, mocking not private and insignificant targets, but the greatest public nuisance of them all—Cleon. His more ambitious target (v. 752 τοῖσι μεγίστοις = "the greatest") requires a correspondingly ambitious comic style with "great" (v. 750 μεγάλοις) words, ideas, and jokes, and a

---

16. For the connection of these terms, cf. Aristotle, *EN* 1128a4–7: "Those who go too far in laughter seem to be clowns (βωμολόχοι) and cheap humorists (φορτικοί), in every way concerned with laughter and aiming at the creation of laughter rather than saying elegant things and not hurting the one mocked." Like Aristophanes, Aristotle opposes this kind of reckless comedy to a more discriminating mode concerned with expression of elegant and decorous things (εὐσχήμονα).

17. See pp. 96–102 and chap. 6 nn.6–7 above. Like the present passage, both *Nub.* 537–38 and *Vesp.* 56–63 are technically correct in what they claim about not doing these things in the first *Clouds* or in the *Wasps*. But these passages are clearly ironic in spirit, since Aristophanes avails himself of these devices elsewhere. On Dicaeopolis' appearance in rags, see chap. 5 n.41 and on Aristophanes' treatment of slave characters, n.42. On the burlesque Heracles in the *Centaur* and later plays, see chap. 5 n.40. Reckford (1979, 197) thinks the "starving Heracles" here may allude to the starving Hierocles who is denied a meal by Trygaeus in vv. 1105–26. Aristophanes certainly does not refrain from attacking poor and starving characters elsewhere; compare the Megarian in *Ach.* 729–835, or Lysistratus, Thumantis, and Cleonymus in the second parabasis of the *Knights* (*Eq.* 1266–73, 1292–99).

"great craft" (v. 749 τέχνην μεγάλην).[18] Using a high-flown Pindaric metaphor, Aristophanes claims to have erected a mighty tower of song (v. 749).[19] The poet's valor and daring are no less than those of Heracles (v. 752),[20] even as Trygaeus (= Comedy) assumed the role of Bellerophon in the prologue. The poet not only wrestles with the Cleon monster as in the *Wasps*, but military terminology pervades the whole parabasis: "warring" (v. 740 πολεμοῦντας), "drove out" (v. 742 ἐξήλασ'), "attacked" (v. 746 εἰσέβαλεν), "with a numerous army" (v. 747 πολλῇ στρατιᾷ), "cut down trees" (v. 747 κἀδενδροτόμησε), "raised a tower" (v. 749 κἀπύργωσ'), "set upon" (v. 752 ἐπεχείρει), "marching across" (v. 753 διαβάς), "do battle" (v. 754 μάχομαι), "making war" (v. 759 πολεμίζων), "held out" (v. 760 ἀντεῖχον), "make attempts" (v. 763 ἐπείρων), "retreated" (v. 763 ἐχώρουν). In summarizing his accomplishments against Cleon, Aristophanes claims to have made war "on behalf of you and the islands" (vv. 759–60); while this principally designates his opposition to Cleon's exploitation of the allies, as in the *Babylonians*, the phrase is itself a citation of the war party's own rhetoric.[21]

There is a marked irony in the use of so much military imagery to describe the poet's actions in the context of a play celebrating the recovery of peace. Surely it is not accidental that the final image is not one of attacking or making war but of retreating from the scene quietly (v. 763). Though once necessary, the time for confrontation is now past; with Cleon dead, the Cleon invective of Aristophanes' earlier plays is something equally to be transcended as the vulgar comic commonplaces, also expressed in military terms, which Aristophanes uses even while presuming not to do so.[22] The dung beetle and everything it

18. The verb ἐποίησε (v. 749) also evokes its secondary sense of "making poetry." On the general concept of poetry as a *technē* in the lyric tradition, particularly Pindar, see Svenbro 1976, 173–212.

19. For song described as building a conspicuous structure, cf. Pindar, *O*.6.1–4, *P*.3.113–5; Aristophanes reuses the image in reference to Aeschylus' grandiloquence (*Ran.* 820, 1004). See Taillardat 1962, 438–39.

20. The "kneading Heracleses" of v. 741 which Aristophanes rejects are clearly meant as a foil for this heroic Heracles he sees as more emblematic for his comic purposes. The reference to a "wrath of Heracles" here and in *Vesp.* 1030 (cf. 1043) may allude to a Cydathenian Heracles *thiasos* of conservative opponents to Cleon who formed the chorus of the *Banqueters*. See the important study of Lind (1985, 249–61).

21. On Aristophanes' parabatic parody of the politicians' rhetoric in this regard, see pp. 120–21 above.

22. Even though political comedy, represented by the attack on Cleon, is clearly superior to the usual *phortika*, *Nub.* 520–27 and *Vesp.* 1043–50 suggest Aristophanes' evaluation of it as less than his intellectual comedy, represented by the first *Clouds*. Indeed, as we have seen in our discussion of the *Knights* parabasis, Aristophanes feels some embarrassment about assuming the role of an invective poet, and the parabases of the *Clouds* and *Wasps* attempt to articulate a higher program.

represents, including Cleon, served a purpose, both in bringing Peace and in creating a successful comedy for Aristophanes. The purpose served, the dung beetle is no longer needed; so he leaves both Trygaeus and Aristophanes free to savor their respective feasts and victories in the second half of the play, the poet's celebration in the pnigos foreshadowing that of Trygaeus.

Self-Citation

One of the most noticeable and problematic features of this parabasis is the almost verbatim repetition of the passage describing Cleon (vv. 751–59) from the parabasis of the *Wasps* (*Vesp.* 1029–37). Some scholars regard this as another sign of the play's hasty composition and imaginative poverty,[23] while others have argued that the *Wasps* passage was interpolated.[24] Our observations concerning the extent and importance of intertextual cross-referencing and self-allusion in Aristophanes, particularly in the parabases, ought to warn us that more is at work here than mere rehash. The decision to repeat a passage can be as deliberate and significant on a metalinguistic level of reference as the composition of a completely new utterance.

It should be noted first that there are some contextually significant differences between the two passages. In *Vesp.* 1029 the poet declines to attack ordinary "men" (ἀνθρώποις); here, he reduces the assault to the diminutive "mannikins" (ἀνθρωπίσκους) and adds women, perhaps reiterating the claims of vv. 739–48 about not making comedy at the expense of slaves or the poor and helpless. We should observe also that v. 753 is completely new; the emphasis on Cleon's odor and association with filth (βορβοροθύμους) cannot but evoke the image of the now

---

23. Cf. Wilamowitz 1935, 290; Whitman 1964, 104; Solomos 1974, 141–42. In fact there was no reason why the *Peace* would have had to be hastily composed; as Landfester (1977, 185–86) notes, the 3–4 months after Amphipolis would be as long a period as Aristophanes normally had for writing a comedy, since he presented two plays in some years. Moreover, as Sicking (1967, 120–22) suggests, the plot outline of the *Peace* may have been conceived even before Amphipolis, with Trygaeus' acquisition of a general peace originally being a wishful fantasy comparable to that of the *Acharnians* or *Lysistrata* rather than celebration of an achieved reality. This would be particularly true if our interpretation of *Vesp.* 1448–49 (see n.35 below) is correct.

24. Cf. Hamaker (1854, 241–48), Müller-Strübing (1873, 170–71), Helmbold (1890, 9), who argue against the possibility of using the past tenses of this passage while Cleon was still alive. But as we have observed (p. 118 above), the reference of this passage is not so much to Cleon himself as to Aristophanes' attack on Cleon in the *Knights;* the past verbs are thus entirely appropriate. For a vigorous refutation of Hamaker's other grounds for excision, see Ehrhardt 1890, 10–13.

departed dung beetle and his food,[25] which among other things referred to Cleon, as we have seen (vv. 43–48). We have already noted the
allusion to the islands in v. 760, added to the corresponding line in *Vesp.*
1037.[26] The inclusion of the allies in this play is entirely appropriate,
since it is produced at the City Dionysia when they are all present (the
Wasps was a Lenaean play and was therefore presented to a purely
domestic audience);[27] moreover, the emphasis of the *Peace* is on the
benefits of peace for all Greece, as represented by the chorus of panhellenic farmers.

But the primary departure from the *Wasps* passage is Aristophanes'
use of the first person here, beginning in v. 754 and continuing until
the end of the pnigos. In the very line in which Cleon is first mentioned
with his familiar epithet "jag-toothed hound" ($\tau\hat{\omega}$ $\kappa\alpha\rho\chi\alpha\rho\delta\delta\sigma\nu\tau\iota$),[28] the
poet himself emerges from the third person to speak directly with the
audience as a visible and audible presence on the stage, thus giving a
special personal imprint to the abuse of Cleon.[29] His attempt to purify
the state of Cleon parallels his earlier undertaking to purify Comedy
aesthetically (vv. 739–51),[30] as we see from the repetition of $\pi\rho\hat{\omega}\tau\sigma\nu$
$\mu\acute{\epsilon}\nu$ beginning each passage (vv. 739, 754).[31] The poet's endeavor is
presented in heroic terms (v. 739 "First, he alone of men stopped his
rivals"; v. 754 "First, of all men I did battle with the jag-toothed hound
itself"). The central difference of course between the *Wasps* and *Peace*
passages is not the internal but the external context: when the *Peace*
was performed Cleon was dead, and indeed it was because of Cleon's
death that there could be a peace and a *Peace*. By virtue of repeating his
strongest purple patch of Cleon hatred and rewriting it in an emphatic
first person, Aristophanes personally claims his share of the credit for
Cleon's downfall and in effect dances a jig of celebration on the dema-

25. On $\beta\delta\rho\beta\rho\rho\sigma\varsigma$ as an image for excrement, see Henderson 1975, 192; for its
association with Cleon, cf. *Eq.* 307, 866.

26. Note also that the bribery theme of *Vesp.* 1036 ($\sigma\ddot{v}$ $\phi\eta\sigma\iota\nu$ . . . $\kappa\alpha\tau\alpha\delta\omega\rho\sigma\delta\sigma\kappa\hat{\eta}\sigma\alpha\iota$) is
dropped here, where it has less polemical relevance; see pp. 120–21, 128 above.

27. Cf. Russo 1962, 211; Cassio 1982, 39–41, especially 40 n.4. Indeed Rohdewald
(1854, 13) thinks it is for the benefit of the bitterly anti-Cleon allies that Aristophanes
repeats the whole passage from the *Wasps*. For the most thorough study of this play's
allusions to the Ionian allies, see Cassio 1985, 105–18.

28. In *Vesp.* 1031 this epithet is already a citation of *Eq.* 1017 (cf. *Eq.* 1030, *Pax* 313).

29. Cf. Strauss 1966, 153. Sifakis (1971b, 37) notes the shift from third person to first
here as also marked by the emphatic present $\mu\acute{\alpha}\chi\sigma\mu\alpha\iota$ (v. 754 "I do battle"), standing out
in a series of otherwise past verbs. Aristophanes emphasizes the continued relevance of
his fight against Cleon and everything Cleon represents, even with Cleon dead.

30. As we have seen (p. 118 above) the idea of political and aesthetic "purification" is
also central to the *Wasps* parabasis.

31. The $\pi\rho\hat{\omega}\tau\sigma\nu$ $\mu\acute{\epsilon}\nu$ of v. 754 is not in the *Wasps* passage and thus seems quite
consciously placed here for structural purposes.

gogue's grave.[32] By this act of self-quotation, Aristophanes reminds us that he was always against Cleon, and that the course of history has now vindicated him.

Aristophanes does not allow his triumphant self-exultation to get out of hand or become overweening. As we have often noticed in Aristophanes' parabases, the poet's assertive *alazoneia* is balanced by a modest, self-deprecatory *eirōneia*. Again borrowing an image from the parabasis of the *Wasps* (*Vesp.* 1025) Aristophanes declares that he does not take advantage of his public success by trying to seduce boys at the wrestling school (vv. 762–63). This statement forswears not only private gain, but also aristocratic mannerisms and sympathies in general, for which pederasty is paradigmatic;[33] as also in the parallel *Nub.* 545 (οὐ κομῶ = "I am not a long-hair [a knight]") Aristophanes balances his profession of superior aesthetic taste and hatred for the popular demagogues with a disclaimer of aristocratic affectation. The pnigos on the contrary emphasizes the poet's common, even unattractive appearance as a bald head, and his solidarity with other equally common looking men.[34] Even after the vigorous self-assertion and credit taking of vv. 754–61 Aristophanes still presents his victory as a victory for all bald men, and the parabasis ends on a note of shared festivity and communal harmony; the feast imagined in vv. 770–74 clearly parallels the feast with which the play itself continues after the parabasis. Unlike Dicaeopolis' private peace, the peace won by the hero of this play is meant to be shared, and the same is true of the poet's victory.

The parabasis' citations of the *Wasps* are not isolated allusions to Aristophanes' previous play. We have already seen from the *Wasps* itself that the poet can sometimes design a play as a rewriting or response to his own earlier work. The idea of a comic plot centered around a dung beetle's flight to heaven originates in the Aesopic fable concerning the dung beetle and the eagle of Zeus, to which Trygaeus alludes when explaining his venture to his children in the prologue (vv. 129–34): the fable illustrates that it is precisely the lowest and most obnoxious

32. Russo (1962, 212) believes Aristophanes presents an aggressive persona in this parabasis to counterbalance the mild and conciliatory tone of the play as a whole. We have observed that the *Knights* parabasis effects the same kind of balance, only in the opposite direction (see p. 76 above).

33. See Robert 1967, 161–62, for the statements on pederasty as reflections concerning the knights and their Laconizing tendencies; on which theme see also Ehrenberg 1962, 100–102; Donlan 1980, 164–68; Carter 1986, 72–73. Σ*Vesp.* 1025, *Pax* 763 (followed by Wilamowitz 1935, 292–93) less plausibly speculate that this may allude to Eupolis' pederastic habits.

34. As we have observed on p. 20 above, the whole chorus probably joins in singing the pnigos, visibly enacting the idea of solidarity with the poet.

creature, like Comedy, who is best able to overthrow the lofty and powerful. Significantly this fable is already alluded to at the end of the *Wasps* (*Vesp.* 1448–49), when Philocleon justifies his violent and offensive behavior by telling witty Aesopic and Sybaritic stories, as his son advised him earlier to do. Indeed Bdelycleon cuts his father off without giving him a chance to finish the story; a choral song follows immediately, then the wild dance of the exodos, leaving it to the next play to complete the fable Philocleon had only begun (*Vesp.* 1448 "as the dung beetle once upon a time . . .").[35]

Not only do Trygaeus' actions pick up on the end of the *Wasps*, but so do those of the chorus. The panhellenic farmers enter the scene with feet dancing wildly out of control in joy over the release from war and deprivation, as Trygaeus tries to restrain them from their loud and riotous celebration (vv. 300–336); the chorus of this play enters effectively in the same condition as they exited the last play when they joined the wild dance of Philocleon and the sons of Carcinus (*Vesp.* 1516–37). The chorus of the *Peace* also identifies itself as a chorus of former jurors, who have dropped their old severity and been rejuvenated by the prospects for peace (vv. 348–53).[36] Where Bdelycleon failed in his attempt to restrain and reform, Trygaeus succeeds. The analogy of the *Peace* with the *Wasps* extends to the allegorical play within the play of War and Turmoil (vv. 236–88); the kitchen implements allegory concerning a war salad of Greek cities ground up by mortar and pestle comes straight out of the Sicilian cheese trial of the *Wasps*, with the cheese-grater, brasier, pots, and pestle as witnesses (see *Vesp.* 936–39).[37] These various allusions to the *Wasps*, all concentrated near the beginning of the *Peace*,[38] contextualize the present play as in some sense a continuation of last year's comedy but with more harmo-

35. Solomos (1974, 141) believes *Vesp.* 1448–49 gave Aristophanes the idea for the plot of the *Peace*. But it is far more likely Aristophanes had this idea for a play before finishing the *Wasps* (see n.23 above) and intentionally holds this until the end of Philocleon's series of fables so as to make an intertextual hint about his next comedy; compare *Ach.* 300–301, where he promises to chop Cleon up for the knights (i.e. in the *Knights*), as noted on p. 34 and chap. 3 n.35. The fable of the dung beetle and the eagle also serves as an intertextual cross-reference to the *Peace* in the parabasis of the *Lysistrata* (*Lys.* 695) as part of the Old Women's advocacy of a peace policy; see p. 194 below.

36. Cf. Russo 1962, 211. Note also that Charinades (named as a member of the chorus in v. 1155) is the name of a wasp juror in *Vesp.* 232.

37. The conception of this scene was also no doubt influenced by *Eq.* 984, characterizing Cleon as a "pestle" and by the general idea of Cleon as someone who "stirs" things up (on which, see Edmunds 1987b, 12). On this scene as a play within the play, see Landfester 1977, 161.

38. Harvey (1971, 362–64) also notes structural and thematic similarities between the prologues of the two plays, both drawing on Euripides.

nious results, as we shall see; whereas the *Wasps* ultimately ends in anarchy and failure, the *Peace* reestablishes a sense of order and common purpose.

The framework of allusion to the *Wasps* is continued in the parabasis odes, which again recall the sons of Carcinus:

O Muse, thrusting away wars,	775
Dance with me your friend,	
Celebrating weddings of gods and banquets of men	
And feasts of the blessed; from the start, these things are a care to	
you.	
But if Carcinus comes	
And asks you to dance with his sons,	
Do not listen or go	785
As a companion to them,	
But consider them all	
Domestic quail, hog-necked dancers,	
Dwarfish, device-seeking shavings of barnyard dung.	790
For their father said of the drama which he had,	
Unexpected, the ferret killed it one night.	795
Such hymns of the fair-haired Graces	
It is fitting for the skilled poet	
To sing, whenever the springtime swallow sits	800
And cries with its voice, and neither Morsimus	
Nor Melanthius have a chorus.	
Him I once heard, chattering with a most bitter voice,	805
When he and his brother	
Had a tragic chorus,	
Both of them	
Sauce-eating Gorgons, skate-hunting Harpies,	810
Loathsome armpit-goaty fish-eating old hag-scarecrows.	
Spitting on them big and wide,	815
O divine Muse, come play out the feast with me.	

(vv. 775–818)

In contrast to their excited entrance chanting trochaic tetrameters (vv. 300–336) the chorus sings stately dactylo-epitrites here, citing well-known verses from the *Oresteia* of Stesichorus.[39] The invocation to the Muse aptly asks her to reject war in favor of celebrating marriages and feasts, and hence parallels the structure of the *Peace* as a whole. But the lofty choral lyric of Stesichorus sinks into bathos with the mention of

39. We are informed of the Stesichorus citations by ΣPax 775, 797, 800.

Carcinus and his sons in vv. 781–82,[40] explicitly naming them as unwelcome participants in the celebratory finale of this play. The absence of Carcinus and his sons helps situate the *Peace* as a departure from the unsuccessful and despairing conclusion of the last play;[41] the *Wasps* ends in a crazy and confused dance symbolizing the ultimate failure of Bdelycleon's quest to civilize and control his father and Aristophanes' quest to reform his theatrical public, but the revel ending the *Peace* affirms the hero's success, along with that of Aristophanes. The Carcinites' characterization as "shavings of barnyard dung" (v. 790) associates them with the recently dismissed dung beetle, and they are quite appropriately eliminated before invading Trygaeus' new world.

Further Exclusions

Another team of brothers, Melanthius and Morsimus, is also described as monsters (Gorgons, Harpies, *etc.*—note the metrical responsion of the list in vv. 809–13 with vv. 788–91) whose "armpit-goaty" (v. 812 τραγομάσχαλοι) smell matches their profession as poets of the "goat-contest" tragedy (see v. 806 τραγῳδῶν);[42] we are again reminded of the dung beetle and the equally foul smelling Cleon monster of vv. 753–59. Tragic dancers and poets like the ones named in these odes have no place in this comedy any more than the tricks of low-comic farce at the other extreme, rejected in vv. 739–48. We note all forms of tragic violence excluded from the second half of the play: blood sacrifice is avoided (vv. 1016–22) and the arms merchants are laughed out of the scene afterwards. Indeed, after this parabasis the communal festivity of the play is defined as much by the people excluded as by those included; the exclusion of the Carcinites and Melanthius and Morsimus from the chorus' celebration here obviously foreshadows

40. Compare the similar perversion of high-flown Pindaric citations in the odes of the *Knights'* second parabasis (see p. 84–86 above, and in general, chap. 2 n.67).

41. On this ode as an allusion to the end of the *Wasps*, cf. Nicole 1884, 163–67, and Russo 1962, 211. But I do not agree with Nicole that Aristophanes is identifying the exodos as the cause of the *Wasps'* failure to win a first prize.

42. Cassio (1985, 21–22) notes the attack upon Melanthius in the other two plays competing at the Dionysia of 421, Eupolis' *Flatterers* (fr. 178 PCG) and Leucon's *Phrateres* (fr. 3 PCG), and concludes there must have been some coordination among the three comic poets. It may just be that the otherwise obscure Melanthius had recently been successful in the tragic competition or was competing this year. In any event he is expelled from the world of Comedy.

this plot development,[43] as the feast imagined in the pnigos adumbrates the play's second half in more positive form. Carcinus' family (see vv. 864, 1083) and Melanthius (see vv. 1009–14) both resurface as objects of caustic allusion in the second half, along with many other familiar Aristophanic targets, such as Ariphrades, Hyperbolus, Theogenes, Chaeris, as well as Morychus, Teleas, Glaucetes, Lamachus, and Cleonymus. The exclusion of undesirables from Trygaeus' marriage and feast does not seem selfish, however, as it perhaps does in the *Acharnians*, since the very establishment of peace here in fact depends on their absence, especially the absence of Cleon, the chief undesirable.

Some critics are troubled by the lack of the usual epirrhemes in this parabasis; they see it as another sign of hasty composition.[44] Yet there are good reasons why parabasis epirrhemes are not needed in this play. We have seen how the odes themselves serve a satirical function similar to that usually filled by the epirrhemes; the odes are longer than usual and confine the conventional hymnic invocation to a ring framing the poetic invective (vv. 775–80, 815–18). In addition to satire one of the other main features of parabasis epirrhemes is a collective self-presentation of the chorus' character, usually in conflict with prevailing social and political norms. This is clearly not appropriate in the *Peace*, since its all-embracing panhellenic chorus includes almost by definition everyone and thus lacks a strongly marked identity.[45] Moreover, social disharmony and group-alienation, as expressed by the Acharnians, Wasps, Knights, and even Clouds, does not belong in a play celebrating reconciliation and union of once antagonistic forces. Happily restored to their farms and prewar prosperity (vv. 550–600) the chorus has nothing to complain about and, with the war terminated, has no advice to give the audience. Cassio has argued that the didactic function of the epirrhemes is here supplanted by Hermes' speech explaining the war's origin (vv. 603–48), which features the usual parabatic address to the spectators, lampooning of rascals, blame for the audience, and complaint of mistreatment (on behalf of the goddess Peace).[46] One also finds the conventional choral satire and complaints in the antepirrheme of the second parabasis (vv. 1172–90).

The emphasis on Pheidias' trial in Hermes' speech and the goddess'

43. Cf. Harriott 1986, 127–28; Reckford 1987, 42–43.
44. See, for instance, the remarks of Solomos 1974, 141–42.
45. Cf. Strauss 1966, 152. Indeed the exact identity of this play's chorus has been a matter of considerable scholarly controversy, on which see Appendix 3.
46. Cassio 1982, 23–25, 43–44 (= Cassio 1985, 84–85). Less convincing is the contention of Landfester (1977, 172–75) that the questioning of Trygaeus in vv. 670–705 and 819–41 takes the epirrhemes' place.

subsequent questions about Sophocles and Cratinus[47] (vv. 693–703) prepare us for the coming parabasis by focussing attention on art (including dramatic art) and its serious political significance. Pheidias emerges as a singularly appropriate figure to blame for the war in this play, dominated as it is by a giant statue of Peace.[48] Aristophanes certainly viewed his own activity as something that was just as consequential for matters of war and peace as Pheidias'; he takes great pains to insist on his lack of greed or self-interested motives such as those of which Pheidias was accused.[49] Whereas Pheidias' art (through Pericles) arguably helped to begin the war, Aristophanes' art (in respect to Cleon) helps put an end to it. Of no such value or importance, however, is the trivial work of Aristophanes' comic rivals, ridiculed in vv. 739–48, or of miserable tragedians like Carcinus' family or Melanthius and Morsimus. It should not surprise us that the poets alluded to immediately after the parabasis odes are the flighty and insubstantial dithyrambists whom Trygaeus saw wandering through the air as he descended back to earth from Olympus (vv. 827–31). These nameless poetasters write poetry having absolutely no contact with the substantive world, and are not only inferior to Sophocles and Cratinus, but are at the very opposite extreme from Aristophanes' self-conception as a poet of transcendental earthiness.[50]

The close integration of the parabasis with its surrounding context is also a notable feature of the play's second parabasis.[51] In the preceding scene (vv. 922–1126), continued after the parabasis (in vv. 1191–96), Trygaeus and his slave perform a sacrifice and proceed to enjoy the feast, barring from it the sycophantic oracle monger Hierocles whose exclusion is highlighted by Trygaeus' invitation to the whole audience to join in the feast (vv. 1115–16).[52] With the second parabasis

---

47. Sophocles' imputed greed (vv. 697–99) parallels the comparable charge against Pheidias (cf. Philochorus, *FGrH* 328F121) and the Spartans (vv. 619–25) in this account of the war's origins. Cratinus' drunkenness, like Sophocles' greed, can be seen as another form of self-indulgence; his grief over seeing winejars broken (vv. 702–3) is also paralleled in Hermes' account of the war's beginning (v. 613).

48. On the statue's significance as a central visual presence on the stage throughout most of the play, see Cassio 1985, 41–50.

49. See especially vv. 762–64 on not seeking sexual favors; note also the apparent modesty and reluctance to undertake self-praise in vv. 734–35. Far from being a thief like Pheidias, the poet has the chorus express its fear of thieves (vv. 729–32).

50. On Aristophanes' criticism of contemporary poetry generally in the *Peace*, see Rohdewald 1854, 19–20.

51. Cf. Moulton (1981, 100) and Cassio (1985, 139–40), who see this parabasis as a generalization of Trygaeus' victory and celebration.

52. Several critics have noted the tendency of this play to involve the audience directly in the celebration (cf. Russo 1962, 215; Dover 1972, 134; Cassio 1985, 37–39, 56–57, 126–28, 141–44; Reckford 1987, 25); note also the presentation of Theoria to

(vv. 1127–90) the chorus takes up the theme, and we are given a lyrical evocation of comfortable domestic pleasures—drinking with friends, kissing slave girls, roasting acorns and chick peas in the fireplace, wearing myrtle crowns, dining on thrush, finch, hare and beestings. The epirrheme is constructed as a series of exhortations, including in the feast the chorus' friends and neighbors—Comarchides, Aeschinades, Charinades; even the slaves are told to cease labor today. But the epirrheme's principle of inclusion is converted into a principle of exclusion in the antepirrheme, which describes a wealthy, swaggering colonel who forcibly enlists unwilling farmers while sparing his influential friends in the city. By focussing on an unattractive individual whose very livelihood is war, the antepirrheme prepares us for the following scene with the arms merchants who attempt to take advantage of Trygaeus (vv. 1197–1264). The colonel described here is not unlike the caricature of Lamachus in the *Acharnians,* and it is no surprise that Lamachus' musical son follows the arms merchants in vv. 1265–94.

In the *Peace* Aristophanes experiments with structural variation[53] and close contextual integration of the parabatic form in a way that already foreshadows the plays of his middle period. In this play, with his personal identity now well established before the Athenian public and the chief object of his comic animus (Cleon) removed, Aristophanes pays his old enemy a retrospective tribute of sorts and prepares to enter a new phase in both Athenian history and his own career as a poet.

---

the Council (= the front row of the audience) in vv. 817–98, or the throwing of sacrificial barley to the audience in vv. 960–67. Muecke (1977, 57 n.39) notes the techniques of audience involvement in the play's prologue.

53. In addition to the lack of epirrhemes in the main parabasis, note also the presence of a short pnigos at the end of each epirrheme in the second parabasis.

CHAPTER 8

From Birds to Frogs

The *Clouds* revision, dating to sometime around 417, is the last extant play in which Aristophanes uses the anapests for the purpose of explicit self-defense.[1] Concomitant with the decline of the personalized parabasis is an abandonment of the "autobiographical" thread in the plots and characters of the later plays. We no longer see the protagonist speaking or acting as a symbolic surrogate for the poet or for Comedy in its social function, although the *Frogs* is a partial exception in this regard, inasmuch as one of Dionysus' many functions within that play is as the patron god of Comedy; even in this case, however, Dionysus is not specifically representative of Aristophanes or of Aristophanic comedy.

The later parabases, again with the significant exception of the *Frogs*, tend to be much more closely integrated into the dramatic plot and action of the play. The *Birds* parabasis demonstrates the Birds' full acceptance of their new status as gods; the *Lysistrata* parabasis enacts the conflict between the two semichoruses over the seizure of the Acropolis; and the *Thesmophoriazusae* parabasis defends women against

1. Fr. 590 PCG preserves part of a commentary on a parabasis, including an anapestic section of poetic self-defense apparently from the same general period as the second *Clouds* (c. 417—see Hofmann 1970, 4–5; Luppe 1971, 96). Although Hofmann and Luppe assign this fragment to the *Anagyros*, Gelzer (1972, 149–51) presents cogent arguments against this assignment; however, see the reply of Luppe (1973, 275– 88). Fr. 30 and 31 PCG, from the *Amphiaraus* (firmly dated to the Lenaea of 414—see *Hyp. Aves*) may be from a poetic self-defense in the parabasis proper (see Whittaker 1935, 89–90), but the choriambic meter is identical to that which Eupolis uses in a parabatic epirrheme (fr. 172 PCG). The same is true of fr. 347–48 PCG (from the second *Thesmophoriazusae*); the paeonic tetrameter is almost certainly used in an epirrhematic passage in fr. 110–11 PCG (from the *Farmers*).

the supposed misogynism of men like Euripides, thus paralleling the speeches delivered in the assembly scene. All of the later parabases show a significant degree of structural variation and experimentation, perhaps parallel with a general tendency in Aristophanic comedy of the middle phase to use new forms and arrangements.[2] We have seen this tendency begin already in the *Peace,* which omits the epirrhemes for reasons we have discussed. The *Birds* features a full parabasis and second parabasis, yet there is no sharp division between the contents of the various sections, all being more or less concerned with the chorus' identity and self-manifestation. Similarly the parabasis of the *Thesmophoriazusae,* which has no odes and only a single epirrheme in addition to the anapests and pnigos, is essentially a unity in its function as a choral self-defense. The parabasis of the *Lysistrata* is quite unique in being a double epirrhematic syzygy split between two semichoruses, with the semichorus of Old Men delivering the odes and epirrhemes, the semichorus of Old Women delivering the antodes and antepirrhemes. The effect is deliberately agonistic and parallels the general confrontation between the sexes in the play as a whole. The parabasis of the *Frogs* is a single epirrhematic syzygy, not at all concerned with the chorus' identity, but with political advice to the city on a matter which at first seems rather removed from the overt subject matter of the play as a whole but is actually connected on a more fundamental level, similar to the way the parabases are used in the earlier plays. The chorus' identity is established in the *Frogs'* parodos, which contains a long section of anapestic tetrameters resembling the absent parabasis proper.

Although the connection between the parabasis and dramatic plot is usually more self-evident in these plays than in those of Aristophanes' earlier period, we will find that the parabasis still plays a crucial role in framing the issues of the play in a way that makes contact with the world outside the theater. As such it still plays a central role as a hermeneutic lens through which the poet intends us to view the dramatic spectacle.

Birds, Gods, and Sophists

There are two predominant schools of thought with regard to the *Birds:* (1) that the play is an escapist fantasy whose plot has little or no reference to contemporary events and is significant precisely as

2. Gelzer (1960, 189–90, 255–65) observes a similar development in regard to Aristophanes' use of the epirrhematic agon, which becomes less formalized and more dramatically integrated in the plays of Aristophanes' middle period, again with the partial exception of the *Frogs.*

Aristophanes' retreat from *littérature engagée*,[3] and (2) that the play is designed as a covert reflection on Athens' overreaching ambition and optimism in undertaking the massive Sicilian expedition, which had departed the previous summer and had as yet no clear result.[4] Much can be said for the view that Peisthetaerus' and Euelpides' quest for *apragmosynē* ("non-involvement in affairs"), which inescapably becomes a reassertion of *polypragmosynē* ("meddlesomeness"), echoes Athens' recent history, abandoning the peace of Nicias for a grandiose military adventure far from home.[5] Still, apart from a few scattered allusions,[6] it is difficult to see in this play, taken as a whole, any systematic allegory concerning the Sicilian expedition.

I would propose a third alternative for the overall interpretation of the *Birds,* namely, that we see it as a reaction not to the Sicilian expedition per se but to the other major event in Athenian affairs of 415, the mutilation of the herms and the profanation of the Eleusinian mysteries, with the resulting atmosphere of accusations, prosecutions, and domestic discord, a reality far more vividly present in the public's eye in the spring of 414 than events in faraway Sicily. Sommerstein has recently and, in my opinion, persuasively revived Droysen's thesis that the much-disputed decree of Syracosius prohibited Comedy from directly mentioning by name any of the individuals convicted in either scandal;[7] it does indeed seem curious that such ripe targets for satire as Alcibiades and the other Athenians involved in these acts are never

3. Cf. Mazon 1904, 110; Croiset 1909, 120–31; Norwood 1931, 241; Gelzer 1960, 259; Händel 1962, 317–20; Murray 1964, 135–36, 155–56; Whitman 1964, 169; Dover 1972, 145; Maxwell-Stuart 1973, 401–2; Torrance 1978, 53; Koelb 1984, 61–64.

4. This view received its most developed articulation in the seminal work of Süvern 1835. Not all later proponents accept the detailed allegory proposed by Süvern, but some form of allusion to Sicily is maintained by Goossens (1946, 51–60), Turato (1971–72, 115–18), Arrowsmith (1973, 141), Solomos (1974, 178–79), Dalfen (1975, 282), van Looy (1975, 181–82), Katz (1976, 353–81), Newiger (1983, 53–55), and Konstan (1990, 186–88). For another interpretation of this play as a political allegory, but not directly connected with Sicily, see Harman 1920, 94–95.

5. For the theme of *apragmosynē* and *polypragmosynē* in the *Birds* see vv. 44, 128, 471, 931, 1026, 1424, and with reference to Athens' intervention in Sicily, see Thucydides 6.87.2–3.

6. Nicias is twice alluded to (vv. 363, 640), as is the messenger ship *Salaminia* (vv. 147, 1203), which summoned Alcibiades back from Sicily to stand trial. Katz (1976, 353–63) argues that the three gods sent to negotiate with Peisthetaerus in vv. 1565–1693 are meant as an allusion to the indecisive troika of generals sent to Sicily in 415; this may be correct, although I am skeptical of his attempt to identify each of the three gods with one of the generals.

7. Sommerstein 1986, 104–5, and Droysen 1836, 59–60. Their arguments are strongly supported by Henderson (1990, 288–90), who cites parallel cases of specific restrictions on comic targets. The only real evidence ΣAv. 1297 presents concerning the decree is Phrynichus, fr. 27 PCG, which merely says the comic poets are prevented from attacking those whom they most wanted to attack; presumably the decree's purpose was to condemn the perpetrators to oblivion.

mentioned in the 1765 lines of the *Birds,* though many other Athenians guilty of far less grievous offenses are ridiculed by name. But as we have seen before in Aristophanes' struggle with Cleon and as we have seen in our own century with many artists from Eastern-bloc countries, nothing focuses creative energies so much as official attempts to stifle them. Syracosius' decree had the effect of merely encouraging the comic poets to seek more creative and indirect ways of criticizing the forbidden targets. It seems that the winning play at this competition, Ameipsias' *Revellers,* may have been directed at the political clubs (ἑταιρίαι) thought to be responsible for the sacrileges.[8] There are good reasons for regarding the *Birds* as also directed against them, albeit in a different way.

While there is some scholarly dispute over the exact form of the protagonist's name (Peisthetaerus, Peisetaerus, Peithetaerus, Pisthetaerus),[9] it is fairly clear that the prefix has to do with "persuasion," and the root -ἑταῖρος with the ἑταιρίαι.[10] As is appropriate, Peisthetaerus is accompanied on his quest by a ἑταῖρος or "fellow club member," Euelpides, whose name means "good hope." They explain to the audience that they are fleeing Athens not out of dislike for the city but because of the excessive litigation and legal prosecutions now current there (vv. 33–45); they wish to find a τόπον ἀπράγμονα (v. 44 "place uninvolved in affairs") and are now seeking the hoopoe Tereus to ask him if he has ever seen such a city. A good many prominent Athenians had recently undergone the same experience as Peisthetaerus and Euelpides, going into self-imposed exile to escape prosecution in connection with the sacrileges;[11] presumably they too sought refuge in appropriate τόποι ἀπράγμονες. It may be more than chance that this play features choral odes lampooning two of the most notable prosecutors in the sacrilege trials, Cleonymus (vv. 1470–81) and Peisander (vv. 1553–64).[12] Indeed, our two city founders here insist on settling somewhere beyond the reach of the *Salaminia* (vv. 145–47; cf. 1203), the messenger trireme that recalled Alcibiades and other accused men from Sicily.

8. See Droysen 1836, 60–61.

9. The first of these alternatives is that found in the MSS and the one which I shall use, although without strong conviction of its correctness.

10. Cf. Harman 1920, 87, and on the *peis* prefix, Dobrov 1988b, 98–103. Reckford (1987, 333) thinks the name alludes to Peisistratus, as is appropriate, considering Peisthetaerus' emergence at the end of the play as a "tyrant" (v. 1708) over the Birds.

11. See Andocides 1.15, 1.44, 1.49, 1.52, 1.55, 1.59. For the identification of Peisthetaerus and Euelpides with such exiles, see Croiset 1909, 121–22.

12. See Andocides 1.27, 1.36, 1.43. The allusions to sycophancy in the scenes surrounding the Cleonymus ode (vv. 1410–69, 1494–1552) as well as the allusion to it in the ode itself (v. 1479) clearly relate to the atmosphere created by these prosecutions. Note also the Decree seller's threat to denounce Peisthetaerus for defiling a stele in v. 1054.

But more important than these specific allusions is the play's overall emphasis on man's relation to religion and the gods. Significantly Peisthetaerus and Euelpides announce that they search for their τόπον ἀπράγμονα carrying a ritual basket, fire pot, and myrtle wreaths (v. 43), so as to make the proper sacrifice when founding their new city.[13] Peisthetaerus indeed uses these implements in sacrificing to the gods later in the play (vv. 848–903); we see the necessity for religion to play a fundamental role in forming and unifying any city. However, it is also significant that the gods to whom sacrifice is made are not by any means the traditional gods of Athenian state religion, but "new gods" (v. 848), not unlike the "new gods" whom Socrates is accused of worshipping (*Nub.* 247–74; Plato, *Ap.* 24B, 26B). The *Birds* as a whole dramatizes not only the abandonment of Athenian democracy, but also the overthrow of the city's traditional religion and piety in favor of a new, artificially constructed system influenced by the radical subjectivism of sophistic teachings. Presuming to create a new democracy in the interests of the Birds (see vv. 1583–85), Peisthetaerus in fact creates a new tyranny (see vv. 1673, 1708) in which he himself holds absolute Basileia ("Sovereignty") and becomes the "highest of the gods" (v. 1765 δαιμόνων ὑπέρτατε), the final words of the play. As was widely suspected in the case of those responsible for the sacrileges of 415, the undermining of traditional religious institutions is a prelude to subversion of the political order.[14] The *Birds* illustrates in comically exaggerated form the ultimate consequences we could expect from the actions of the impious—the overthrow of Zeus and the elevation to divinity of anything the individual thinker desires, including tiny birds and even the thinker himself.

Aristophanes uses the *Birds* to explore the consequences as well as the causes of such impiety. The loss of respect for the city's most hallowed institutions was attributed by many to the contemporary influence of the sophists and their teaching, patronized particularly by the upper classes of Athenian society.[15] The *Birds* makes direct reference to a wide range of contemporary thinkers whose influence was

---

13. This is the interpretation of Σ*Av.* 43. I do not agree with Hamilton (1985, 235–39) in seeing these implements as sympotic, which is irrelevant to the context, or in believing that vv. 47–48 proves that Peisthetaerus and Euelpides expect to join an existing city rather than found a new one: v. 48 in fact expresses doubt of any *apragmon* city currently existing.

14. See Thucydides 6.27.3, 6.28.2, 6.61.1–4. While most modern historians reject the existence of any plot to overthrow the democracy at this time, the political leanings of the *hetairiai* responsible were certainly oligarchic; see Aurenche 1974, 89–101; Kagan 1981, 205–9; Ostwald 1986, 329–30, 549–50.

15. On the connections between sophistic teaching and the profanations, see Guthrie 1969 III, 245; Kagan 1981, 205–9; Ostwald 1986, 324–30.

seen in one way or another as atheistic, such as Prodicus, Diagoras of
Melos, Socrates and Chaerephon, Gorgias and Philip, the astronomer
Meton, the dithyrambist Cinesias.[16] The very name of Peisthetaerus'
new city, "Cloudcuckooland" (v. 819 Νεφελοκοκκυγία), evokes Aristophanes' other famous play attacking contemporary intellectuals, the
Clouds (Νεφέλαι), as is clear from Tereus' line deriving the name "from
the clouds and midair (μετεώρων) places" (v. 818).[17] The recent actions
of Alcibiades, Critias, and others seem to have realized Aristophanes'
worst fears about the potential effects of Socrates' and others' teachings.[18] Thus Aristophanes' return to many of the *Clouds*' themes is
entirely understandable, only here with the ethereal Birds in the place
of the ethereal Clouds as the new gods and the hero Peisthetaerus in
the place of Socrates as the master sophist who reveals their divinity.
But whereas Socrates and the *bomolochos* Strepsiades were ultimately
working at cross-purposes leading to failure for both in the *Clouds*,
Peisthetaerus is himself the unquestioned protagonist in the *Birds*,
accompanied by the naive and gullible *bomolochos* Euelpides; what we
see is Peisthetaerus experiencing the ultimate triumph of a sophistic
will to power which the miserable Socrates and Strepsiades could only
dream of.

The identification of Peisthetaerus, "the persuader of aristocratic
companions/club-men," with the doctrines and techniques of the sophists seems quite clear. He is presented to the Birds as a subtle speaker (v.
318 λεπτὼ λογιστά), an "old man of new ideas" (vv. 255–57 πρέσβυς
καινὸς γνώμην . . .) from "wise" (v. 409 σοφῆς) Greece and is congratulated with the epithet *sophos* in numerous passages.[19] The Birds, pre-

16. The Clouds' condemnation of Meton's calendar reform (*Nub.* 607–26) suggests
that Aristophanes regarded it along with Socrates' speculations as something contrary to
Athenian religious tradition. On Cinesias' impiety, see Strattis, fr. 18 PCG; Athenaeus
12.551a (citing Lysias); Pickard-Cambridge 1962, 44–45; Dodds 1951, 188–89; Woodbury 1965, 210; Turato 1971–72, 127–31. Andocides 1.35, 1.63, and ΣAv. 766 tell us his
father Meletus was one of the violators of both the herms and the Mysteries.

17. For interest in the μετέωρα as a leitmotif in the *Clouds* symbolizing atheistic
naturalism see *Nub.* 228, 264–66, 333, 360, 404–7, 489–90, 1283–84. On the term and
its significance in both plays, see Newiger 1957, 55–56. For the general relation between
the *Clouds* and *Birds,* see the detailed discussion of Gelzer 1956, 79–82.

18. That Socrates' influence in fact was blamed for the actions of Alcibiades and
Critias is recorded by Xenophon, *Mem.* 1.2.12; Xenophon spends considerable effort in
exculpating Socrates from any responsibility for their actions. See also Aeschines' defense of Socrates' condemnation (1.173), which suggests that Critias and his followers are
what Socrates' accusers had in mind when charging the philosopher with "corrupting the
youth." The essentially antidemocratic character of Socrates' teachings and followers has
recently been highlighted by Stone (1988).

19. See vv. 362–63, 427–31, 1271–75, 1401. On Peisthetaerus' sophistic character,
see Süvern 1835, 33–34, and Gelzer 1956, 80. Like any clever rhetorician Peisthetaerus
also criticizes his opponents for being "sophists" (vv. 1619, 1646). It is significant that the

viously "unlearned" (v. 471 ἀμαθής), address Peisthetaerus as their teacher (v. 548) and come to rely upon him for guidance in fulfilling the desire for power he has awakened in them (vv. 539–49). Like the sophists his teaching proceeds by *epideixis* (v. 483), exemplary demonstration.[20] Tereus had taught the Birds the rudiments of human language (vv. 199–200) and encouraged them to learn more refined arts from the two human visitors; although they belong to an enemy race, enemies can also teach valuable lessons, as in warfare (vv. 371–82). As with Protagoras, Prodicus, and other sophists,[21] Peisthetaerus is especially concerned to teach the Birds about the origins of civilization, when the cock was first king of the Persians (vv. 481–85) and the kite ruled over the Greeks (vv. 499–501). Peisthetaerus explains human belief in the gods as a function of *nomos* or "convention," rather than as anything rooted in nature; the ultimate relativity and reversibility of human values is demonstrated by men once having regarded the Birds as gods and now seeing them merely as animals and pests (vv. 520–38). But this arbitrary belief can just as easily be changed back into reverence for the Birds as gods and rejection of the Olympians (vv. 561–87). Even as health and sickness are not absolutes but only states of perception in which a man either "fares well" (v. 604 ἢν εὖ πράττωσ') or "fares ill" (v. 605 κακῶς πράττων),[22] the gods are whatever men at any historical moment consider to be gods. Peisthetaerus' teaching of the Birds covers the full range of sophistic concerns: the theory of culture and religion, nature and convention, language, the relativism of perceptions.

The sophistic issues are highlighted in the parabasis; this exposure gives the Birds the opportunity to appropriate and extend Peisthetaerus' teachings in the agon. Like Pheidippides in the *Clouds* the Birds show themselves to be fast learners; ignorant of their own divinity only a little while earlier, they are now able to produce a detailed cosmogony and theogony to challenge Hesiod, the Orphics, and Prodicus. The

---

Birds uses the terms *sophos* and *kainos* more than any other play of Aristophanes except the *Clouds;* cf. Moulton 1981, 35.

20. On the sophistic method of *epideixis*, see Guthrie 1969 III, 41–44, and Kerferd 1981, 28–29.

21. Sophistic and pre-Socratic interest in the origins of civilization can be inferred from the accounts in Plato, *Prot.* 320C–323C, Diodorus Sic. 1.8.1–7, and the *Sisyphus* fragment often attributed to Critias (= 88B25 DK). See Havelock 1957, 104–24; Reinhardt 1960, 114–32; Cole 1967, 1–147; Guthrie 1969 III, 60–68; Kerferd 1981, 140–42. For the influence of these theories on the *Birds*, see de Carli 1971, 50–54.

22. For Protagoras' doctrine concerning the relative truth of all such quality perceptions, see Kerferd 1981, 83–100. The connection of inner health with external well-being is implied in the concept of πλουθυγιεία (v. 731).

extemporaneous nature of this protohistory travesties the entire genre
of speculation about the origins of man and the cosmos:

> O dear, shrill,
> Dearest of all birds,
> Fellow of my songs,
> Nightingale brought up with me,
> You've come, you've come, you've been seen;   680
> Bringing to me your sweet voice
> Now playing the fair-toned
> Flute with your springtime voice,
>   Begin the anapests.

Come, you men of dim lives by nature, like to the race of leaves,   685
Little accomplishing, castings of mud, shadowy-formed strengthless
        tribes,
Wingless, ephemeral, wretched, mortal, dreamlike men,
Hold your attention to us, the ever-being immortals,
Ethereal, unaging, caring for imperishable things.
Then, hearing correctly from us everything about heavenly affairs,   690
And knowing correctly the nature of birds, the birth of gods, rivers,
        Darkness and Chaos,
You can tell Prodicus for me that he should go off and weep forever
        more!
First there was Chaos and Night, black Darkness and broad
        Tartarus,
And there was no earth nor air nor heaven. But in the boundless
        folds of Darkness
Black-eyed Night first begets a wind-egg,   695
From which longed-for Eros grew with the revolving seasons,
Glittering with two golden wings on his back, like wind-swift eddies.
Mingling with winged Chaos at night in broad Tartarus,
He hatched our race, and first brought us to light.
There was up to now no race of immortals, until Eros mingled all
        things together;   700
When some things mingled with others, Heaven, Ocean, and Earth
Were born, and the imperishable race of all the blessed gods. Thus,
        we are
By far the oldest of all the blessed ones. That we are children of
        Eros
Is clear by many signs: we fly and are present with those in love.
On account of our strength lovers have at the end of their youth   705
Penetrated the thighs of many pretty boys who once said no,
One giving a quail, another a purple gallinule, another a goose,
        another a Persian cock.
Mortals have all their greatest benefits from us Birds.
First, we show them the seasons of Spring, Winter, and Fall—

Time to sow, when the croaking crane crosses over to Libya;   710
Time for the shipowner to hang up his rudder and sleep,
And then for Orestes to weave an overcoat, so that he doesn't have
        to steal one when cold.
But after this, the kite signals another season, when he appears—
When it is time to comb out the flocks' springtime fleece. Then the
        swallow shows,
When it is right to sell one's overcoat and buy a lighter robe.   715
For you, we are Ammon, Delphi, Dodona, and Phoebus Apollo.
It is only after coming to the Birds that you turn to all affairs,
To a business-trip, to earning a living, to a man's marriage.
And you consider a "bird" everything which you examine for
        prophecy:
An utterance is a "bird" to you, you call a sneeze a "bird,"   720
An encounter a "bird," a voice a "bird," a servant a "bird," an ass a
        "bird."
Aren't we clearly the prophet Apollo for you?
        Therefore, if you consider us gods,
        You will have for your use prophets, Muses,
        Breezes, seasons, winter, summer,   725
        Moderate heat. We will not run away
        And sit among the clouds
        Puffing ourselves up like Zeus;
        But being present here, we shall give to you
        Yourselves, your children, and children's children   730
            Health and wealth,
        Happiness, life, peace,
        Youth, laughter, choral dances, banquets,
        And birds' milk—with the result that
        You can be exhausted with all the good things.   735
            So you will all be wealthy.

(vv. 676–736)

The close integration of this parabasis with the dramatic context is
apparent. The Birds' history of their origins fleshes out Peisthetaerus'
argument about their antiquity relative to the gods (vv. 465–78; cf. vv.
702–3) with an elaborate revisionist cosmogony in the style of the
Orphics.[23] Just as human beings imagine the gods in anthropomor-
phic terms the Birds see their original forebears as winged and aerial
creatures, "blackwinged Night" (v. 695), "wind-egg" (v. 695), "Eros,
glittering with two golden wings on his back, like windswift eddies" (vv.

23. For Orphic influence here, especially with respect to the cosmic egg and birth of
Eros, see Pollard 1948, 374–75; Hofmann 1976, 184–85, 190 n.1; West 1983, 111–12,
201; Zannini Quirini 1987, 134–45. Of course, the basic starting point of this cosmogony, as of all Greek cosmogonies, is Hesiod.

696–97), "winged Chaos" (v. 698). Of course, the whole genealogy is impossible, since the "wind-egg" from which Eros is born is by definition a sterile, unfertilized egg[24] unable to give birth to anything. The Birds themselves are born from the union of Eros and Chaos (= "gap," "yawn," "void") taking place in the depths of Tartarus, the place of death; such an origin explains their lightness and lack of substance, indeed, their unreality. The rest of the universe, however, is born in a more conventional way, "when some things mingled with others" (vv. 701–2). The notion of Eros "mingling all things together" (v. 700) is distinctly Empedoclean in nature, even as the picture of "boundless ($\dot{\alpha}\pi\epsilon\acute{\iota}\rho o\sigma\iota$) folds of Darkness" reminds us of Anaximander's *apeiron*.[25] This whole scheme is itself a skillful fusion of Hesiod's *Theogony*, Orphism, pre-Socratic cosmogony, and sheer nonsense.

One thinker is designated by name in this passage, the sophist Prodicus (v. 692). It has been noted that the repetition of the adverb "correctly" ($\dot{o}\rho\theta\hat{\omega}\varsigma$) in vv. 690 and 692, where it is the word immediately before Prodicus' name, alludes to Prodicus' doctrine of "correctness" in language ($\dot{o}\rho\theta\acute{o}\tau\eta\varsigma$ or $\dot{o}\rho\theta o\epsilon\pi\epsilon\acute{\iota}\alpha$).[26] These allusions are more than simply passing references to his supposed "atheism."[27] Aristophanes may have seen something in common between such popular quack religions as Orphism and the "atheistic" teachings of the sophists, for in different ways both had the effect of denying traditional beliefs and undermining the city's established religious institutions.[28] Prodicus' doctrines on the origin of religion are in fact quite relevant to the Birds' claim to being the original divinities. Prodicus claimed that men first regarded as gods those things in the perceptible world that benefited and nourished them—the Sun, Moon, rivers, lakes, the four elements, bread, wine—and that these elements later came to be identified as the

24. See Whitman 1964, 184; Hofmann 1976, 191–92. In this case it cannot be an egg fertilized by wind, since air has not yet been created; or if this is the meaning, then the whole process is still impossible, since there is no wind to fertilize.

25. For Empedocles, see 31B17.7, B20.1–3, B21.8–14, B22.1–5, B26.3–5, B35 D–K, on the elements coming together to form things through the force of *Philotēs*. For Anaximander's *apeiron*, see 12B1 D–K and the discussions of Guthrie 1962 I, 83–87, and Kahn 1960, 231–39.

26. See Hofmann 1976, 181. Nestle (1936, 162) also notes that the repetition of $\dot{\omega}\rho\alpha$ (vv. 696, 705, 709, 714, 725) and the emphasis on the Birds' role as seasonal signs in vv. 709–15 may allude to the title of Prodicus' treatise (Ὧραι).

27. Henrichs (1976, 21) suggests that Prodicus was not, strictly speaking, seen as an atheist by his contemporaries, because he at least granted some of the gods a past human existence.

28. For the harmful effects of merchandising religion among the public, see Plato, *Rep.* II 364B–365A. Note the contempt with which oracle sellers are treated, both here in vv. 959–91 and in *Pax* 1052–1126 (cf. *Eq.* 997–1110).

Olympian gods.[29] Indeed, the Birds' chief argument here for their divinity is precisely their usefulness to men, as love gifts (vv. 703–7), seasonal indicators (vv. 709–15), prophetic signs (vv. 716–22), musicians (vv. 723–26), general givers of bounty (vv. 727–36). This theme has also been adumbrated in Peisthetaerus' discourse to the Birds emphasizing their usefulness to men, particularly in agriculture (vv. 586–91) and prophecy (vv. 592–626). And it is taken up again in the second parabasis, especially vv. 1058–70 on agriculture and vv. 1102–13 on other benefits. Soon after the parabasis we discover the Olympian gods to be themselves identified with different species of birds (vv. 863–88), apparently giving further demonstration to Prodicus' doctrine that worship of the Olympians evolved from primeval worship of natural elements and forces.[30] The echo of the *Prometheus Bound* at the beginning of the parabasis (vv. 686–87 "little accomplishing . . . ephemeral . . . dreamlike men"; cf. *PV* 547–49)[31] has put us into a context of viewing the human race in its helpless infancy, dependent on outside help, whether by gods or by birds; it therefore should not surprise us that the parabasis proceeds to encompass Prodicean anthropology as well as Orphic cosmogony.

By emphasizing the Birds' identity as Muses (v. 724) and their ability to give "youth, laughter, choral dances, banquets" (v. 733), the pnigos prepares for the choral performance and display of the parabasis odes. These also emphasize the Birds' connection with the Muses (vv. 737–39, 782) and Graces (v. 781) and show them actively celebrating gods such as Pan, Cybele, and Apollo:

> O Muse of the thicket,
> Tio tio tio tio tio tio tiotinx,
>   Intricate Muse, with whom I
> Among the mountain dells and ridges,   740
>   Tio tio tio tiotinx,
> Sitting on the leafy-headed ash-tree,
> Tio tio tio tiotinx,
> Through my shrill throat display
> The sacred laws of melody to Pan   745
> And holy dances to the Mountain Mother,

29. See Prodicus, 84B5 D–K, and Nestle 1936, 160–63; Untersteiner 1954, 209–11; Guthrie 1969 III, 238–42; Kerferd 1981, 169.

30. The identification of the Olympians with bird species has also been made by Peisthetaerus in vv. 514–19.

31. For the allusion, cf. Herington 1963, 237–38; Rau 1967, 176–77; Hofmann 1976, 179–80.

Totototototototototinx.
Thence, just like a bee,
Phrynichus always fed on the fruit of ambrosial melodies,
        Bearing away his sweet song.   750
        Tio tio tio tiotinx.
O spectators, if one of you wishes to spend the rest of his life
Happily, along with the Birds, let him come to us.
As many things as are constrained by custom out there, called
        "shameful,"
These are all noble among us Birds.   755
If out there it is by custom shameful to strike one's father,
It is noble among us, if anyone runs up to his father
And strikes him, saying, "Raise your spur, if you fight."
If anyone of you happens to be a branded runaway,   760
He will be called a dappled attagen among us.
If anyone happens to be a Phrygian no less than Spintharus,
He will here be a finch (*phrygilos*), of the race of Philemon.
If he is a slave and a Carian like Execestides,
Let him grow ancestors among us, and his clansmen are revealed.   765
If the son of Peisias wishes to betray the gates to those in disgrace,
Let him become a partridge, chick of his father,
Since among us, it is not shameful to escape like a partridge.

        Such as this the swans,
        Tio tio tio tio tio tio tiotinx,   770
            Sending forth a commingled voice,
        Rustling with their wings, called out "Apollo,"
            Tio tio tio tiotinx,
        Sitting on a slope by the river Hebrus.
            Tio tio tio tiotinx,   775
        Through the ethereal clouds came the cry.
        The varied races of beasts cowered,
        And the windless clear sky extinguished the waves,
        Totototototototototinx.
        All Olympus thundered,   780
And amazement took hold of the lordly gods; the Olympian Graces
        And Muses raised up their triumphant song.
            Tio tio tio tiotinx.
There is nothing better or sweeter than to grow wings.   785
If anyone of you spectators suddenly became winged,
And then, being hungry, was bored by the tragic choruses,
Flying away, he would go home and take his meal,
And then, being full, would fly back to us again.
If any Patrocleides among you happens to need a shit,   790
He wouldn't foul his garment, but would fly up,
Fart off, take a breather, and then fly back again.

> If there is anyone of you who happens to be committing adultery,
> And then sees the woman's husband in the front-row Council-seats,
> He again would fly up, taking wing away from you,   795
> Would then screw, and from that place fly back again.
> Isn't it worth anything to become winged?
> See how Dieitrephes, having only wicker-flask wings,
> Was elected phylarch, then hipparch, then coming up from nothing
> Undertakes great affairs of state, and is now a shrill-voiced
>   horsecock.   800
>   (vv. 737–800)

The force of the Birds' music as described in the antode seems almost more powerful than the gods themselves, calming the beasts and waters (vv. 776–78) and shaking Olympus (vv. 780–81). The significance of the allusion to Phrynichus in the ode (vv. 748–50) is not altogether clear. Kakridis argued that the odes are a cento of citations from a bird *hyporchema* of Phrynichus,[32] but the evidence is insufficient to conclude that such a poem ever existed. Other critics[33] may be correct in interpreting the allusion as designed to evoke a style of poetry like Phrynichus', soft, sensual, and Ionian, in keeping with the allusion to the oriental Mountain Mother (vv. 745–46), or later to Phrygians and Carians (vv. 762–65).

In the epirrhemes the Birds offer the audience a world with complete latitude and freedom for self-indulgence of every kind. Whereas the anapests focussed on cosmogony and the evolution of religious beliefs, the epirrhemes explore sophistic anthropology further with the opposition between *nomos* and *physis*, "convention" and "nature."[34] The epirrheme insists upon the distinction between *aischron* (vv. 755, 757, 768 "shameful") and *kalon* (vv. 756, 758 "noble") being purely a matter of *nomos* (vv. 755, 757); everything "shameful" among men is "noble" among the Birds and hence not restrained or forbidden (vv. 755–56). In what appears to be a direct intertextual echo of the *Clouds*,[35] the Birds tell us that even father-beating is noble among them, however dishonorable it may be among men in general. Similarly Athenian anxieties about racial purity and citizenship are shown

32. Kakridis 1970, 48–51.

33. Cf. Giner and de Hoz (1979, 114–16) relying on Aristophanes' characterization of Phrynichus' style in *Vesp.* 219–20.

34. For this opposition in Aristophanes, see p. 124 above and the references therein. With regard to the *Birds* specifically, see de Carli 1971, 49–53, and Konstan 1990, 189–203.

35. Pheidippides' father beating (*Nub.* 1321–1446) is the climactic turning point of that play, in which Strepsiades sees his whole enterprise turn to his own disadvantage. Significantly Pheidippides also evokes the example of cocks striking their fathers to demonstrate the relativity of *nomoi* (*Nub.* 1421–29).

to be only a matter of convention; the Birds welcome to their new city even the lowest Phrygian or Carian slaves like Spintharus or Execestides (vv. 762–65).[36] They will open their city up to the *atimoi* (vv. 766–68), those recently in exile from Athens for the sacrileges of 415. Peisthetaerus and Euelpides are themselves such *atimoi,* as we have seen, and the founding of their new city is itself an act of impiety toward the traditional gods.

In contrast to the epirrheme's emphasis on matters of *nomos* the antepirrheme lists the various ways in which the spectators would be free to satisfy the demands of their *physis* if they had wings.[37] Our attention shifts from political liberty to personal liberty. Bodily needs for food (vv. 786–89), excretion (vv. 790–92), and sex (vv. 793–96) can be fulfilled at will and without inhibition. The verbal parallelism implies the equivalence of all these bodily processes; even if sex takes the form of adultery, with an important man's wife no less, it is just as natural and acceptable in this context as eating and defecating.[38] By satisfying his need for drink with "winged wicker wine flasks," Dieitrephes is elevated to the posts of phylarch, hipparch, and "horse-cock" (vv. 798–800); the ascent to ultimate political power through self-indulgence foreshadows Peisthetaerus' acquisition of power by marrying Basileia. This antepirrheme presents a fantasy world of total wish fulfillment, not unlike the one imagined by Peisthetaerus and Euelpides at the beginning of their adventure (vv. 127–42), where friends share only their happy moments and not their times of need, and where fathers willingly offer their sons as *paidika.* Significantly wings allow men to leave Tragedy behind (v. 787), and with it all care, grief, and social restraint.

The epirrheme's theme of citizenship and the antepirrheme's enumerated advantages of wings together serve as effective introductions to the play's second half, which exhibits a long series of foreign visitors attempting to profit from the Birds' new city.[39] Peisthetaerus even has

36. The citizenship question, particularly with regard to Execestides, appears to be a topical leitmotif in this play; cf. vv. 11, 30–35, 1527.

37. For the concept of *physis anangkaia* articulated here, cf. *Nub.* 1075–78 (in connection with the Lesser Discourse's justification of adultery), Thucydides 5.105.2 (in connection with the Melian dialogue), Democritus, 68B278 D–K (in connection with the sexual drive), and the comments of Heinimann 1945, 167–68; Guthrie 1969 III, 99–101; Turato 1971–72, 123–24.

38. Concerning the sequence of verbal parallelisms which tend to equate these three acts, see the analysis of Giner and de Hoz 1979, 126–27. On the importance of the erotic element in this play, see Arrowsmith 1973, 130–41, and Paduano 1973, 120–21.

39. See the remarks of Paduano 1973, 125–27. And as Dobrov (1988b, 168) notes, the antepirrheme, with its final image of Dieitrephes transformed into a "shrill-voiced horsecock," leads directly into Peisthetaerus' and Euelpides' reentry onstage in bird form.

loads of feathers brought onstage to equip the new immigrants with wings (vv. 1305–36). Despite the parabasis' open invitation to new settlers of every sort, however, Peisthetaerus actually admits no one to his city. We can certainly understand his rejection of the first group that comes to him; the oracle seller, the urban planner Meton, the Athenian inspector, and the sycophantic decree seller are all characters who try to impose external laws and restrictions of one sort or another on the new city, thus annihilating its freedom from restrictions.[40] None of these are really interested in becoming part of Cloudcuckooland. Even the Pindaric poet, who is treated rather sympathetically by Peisthetaerus, comes as an itinerant seeking monetary profit from his ready-made encomiastic poetry; only moments after the foundation of Cloudcuckooland (see vv. 917–23) he is already celebrating it in terms identical with those in which he celebrates every other city. Hence his poetic *nomos* is as constricting and foreign as the legal, architectural, and religious *nomoi* of the other parasites.

On the other hand the second group of visitors (the young man, Cinesias, and the sycophant) are all people who desire to live in Cloudcuckooland permanently, precisely because of its freedom and lack of conventional Hellenic *nomoi*.[41] But Peisthetaerus rejects them too, sending the young man off to military service, insulting Cinesias, and beating the sycophant. The rejection of the young man who wishes to strangle his father and inherit a fortune (vv. 1351–52) strikes us as particularly strange after the parabasis' specific evocation of father beating as the primary example of what is permitted in bird *nomos* but not in human *nomos* (vv. 757–59), alluded to here by the young man's reference to the desirability of bird *nomoi* (v. 1345). Peisthetaerus gives the young man some "fatherly" advice not to beat his father and instead provides him with wings to undertake a more patriotic and socially useful way of releasing his aggressive energy—by military service in Thrace (vv. 1360–69). In like manner he tries to use Cinesias in training tribal choruses (vv. 1405–7) and with his "noble words" attempts to turn the sycophant toward "lawful work" (v. 1450 ἔργον νόμιμον).

Some critics interpret this anomaly between the programmatic invi-

---

40. See Turato 1971–72, 124–25; Reckford 1987, 337.

41. Turato (1971–72, 132–33) sees the three newcomers here as violators of each of the three fundamental "unwritten laws" of Greek culture: respectively, (1) honoring parents, (2) worshiping the gods, and (3) obeying the laws. I would note, however, that although Cinesias' well-known impiety was probably part of the reason for his inclusion here, it is not emphasized in the context so much as his free dithyrambic verse which violates all traditional poetic nomoi; that Aristophanes saw a connection between poetic style and general moral principles is demonstrated by the agon in the *Frogs*. See especially p. 212–13 below.

tation of the parabasis and Peisthetaerus' actual practice as evidence of the hero's recognition that law is a necessary and integral part of any organized society. Some have even seen Cloudcuckooland as a utopian "just society,"[42] although we are dealing with at least two mutually contradictory versions of Utopia here. We should be more suspicious of Peisthetaerus' motives, in view of his subsequent manipulation of the Bird state to his own advantage, eating dissident Birds and even at the end establishing himself as a "tyrant" (v. 1708) with absolute Sovereignty (*Basileia*) over them.[43] He may not be defending the claims of morality here so much as using them to consolidate his own social control over Cloudcuckooland. At this point in the play even his old friend Euelpides has disappeared;[44] Peisthetaerus' ideological fervor is no longer undercut by the lightness of his friend's humor, and the new Bird city emerges more and more as the private fiefdom of one man. The parricide, dithyrambist, and sycophant introduce potentially disorderly and subversive influences into his ideal state which, unless channeled into appropriate activities, could threaten his power even more than the foreign parasites whom he had rejected before. Indeed, Peisthetaerus is himself identified as an "old man" (vv. 255, 320, 337) and establishes his position with the Birds by using arguments appealing to the patriarchal authority of antiquity and ancestors (vv. 472–75; cf. vv. 540–43). It is thus not surprising that he resists the young man's antipatriarchal iconoclasm. Master sophist that he is, Peisthetaerus is able to come up with a counterargument to any contention and can cite another bird *nomos,* that of the stork's obligation to nurture its father (vv. 1353–57), to counter the bird *nomos* on which the young man relies.[45] As Peisthetaerus says, "there are many bird laws" (v. 1346 πολλοὶ γὰρ ὀρνίθων νόμοι); the sophistic concept of legal relativism is most convenient, since it allows him to find support in the body of bird *nomoi* for any position he wishes to take.

The sophistic theory of *nomos* may seem to liberate individuals from any moral obligation to obey absolute *nomoi;* by the same token it also liberates unscrupulous rulers to impose any *nomoi* which they find to be

42. For the former view see Turato 1971–72, 141–43; for the latter see Gigante 1948, 21–23; Reckford 1987, 334–35, 340; Zannini Quirini 1987, 86–87.

43. The eating of the Birds is done in the name of preserving democracy (vv. 1583–85), as the Olympians are overthrown in the name of restoring the Birds to supremacy (vv. 549–50). On Peisthetaerus' demagogic use of popular ideals for selfish purposes, cf. Strauss 1966, 185–87; Solomos 1974, 176; Dalfen 1975, 277–78.

44. Strauss (1966, 173–74) has rightly emphasized the importance of Euelpides' disappearance as a turning point in the plot's development.

45. This patriarchal bird *nomos* has already been adumbrated in vv. 472–75. For the general reestablishment of patriarchal authority here, with new gods merely taking the place of the old, see Paduano 1973, 129–31.

in their self-interest. The dream of absolute personal freedom from *nomos* which the Birds offer in the parabasis is dissolved into rule by arbitrary and capricious application of *nomos,* just as the prologue's dream of a τόπον ἀπράγμονα (v. 44) turns into its exact opposite.[46] Even so, our own century has witnessed many hopeful revolutions of social liberation transform themselves into the most oppressive forms of despotism and totalitarianism. The Birds' Utopian just society is revealed to be a negative anti-Utopia comparable to those of George Orwell or Aldous Huxley.

In the second parabasis these issues of law, nature, and freedom are also explored with direct contextual relevance.

Now all mortals will sacrifice
With votive prayers
To me, seeing all and ruling all.   1060
For I look upon the entire earth,
And I preserve bounteous harvests
By killing the offspring of many-tribed
Beasts, all of those which
With all-devouring jaws consume the fruit swelling from the
    bud
Both on the ground and sitting in trees.   1066
  I kill those who destroy fragrant gardens
  With their most-hated depradations;
Both creeping and biting things, as many as there are,
Are all destroyed in slaughter beneath my wing.   1070
On this day, indeed, proclamation is made,
If anyone of you kills Diagoras the Melian,
He receives a talent, and if anyone kills
One of the dead tyrants, he receives a talent.   1075
Even we now wish to proclaim here the same kind of thing.
If anyone of you kills Philocrates the Sparrow-man,
He will receive a talent, and if he brings him in alive, four talents,
Because he sells finches seven to the obol, stringing them together,
He exhibits and tortures thrushes by blowing them full of air,   1080
He stuffs feathers through the noses of blackbirds,
And collecting pigeons together in confinement,
He forces them to act as decoys, bound in the net.
These things we wish to proclaim. And if someone of you raises
    birds
Enclosed in his courtyard, we bid you to release them.   1085
And if you don't obey, collected together by the Birds,
You in turn will act as decoys for us, confined in our chains.

46. For an interesting Freudian explanation of the inversion, see Paduano 1973, 141.

> Happy tribes of winged
> Birds, who in winter
> Need not wrap up in cloaks!   1090
> Nor in summer, does the warm
> Far-shining sunbeam make us hot.
> But I dwell in the folds
> Of flowery meadows and leaves,
> When the godlike cicada cries out its sharp song,   1095
> Sun-mad with the noontime heat.
> And I winter in the hollow caves
> Playing with the mountain nymphs;
> And we feed on the springtime maidenly
> White myrtle-berries and garden-flowers of the Graces.   1100
> We wish to say something to the judges concerning victory—
> How many benefits, if they judge us best, we shall give them,
> So that they will receive gifts much greater than those of Paris.
> First, especially where every judge commands,   1105
> The Laureian owls will never leave you behind;
> Rather, they will dwell inside and build nests
> In your purses and leave little coins.
> Then, in addition to this, you will live as if in great temples,
> For we will roof your houses spread-eagle style.   1110
> And if, winning an office, you wish to steal something,
> We will put a sharp little hawk into your hands.
> If you are dining somewhere, we will send you big bird-crops.
> But if you don't judge in our favor, build little moon-shields to
>   carry
> Just like statues; whoever of you doesn't have a moon,   1115
> Whenever you have a white robe, then especially you will pay
> The penalty to us, shitted upon by all the Birds.
>
> (vv. 1058–1117)

This parabasis comes between the two sequences of visitors to Cloud-cuckooland and helps reinforce some of the theoretical issues raised in the main parabasis. The ode and antepirrheme reiterate the theme of the Birds' benefit to humankind, emphasized in the anapests (vv. 708–36). The conditional phrase of v. 1103, requiring the judges to honor them, echoes that of v. 723 similarly predicating the Birds' benefactions on men's honoring of them. The same conditional structure occurs in the second parabasis of the *Clouds* (*Nub.* 1115–30), also promising the judges many benefits for their recognition of the Clouds' divinity by honoring the chorus with victory, and threatening them with inopportune rain and hail should they fail to do so. The Birds threaten to punish the judges with a similar form of aerial bombardment; this antepirrheme indeed seems to function as another intertextual echo of the *Clouds,* whose chorus resembles that of the Birds, not least in its capacity as a glorified projection of human fantasies and desires.[47] The echo gains particular point in that the threats of the Clouds were ignored by the judges who gave the play third prize; the Clouds' threats are here renewed in an even more unpleasant form.

The specifically agricultural benefits enumerated in the ode may also echo the *Clouds'* second parabasis, whose emphasis is agricultural (*Nub.* 1117–20, 1123–25), but even more clearly, the ode evokes the first benefit of the Birds to mankind that Peisthetaerus listed in vv. 588–91, ridding the fields of destructive insects and pests. In effect this is what Peisthetaerus has just finished doing in the iterated type scenes leading up to the second parabasis; one by one he has removed from the stage various parasites who endanger the fertility and freedom of his new polity. The epirrheme proceeds to illustrate this process of pest removal with specific examples. At the beginning of the dramatic festivals decrees against state enemies are announced, such as those against Diagoras of Melos or the tyrants.

The allusion to Diagoras here is similar in function to the one concerning Prodicus in the main parabasis. On the surface it appears to be merely a passing foil; but considering Diagoras' fame in antiquity as a denier of the gods[48] and this play's overall concern with the overthrow of traditional religion, we may be justified in regarding the allusion as more programmatic. In the Birds' view Diagoras' atheism is no more a threat to the city than the long-dead tyrants, since Diagoras' denial applies only to the Olympian gods against whom the Birds themselves are in revolt.[49]

Far more of a threat is the bird catcher and taxidermist Philocrates who is responsible for dishonoring and maltreating the new gods and whose very name (= "lover of power") recalls the tyrants.[50] With his

47. See p. 89 above and n.8.

48. The definitive treatment of Diagoras remains that of Jacoby (1959), who dates his condemnation to 433/32, and accepts his authorship of a pamphlet titled Ἀπο-πυργίζοντες Λόγοι, denying the existence of gods. Woodbury (1965, 178–211) challenges Jacoby's conclusions, but is clearly mistaken in his dogmatic assumption (198–99, 206) that a dithyrambic poet could not also write a prose treatise or have unconventional religious ideas. Still less satisfactory is the view of Rosenmeyer (1972, 232–38) that the whole tradition of a decree against Diagoras is a scholiastic fiction; this is disproven by Lysias 6.17–18, as Ostwald (1986, 275 n.287) notes. Katz (1976, 372–73) raises the interesting possibility that v. 1576 (ὁ τοὺς θεοὺς ἀποτειχίσας) and the general idea of a fortified city blockading the gods are inspired by the title of Diagoras' work; Jacoby (1959, 30) also sees a possible allusion in *Nub.* 1024 (καλλίπυργον σοφίαν . . . ἐπασκῶν).

49. We should not make the mistake of assuming that this was also Aristophanes' view as, for instance, Rosenmeyer (1972, 235–36) does.

50. Philocrates is a common enough name in ancient Athens; in this case the name fits so well that he is likely to be a character of Aristophanes' invention. It is worth noting

snares and nets Philocrates restrains and constricts the Birds' natural
liberty, expressed with lyrical rapture by the antode. Thus we see the
Birds set a price upon his head, using the proscriptive powers of *nomos*
to guarantee their own free expression of *physis*; in a reversal of the
conventional order they even threaten to imprison men just as they
have been imprisoned (vv. 1084–87). At the same time the Birds are
still capable of encouraging and assisting unrestrained human greed in
the antepirrheme; they exhort their favorite men to steal whatever
they like while holding public office (vv. 1111–12), thereby reaffirming
their open invitation to human self-indulgence and *ponēria* in the
epirrhemes of the main parabasis. This arbitrary application and violation of *nomoi* as dictated by self-interest, especially the self-interest of
rulers, prepares us for Peisthetaerus' effective manipulation of *nomos*
and political power in the following scenes.

Because the *Birds* is a long play with so many impostor scenes in the
second half, there is a need for other choral interludes beyond the
second parabasis. Thus we perceive a connected system of four odes
consisting of strophe and antistrophe in vv. 1470–93 and a metrically
identical strophe and antistrophe in vv. 1553–64 and 1694–1705.
Here we have a continuation of the themes presented in the parabases:
the ambiguity of *nomos*, the deleterious impact of social parasites and
sophists. All four display an ethnological interest in strange places and
peoples, beyond Cardia (vv. 1474–75 "Heartland"), the land of darkness (vv. 1482–84), the land of the Shadowfeet (vv. 1553–54), and the
race of the Englottogasters (vv. 1694–96 "Tongue-stomach men").[51]

Among the wonders of the world the first strophe enumerates the
great Cleonymus tree, which sends out sycophantic fig shoots in the
spring,[52] but sheds shields in the fall:

> We have flown to many new   1470
> And wondrous places
>   And seen terrible things.
> For there is a strange tree

---

his identification in v. 14 as the merchant from whom Peisthetaerus and Euelpides
purchased their guide birds; thus we see that Peisthetaerus' ambitions for power go back
to the beginning of the play.

51. On the repeated ἔστι τις . . . formula initiating each ode and the thematic
connection of the four odes, see Moulton 1981, 29–46. Whitman (1964, 194) aptly notes
the analogy of these strange places to Cloudcuckooland; we should certainly reject the
view of Harman (1920, 97) that they are "topical gibberish . . . designed for the purpose
of diverting too critical attention from the dangerous scenes which they enclose."

52. In the context συκοφαντεῖ clearly puns on σῦκα φαίνει or something of the sort,
relating to figs.

> Having grown beyond Cardia,
> > Cleonymus by name,   1475
> > In no way useful,
> > But especially big and cowardly.
> In spring, this always
> Buds and sends out sycophant-shoots,
> But in winter, it again   1480
> > Sheds its shield-leaves.
> > > > (vv. 1470–81)

The allusion to sycophancy is immediately appropriate inasmuch as
Peisthetaerus has just finished whipping a sycophant off the stage in vv.
1462–69, and in the scene following the odes Prometheus appears as a
divine sycophant revealing the plans of the gods.[53] It has a historical
basis too, since Cleonymus had just proposed a decree rewarding
informers with 1,000 drachmas for information regarding the profanation of the mysteries.[54] This decree and the subsequent decree
of Peisander helped foster an atmosphere of denunciations, accusations, plots, and counterplots in which prominent Athenians were condemned by the testimony of metics and slaves, with the most extravagant accuser, Diocleides, eventually being shown to have fabricated his
entire story.[55] In this environment the self-proclaimed upholders of
nomos turn out to be cunning manipulators and violators of *nomos*. The
ode illustrates the point effectively by recalling that Cleonymus, now
presuming so ostentatiously to act as a guardian of public morality, was
himself guilty of violating it when fleeing in battle.[56] In the same way,
the sycophantic Prometheus turns out to be a coward (see vv. 1494–
1512).

Cleonymus' satiric counterpart in the antistrophe is a figure of similar ambivalence whose dual nature conceals criminality beneath re-
spectability:

> There is a place far away
> Near darkness itself

53. The sycophant (v. 1424 πραγματοδίφης) and Prometheus (v. 1507 φράσω σοι
πάντα τἄνω πράγματα) are both characterized as part of the world of *polypragmosynē;* this
may also be alluded to with the many δεινὰ πράγματ' (v. 1472) which the Birds claim to
have seen in the intervening lyric.

54. See Andocides 1.27; Cleonymus' proposal was exceeded by Peisander's decree to
make the reward 10,000 drachmas (implicitly alluded to by his presence in the next
strophe of the system).

55. Cf. Andocides 1.37–42, 65–66; Plutarch, *Alcibiades* 20.5.

56. Aristophanes repeatedly alludes to Cleonymus' Archilochian "throwing his
shield away" in battle (cf. *Nub.* 353–54, *Vesp.* 15–27, 592–93, 822–23, *Pax* 444–46, 673–
78, 1295–1304), perhaps at Delium.

> In a region barren of lamps,
> Where men dine together   1485
> With heroes and are with them
>   Except in the evening.
>   Then it is no longer
>   Safe to encounter them.
> For if someone of mortal men should at night   1490
> Meet with the hero Orestes,
> He would be left naked, struck by him
>   All over the right side.
>
> (vv. 1482–93)

Orestes the cloak thief has already been alluded to in the main parabasis (v. 712) and at least implicitly by Euelpides' story concerning the robbery of his garment in vv. 492–98. He illustrates that a hero in name can be a common street thug in practice.[57] Shrouded in the darkness of night any man can turn out to be a criminal, like the prominent Athenians who committed the sacrileges of 415. And so, given the cover of secrecy, even Prometheus can betray the gods, as we soon see (vv. 1494–1512, 1549–51).

The atmosphere of gloom and darkness is also evoked immediately after the Prometheus scene with the ode on Socrates' necromancy in the land of the Shadowfeet:

> Among the Shadowfeet there is
>   A lake, where unwashed
>   Socrates conjures up spirits.   1555
> There even Peisander came,
> Asking to see the spirit which
>   Left that man behind, still living.
>   Having as sacrificial victim
> A camel-lamb, of which he cut the throat   1560
> Just like Odysseus, he went away.
> And then there came up for him from below
> Toward the bloody neck of the camel
>   Chaerephon the bat.
>
> (vv. 1553–64)

Peisander, like Cleonymus, was one of the democratic politicians most eager to obtain information about the sacrileges at all costs, even with huge rewards and torture of free citizens.[58] His desire to interrogate

57. Müller-Strübing (1873, 32–36) plausibly argues on the basis of Isaeus 8.3, 8.44 that "Orestes" was a generic name for criminals.
58. See Andocides 1.27, 1.36, 1.43.

the ghost of Chaerephon[59] may represent the extremes to which his prosecutorial zeal has taken him. Indeed, Socrates' necromancy constitutes a private mystery ritual[60] not unlike the private rituals at which the Eleusinian mysteries were supposedly parodied.

Socrates himself is an appropriate satirical object here, given our previous observations about the importance of sophistic doctrine in this play and given the *Birds'* close relation to the recently revised *Clouds*.[61] Socratic followers such as Critias and Alcibiades played a prominent role in the profanation of the mysteries, and the enthusiasm of such young aristocrats for Socrates' teaching is alluded to in vv. 1280–85:

> Before you settled this city,
> All men at the time were mad for Sparta,
> Wore their hair long, were hungry, were dirty, were Socrates-like,
> Carried club-staffs, but now turning around
> They are bird-mad, and with pleasure
> Do in imitation everything which the Birds do.

Socrates' dirty, unwashed appearance (alluded to here in vv. 1554–55; cf. *Nub.* 837) is familiar as is the poverty and hunger of his school (cf. *Nub.* 175, 185–86, 416, 441). Here these habits are assimilated to the traditional customs of the Spartans and are taken to be signs of pro-Spartan sympathy, as was commonly suspected of Athenian aristocrats.[62] In fact this passage may allude to Alcibiades' defection: Plutarch tells us that he adopted Laconian customs of grooming, exercise, and diet after arriving in Sparta.[63] The passage implies that the same kind of people who used to follow Socrates are now "mad for the Birds," eager to adopt bird customs; the inference to be drawn is that the characters who soon appear onstage (the parricidal young man, Cinesias, the Sycophant) are similar to Socrates' trendy followers,[64] and

---

59. I agree with Cavaignac (1959, 246–47) that the demonstrative ἐκεῖνον in v. 1558 is more likely to refer to Socrates than to Peisander, and thus that the ψυχή refers to Chaerephon who may have died recently. However, the passage may also be meant to have a secondary reference to Peisander's own spirit.

60. Aristophanes also connects Socrates' teaching with the language and procedures of initiation into mysteries in the *Clouds* (*Nub.* 254–74, 497–508). On the travesty of Socrates' notion of *psychagogia* in this ode, see Hofmann 1976, 210–11; Sommerstein 1987, 300–301.

61. For other possible Socratic references in the *Birds*, see Stark 1953, 77–89.

62. Peisthetaerus and the Birds have already been associated with laconizers by Euelpides' proposal to name the new city Sparta (vv. 813–14).

63. Plutarch, *Alcibiades* 23.3–4.

64. Note that the same verb ὀρνιθομανῶ ("I am mad for the Birds") is used by the young man in v. 1344.

that Peisthetaerus' revolt against conventional religion and morality is very much the same kind of thing as what Socrates and the other sophists promote. Indeed, Peisthetaerus is twice congratulated with the address ὦ σοφώτατε and other honorific vocatives in vv. 1271–73; vv. 1274–79, immediately leading up to the passage on bird madness, make it clear that his personal magnetism and charisma, like Socrates', have been responsible for these new developments in fashion.

The connection of sophistry, rhetoric, and sycophancy is most sharply articulated by the final antistrophe of the series:

There is in Phanae near
   Waterclock a criminal   1695
   Race of Tongue-stomach men,
Who with their tongues
Reap and sow and harvest
   And gather figs;
   They are barbarians by race,   1700
Gorgiases and Philips,
And because of those horse-loving
Tongue-stomach men,
Everywhere in Attica,
   The tongue is cut out.   1705
(vv. 1694–1705)

This attack on Gorgias and the Englottogasters ("Tongue-stomach men," i.e. men who feed themselves by the art of speaking) is itself quite appropriately made through a string of clever wordplays: Phanae plays on the verb φαίνειν ("to denounce"), Klepsydra refers to the law court's waterclock, "gather figs" (συκάζουσι) puns on the word "*syco*-phant," "horse-loving" (φιλίππων) on the name Philip. Of all the sophists Gorgias was the greatest rhetorician, for whom the persuasive power of *logos* was supreme.[65] We should not forget that Gorgias' original prominence in Athens derived from his leadership of an embassy from Leontini in 427, which convinced Athens to undertake its first direct involvement in Sicilian affairs; indeed, it was ostensibly to settle matters in Leontini and Segesta that Athens was undertaking its much larger expedition contemporary with this play.[66] As in the case of Socrates, however, Gorgias' true danger was not simply his own eloquence, so much as it was his spawning a whole race of imitators, not

---

65. For Gorgias' theory of the irresistible persuasive power of *logos*, see especially the *Encomium of Helen* (82B11 D–K); cf. Segal 1962, 99–155; de Romilly 1973, 155–62; Kerferd 1981, 78–82.

66. See Diodorus Sic. 12.83.2.

only Philip but many Gorgiases and Philips (v. 1701), an entire γένος of "Tongue-stomach men." Even though many of this race were native Athenians, Aristophanes views the New Rhetoric as something fundamentally un-Athenian and foreign, like Gorgias himself; it is in fact so foreign that the "Tongue-stomach men," despite their obvious facility in speaking the Greek language, are properly considered a race of *barbaroi* (v. 1700).

Gorgias is apt as the culminating figure in the list of intellectual villains whom the chorus attacks in this play. Although Süvern was wrong in trying to make a direct allegorical identification of Peisthetaerus with Gorgias,[67] there is clearly some truth in the general parallel. Peisthetaerus' creation and triumph are products of language, and some critics have observed that this is fundamentally a play about the power of language.[68] In the immediately preceding scene Peisthetaerus used his resources of legal argument and sophistic persuasion to convince the divine Heracles of his inability to inherit Zeus' estate and the resulting advantage of delivering Zeus' Sovereignty (Basileia) to Peisthetaerus. Even the gods have come to view themselves as mortals who die and inherit (vv. 1642–45) and are thus subject to the complexities of Athenian inheritance law (vv. 1656–66). It is from this subordination to legal process and rhetorical skill that the gods really lose sovereignty over the universe. Even the Birds, whom Peisthetaerus set out to install as new gods, prove in the end to be mere naive tools useful in the sophist's own acquisition of power:[69] he is addressed as "chief magistrate" (v. 1123 ἄρχων) of the new city, he eats dissident Birds (vv. 1583–85),[70] he promises to make Heracles a "tyrant" (v. 1673 τύραν-

67. Süvern 1835, 35–41.

68. Cf. Whitman 1964, 172–78, 198–99; Moulton 1981, 41–43; Koelb 1984, 61–80. Note especially vv. 1437–50 on the power of *logoi* to give men new wings and transform their nature.

69. Peisthetaerus' use of religious beliefs to gain power has much in common with the radical sophistic view that the gods and morality were merely inventions of πυκνός τις καὶ σοφὸς γνώμην ἀνήρ for the purpose of consolidating social and political control: see the fragment from the satyr play *Sisyphus*, probably produced the year before the *Birds*, and attributed by many to the sophist Critias (= 88B25 D–K), one of those involved in the sacrileges of 415. On the question of Euripidean vs. Critian authorship, see the recent discussions of Dihle 1977, 28–42; Scodel 1980, 122–37; Winiarczyk 1987, 35–45. Critics have failed to recognize the possibility that the satyr play was written by Critias but produced along with Euripides' Trojan trilogy of 415, and that this may have given rise to the confusion in the doxographical tradition. For Aristophanes' familiarity with the *Sisyphus*, see de Carli 1971, 52–54.

70. Peisthetaerus' cooking and eating of the Birds actualizes the threat made symbolically and theatrically during his first confrontation with the chorus, as he brandishes the cooking pot and spit to defend himself against the Birds' attack (vv. 356–99). As we have seen, the χύτρα is thematically significant: it is one of the sacrificial implements Peisthetaerus and Euelpides carry onstage at the play's beginning (v. 43), is used to fight

vov) who can enjoy the Birds' milk, and he himself marries Sovereignty to become the absolute "tyrant" (v. 1708) of the universe. Unlike Trygaeus' marriage to Opora, which has a communally shared component (= Theoria), Peisthetaerus' marriage to Basileia at the end of the play is the purest assertion of unshared and unlimited self-gratification.

The parabases and choral odes of the *Birds* help to clarify the play's significance by drawing attention to the fundamental unity of Athens' contemporary problems: overweening military ambitions, loss of reverence for the city's traditional gods and institutions, the rise of sycophancy and manipulation of the legal system—all rooted in the sophistic delusion that Man himself can somehow become God.

Women in the City

Like the *Birds*, Aristophanes' *Lysistrata* and *Thesmophoriazusae* feature parabases fully integrated with the action of the play. They do not present political or aesthetic programs so much as the chorus' self-definition and defense, which is in each case central to the play's thematic development. The Birds assist in erecting a counter-Athens outside the city, and the women of the two later plays concoct a counter-Athens within the city, even within the most private confines of the *oikos*. The women of the *Lysistrata* conspire with political motives in view, while those of the *Thesmophoriazusae* are more concerned with addressing a literary and artistic issue. There are those who perceive the conspiratorial plots and counterplots of these plays as a reflection of the oligarchical revolution soon to seize Athens in June of 411.[71] Yet these events seem rather unlikely to have been in any way a primary inspiration for the plays, which must have been conceived several months before Peisander's first speech to the Assembly; the plays make some allusions to Peisander, the Samian generals, and proposed constitutional reforms,[72] but these passages were clearly late additions to bring the plays up to date at the time of performance. To the extent that the women's machinations resemble oligarchical attempts to gain

---

off the Birds (vv. 357, 386, 391), to sacrifice to the Birds (vv. 848–903), and finally to cook the Birds (vv. 1583–85, 1688–91). Auger (1979, 82–87) examines the inversions of the sacrifice theme in this play and sees it as the vision of a pre-Promethean, pre-sacrificial Golden Age corrupted into a cannibalistic tyranny in which all distinctions between man, god, and animal are erased; on the general corruption and "auto-destruction" of comic utopias in the later plays of Aristophanes, beginning with the *Birds*, see the interesting remarks of Carrière 1979, 105–10.

71. See Töttössy 1962, 273–82; Reckford 1987, 304–5.

72. See *Lys.* 313, 489–92, *Thesm.* 335–39, 356–67, 1143–44.

power, the resemblance must be attributed to the general rumors and gossip about oligarchical conspiracy current ever since 415 and not to the events of 411, which later fulfilled those rumors.

More significantly both plays of 411 deal with women. Aristophanes may have meant to suggest something about the effeminization of Athens' political and cultural leadership in the aftermath of the Sicilian disaster and the subsequent allied defections. Responsible figures like the Proboulos of the *Lysistrata* appear weak and discredited; it is fitting that his emasculation and humiliation should take the form of being dressed up as a woman working at the loom (*Lys.* 530–38), even as the women take charge of civic affairs and reveal themselves as the true examples of "courage" (*Lys.* 545) and "manliness" (*Lys.* 549). By the same token Athens' literary elite appear in the *Thesmophoriazusae* in the guise of women unable to agree on an effective course of action, while the women themselves assemble and deliberate in a prudent and or-derly way making proper use of the civil procedures and institutions ordinarily operated by men.[73] In the topsy-turvy inversion of comic fantasy men have become dependent and helpless women who beg to be rescued from disgrace, while the women take command of affairs and confer pardon on their delinquent male counterparts from a position of strength.

Aside from the political point of this representation, there is also a significant literary background to Aristophanes' concentration on the female perspective in these plays. Lysistrata is the first heroine whom we see in Aristophanic comedy and, so far as we can reconstruct, she may have been the first heroine in Attic Old Comedy; *Lysistrata* and *Thesmophoriazusae* are the first comedies we know to have centered upon women's role in society.[74] Critics have noticed the contrast of Lysistrata's rather austere, businesslike, and even humorless person-ality with the usual clownishness and selfish extravagance of Aristoph-anes' other comic heroes.[75] Her name is generally accepted as inten-tionally calling to mind the name of Lysimache, the long-standing and

<hr>

73. Note the references to the women's *ecclēsia* (*Thesm.* 295–311, 329–31) and *dēmos* (*Thesm.* 335–36, 1145–46), and see the discussion of Haldane 1965, 39–46.

74. Prior to this, women's role in Comedy seems to have been at most marginal and decorative. See Tschiedel 1984, 29; Henderson 1987, xxviii.

75. Lysistrata tells us very little about herself or her family background, and there is a notable lack of humanizing detail, although *Lys.* 510–20 suggests that she has a husband. Cf. Whitman 1964, 201–2; Strauss 1966, 198–99; Solomos 1974, 188; Henderson 1980, 171, 187–88; Henderson 1987, xxxvii; Foley 1982, 8–9; Tschiedel 1984, 33–34. Wilson (1982, 157–58) begs the point in suggesting that any woman who presumes to be serious necessarily seems funny to a male audience, although he correctly points out the humor in some of Lysistrata's remarks; her humor seems to me to be that of someone very much in control of the situation.

prominent priestess of Athena Polias; many have even interpreted
Lysistrata as a comic incarnation of the goddess Athena herself.[76] To
the all-male audience of the ancient theater,[77] such a forceful and
commanding female figure must have been striking, particularly in her
successful inversion of traditional social and sexual hierarchies.

The *Thesmophoriazusae* reminds us that the provenance of a figure
like Lysistrata, so uncharacteristic of Comedy, is rather to be found in
Tragedy, and particularly in the psychological drama of Euripides.[78]
Far from being the misogynistic hermit the Thesmophoria women and
comic tradition generally portray,[79] Euripides was throughout his career a keen student of the feminine personality and its emotional
complexity; even when presenting traditionally villainous women such
as Medea, Phaedra, or Stheneboea, Euripides reveals them as tor-
mented spirits with their own pathos and emotional appeal. In the year
immediately preceding 411 he created especially sympathetic portrayals of feminine suffering in the *Helen* and *Andromeda,* parodied at
length in the *Thesmophoriazusae.* By presenting Helen, the archetypal
"bad woman" of Greek literature, as the innocent victim of mistaken
identities Euripides makes an ideological statement with distinctly fem-
inist overtones.[80] The *Thesmophoriazusae* depicts Euripides himself as a
similar victim of mistaken identities, misunderstood as a woman-hater
by women who of course never saw his tragedies, while in fact being a
champion of women, as manifested by his roles as Menelaus and
Perseus coming to rescue their respective women.[81] By the end of the
play Euripides convinces the women of his intention in the future not

76. The identification with Lysimache was first made by Lewis (1955, 1–8) and is
corroborated by the allusion to her in *Lys.* 554. Henderson (1987, xxxviii–xl) accepts the
allusion to Lysimache, but cautions against thinking actual portraiture is involved here.
On Lysistrata as Athena see Newiger 1980, 235–36; Foley 1982, 9–10; Henderson 1980,
188; Henderson 1987, xxxviii. For the general importance of Athena and her cult within
this play, cf. Elderkin 1940, 391–93; Bodson 1973, 5–27; Loraux 1980/81, 141–43.

77. Several passages in Aristophanes strongly suggest that women were not present
in the theater. For discussions, cf. Box 1964, 241–42, and Wilson 1982, 158–59.

78. For Euripides as Aristophanes' inspiration in treating women as central figures,
see Tschiedel 1984, 44–49. Miller (1947, 180–81) calls special attention to the defense of
women's superiority in the *Melanippe Desmotis* (Page, *GLP* I, 112–14), based on their role
as managers of household economy and key figures in religious ritual; these are clearly
the two principal bases for Aristophanes' depiction of women as responsible beings with
a constructive role in the city's political affairs.

79. It is certainly comic tradition, including but not limited to the *Thesmophoriazusae,*
that is behind the anecdotes in *Vita Eur.* 62–78, 90–108.

80. See Zeitlin 1981, 189–90, 201–4, on Helen's significance here as a symbol for the
process of literary transformation itself. Just as Helen's reputation is transformed, Euripides undertakes to transform his own.

81. On Aristophanes' consciousness of Euripides' actual favorable attitude toward
women, cf. Paduano 1982, 113–15; Tschiedel 1984, 42–49. Indeed Murray (1964, 117–
18) finds this play quite complimentary in its attitude toward Euripides.

to be a threat to their reputation (*Thesm.* 1160–67). Certainly he never really was an enemy of women; it is significant that the man on whom he relies in dealing with them is his κηδεστής or "in-law" (*Thesm.* 74, 584, 1165), a connection by marriage calling attention to Euripides' conventional and normal relationship with the female species. The *Thesmophoriazusae* is not a play about Euripides' hatred of women but about popular misunderstandings of Euripides, in the same sense that the *Clouds* dramatizes popular misunderstandings of Socrates and other intellectuals.[82]

Like the Socrates of the *Clouds* Euripides is himself mostly to blame for being misunderstood. The delicate emotional and psychological nuances of his tragic characterization are much too subtle and refined for most members of his audience, to whom Phaedra and Stheneboea are simply wanton, destructive paradigms of female libido. The average theatergoer returns home from a day of Euripidean tragedy and suspects his wife of adultery or theft (*Thesm.* 395–432). Like Socrates, Euripides is accused of inducing men not to believe in the gods (*Thesm.* 450–51). Euripides' own kinsman and agent among the women does not challenge the popular judgment concerning Euripides' attitude toward women, but like the husbands whom the first woman complained about, defends such a negative valuation as true (*Thesm.* 466–519). After the parabasis Euripides himself comes onstage in tragic costume playing the role of Menelaus rescuing Helen and Perseus rescuing Andromeda. But even Euripides' heroic guise as a savior of women does not convince his audience that he has sincere intentions.[83] Again like Socrates, Euripides fails to understand the nature of his audience and overestimates its capabilities.

The kinsman can be rescued only when Euripides comes back in distinctly comic costume as an old bawd with a dancing girl for sale to the Scythian guard.[84] Euripides' delicate portrayals of female suffering fail to create a convincing dramatic illusion with the coarse and unsophisticated male audience symbolized by the Scythian; what does succeed in deceiving this audience is the blatant appeal to physical self-gratification, with the woman depicted exclusively as a sex-object. Aristophanes here represents the same conflict between highbrow dra-

---

82. In this regard Paduano (1982, 109–10) correctly sees the in-law's relation to Euripides as comparable with Strepsiades' relation to Socrates.

83. Euripides' attempts to involve Critylla or the Scythian as characters in the plots of his metatheatrical performances (*Thesm.* 897–99, 1115–27) both fail. See Paduano 1982, 124–26.

84. On the comic character of this stratagem and its status as a reflection on the "barbaric nature" (*Thesm.* 1129) of the theatrical audience, cf. Rau 1967, 89; Zeitlin 1981, 173, 191–93; Paduano 1982, 106; Tschiedel 1984, 46.

matic sophistication and lowbrow audience appeal that characterized his earlier reflections on his own work, particularly in the *Clouds* and *Wasps*. Euripides could just as well be speaking for Aristophanes himself in saying, "In vain you would waste new and clever things by presenting them to dumb men, but it is necessary to present some other fitting device to this man" (*Thesm.* 1130–32). The ultimate failure of Euripides' tragic intrigues, though, and the success of his final comic maneuver suggest that the transformation of attitude Euripides is here trying to effect can be accomplished through Comedy better than through Tragedy.[85] The new, softer, more romantic portrayals of women in the *Helen* and *Andromeda* of 412 probably influenced Aristophanes in turning his attention to women's themes in 411; however, Aristophanes felt that he could be more successful than Euripides in using female dramatic figures to influence dominant social, political, and literary values.

In this sense the *Thesmophoriazusae* is not only a play about Euripidean tragedy but also a metadramatic statement about Aristophanes' own use of women in the comedies of 411. The *Lysistrata* and *Thesmophoriazusae* are intimately linked in both conception and execution and must be viewed in terms of a close intertextual relationship in which each play alludes to the other and comments upon the other. As well as sharing the same general concerns the plays possess numerous parallels and cross-references of a more specific nature. Lysistrata opens the play by lamenting the reputation women have among men as the "perpetrators of every evil" (*Lys.* 12 πανοῦργοι), and Kalonike interrupts to declare that women indeed are the perpetrators of every evil. The *Lysistrata* goes on to prove, at least implicitly, that women are not so evil, but the issue of women's reputation among men for doing evil is addressed much more programmatically in the *Thesmophoriazusae*. Kalonike's joke about women being actually as evil as men suspect parallels the argument made by Euripides' in-law in the guise of a woman speaking at the Assembly (*Thesm.* 466–519). Similarly Lysistrata's frustrated statement regarding women as a despicable race who are quite fittingly the subjects of Tragedy (*Lys.* 137–38) points to the

---

85. Zeitlin (1981, 171–75) is illuminating on this play's use of gender reversal to represent genre reversal: just as men can act the role of women (and vice versa), Tragedy can act as Comedy (and vice versa). We have already discussed the significance of Dicaeopolis' (= Comedy's) donning tragic costume to discuss serious issues in the *Acharnians*. In this play we see just the opposite, as Euripides (= Tragedy) dons comic costume to make his point; this reversal of the *Acharnians*, consciously evoked by the extended *Telephus* parody (see p. 44 above) may be meant to reflect Euripides' progression from the hard tragic paradigms of plays like the *Medea, Hippolytus,* and *Heracles* to the tragicomic style of many later plays (*Helen, Ion, Iphigenia in Tauris*).

Thesmophoriazusae, as do the references to women as a race hated by Euripides (*Lys.* 283, 368–69). The line about "no creature so shameless as women" (*Lys.* 369) finds a close parallel in *Thesm.* 531–32, and they must both be based on a Euripidean archetype.[86] Critylla is named as a member of the old women's chorus in *Lys.* 323, and is one of the actors in the *Thesmophoriazusae* (see *Thesm.* 898) set to guard Euripides' in-law. Cleisthenes is alluded to as a fellow conspirator of the women in *Lys.* 621 and appears onstage in that role in *Thesm.* 574–654. The dressing of the Proboulos in female costume (*Lys.* 530–38) has obvious counterparts in the *Thesmophoriazusae,* which makes much of the man-dressed-as-woman theme. The woman who uses a helmet to feign pregnancy in *Lys.* 741–59 bears a distinct analogy to the woman who dresses up a wineskin as her baby in *Thesm.* 689–759; the women employ a ruse to indulge themselves in violation of the respective prohibitions of the sex strike and the Thesmophorian day of fasting.[87] The civic role of women in performing religious rituals (*Lys.* 641–47) and their contributions to the city as mothers (*Lys.* 651; see *Thesm.* 832–39) are also themes bulking large in the *Thesmophoriazusae.*

Although both plays quite certainly date to 411,[88] the relative chronology of the *Lysistrata* and *Thesmophoriazusae* is open to some doubt: arguments based on political allusions within the plays are inconclusive. I concur with the most frequent modern dating of the plays, which assigns *Lysistrata* to the Lenaea and *Thesmophoriazusae* to the City Dionysia of 411, but I believe the grounds on which it is usually advanced to be insecure and in some cases erroneous.[89] Of far more use in establishing the priority of the *Lysistrata* is consideration of intertextual relation of the two plays as described above. Most of the specific points

86. The context of the line in the *Lysistrata* clearly suggests that it is Euripidean parody, and it is labelled fr. 882a by Snell. Cf. Rau 1967, 199. Rogers (1904, 59) traces *Thesm.* 531–32 back to the *Melanippe Desmotis* fragment cited in n.78 above. Euripides of course may formulate this idea in more than one passage.

87. The scene in the *Thesmophoriazusae* seems intended as a complex play of intertextual echoes. The idea of baby kidnapping to extricate oneself from a difficult situation is primarily meant to evoke Euripides' *Telephus,* which is the subject of extended parody in the *Thesmophoriazusae* (cf. Miller 1948, 174–83; Rau 1967, 42–50). But the motif of using a beloved inanimate object instead of a real baby clearly derives from the parody of the *Telephus* in the *Acharnians,* in which Dicaeopolis kidnaps the Acharnians' coal basket (*Ach.* 325–57). What is unique to the *Lysistrata* is the idea of disguising such an object as a baby and insisting it actually is one; on the connection of the two passages, see Henderson 1980, 205.

88. Sommerstein (1977a, 112–13, 116–19) convincingly refutes the arguments of Rogers (1904, xxviii–xxxviii) and Rhodes (1972, 185–86, 190) in favor of dating the *Thesmophoriazusae* to 410. Few will be convinced by the recent arguments of Vickers (1989, 41–52) who advocates the 410 date based on what he perceives as a series of covert allusions to Alcibiades' activities.

89. See Appendix 4.

of contact between the plays are cases in which the *Lysistrata* makes brief allusion to themes that receive greater elaboration and development in the *Thesmophoriazusae*. One might of course interpret these as cross-references to an earlier play; however, their significance does not seem to be particularly enriched by such a reading, in the way, for instance, that certain passages in the *Peace* are enriched when viewed as echoes of the *Wasps*. The jokes about Cleisthenes or the Proboulos in drag or women actually being as bad as men think they are would be rather stale if these themes have already been milked as thoroughly as they are in the *Thesmophoriazusae*. What seems more likely is that Aristophanes would first try out these topics as quick jokes in the *Lysistrata* to test whether they rouse a laugh, and later expand them in the *Thesmophoriazusae*. The really decisive allusions are those to Euripides as a hater of women (*Lys.* 283, 368–69; cf. 137–38); as we have seen, one of the primary points of the *Thesmophoriazusae* is to show that Euripides is not in fact a hater of women, or at least is no longer one. In light of Euripides' promise at the end of the play (*Thesm.* 1160–63) never in the future to speak ill of women, *Lys.* 283 and 368–69 would not work as retrospective allusions to the *Thesmophoriazusae*, whereas they do work as anticipatory hints pointing forward to Aristophanes' next play whose beginning is predicated on popular assumptions concerning Euripides as a woman hater.[90]

There are also a number of more general reasons why the *Lysistrata* appears to be the original model for a women's play and the *Thesmophoriazusae* its humorous sequel. *Lysistrata* introduces the idea of women organizing themselves politically as a novel and striking concept, and the play's prologue illustrates the many difficulties involved in such an enterprise. The *Thesmophoriazusae* on the other hand takes it for granted that the women can hold, with official sanction and support, a deliberative assembly at which they condemn specific enemies of the people; to this extent the plot seems to presuppose a more advanced stage of organization and political development, less surprising if coming as a follow-up to their success in the *Lysistrata*.[91] The *Lysistrata* uses women to make what in a qualified sense is a serious political point about the war and its deleterious effect on domestic concord, both metaphorical and literal.[92] The *Thesmophoriazusae*, on

90. Russo (1962, 298–99) briefly notes these allusions and believes the *Lysistrata* was written earlier than the *Thesmophoriazusae* although presented at the same contest. I do not agree with Sommerstein (1977a, 118) that the allusions work just as well in either direction.

91. On this relation between the two plays, see Wilamowitz 1893 II, 352.

92. See Newiger 1980, 233–36, and Erbse 1982, 101–2. Westlake (1980, 43–44) is wrong to dismiss Lysistrata's woolworking simile (*Lys.* 574–86) simply as an irrelevant

the other hand, does not use women for such a serious purpose, but is a more humorous treatment of feminine identity as an issue per se;[93] the heroine of the *Lysistrata* is efficient, principled, and earnest, while the hero of the *Thesmophoriazusae* is a clownish, bumbling fool. The *Lysistrata* presents an impressive women's conspiracy, whereas the *Thesmophoriazusae* is a play about male attempts to thwart a women's conspiracy. It would in fact be accurate to characterize the *Lysistrata* as about women and the *Thesmophoriazusae* about men's attitudes toward women. In the *Lysistrata* the change in women's social position is purely temporary; the *Thesmophoriazusae* seems to point toward a more fundamental and permanent shift in their status and valuation.

This developmental relation between the treatment of women in the two plays is clear from the respective parabases: nothing in the *Lysistrata* parabasis gains from assuming the priority of the *Thesmophoriazusae* whereas the *Thesmophoriazusae* parabasis builds on themes from the *Lysistrata* and in many ways seems to be an *apologia* for both plays. The *Lysistrata* parabasis is closely integrated with the progression of the play's plot, presenting no anapests, but a double epirrhematic syzygy, with the two odes and epirrhemes delivered by the Old Men's semichorus, the two antodes and antepirrhemes delivered by the Old Women's semichorus. As such, the unique form of the parabasis seems designed to reflect the immediately preceding epirrhematic agon between Lysistrata and the Proboulos (*Lys.* 476–607),[94] and more broadly, the division of the whole city into unreconciled factions. The first syzygy concerns the women's background and motives:

<pre>
O. M.: No longer is sleep the task for any man who is free,
        But let us strip, O men, for this action.   615
        For already these things seem to me
        To carry the whiff of more and greater affairs,
        And I smell especially the tyranny of Hippias:
        I very much fear that some of the Spartan men,   620
        Having come here to Cleisthenes' house,
        Are treacherously inciting these god-detested women
        To seize our money and pay,
            From which I was accustomed to live.   625
</pre>

---

digression, since the lack of harmony at home is precisely what the women's sex strike symbolizes. Although the famous éssay of Gomme (1975, 75–98) is right in warning us not to search for systematic political programs in Aristophanes, this does not prevent us from finding serious attitudes and judgments about the contemporary situation; see the corrective remarks of Ste. Croix 1972, 356–71, and Henderson 1990, 271–75.

    93. See Tschiedel 1984, 43–45.

    94. See Moulton 1981, 58.

For already these women chastise the citizens terribly,
And, although women, blather about bronze shields,
And make treaties against us with Spartan men,
Whom one can trust no more than an open-mouthed wolf.
Men have woven these plots against us for the sake of tyranny.   630
But they won't be tyrants over me, since I shall keep guard
And in the future carry my sword in a myrtle branch,
And I will shop among the arms-merchants next to Aristogeiton,
And thus I will stand beside him. For it falls to me
To strike the jaw of this god-detested old woman.   635

O. W.: Not even your mother will recognize you returning home.
        But, dear Old Women, let us first put these things on the
            ground.
        For we, all ye citizens, are beginning
        A speech useful to the city.
        Fittingly, since it splendidly nourished me in luxury: 640
        Seven years old, I was a holy relic-carrier,
        Then at ten years old, I was a sacred wheat-grinder for the
            founder,
        And shedding the saffron veil, I was a bear at the
            Brauronia.   645
        And once, being a fair young girl, I carried the basket,
            Bearing a string of figs.
Don't I owe it to the city to advise something useful?
If I have been born a woman, don't begrudge me this,
If I bring in something better than the present affairs.   650
I have a share of the burden, for I contribute men.
But you wretched Old Men have no share of it, since
Having squandered the so-called "ancestral contribution"
From the Persian Wars, you don't bring in new tax-contributions,
And we are in danger of being destroyed by you besides.   655
Is this reason for you to grumble? If you cause me any pain,
I will shatter your jaw with this rough boot.

                                            (*Lys.* 614–57)

The Old Men believe the women's seizure of the Acropolis is part of a
broader conspiracy (*Lys.* 616–17). In this they are of course correct,
although they are wrong to suppose the conspiracy to be the work
either of would-be tyrants (*Lys.* 618–19, 630–34) or of the Spartans
(*Lys.* 620–25, 628–29). One could easily dismiss the talk of tyranny as
the usual cant of old democrats (see *Vesp.* 488–507, *Av.* 1074–75); it
may, however, have a special point after Peisander's first proposals for
constitutional reform when many in Athens caught "the whiff of more
and greater affairs." The Old Men significantly see the women's actions

as a plot woven by "men" (*Lys.* 630 ἄνδρες; see 621, 628); they refuse to accept that women are capable of thinking and acting on their own initiative.

The Old Women on the other hand respond by establishing their right as women to address the city on serious issues (*Lys.* 638–40, 648–60). Their first argument rests on their important civic contribution to the city's cults and rituals: as little girls, the women served in the Arrephoria, the office of sacred wheat grinder for Athena, the bear rites of Brauron, and the Canephoria of the Panathenaic procession (*Lys.* 641–47).[95] All of these ritual offices characterize the women's youth or childhood, suggesting that they have long ago paid their dues to the city, just as the Old Men claim credit for their long past military services. The women do not mention here their role in the most prominent women's festival, the Thesmophoria; if this passage were meant to refer back to the *Thesmophoriazusae*, it would surely have been included as the final term. Its omission suggests rather that Aristophanes is here building the background for his next play by reminding the audience of women's ritual function and its general civic importance.[96] Another theme expanded upon in the *Thesmophoriazusae* is that of women's contribution to the state in giving men to the war effort, sons and husbands (*Lys.* 651). This idea receives specific elaboration in the epirrheme of the *Thesmophoriazusae* parabasis (*Thesm.* 830–45), where it is argued that mothers should be esteemed in relation to their sons' military achievements, whether good or bad. Since the *Thesmophoriazusae* is not otherwise concerned with military matters, the direction of influence seems clear.

The last two verses of each epirrheme present a physical threat and challenge to the other semichorus. In the second syzygy the mutual threats are elevated to virtually the whole content of the passage, with the political commentary of the first syzygy dropped in favor of a humorous and ribald tone;[97] the movement from first to second syzygy thus parallels the progression of a typical parabasis from epirrheme to antepirrheme.

> O. M.: Aren't these affairs a matter of much presumption?
>   The business seems to grow more and more.   660

---

95. On this passage and the various offices listed in it, cf. Brelich 1969 I, 229–90; Sourvinou 1971, 339–42; Stinton 1976, 11–13; Parke 1977, 140–43; Loraux 1980/81, 134–36; Foley 1982, 11–12.

96. Again, vv. 8–18 of the fragment from Euripides' *Melanippe Desmotis* (cited in n.78 above) were probably the inspiring influence for this idea.

97. On the difference in character between the two syzygies, see also the remarks of Moulton 1981, 67.

But the affair must be repelled by any man with balls.
Let us take off our vest, since it is right that a man
Now smell like a man, and not be all wrapped up.   665
Now come, men of white feet,
    We who came to Leipsydrium
    When we were still young,
    Now, now it is necessary to be young again and take wing
        again   670
Over all our body and shake off this old age.
For if one of us gives even a small handle to these women,
They will omit nothing in their easy handiwork:
They will even build ships, and will undertake
To sail against us and do battle, just like Artemisia.   675
If they turn to horsemanship, I'll write off the knights,
For a woman is a most horsey and well-seated thing,
Who will never slip off a running mount. Look at the Amazons
Whom Micon painted on horseback fighting with men.
But it is appropriate for us to take this little neck   680
And fit it into the drilled wood of all these women.

O. W.: If you inflame me, by the two gods,
    I'll let loose my pig, and I'll make
    You today call your demesmen for help, with your hair
        sheared off.
    Let us take off our clothes more quickly, O women,
    So that we may smell like angry women with clenched teeth. 690
    Now let one of you come near me,
        So that he'll never again eat garlic
        Or black beans.
        I'm angry, and if you only speak ill of me,
    Like the dung-beetle and mother-eagle, I'll hatch your eggs. 695
I wouldn't even think of you, as long as my Lampito lives,
And the dear Theban girl, noble Ismenia.
For there will be no force in it, not even if you vote seven decrees,
O wretched man, you who are hated by all and even by your
    neighbors.
Yesterday, preparing a little feast for Hecate,   700
I asked the neighbors for a companion for my girls—
A useful and much-loved child, the Boeotian eel.
But they said that they wouldn't send it on account of your decrees.
Don't stop from these decrees of yours, until
Someone grabs hold of your leg and takes you off your high horse.   705
                                          (*Lys.* 658–705)

Like the Acharnians and Wasps, the Old Men here rely on their military accomplishments in the distant past as tokens of their present

strength and value. Having just been taunted by the Old Women as noncontributors to the present war effort (*Lys.* 652–55) who merely squander the city's resources and themselves consume much in jury pay (see *Lys.* 624–25), the Old Men defend themselves by recalling their exploits in fighting the tyrants at Leipsydrium. The men reinforce their claim of military valor with a series of sexual double entendres aimed at the women:[98] military aggression is expressed in terms of manifest virility (*Lys.* 661 "any man with balls") and phallic subjugation of the female whose proper place, it is implied, is in a submissive rather than a dominant ("horse-riding") sexual posture. Here again we are reminded of the Wasps whose fierceness and claims to military valor were supported visually by their phallic sting.[99] As in the case of the Wasps the Old Men's phallic potency is a thing of the past, and their wish for a rejuvenation in which they can "take wing"[100] again is idle fantasy. Actually the Old Men's historical memories may be just as much a matter of hollow dreams: Leipsydrium was in fact a defeat for those fighting the tyrants, and like the Old Men's other historical memories (Cleomenes, Hippias, Aristogeiton), it occurred over 100 years ago. The Old Men would have to be at least 120 to have fought at Leipsydrium, all the more strange in that *Lys.* 636 implies that their mothers are still alive. Aristophanes seems to have gone out of his way here to suggest, even more than with the Marathon veterans of the *Acharnians* and the Salamis veterans of the *Wasps*, that the Old Men and the ideals which they represent are buried so deep in the past as to be completely irrelevant to the contemporary situation. The Old Men are no longer positive paradigms of Athens' former greatness, as in the earlier plays, but are now so remote that even their memories lack credibility.

In response to the men's sexual harassment the Old Women threaten to release their "pig" (*Lys.* 682–83), by which they refer simultaneously to their anger and the female genitalia.[101] And at the end of the

98. For the double entendres in this passage and its overall significance, cf. Henderson 1975, 114, 119, 122, 160, 163, 165; Henderson 1980, 204; and Henderson 1987, 159–60. The Old Men's sexual threats have already been anticipated in *Lys.* 619 and 632 (of the first syzygy), and symbolically by their attack on the Acropolis' gates with long beams in the parodos (cf. Henderson 1975, 95–96).

99. See p. 122–23 above.

100. The winged phallus bird was common in Greek iconography (see for instance *ARV* 279.2); for discussion of the wing = phallus metaphor in Aristophanes, see Arrowsmith 1973, 136–37; Henderson 1975, 128–29. It has not, however, been recognized that *Lys.* 668 may also be such a double entendre. Given the general context, and especially *Lys.* 661 (ἐνόρχης) and 664 (οὐκ ἐντεθριῶσθαι πρέπει, cf. Henderson 1975, 119; Henderson 1987, 159), it seems likely to bear such a meaning here also.

101. Cf. Henderson 1975, 132; Henderson 1987, 161; as he notes, this ambiguity seems to be recognized by Σ*Lys.* 683 also.

antepirrheme they threaten to pull the men off their horses (*Lys.* 704–5), perhaps again referring to a sexual position. By and large, however, the women's tone is not as bellicose as the Old Men's, since their orientation is ultimately toward peace and reconciliation. If maligned by the men they will act as the dung beetle did with the eagle (*Lys.* 694–95). The Aesopic fable not only makes a point about the smaller and seemingly weaker creature defeating the stronger; it is also the fable that provided the idea for Aristophanes' *Peace* (see *Pax* 129–34, *Vesp.* 1448–49).[102] We should thus see the fable's presence here as a significant intertextual signpost, as it was in *Vesp.* 1448–49. The antepirrheme alludes to another significant creature in Aristophanes' comic bestiary, the famous Boeotian eel of the *Acharnians* (*Lys.* 702; see *Ach.* 880–94), symbol of all the sensual pleasures of which Dicaeopolis was deprived by war.[103] The women thus make significant intertextual allusions to Aristophanes' two other prominent peace plays. The imagery of a friendly neighborhood feast that includes even the Spartan and Boeotian "neighbors" is very much in keeping with those plays' atmosphere of communal celebration and rich sensual gratification; it also points forward to the joint feast with the Spartans at the end of the *Lysistrata* itself (*Lys.* 1216–1321). The echoes of the *Acharnians* and the *Peace* are not limited to this parabasis: in the prologue (*Lys.* 61–68) Lysistrata expects the women from Acharnae to be the first and most eager arrivals, but instead sees the women from Anagyros.[104] And at the end of the play the allegorical figure of Diallage ("Reconciliation"), whose body is divided between the Spartan and Athenian in a three-way act of copulation (*Lys.* 1114–88), clearly recalls Theoria in the *Peace,* who also becomes a communally shared sexual object (*Pax* 868–909). One of the principal points of the *Lysistrata,* echoing the other peace plays, is the impossibility in a time of war of the sensual pleasures human life normally takes for granted and the necessity of peace for their restoration.

The parabasis as a whole is structured in such a way as to form a transition from the Acropolis seizure plot that has dominated the play since the parodos back to the sex-strike plot which was Lysistrata's original proposal in the prologue.[105] The first syzygy dealt with the Old Men's fears of conspiracy against the *dēmos* and especially with the

---

102. On *Vesp.* 1448–49 as a forward-looking allusion to the *Peace,* see p. 151 above.

103. The Boeotian eel has already been called to our attention in the prologue by the remark of Kalonike (*Lys.* 35–36).

104. This of course alludes to Aristophanes' *Anagyros,* produced sometime between the *Peace* and *Birds* (cf. Geissler 1925, 50). On these two allusions, see p. 35 above.

105. On the coordination of these two separate plots in the play, cf. Hulton 1972, 32–36; Vaio 1973, 371–72; Henderson 1980, 185–86.

money stored in the treasury (*Lys.* 624–25, 653–55), thus continuing the themes of *Lys.* 240–613. On the other hand the second syzygy is more explicitly sexual in language and theme, looking forward to the resumed emphasis on the sex strike in the scenes following the parabasis; and the allusion to Lampito and Ismenia as neighbors in *Lys.* 696–97 also orients our attention in this direction.[106] The yearned-for Boeotian eel which is not there, like the Old Men's desired youth and sexual potency which are not there, is a metaphorical equivalent for the privation of sexual fulfillment (and other forms of fulfillment) which the war has caused. The same idea of sensual fulfillment offered and denied is reiterated in the later odes of the unified chorus;[107] there the audience is invited to borrow money from a lender who has none (*Lys.* 1049–57), to attend a feast not going to take place (*Lys.* 1058–71), to receive clothes, money, and grain which are not there (*Lys.* 1189–1215). All of this is no different from Myrrhine's invitation to Cinesias to enjoy sex that does not take place. The parabasis unifies this theme of disappointed expectation and gives the Old Women the chance to insist on its direct connection with the Assembly's unwise decrees (*Lys.* 698, 703–5); the second person addressed by the Old Women here is not only the semichorus of their male counterparts but is also the entire male audience, which is in truth the group responsible for the war's continuation and hence for its own misery and deprivation.[108]

We witness such a direct address to the male audience in the parabasis of the *Thesmophoriazusae.* This parabasis is truncated, consisting as it does of anapests, pnigos, and a single epirrheme.[109] Nevertheless it offers a neatly unified focus on the women's self-defense and criticism

106. See Russo 1962, 262–63.

107. The choral interlude of *Lys.* 1043–71, with its comic vignettes and address to the audience, in many ways serves the function of a second parabasis; indeed *Lys.* 1043–48 explicitly reject the topical abuse and satire the audience would usually expect at this point in the play (compare the ironic rejection of personal abuse at the beginning of the *Knights'* second parabasis, *Eq.* 1264–73; also, cf. *Thesm.* 963–65). For a general discussion of these odes, see Moulton 1981, 24–28.

108. In this sense we find the element of political advice common at the end of parabasis epirrhemes (cf. *Ach.* 713–18, *Nub.* 587–94, *Vesp.* 1117–21, *Ran.* 700–705, 734–37). We need not see it as absent or displaced onto Lysistrata's speeches, nor should we view it as properly belonging to parabasis anapests, as argued by Gelzer (1959, 28–29), Solomos (1974, 185), Westlake (1980, 43–44), Henderson (1987, xxix, 130, 141).

109. The absence of a lyric element in this parabasis may be compensated for by the elaborate cletic hymns and invocations of *Thesm.* 947–1000, 1136–59. Cf. Wilamowitz 1893 II, 349; Gelzer 1970, 1473; Dover 1972, 171; Hansen 1976, 184. Gelzer (1970, 1470) calls *Thesm.* 947–1000 a "second parabasis." The hymns are not purely decorative but bear implicit political comments comparable to what we sometimes find in parabasis hymns; note especially *Thesm.* 1140–47. Nevertheless they would have been disruptive in the context of this particular parabasis with its unitary emphasis on the women's self-justification.

of men. Since the agonistic structure and war-centered thematics of the
Lysistrata parabasis precluded a programmatic treatment of the wom-
en's interests, this parabasis in many respects serves that purpose for
both plays:

> We, therefore, will step forward and speak well of ourselves,   785
> Even though everyone speaks much ill of the female race,
> That we are entirely bad for men and that all bad things come from
> > us—
> Strife, disputes, discord, difficulties, pain, war. Come on now,
> If we are an evil, if we are truly an evil, why do you marry us,
> And tell us not to go out or be caught peeking out—   790
> Why do you want to protect this evil with so much zeal?
> And if your wife goes out anywhere, and then you catch her
> > outdoors,
> You rave like a madman, when you ought to rejoice and make
> > libations,
> If truly you found this evil gone and not inside your house.
> And if we fall asleep at a neighbor's house after making sport and
> > tiring ourselves out,   795
> Every man seeks out this evil when returning home to his bed.
> And if we peek out the door, you try to look at this evil;
> And if, in modesty, she retires, every man desires much more
> To see this evil peeking out again. So we are clearly
> Much better than you, and there is a test available to be examined.   800
> Let us try this test to see which of us is worse. We say that you are,
> You that we are. Let us examine and compare in regard to each
> > thing,
> Placing side by side the name of each woman and each man.
> Charminus is less than Nausimache; their deeds are evident.
> And indeed, Cleophon is altogether worse than Salabaccho.   805
> For a long time, none of you undertake to make war
> On Aristomache, that woman at Marathon, or Stratonike.
> And is any of last year's council-members, handing his office over to
> > another man,
> Better than Euboule? You yourself wouldn't say this!
> And so, we claim to be much better than men.   810
> No woman would come to town in a chariot after stealing
> Fifty talents of public funds; but if she secretly filches at most
> A measure of grain from her husband, she gives it back the same
> > day.
> > But we could show many of these men
> > Doing these things.   815
> > And in addition to these things, we could show

Them, rather than us, to be gluttons and cloak-thieves
And clowns and slave-merchants.
And indeed, they are worse than us
In saving their patrimony: 820
For among us, on the contrary,
Weaving rod, wool-baskets, and parasol
    Are still safe even now.
But among these husbands of ours,
Many lost their inherited "rod"   825
Along with the spear-head itself,
And many others threw
    The "parasol" from their shoulders
    Among the armies.
We women would justly blame our husbands   830
For many things, but one thing most of all.
For it is right that one of us should receive some honor,
If she gives birth to a man who is useful to the city—a colonel or
    general,
And that a seat of honor be given her at the Stenia and Skira
And at the other festivals which we conduct;   835
But if some woman gives birth to a cowardly and base man—
Either a base trierarch or a bad ship-captain,
She, with her hair cut short, should sit behind the woman
Who begat a courageous man. Therefore, O city, it is right
That Hyperbolus' mother, dressed in white robes and hair let-
    down,   840
Should sit near Lamachus' mother and loan out money.
If she loans money to anyone and asks for interest,
It is in this way fitting that no one give interest to her,
But all men should forcibly take the money away, saying this:
"You are one to claim interest, begetting such an 'interesting' son!"   845
                                        (*Thesm.* 785–845)

As we have noted, the *Thesmophoriazusae* is a play less about women
(like the *Lysistrata*) than about men's attitudes toward women, and
seems intent on effecting a change in those attitudes. The first woman
to speak at the Assembly (*Thesm.* 383–432) denounces Euripides for
causing husbands to distrust their wives both in sexual matters and in
affairs of household economy. The parabasis responds to these suspicions not so much by denying them as by accusing men in turn. If wives
are guilty of peeking out into the street to attract the attention of
men, men are guilty of paying attention (*Thesm.* 797–99); and if wives
may be guilty of temporary household thefts men are guilty of much

greater political thefts (*Thesm.* 811–13). The argument here, like the play as a whole,[110] achieves credibility by conceding the women's peccadillos and emphasizes their trivial nature in comparison with men's own faults.

The women ask rhetorically why, if they are such a great evil as misogynistic poetry from Hesiod through Semonides to Euripides suggests, do men marry them? Why complain about their absence? Why require their presence in bed? These lines gain added point and emphasis if the Athenian audience had just seen, within the space of the last two months, Aristophanes' dramatization in the *Lysistrata* of what the world would be like for men should their wives in fact be absent. Men's distrust of women would then be perceived to be just as divisive to family life as the war.

To see the women turn to the subject of war and politics is not astonishing. They claim a right to speak on these matters and even to be superior to men (*Thesm.* 799–810):[111] Nausimache ("Battleship") is best in naval warfare, Salabaccho ("Trumpeter") in voice, Aristomache ("Best in Battle") and Stratonike ("Victory of the Army") in battle, Euboule ("Good Counsel") in political counsel.[112] The claim of women to superior political and military wisdom has not been justified by anything in this play; but again it gains point and emphasis when seen against the background of the *Lysistrata,* in which significantly named women like Lysistrata ("Disbander of Armies") and Kalonike ("Fair Victory") in fact prove to be superior to men in resolving the war.[113] In the pnigos the women criticize men for being less able to preserve their patrimony (*Thesm.* 819–20), an allusion to all the money spent on the war, and especially to the last remaining resource of the treasury, the

110. Similarly the first woman who speaks against Euripides in the Assembly refers to supposititious children (*Thesm.* 407–8) and household thefts (*Thesm.* 418–28) as rights women should be able to take for granted. The wineskin baby in *Thesm.* 689–759 combines both motifs in visible form.

111. Again we should note the influence of the *Melanippe Desmotis* fragment (see n.78 above), especially v. 3: αἱ δ' εἰσ' ἀμείνους ἀρσένων. δείξω δ' ἐγώ.

112. There has been great controversy over the particular allusion involved in *Thesm.* 808–9, in which Euboule is said to be superior to "one of last year's councillors, handing his office over to another." Some think it alludes to the appointment of Probouloi (cf. Wilamowitz 1893 II, 344–45, and *HCT* V, 188), others to the resignation of power by the 500 in 411 (cf. Rogers 1904, xxxiii–xxxiv), others to some unnamed individual who resigned office (cf. Sommerstein 1977a, 116–17, but if he is a specific individual, why is he not named, like Charminus or Cleophon?). Van Leeuwen (1904, xi–xii) tries to solve the problem by deleting *Thesm.* 809 as an interpolation. I think Croiset (1909, 146) is right in merely referring the statement to the annual nature of the office, as compared to Euboule's absolute and enduring embodiment of political counsel.

113. Loraux (1980/81, 145–46) associates the Cratylinian interest of this passage with the names of the *Lysistrata.*

special 1,000 talent emergency reserve fund that was tapped in the aftermath of the Sicilian disaster[114] and that the Old Women criticized the Old Men for squandering, along with the rest of Athens' revenue, in *Lys.* 652–55. The issue receives comic treatment in the lines following wherein the women contrast their ability to keep their shuttle (*Thesm.* 822 κανών) and parasol (*Thesm.* 823 σκιάδειον) with the inability of many men to hold onto their spear (*Thesm.* 825 κανών) and shield (*Thesm.* 829 σκιάδειον). As in Lysistrata's famous wool-working simile (*Lys.* 574–86), the women's weaving equipment becomes a symbol of their domestic common sense, which also applies to political affairs. The *Lysistrata*'s whole plot of seizing the Acropolis and treasury is based on this very idea of women's household management skills enabling them to conduct the city's finances more prudently than their wasteful and extravagant husbands (see *Lys.* 488–95).[115] The epirrheme concludes the development of ideas by advising the city not only to honor good men and dishonor bad men, but also to honor and dishonor respectively the mothers of good and bad men, because their influence was strong and decisive in shaping their sons. Like *Thesm.* 819–29 this emphasis on the maternal role in contributing men to the war effort develops an idea first introduced in the parabasis of the *Lysistrata* (*Lys.* 651). Although motherhood figures, the war does not bulk large as a theme elsewhere in the *Thesmophoriazusae.*

One might argue that the cross-references to the *Lysistrata* in this parabasis are anticipations rather than allusions and that the cross-references in the *Lysistrata* itself are the opposite. To some extent the judgment of priority is subjective, but the preponderance of evidence suggests, as we have contended, that the *Thesmophoriazusae* builds on themes first touched on in the *Lysistrata,* and that its parabasis serves effectively as a comment on both plays in a way the *Lysistrata* parabasis cannot. In both cases, however, the parabasis functions as a critical focus for the consequences of women assuming an active and outspoken role in the city.

Debased Coinage

Because the *Frogs* is not only our last surviving work of Old Comedy but is itself concerned with the decline both of Athenian drama and

114. See Thucydides 8.15.1. On the theft and corruption accompanying the distribution of this fund (also alluded to in *Thesm.* 811–12), see Wilamowitz 1893 II, 346–47, interpreting Antiphon 6.35, 6.50.

115. On this idea, see the discussion of Rosellini 1979, 15–16, and on the general parallel of *oikos* and *polis,* see Foley 1982, 6–12.

political greatness, it occupies a special place in the history of Greek literature. Even more than Euripides' *Bacchae* or Sophocles' *Oedipus at Colonus*, the *Frogs* stands as a retrospection on an era coming to a close, in both literature and politics. Aristophanes' chief prototype for the idea of a descent to Hades to retrieve great figures of the past who could assist Athens in its present difficulties was Eupolis' *Demoi*, which brought back to life Solon, Miltiades, Aristides, and Pericles.[116] Aristophanes makes the significant shift of bringing back to Athens a tragic poet, not a statesman, in order to reflect the recent deaths of Sophocles and Euripides. But the *Frogs* is from beginning to end imbued with political as well as poetic themes, and Dionysus' final choice of Aeschylus seems to be determined more by political symbolism than by aesthetic superiority. The play's choruses and parabasis perform a pivotal role in coordinating its political and literary dimensions.

In the *Frogs* we also discover a generic concern about Comedy itself, a matter mostly absent in *Birds, Lysistrata,* and *Thesmophoriazusae,* but quite important in Aristophanes' earlier plays, as we have seen. Segal has discussed the development of Dionysus within the play as the god of Comedy who progressively assumes his role after much self-doubt and many changes of identity.[117] In this respect he resembles some of Aristophanes' earlier protagonists, such as Dicaeopolis, the Sausage seller, Bdelycleon, or Trygaeus, who emerge as symbolic figures for Aristophanic Comedy, in their different ways combining lofty ambitions with earthy means of accomplishment. Dionysus' character expresses the same duality and ambivalence, oscillating as it does between bravado and effeminate cowardice, between the heroic costume of the great Heracles and the mundane garments of a slave.

The overall movement of the play progresses from a farcical first half with a weak and uncertain Dionysus to a more serious second half, in which Dionysus assumes the role of judge and mediator. Critics have on occasion been troubled by the *Frogs'* atypical structure, with the major agon coming after the parabasis and the series of farcical genre scenes coming before; they have also had difficulty in discerning any clear connection between the thematics of Dionysus' journey in the first half and the tragic contest in the second half of the play.[118] Aristopha-

116. The *Demoi* almost certainly dates to 412 (cf. Geissler 1925, 54–55). An embassy to Hades to retrieve dead poets also appears to be part of Aristophanes' *Gerytades* (cf. fr. 156 PCG) but this play may postdate the *Frogs;* on the uncertainty of its date, see *PCG* III, 2, 101.

117. Segal 1961, 208–15, 227–28. Cf. Whitman 1964, 239; Reckford 1987, 408.

118. For criticism of the play's structure, see Fraenkel 1962, 163–88; Hooker 1980, 169–70; Harriott 1986, 106–16; and for defense, see Heath 1987, 44–48. As will be clear from my discussion, I do not agree with their mechanical explanations of why Aristophanes chose the present form and structure.

nes may have structured the play as he did precisely to make a point about the relation of the comic and serious (as the chorus puts it in vv. 391–92, "saying many funny things [πολλὰ μὲν γέλοια] and many serious things [πολλὰ δὲ σπουδαῖα]") and the necessity of approaching the serious through the comic. It has been observed that the part of the play before the parabasis features all the well-worn comic topoi Aristophanes abjures elsewhere: the glutton Heracles (vv. 503–73), slave beating (vv. 610–73), primitive animal choruses (vv. 207–68).[119] The slave Xanthias opens the play by asking Dionysus whether he should say "one of the customary things the spectators always laugh at" (vv. 1–2) and Dionysus consents, prohibiting only the use of certain grossly physical terms and jokes that are nevertheless used in the very act of banning them, and indirectly, later on (see vv. 479–91).[120] The simultaneous disavowal and use of these clichés foreshadow the slapstick technique of the section as a whole. As in so many other cases Aristophanes ironically announces his disdain for the very devices he employs, thus profiting from their theatrical value and at the same time appearing to be above them.

The same dialectic between the low comic and its more serious transcendence is also apparent in the play's double chorus, which first appears as lowly Frogs and later as mystic Initiates. After paying Charon a fee of two obols (= the price of theater admission)[121] Dionysus encounters an invisible, but highly audible chorus of Frogs,[122] from whom the play takes its title. The Frogs offer an amusing and colorful spectacle, even if not seen, and recall the old animal choruses that poets like Magnes used to present.[123] Dionysus' attempt to com-

---

119. For Aristophanes' disavowal of interest in these, cf. *Eq.* 522–23 (ridiculing Magnes), *Nub.* 541–43, *Vesp.* 60, *Pax* 741–47. On the use of these topoi here, see Cantarella 1962, 128–29; Redfield 1963, 432; Solomos 1974, 211.

120. See chap. 5 n.43 above.

121. Cf. Whitman 1964, 235, and Demand 1970, 85. What follows is thus a sort of play within the play. Charon's usual fee of course is one obol.

122. The invisibility of the Frogs has, I think, been rather conclusively demonstrated by Allison 1983, 8–20.

123. See *Eq.* 522–23 and in general, Sifakis (1971b, 71–102), who regards theriomorphic choruses as fundamental to the early history of Attic comedy. The Frogs seem to be a more archaic kind of animal chorus than the others employed by Aristophanes, in the sense that they are actually frogs and nothing more. The Knights and Wasps are both actually choruses of Athenian citizens, and the Birds are at least symbolically Athenian citizens. Frogs had earlier been used as comic choruses by both Magnes (cf. *Eq.* 523) and Callias (cf. *PCG* IV, 42). The invisibility of the Frogs here may be meant to indicate something about the disappearance of Old Comedy and its extravagantly costumed choruses; contrast the Frogs with the chorus which *is* visible, Eleusinian Initiates dressed in rags (vv. 405–10), perhaps making a point about the financial exigency now pressing dramatic production. It is not that lack of resources forced Aristophanes to make the Frogs invisible, since Comedy seldom contained two choruses even in prosperous times; rather Aristophanes conceived the idea of presenting a traditional comic chorus that

pete with their croaking as he rows across the lake itself evokes reminiscence of Eupolis and possibly of other poets.[124] That Dionysus' contest with the Frogs is a comic equivalent of the contest between the two tragic poets after the parabasis has often been recognized. Many have seen the Frogs as symbols of the new dithyrambic poets or as just bad poets in general,[125] but they are probably better viewed as symbols of traditional Old Comedy, particularly in its most extravagant and farcical aspects.[126] It is well worth noting that the Frogs combine their raucous ugliness with lyrical pretensions: Charon introduces them as nothing less than "frog-swans" (v. 207) who sing "the most beautiful melodies" (vv. 205–6).[127] As in comic parody they mix the sublime with the ridiculous. To recognize the symbolic polarities the frog archetype evokes one need only think of the many fairy tales in which frogs turn into beautiful princes or princesses.

In fact Aristophanes' frog chorus undergoes such a metamorphosis. The Frogs' marsh is merely a dark region through which Dionysus passes on his heroic pilgrimage, and when, scarcely fifty lines later, the chorus comes into the orchestra in visible form, they are revealed to be not slimy green Frogs, but pure and holy mystic Initiates.[128] The Frogs' onomatopoetic *brekekekex koax koax* is replaced by an equally resonant and far more mellifluous cry of *Iacch' O Iacche!* The two forms of this play's chorus thus mirror the dialectic between man's physical, animal nature and his transcendent, spiritual side, a dialectic essential to the comic view of the world, aptly represented elsewhere by the image of flying to heaven on a dung beetle's back. Comedy depends on a recognition of man's corporal frailties as displayed here in carrying heavy

---

could not appear, with a view to making a statement about financial constraints and the decline of Comedy (cf. vv. 367–68).

124. For the rowing scene in Eupolis' *Taxiarchoi* as a model for the *Frogs*, cf. Wilson 1974, 250–52; Handley 1982, 24–25; Allison 1983, 11–13; and chap. 4 n.55 above.

125. Cf. Defradas 1969, 25–27; Demand 1970, 86–87; Solomos 1974, 215; Henderson 1975, 93. Against the idea of parody in the Frogs' song, see Campbell 1984, 164–65.

126. For the Frogs' symbolic significance in this regard, see the interesting discussion of Reckford 1987, 408–13, especially 412.

127. On the elements of high lyric in the Frogs' song, see Segal 1961, 222; Wills 1969b, 316; Campbell 1984, 165.

128. The Initiates are generally considered to be Eleusinian, as is strongly suggested by the hymn to Demeter in vv. 385–95; see Σ*Ran.* 320, 354, and Lapalus 1934, 1–20. However, Tierney (1935, 199–202) criticizes this view and proposes that they are Orphic initiates. There may be some syncretism of associations here. Hooker (1960, 116–17) is probably right in seeing their procession as modelled on that to the Lesser Eleusinian Mysteries at Agrai taking place in the month of Anthesterion and located across the river from the sanctuary of Dionysus in the Marshes. Sartori (1974, 437–38) less convincingly holds that allusion is being made to Alcibiades' military protection of the Greater Eleusinian procession in 407 (Xenophon, *Hell.* 1.4.20; Plutarch, *Alc.* 34).

burdens like Xanthias, rowing nonstop across a huge lake like Dionysus, desiring and being deprived of the food and dancing girls offered by the Hostess, or being whipped by Aeacus to test sensitivity to pain. Even amid these physical stresses and limitations, however, the chorus of Initiates offers an idealistic vision of self-fulfillment in which old age can disappear (vv. 345–53), where the chorus can play and dance all day (vv. 388–90) and live happily dressed in rags and torn sandals (vv. 405–10). Invoked by his mystic title Iacchus, Dionysus is reminded of his ability to complete the long journey to this place absolutely "without toil" (vv. 402–3 ἄνευ πόνου), with the implication that the discomfort and toil he has experienced in the rowing scene were illusory. The mystery-religions of which the Initiates are representatives aim ultimately at the overcoming of death itself, the greatest physical limitation of all. This idealized, utopian version of the world as it ought to be is as much an essential aspect of Comedy as the other more realistic and mundane perspective with its emphasis on man's physical appetites and susceptibilities. Thus each chorus initiates an important register of comic meaning, one more democratic and commonplace, with an accent on pure entertainment value, the other more elitist and *sophos,* using Comedy as a vehicle to articulate a higher agenda.

The utopian aims of Comedy are always connected with a purification of the state from social pests and undesirables.[129] In this aspect Comedy may seem conservative and aristocratic, like the select band of Initiates who in an extended anapestic section of the parodos define themselves by contrast with the malefactors excluded from their company:

> He ought to speak piously and stand aside from our choruses,
> Whoever has no experience of such teachings or is not pure in
>   thought,   355
> Or has never seen the rites of the noble Muses or danced in them,
> And has not been initiated into the Bacchic rites of tongue special
>   to bull-eating Cratinus,
> Or delights in clownish sayings which come at the wrong time,
> Or whoever does not dissolve hateful faction and is not well
>   disposed to his fellow citizens,
> But arouses and fans the flames, desiring private gain,   360

129. The image of social purification or catharsis is quite clear in v. 355, in which the chorus commands anyone who "is not pure in thought" (γνώμῃ μὴ καθαρεύει) to stand aside; compare the *Wasps* parabasis (especially vv. 1015, 1043–45), and our remarks on p. 118 above. For the general connection of utopian poetry since the time of Hesiod with this type of social criticism, see Auger 1979, 71–72; Carrière 1979, 102–4.

Or takes bribes as a magistrate, while the city is in rough weather,
Or betrays a fortress or ships, or exports contraband
From Aegina, being a wretched customs-man like Thorycion,
Sending over to Epidaurus oar-pads and sailcloth and pitch,
Or persuades someone to contribute money for the enemies' ships,   365
Or shits on the Hecate-shrines while singing with dithyrambic
        choruses,
Or as an orator nibbles away at poets' pay,
Because of being laughed at in the ancestral rites of Dionysus.
To all these I declare and again declare and again a third time
        declare
That they should stand aside from the mystic choruses. But you
        now awaken the song   370
And our all-night vigils which are fitting at this festival.

                                                     (vv. 354–71)

It is significant that the ill-doers excluded from the mystic band combine those who are aesthetically ignorant with those who have betrayed
the city politically. Vv. 356–57 reject those who are unfamiliar with the
rites of the Muses or are uninitiated into the Bacchic mysteries of
Comedy, as represented by Cratinus, the great prototype of politically
engaged comic poetry.[130] The rejection of those who laugh at inopportune clownish jokes (v. 358) appears specifically aimed at the kind of
vulgar comedy which the Frogs symbolize and which Dionysus dis-
paraged in the prologue; the Initiates seem to be assimilating themselves to the *sophoi* of good taste whom Aristophanes in the parabases
of the *Clouds* and *Wasps* professed to be his ideal audience. Vv. 359–65
turn attention to those guilty of political crimes such as revolution,
bribery, misappropriation of tax revenues and helping the enemy with
money, goods, or information. But vv. 366–68 combine the civic and
artistic realms by excluding impious dithyrambic poets, an evident
allusion to Cinesias,[131] and orators who propose reducing dramatic
poets' pay after being ridiculed in Comedy. This acts as a humorous
anticlimax to the whole series of crimes and also introduces a serious
point about the decline of drama being inextricably linked with the
decline of political morality and leadership in Athens. Just as the lust
for ever scarcer money corrupts political officeholders and merchants
of trade, the lack of money has led to a decline in the quality of drama,
although the ragged chorus of Initiates does its best. This connection

130. See p. 74 above.
131. Cf. Σ*Ran.* 366, van Leeuwen 1896, 67; Kock 1898, 92; Stanford 1963, 107. On
Cinesias' impiety, see n.16 above.

between political and poetic debasement adumbrates the major themes of the coming parabasis and agon.

In many ways the anapestic tetrameters here function as a parabasis both formally and thematically.[132] Comedy's role as an instrument of purification for the benefit of a selective audience of *sophoi* is familiar from the anapestic parabases of the *Clouds* and *Wasps*, as we have seen. Since there are no anapests in the actual parabasis of the *Frogs* we can legitimately consider this section as their displaced equivalent. It is not concerned with a defense of the poet himself so much as with establishing the identity and credentials of the chorus, as is usual in the epirrhemes, though also evident in the anapests of the *Birds* and *Thesmophoriazusae*. What resembles the anapests of the earlier plays, however, is this chorus' implicit identification with and defense of Comedy as a generic phenomenon. In these lines the coryphaeus speaks for the chorus not only as Dionysiac initiates but specifically as initiates in the Dionysiac mysteries of Comedy. Preceding and following the anapests are lyric hymns to both Iacchus, the mystic Dionysus, and Demeter, goddess of the Eleusinian mysteries, interspersed with topical abuse of undesirables such as Thorycion (v. 383, already mentioned in v. 363 of the anapests), Archedemus (vv. 420–25; cf. v. 588), Cleisthenes (vv. 426–31; cf. vv. 48, 57), and Callias (vv. 432–34).

Because the Frogs' chorus in many ways delivered the play's real parodos, the Initiates' parodos can act as a sort of preliminary parabasis. And since this preliminary parabasis gives scope to the comic self-defense, choral self-presentation, and hymnic invocations customary in parabases, the real parabasis is free to concentrate on political advice to the city, with the authority and credentials of the chorus already well established:

> O Muse, come to our sacred dances and arrive for the
>   pleasure of my song,
> So that you can see the great crowd of people, whose
>   Countless forms of wisdom sit
> More eager for honor than Cleophon, upon whose
>   chattering lips
>   The Thracian swallow   680
>   Makes a terrible noise
>   Sitting on a barbarian leaf.

---

132. Cf. Pieters 1946, 23–24; Sodano 1961, 51; Whitman 1964, 230; Strauss 1966, 246; Horn 1970, 137; van der Valk 1981–82, 125; Zimmermann 1985 I, 125; Reckford 1987, 415–17; and our remarks on pp. 26–27 above.

It sings a mournful nightingale's song, that he will be
    destroyed,
      Even if the jury's votes are equal.   685
It is just for the sacred chorus to advise and teach
Good things for the city. First, it seems right to us
To put all the citizens on an equal level and remove their fear,
And if anyone made a mistake, being tripped up by Phrynichus'
    tricks,
I say that it should be possible for those who then slipped up   690
To make their case and atone for their previous mistakes.
Then I say that no one should be disgraced in this city;
For it is shameful that those fighting one naval battle
Should immediately become Plataeans and masters instead of
    slaves.
And I would not even be able to say that this matter is wrong;   695
Rather I agree with it, for you did this alone correctly.
But in addition to these men, it is fitting that you forgive those who
Fought many naval battles along with you, as their fathers did, and
    are of good stock,
Accused only in this one misfortune.
But, O naturally wisest men, giving up this anger   700
Let us willingly obtain as kinsmen all men,
Citizens with full rights, whoever fights with us at sea.
But if we puff ourselves up and are too proud in this matter,
Especially when we have the city in the arms of the sea,
At some later time we will not seem to have planned well.   705

    If I am right in seeing the life or manner of a man who will
      soon lament,
    Not much time will be wasted by this monkey who hinders us
      now,
      The little Cleigenes,
    The most wicked bath-man, of as many as control the ash-
      mixed   710
      False-soda lye
      And Cimolian clay.
    Seeing these things, he will not be
    Peaceful, fearing lest he also be stripped of his cloak, walking
      home drunk   715
      Without his magistrate's rod.
The city has often seemed to us to have suffered
The same thing in regard to the good and noble citizens
As in regard to the old coinage and newer gold.   720
These coins are not adulterated,
But the finest of all coinages, as it seems,
Alone correctly minted and assayed

Everywhere among the Greeks and barbarians.
But we use them not at all, preferring these base coppers   725
Minted yesterday and the day before by the worst process.
Even so, we maltreat the citizens whom we know to be well-born
And restrained men, just, good, and noble,
Brought up with wrestling, choruses, and music;
Instead, we use for all things the brazen, foreign, and red-haired,   730
Base men of base parents,
The latest arrivals, whom before this the city
Would hardly even have used as scapegoats.
But even now, foolish men, change your ways
And use the good men again. For then, if you succeed,   735
It is praiseworthy; if you trip up on something, it is at any rate on a
      good piece of wood;
Even if you suffer some calamity, wise men will think it a calamity.

(vv. 674–737)

Here the elite chorus addresses the audience as people of elite under-standing (v. 700 "O wisest ones [σοφώτατοι] by inborn nature"; vv. 676–78 "the great crowd of people, whose countless forms of wisdom [σοφίαι] sit more eager for honor than Cleophon")[133] who are concerned about how they will appear to the elite of future generations (compare vv. 705 and 737, the last line of each epirrheme). Within this framework of encouragement to the audience[134] the chorus urges a restoration of full political rights to all the former supporters of the oligarchic revolution in 411. This group includes many of Athens' best and brightest citizens whose leadership is sorely needed in this period of continuing vulnerability for Athens. When Athens has been willing to give citizenship to slaves for fighting in the recent battle of Arginusae, it is unjustifiable to withhold the full franchise from men who are of good family, who have served in many such naval battles, and whose ancestors have served in such battles (vv. 693–98).

Aristophanes' concern for the oligarchs here certainly does not stem from any fondness or affection for that group; as we have noted, several passages in the *Lysistrata* and *Thesmophoriazusae* suggest that he viewed the proposed constitutional changes and brewing revolution of 411 with suspicion. Nor was Athens' military situation nearly as desperate in the wake of the victory at Arginusae as it had been a year earlier. Rather what inspired Aristophanes' call for rehabilitation of the oli-

133. On the contrast between the positive stance of the ode and epirrheme and the more admonitory tone of the antepirrheme, which addresses the audience as "foolish men," v. 734 ὦνόητοι, see van der Valk 1981–82, 110.
134. Compare this with the similar technique of rhetorical protreptic in the parabases of the *Clouds* and *Wasps* (see pp. 94 and 116 above) and, in general, p. 18 above.

garchs were two troubling events in the immediate aftermath of Arginusae: the trial and execution of the victorious generals for failing to rescue shipwrecked survivors,[135] and the rejection of reasonable peace terms offered by the Spartans. The first action provides a searing example of the Athenian public's readiness to be led by cunning demagogues into quick condemnation of the city's most experienced and effective leaders; before this incident the *dēmos* had unbalanced the Sicilian expedition with the recall of Alcibiades and driven many other notable citizens into self-imposed exile to escape the torrent of accusations stemming from the mutilation of the herms and profanation of the mysteries. Alcibiades had found favor in Athens again and lost it once more after the battle of Notium in 407, disappearing into a final self-exile at his fortress in the Chersonese. Year after year new boards of generals were elected, often passing over experienced and successful commanders such as Thrasybulus because of past connections with the oligarchs; as soon as the new commanders gained experience they too were disgraced. The disenfranchisement of the oligarchs was merely one more in a long series of actions by which popular opinion deprived the state of skilled leadership and, what may be worse, intimidated other good men from offering leadership. In turn, this lack of truly public-spirited leadership was responsible for Aristophanes' other great disappointment that year and, as it proves to be in the end, a decisive mistake—rejection of peace with Sparta.[136]

The result of driving out good leaders is that inevitably bad leaders will take over. Aristophanes refers quite appropriately to the emancipation of slaves after Arginusae as slaves being "masters instead of slaves" (v. 694). The decline in the quality of Athens' political leaders, hinted at already in the anapestic section of the parodos, makes it seem as if slaves in fact were now the masters of the city. One remembers Cleon in the *Knights* represented as the Paphlagonian slave who rules master Demos; and in the present context the ode implies that the demagogue Cleophon was the son of a Thracian slave woman (vv. 680–

135. The various references to Archedemus "who is now a demagogue among the corpses above" (vv. 423–24; cf. v. 588), Theramenes who is noted for his ability to change positions to his advantage (vv. 541, 967–70), and Erasinides (vv. 1195–96) suggest that Aristophanes strongly disapproved of the generals' condemnation. See Sartori 1974, 425–32. The joke about Cleisthenes' mourning for Sebinus (vv. 426–31) may also allude to the large number of mourning "relatives" who showed up at the Assembly, many of whom were suspected of being fraudulent hirelings (Xenophon, *Hell.* 1.7.8; cf. Diodorus Sic. 13.101.6).

136. The final lines of the play (vv. 1531–33) make it quite clear that Aristophanes favored the recent peace proposals; see Sartori 1974, 433. On the advantages of accepting Sparta's peace terms at this time, see Kagan 1987, 377–79.

82) and thus not a true Athenian citizen.[137] The exchange of costumes back and forth between Dionysus and his slave Xanthias has already suggested a dramatic blurring of the distinctions between slave and master; on one level this may reflect the current state of social relations between former slaves and their masters,[138] but on another level it serves as a comment on the total breakdown of traditional social differentiation in an era when the lowliest tradesmen, like the lyre maker Cleophon and bath man Cleigenes, lead the state and the old-line aristocracy is completely excluded from having a voice in the city's affairs.

The idea that worse men are taking the place of better men in politics is expressed more clearly in the antepirrheme (vv. 727–33) and illustrated with the memorable metaphor of debased coinage (vv. 718–26). Unlike the old silver coinage and the recent special issue of gold coins (= "the well-born, restrained, just, good, and noble citizens"[139]), Athens' present currency is a cheap alloy of silver-plated copper, seemly in appearance but hollow in substance. Even so, the city's present leaders, rather than coming from families with long traditions of public service, are new arrivals on the political scene, "base men of base parents" (v. 731), "foreign and red-haired" (v. 730). The image of adulterated coinage is foreshadowed in the antode by the demagogue Cleigenes' debased laundry ash (vv. 710–12), as in the ode by Cleophon's allegedly half-breed ancestry.

Cleophon and his slave mother are reminders of another "new man" and his infamous mother, the poet Euripides, identified in comic tradition as son of a greengrocer woman.[140] Euripides' new poetry is re-

137. According to Σ*Ran.* 681 (= fr. 61 PCG), Plato claimed Cleophon's mother was a Thracian.

138. See Segal 1961, 216; Sartori 1974, 424–28; Solomos 1974, 211–12; Konstan 1986, 302–3.

139. I am relying here on the most common modern interpretation of this line as elaborated, for instance, by Bergk (1873, 131–36) and Thompson (1966, 339–43). Van der Valk (1981–82, 116–17), however, has proposed that the καινὸν χρυσίον (v. 720) does not refer to the new gold coins minted out of the gold plating from the statue of Nike in the Acropolis, but simply uses χρυσίον in the generic sense of "money" and thus refers to the newer silver-plated coppers. Against this view, we note that the following vv. 721–24 (τούτοισιν οὖσιν . . .) refer only to good coinage, and the parallel ἔς τε . . . in v. 719 refers only to good citizens, not good and bad, unless we emend καλοὺς to κακούς. Even if the gold coins were only used for foreign exchange, as van der Valk claims, everyone in Athens knew about their minting; for van der Valk's interpretation to be good Greek we should expect a μὲν/δέ coordination, not the adversative ἀλλά in v. 725, which marks a sharp break with everything preceding it. The same objections apply to the old interpretation going back to the scholia (Σ*Ran.* 725), that the gold coins are bad because they are easily counterfeited by copper coins; this interpretation obscures the whole contrast between good and bad citizens.

140. Cf. *Ach.* 475–78, *Eq.* 19, *Thesm.* 387, 456, *Ran.* 840.

garded as in many ways a cheapening and debasement of the dramatic art analogous to what demagogues like Cleophon and Cleigenes have done in the political realm. It is no surprise that the coinage metaphor is applied to his poetry, as his "private gods" are called a "new coinage" (v. 890 κόμμα καινόν);[141] a few lines earlier, dramatic poets are called "aphorism-minting men" (v. 877 ἀνδρῶν γνωμοτύπων), all of which harks back to the prologue, with Dionysus wanting to "test the metal" of Iophon's poetry (v. 79 κωδωνίσω; cf. v. 723).

Indeed everything about the contest between Euripides and Aeschylus translates back into the poetic sphere the political contrast foregrounded by the parabasis.[142] Euripides is of course the newer poet associated with Socratic and sophistic subtlety (λεπτολογία)[143] and supported in his bid against Aeschylus by the mob of "muggers, purse-snatchers, parricides, and break-in artists" who form the majority in Hades (vv. 771–78); it is no wonder that he numbers among his chief students the Socratic Cleitophon and the "clever Theramenes" (v. 967) who had recently inflamed the Athenian rabble to demand the trial and execution of the generals at Arginusae and who in this play is twice referred to for his ability to twist himself out of difficulty (vv. 538–41, 967–70; cf. vv. 775, 957, on Euripides' verbal "twisting"). The older Aeschylus is supported by the "few good men" (v. 783 ὀλίγον τὸ χρηστόν) including the recently deceased Sophocles (vv. 786–94); the parallel with the neglected "good men" (v. 735 χρηστοῖσιν) of the just finished parabasis is evident, especially as v. 783 invites comparison with contemporary politics through the tag ὥσπερ ἐνθάδε ("just like here").

Aeschylus' politics naturally reflect the more conservative, aristocratic values of the Marathon and Salamis generations, but Euripides self-consciously proclaims himself as the poet of radical democracy (v. 952 δημοκρατικόν), affording equal opportunity for speech and character interest to all, be it woman, old woman, slave, master, or maiden

---

141. On the continuing allusion here to the debased coinage mentioned in the parabasis, see Taillardat 1962, 471.

142. Cf. Redfield, 1963, 434–39; Whitman 1964, 238–39; Sartori 1974, 419–20.

143. Cf. vv. 774–76, 826–29, 901–2, 956; similar terms are used in *Nub.* 153, 229–30, 320, 359, 741–42, 1404, 1496. On the *leptos* terms, see Denniston 1927, 119. Note also Cratinus, fr. 342 PCG, where Aristophanes and Euripides together are derided as ὑπολεπτολόγος. The chorus' final ode characterizes Aeschylus' victory over Euripides as a triumph of "common sense" (σύνεσις, cf. vv. 1482–90) over Socratic chatter (vv. 1491–99). For the general parallel of this agon with the one in the *Clouds,* casting Aeschylus as a more successful version of the Greater Discourse, Euripides as the Lesser Discourse, cf. Strauss 1966, 254; Dover 1972, 183–84; van der Valk 1981–82, 103–5; Reckford 1987, 426–28.

(vv. 949–50).[144] As befits a properly democratic poet, Euripides' drama
is realist in orientation, relying only on what is familiar to the experience of his audience:

> . . . Bringing onstage domestic affairs, which we experience and are
>   familiar with,
> And on which I could be refuted—for these men, knowing about
>   these things,
> Could test my art. But I never talked big,
> Striking people out of their minds, nor did I frighten them,
> Creating Cycnuses and Memnons with bell-and-cheekpiece-horses.
>
> (vv. 959–63)

As Euripides accuses Aeschylus of preoccupation with the fantastic and
unnatural, Aeschylus can in turn characterize Euripides' democratic
realism as fixation on the degraded: whorish women, kings in rags,
panders, incest, suicide (vv. 1043–44, 1063–64, 1079–82). Aeschylus
traces the city's moral decline (vv. 1050–51, 1065–66, 1069–72), athletic indolence (vv. 1070–71, 1087–88), and dependence on demagogues (vv. 1083–86) to Euripides' drama, which in his view provides
people with evil models which they feel justified in imitating. Not
unlike Plato in the *Republic*,[145] Aeschylus is concerned with the effect
of drama on its audience and so believes that poetry should offer positive paradigms of behavior for the public to follow, such as examples
of martial valor, and should conceal evil paradigms lest people be
tempted to imitate them as models (vv. 1053–56). Drama should therefore not be open democratically and indiscriminately to representation
of everyone, but must restrict itself to presenting good men and "saying good things" (v. 1056 χρηστὰ λέγειν), that is, giving useful advice to the city as the select Initiates do in the parabasis (vv. 686–87
χρηστὰ . . . συμπαραινεῖν καὶ διδάσκειν). Such a practice of course is
no more true of Aeschylean than of Euripidean drama; all the same
Aristophanes finds the aristocratic Aeschylus an appropriate mouthpiece for this more selective and idealistic conception of drama's role,
in contrast to the hyperrealism of Euripides. There is a certain authoritarianism implicit in this idea of exclusiveness as there was in the

---

144. Euripides' close collaboration with the slave Cephisophon (vv. 944, 1408, 1452–
53) also suggests hyperegalitarian sympathies and a lack of sensitivity to distinctions of
class and status. Cf. Walsh 1984, 92.

145. Of course this is a theory having its roots far back in poetic tradition: compare,
for instance, Pindar, *N*.5.16–18, *N*.7.14–16, fr. 42 S–M and my remarks in Hubbard
1985, 102–6.

oligarchs of 411; neither Aeschylus' views nor Euripides' here should
be completely identified with those of Aristophanes.

The contrast between the democratic Euripides and the elitist Aeschylus extends into the stylistic realm as well. Euripides prides himself
on clarity and straightforwardness, on making his work accessible to
everyone; in his prologues a character always comes forward to explain
for the audience the background and circumstances of the play (vv.
945–47). Indeed, Aeschylus mocks Euripides' expository prologues for
their formulaic uniformity and predictability by showing that the same
phrase can be tacked onto any of them (vv. 1206–47). Aeschylus on the
other hand seems too little concerned with the comprehensibility of his
poetry and at times inclines to willful obscurantism; silent characters
like Niobe and Achilles sit onstage for hundreds of lines saying nothing
(vv. 911–20), and when they finally speak they use long and redundant
words the spectators cannot understand (vv. 923–26).[146] In the battle
of prologues Euripides accuses Aeschylus of being "unclear" (v. 1122
ἀσαφής) and proceeds to illustrate his charge by carefully dissecting
the prologue of the *Choephori,* revealing its ambiguities and redundan-
cies (vv. 1124–74). Many of Euripides' criticisms here are in fact quite
trenchant, and Aeschylus' densely packed style has often seemed difficult and taxing to modern students as well. Aeschylus' pretentious and
recherché diction unquestionably demands the understanding of a more
literary and sophisticated audience than Euripides' rather pedestrian
and commonplace rhetoric. Both stylistic tendencies contain faults.
Each, however, also has its merits: it bears noting that Aristophanes
himself makes use of expository prologues as well as exotic big words
like those of Aeschylus.

Another stylistic area in which the political contrast between the two
poets becomes apparent is in their metrical practice. Aeschylus' conservative traditionalism is reflected appropriately in a conservative use of
meter, adherence to regular patterns and chaste rhythms, without
deviation from the established rules of good usage. Euripides criticizes
Aeschylus' lyrics for metrical uniformity, showing that they end in a
paroemiac clausula (vv. 1261–77) or have a monotonous musical ac-
companiment (= *toflattothrat toflattothrat,* vv. 1281–95). Aeschylus on
the other hand parodies Euripides' lyrics as thoroughly undisciplined
and aimless; the long, unresponsive Euripidean lyric delivered in vv.
1309–63 wildly mixes Aeolic, anapestic, dactylic, iambic, and cretic
rhythms into an irrational medley of meters and moods reminiscent of

146. Aeschylus' fondness for big words and metaphorical density is also ridiculed in
the ode introducing the contest (vv. 814–42). In addition, cf. vv. 902–4.

the new dithyrambic style at its worst. In the earlier battle of the prologues Aeschylus' refrain "lost his oil flask" (ληκύθιον ἀπώλεσεν) not only reflects the formulaic nature of Euripides' expository prologues and the banality of Euripidean diction but also makes a metrical point about Euripides' fondness for resolution, particularly in the fourth foot, at which place it is normally avoided.[147] Euripides' desire to defy convention and break metrical laws forms part of the same modernist iconoclasm Aeschylus considers responsible for the dissolution of moral values and laws in Athenian society as a whole.

The penultimate contest between Aeschylus and Euripides consists in a fantastic "weighing of words," modelled on the famous weighing of souls in Aeschylus' *Psychostasia.* Though on one level this contest is an absurd literalization of the figural metaphor of "weight," on another level it makes a serious point in characterizing Euripides' words as insubstantial and trivial in comparison with Aeschylus' gravity of both expression and purpose. Like the sophists and demagogues Euripides is concerned with Peitho and the power of language in its own right (v. 1391), while Aeschylus is concerned with real issues of life and death (vv. 1392, 1403). Still, Dionysus is unable to make a decision between the two poets on the basis of purely aesthetic criteria, declaring that he considers the one "wise" (v. 1413 τὸν μὲν γὰρ ἡγοῦμαι σοφόν) and takes pleasure in the other (τῷ δ' ἥδομαι). There has been considerable disagreement among commentators as to which of the two poets is which here; on the basis of the preceding discussion I believe the elitist Aeschylus must be the one designated as "wise," concerned as he is with substantive betterment of the young through positive poetic paradigms (vv. 1053–56); Euripides, on the other hand, gives pleasure, since he is concerned with appealing to the widest possible audience on a level they can understand without serious moral or intellectual exertion.[148]

147. On the almost extravagant fondness for resolution in the latest plays of Euripides, see Ceadel 1941, 66–89; for the extreme rarity of fourth foot resolution in Aeschylus, see the figures in Ceadel 1941, 84, and Schein 1979, 81. For the various other implications of this joke, cf. Whitman 1969, 110–11, and Henderson 1972, 133–43, although I tend to agree with the latter in not wanting to see the oil flask as a phallic object.

148. Aeschylus is characterized as *sophos* ("wise") in both vv. 1154 and 1519 (cf. 1482–90). Cf. Dover 1972, 187. Of course Euripides is also *sophos* ("clever," cf. vv. 776, 1451 σοφώτατος, really "too clever"). The language of *sophia* is commonly used of both poets together (cf. vv. 872, 882, 896, 1104–8, 1370) although they clearly represent different kinds of *sophia* (see our discussion of the term and its ambiguities on p. 95–96 above). As an antithesis to "pleasure" Dionysus probably means *sophos* in the more serious, didactic, Aeschylean sense here; the other kind of *sophia* ("cleverness") is itself too close to being a form of intellectual amusement. Also in support of this interpretation, Hurst (1971,

Dionysus' final decision must be made on political grounds, and as we might expect he returns to the issues raised by the parabasis in posing his questions to the two poets. Although Alcibiades was not one of the disgraced aristocrats of 411, the vicissitude of his political fortune in Athens was in many ways analogous. Alcibiades was an ambitious and self-serving individual, not unlike many of the oligarchs; all the same, he had over the years proven himself capable of shrewd diplomatic maneuverings and occasional military genius, qualities Athens sorely needed at the time. In retrospect we can say that Alcibiades' leadership might have saved the Athenian fleet from its disastrous errors at Aegospotami later that year.[149] Given the background of the parabasis and its call for restoration of the *atimoi* one can hardly doubt Aristophanes' cautious approval of Alcibiades' recall, whatever his reservations about Alcibiades' flamboyant character. Euripides' negative response to the recall seems to represent the popular judgment of Alcibiades as "resourceful for himself, helpless for the city" (v. 1429). On the other hand Aeschylus' qualified support is expressed in terms that reveal his more aristocratic orientation: "it is not fitting to raise a lion cub in the city, but if one does raise it, one must be subject to its ways" (vv. 1431–32).[150] There is some truth both in Euripides' suspicion and in Aeschylus' advice, but Dionysus ultimately expresses the

---

231–40) notes the $\mu\grave{\epsilon}\nu/\delta\acute{\epsilon}$ coordination as always referring the *men* term to the last speaker, the *de* term to the first speaker. In favor of the opposite view Marr (1970, 53) and Walsh (1984, 86–87) equate "taking pleasure" with Dionysus' intention to choose "whomever his soul wishes" in v. 1468 (= Aeschylus), but the soul's volition can just as well be an intellectual matter as a hedonistic one. Dionysus' "desire" ($\pi\acute{o}\theta os$) for Euripides in vv. 52–54 suggests that he is rather the one who appeals on the emotional, pleasure-oriented level. Clearly the *sophos* of v. 1413 must be the same as that of v. 1434, on which see our discussion below.

149. On Alcibiades' rebuffed attempts to advise the Athenians to move their camp from Aegospotami to Sestos and his proposals to supply Thracian allies, see Xenophon, *Hell.* 2.1.25; Plutarch, *Alc.* 36.5–37.2; Diodorus Sic. 13.105.3; Nepos 7.8.

150. Marr (1970, 53–55) may be correct in reassigning v. 1424 to Aeschylus, but he is wrong in reversing the speakers of the two answers; v. 1424 and vv. 1427–29 do not necessarily have to be spoken by the same person. Throughout the contest Euripides always speaks first, Aeschylus last; under Marr's reversal this passage would be the sole exception. Marr's proposal would also give the lion cub metaphor to Euripides on the grounds that it is a parody of the famous *Agamemnon* ode (*Ag.* 717–36); however, the purpose of this phase of the contest is not for each poet to parody the other, as in the section on prologues or lyrics, so much as to give his own opinion about contemporary politics in his own characteristic style. Marr's chief reason for wanting to switch the answers is to make it possible for Aeschylus to be the "clear" one, and Euripides the "clever" one, thus being consistent with vv. 1445 and 1451. But as I argue below, Euripides' lack of clarity in that passage is an intentional response to Dionysus' judgment in v. 1434.

poet's view in saying that Aeschylus again has spoken "wisely" (v. 1434 ὁ
μὲν σοφῶς γὰρ εἶπεν), Euripides "clearly" (ὁ δ' ἕτερος σαφῶς).[151]

In reaction to this verdict Euripides responds to Dionysus' second
question about general advice for the city's salvation by supplying an
answer which is less clear and, he hopes, more wise: the city will be
saved "when we consider trustworthy the things now distrusted, and
untrustworthy the things which are trusted" (vv. 1443–44). Dionysus
now asks him to be more clear (v. 1445 σαφέστερον) and less learned
(ἀμαθέστερον).[152] Euripides replies by explaining that the city should
distrust the citizens whom it now trusts and use the citizens whom it
does not now use; if the city fares ill at present, how could it fail to fare
better by doing the opposite of what it is now doing (vv. 1446–50)?

Critics have generally seen Euripides' advice here as equivalent to
what the poet recommends in the parabasis;[153] but it does not square
with what Euripides has just said about Alcibiades in vv. 1427–29. If
Euripides truly believes the city should use those whom it is not using,
would this not also include the recall of Alcibiades? What Euripides is
recommending here is something quite different from what the chorus
advised in the parabasis; the parabasis did not merely advise the city to
use men different from those it is currently using, but to use "good
men" (v. 735 χρῆσθε τοῖς χρηστοῖσιν), a distinction nowhere made
in Euripides' answer. Indeed, it is left to Aeschylus to ask about the
moral quality of the men the city is now using, whether good (v. 1455
χρηστοῖς) or bad (v. 1456 πονηροῖς). Euripides' interest seems rather to
be in continually using new men merely for the sake of using new men;
this concept receives its *reductio ad absurdum* with Euripides' ridiculous
new idea of using Cleocritus and Cinesias airborne to bombard the

---

151. The judgment is clearly parallel to that of v. 1413, with the *men* term again
designating the last speaker, the *de* term the first speaker. Although both answers are
indirect, Euripides' hostility toward Alcibiades is quite unambiguous and clear; Aeschylus' is expressed through metaphor and enigma, approving of Alcibiades' return without
approving of Alcibiades. As Dover (1972, 187) notes, this metaphorical answer is *sophos*
in the sense of using a poetic figure and thus displaying "poetic skill." On the allusive
complexity of Aeschylus' answer, see also Moorton 1988, 351–54, and Walsh 1984, 94–
95; the latter, however, curiously holds Euripides to be more *sophos*, as do most commentators, following Aristarchus (ΣRan. 1413), in regard to this line and v. 1413; cf. van
Leeuwen 1896, 205–6; Kock 1898, 209, 212; Radermacher 1954, 335. Tucker (1906,
255) fudges the issue by accepting Meineke's emendation of σαφῶς to σοφῶς, as does
Stanford (1963, 192–94) by suggesting intentional ambiguity.

152. Note that this term characterizes Euripides' answer as learned without necessarily being wise. In v. 1451 he is *sophos* in the sense of inventive "cleverness," like
Palamedes, not in the sense of broader "wisdom."

153. See Croiset 1909, 161; Harsh 1934, 184; Strauss 1966, 260; Wills 1969a, 54;
Sommerstein 1974, 27; Erbse 1975, 57; Walsh 1984, 96; Heath 1987, 21 n.36.

enemy's ships with vinegar bottles (vv. 1437–41).[154] It is not sound or intelligent advice to tell the city that it should simply do "the opposite" (v. 1450 τἀναντί') of what it is currently doing, if it is currently having problems. Indeed, Euripides' advocacy of perpetual questioning and distrust of those in authority and his proposal here that leaders and policies should continually and indiscriminately be changed are not the answer but precisely the problem with Athenian politics.[155] In the parabasis the chorus did not propose the bringing in of new leaders to replace those now in power, but the bringing back of old leaders. Aeschylus' response to Dionysus' question is much more in this spirit; Athens will not hold off the enemy by appointing new generals every year but by returning to a form of its traditional Themistoclean and Periclean policy, using ships to attack the enemy's homeland instead of trying to defend Attica and the empire (vv. 1463–65).[156] This advice ultimately may not be any more practical than Euripides', but its intellectual affinities are evident.

Euripides' not distinguishing between good leaders and bad leaders, but merely between new and old ones, points to a fundamental deficiency in his moral vision. Like Aeschylus he professes to aim at the betterment of citizens through his drama (vv. 1009–10); yet he seems rather unconcerned with the effects of his plays on the audience and the future behavior of its members. Like Socrates, he may not be selective enough in the audience at which he aims and may release dangerous ideas into the hands of those who will misuse them. We have already seen the negative consequences of Euripides' carelessness in

154. There have been numerous unnecessary attempts to delete or rearrange these lines, going back to Aristarchus and Apollonius (ΣRan. 1437); for a history of the critical controversy, see Dörrie 1956, 296–319, and MacDowell 1959, 261–68. However, as we have argued, vv. 1437–41 are merely an absurd way of expressing the advice given in vv. 1443–50; the connection of the two answers (with a partial disavowal of the first) is implied by v. 1453, although I agree with the critics who reassign the first half of v. 1454 to Dionysus. Since Dionysus has criticized Euripides in v. 1434 for being clear at the expense of *sophia*, which Euripides interprets as "cleverness," Euripides now tries self-consciously to be evasive and clever.

155. On Euripides' tendency to question everything, see vv. 971–91. Athens' continuous lust for new leaders, regardless of quality, is an issue in Aristophanic comedy from the beginning to the end of his career. It was the focal issue of the *Knights*, paralleled in the parabasis by the public's continuous lust for new comic poets, and is later the problem giving rise to revolt in the *Ecclesiazusae* (see especially *Eccl.* 215–28, and the remarks of Saïd 1979, 35). And of course it is also what the *Frogs* parabasis attacks.

156. Sommerstein (1974, 25–26) argues that Aeschylus is actually proposing to attack former allies like Chios, which had revolted and in this sense become "the enemies' land." It is also quite possible, however, that he really means attacking Laconia; as we know from the *Babylonians*, Aristophanes was never a great supporter of the Athenian empire and may, with the phrase ἀπορίαν δὲ τὸν πόρον, be proposing to give it up completely in favor of a purely offensive strategy.

this regard in the *Thesmophoriazusae*. Here we witness Euripides' ideas come back to haunt him, as Dionysus justifies his decision to bring Aeschylus rather than Euripides back to life by quoting some of the many relativistic and sophistic aphorisms found in Euripides' plays (vv. 1471–78).[157]

In the final analysis Euripides' drama is inferior to Aeschylus' because it has lost all sense of poetic presence, that is, the notion of the poet having a special personal relationship with his audience thanks to which he communicates with them through his works. Euripides' drama found itself in an age that began to experience the widespread diffusion of reading and writing; not only is Euripides himself associated with a library of books (v. 943, 1409), but Aeschylus accuses him of filling the whole city with scribes (vv. 1083–84). Everyone goes into the army having books these days (vv. 1113–14) and literary knowledge becomes democratized for better and for worse.[158] Indeed, the whole plot of this play is set in motion by the desire (v. 53 πόθος) Dionysus conceives for Euripides while reading the *Andromeda* aboard a ship in Cleisthenes' navy. But the rise of the text is also the fall of the theater, the decline of the living stage presence, the desacralization and decontextualization of the work of art.[159] The political topicality and relevance of the work, and hence its didactic force, are substantially lost when uprooted from its original context and reproduced in a non-living, devitalized form. The poet is removed one step further from his audience, and the lines of communication become even more faint and indistinct.[160] The work can be read, reread, and misread with more

157. On this reversal, see Whitman 1964, 245; Strauss 1966, 260–61.

158. On one level the whole ode of which this statement is a part (vv. 1099–1118) is protreptic flattery of the audience's *sophia* comparable to what we find in the parabasis (see n.134 above). On another level, however, the idea of soldiers reading books while on campaign is a typically Aristophanic incongruity, as it clearly is when Dionysus reads the *Andromeda* aboard a trireme in vv. 52–54 (see Woodbury 1976, 349–51). Aristophanes perceives the decline of the old, aristocratic system of choral and gymnastic education *pari passu* with the increased reliance on written instruments as behind the general decline in Athenian military leadership and power (see Aeschylus' connection of these phenomena in vv. 1083–88). For an anthropological view of the general cultural changes involved in Greek society's transition from orality to widespread literacy, see Goody-Watt (1968, 42–68) who emphasize especially the association of writing with the spread of democracy, individualism, and skepticism; on Aristophanes' attitude to the same transformation, see Denniston 1927, 117–18, Walsh 1984, 89–90, and particularly Havelock (1982, 283–92), who sees the basic contrast between Aeschylus and Euripides as between a fundamentally oral poet and one whose consciousness was increasingly conditioned by writing and literacy.

159. For a relevant theoretical discussion of a similar phenomenon, see Walter Benjamin's "Das Kunstwerk im Zeitalter seiner technischen Reproduzierbarkeit," in Benjamin 1974 I, 2, 431–508.

160. On the connection between the advent of literacy and the tendency to view

and more remoteness from the poet's original moral intent. Aeschylus, who lived in an age before the phenomenon of the mass-produced dramatic text, is clearly uncomfortable with this process of estrangement between author and work and insists on the primacy of poetic presence:[161] at first he declines to give Athens political advice from the realm of the dead, insisting that he can do so only once he is present in Athens itself speaking directly to the public through living drama (v. 1461).[162]

The issue of poetic presence was equally important to Aristophanes himself. Even in those plays which lack the full anapestic parabasis presenting the poet's persona directly, the parabasis still serves to articulate a framework of understanding that allows the poet to communicate his views to the audience through the dramatic work. Nevertheless Aristophanes was perhaps already aware of a coming time when he could not do even this much. The tension between Aeschylus and Euripides, traditionalism and modernism, idealism and naturalism, moralism and relativism, poetic presence and poetic absence, elitism and democracy, "being wise" and "giving pleasure," is a tension internal to Aristophanic comedy itself. Dionysus' final decision gives precedence to the former set of qualities, but it is up to the very end a close call; for all of Euripides' vices, his values represent a necessary and integral aspect of the dramatic art, which must properly consist of a well-tempered dialectic between "Aeschylean" and "Euripidean" tendencies. Aristophanes' own drama aims to embrace Aeschylus' fantastic imagination and moral purpose without his obscurantism and seeming authoritarianism; it favors Euripides' everyday realism without his apparent moral indifference. Although an unrelenting critic of modernism Aristophanes was himself in many ways a modernist. And although an unrelent-

---

poetry as entertainment rather than instruction, see the acute remarks of Havelock 1982, 266.

161. Aeschylus not only sneers at all the scribes with whom Euripides has filled the city (vv. 1083–84), but at the end of the weighing contest he declares that only two of his sayings will outweigh Euripides, together with his family, his amanuensis Cephisophon, and all his books (vv. 1407–10). Cf. Havelock 1982, 287.

162. There is no need to consider Aeschylus' reluctance here as out of character for a pious and patriotic poet (as Kock [1898, 215] and Dörrie [1956, 311–12] do), nor do we need to delete vv. 1463–65 as Wills (1969a, 49–53) does on the grounds that Aeschylus cannot both answer and refuse to answer; Wills misinterprets the limitation involved in v. 1462 μὴ δῆτα . . . γ', ἀλλ' . . ., which assents to Aeschylus giving advice in the world above, but insists on his answering this particular question now from the world below. Nor need we delete vv. 1437–41 on the grounds of Euripides having two answers compared to Aeschylus' one (see n.154 above). Rather the poets' responses are perfectly balanced: Euripides tries to evade answering by first giving a non-serious answer and Aeschylus demurs because of being too remote from the situation (note his questions in vv. 1454–59).

ing critic of democracy Aristophanes was unquestionably a democrat, not an oligarch. We have observed that the *Frogs* itself has a farcical side, symbolized by the Frogs, designed to entertain the broadly democratic audience proper to Attic comedy; this aspect is no less necessary to Comedy than the more serious, didactic, and utopian side represented by the select band of Initiates. Similarly the appeal of the parabasis for restoration of political rights to the disgraced oligarchs does not exclude Aristophanes' simultaneous approval of the extension of citizenship to the slaves who fought at Arginusae (vv. 695–96); he merely asks that the upper classes be accorded the same treatment as the lower classes of society. The problem of reconciling the lower and higher purposes of Comedy is one that concerned Aristophanes throughout his career, particularly in the *Clouds* and the period immediately thereafter. Only in the *Frogs* does it receive a final resolution and become part of a more holistic view encompassing Comedy, Tragedy, Athenian politics, and society's moral character.

The hypothesis records that Dicaearchus reports the *Frogs* to have been accorded the singular honor of a second performance because of the advice it proffers in the parabasis. But as we have seen, the advice of the parabasis is inextricably linked with the aims of the play as a whole.

CHAPTER 9

Comic Autobiography and the Mask of Aristophanes

As we have observed, the parabasis offers a self-reflective interlude in the middle of the play, in which the identities of both chorus and poet are displayed, thematic threads relevant to the play are drawn together, and the play's significance within its social and historical context is often clarified. This moment of poetic self-analysis is both aloof from the dramatic action and at the same time part of the dramatic structure, as well as the intellectual framework of the play. We have further observed that those early parabases which defend the poet himself help set up a parallelism between the poet's glorified persona and major characters involved in the dramatic action of each play: Dicaeopolis, the Sausage seller, Socrates, Bdelycleon, Trygaeus. In this sense Aristophanes' early plays can be called "autobiographical," not because they actually portray events in the poet's life, but inasmuch as they project the poet's personal wishes and fantasies into a fictionalized confrontation with the political, social, and intellectual currents of his day. The poet himself thus becomes the chief comic hero, reappearing onstage each year in different poses and costumes.

Much has been written about Aristophanic comedy as representing the triumph of the "little man" against Athens' power elite.[1] The little man, however, does not represent any specific social class so much as he is the poet's dramatized conception of his own role. Aristophanes represents in the form of Dicaeopolis not just the petty agrarian ele-

---

1. See, for example, Whitman 1964, 2, 52; Dover 1972, 32; Torrance 1978, 37; Sutton 1980, 17–18. This view ultimately goes back to the treatise of the "Old Oligarch" (Ps.-Xenophon, *Ath. Pol.* 2.18), who says that Comedy must attack the rich and powerful, not the *dēmos*.

ment of Athenian society bottled up within the city walls against its will, but every Athenian who, like himself, was tired of Cleon's militant pro-war policies and resistance to negotiating peace on reasonable terms.[2] Dicaeopolis' identification with Aristophanes in their mutual antagonism to Cleon is made clear by several of the protagonist's speeches and highlighted in the parabasis by parallel statements about the poet. Dicaeopolis' speech with his head on the chopping block is a vivid metaphor of the poet's boldness in undertaking to present unpopular views before a hostile audience. The Acharnians' conversion from opposition to sympathy with his views is meant to be paradigmatic of his intended effect on the theatrical audience as a whole. Again these connections are highlighted in the parabasis by the poet's insistence on the importance of free speech and self-criticism to a society's resourcefulness and success.

But it is important to remember that Aristophanes presented the *Acharnians* (425 BC) only under the cover of Callistratus and hence could jokingly boast about his world fame reaching to the King of Persia when he was as yet little known even in Athens. The *Acharnians* is in many ways intended as a complex play on identities, and only in the next play does the poet come fully forward in his own right, introducing himself to the public with flair and aplomb, but also with an unexpected modesty. The *Knights* (424 BC) continues the theme of Aristophanes' boldness in opposition to Cleon but against a very different background; the agrarian protagonist and chorus of the earlier play are replaced by a very urban protagonist straight from the *agora* and an aristocratic chorus. Together the upper class Knights and lower class Sausage seller form an effective synergism reflecting the use of a "lower class" poetic medium, Comedy, to enact the antidemagogic program of a well-educated upper class poet like Aristophanes.[3] The Sausage seller's initially reluctant emergence from nowhere to challenge Cleon in vulgarity is a projection of the poet's emergence from behind the cloak of working under a producer to present this play to the public on his own. The parabasis parallels the play's political contest between the Sausage seller and Paphlagon to the dramatic contest

---

2. As Carter (1986, 81–98) has shown, oligarchical writers of the late fifth century made the peasant farmer like Dicaeopolis into an idealized type embodying the virtues of *apragmosynē* and political stability, as opposed to the meddlesome and unstable urban masses. The "little man," particularly in the form of the small landholder, was therefore as much an ideological topos as a class reality.

3. Ste. Croix (1972, 357–62) has argued convincingly for Aristophanes' prejudices as essentially those of someone with upper-class upbringing. But as Ste. Croix acknowledges, this does not mean he lacked sympathy for the poor nor does it suggest the upper classes to have been themselves exempt from his satire.

between Aristophanes and Cratinus; in both cases the public is a fickle master.

With the *Clouds* Aristophanes' fears about the vicissitude of public favor were realized, as he saw the play relegated to a humiliating third prize at the Dionysia. Although the *Clouds* as originally produced in 423 BC may have been quite different in tendency and significance from the later version we now possess, the original play clearly seems to have been intended in some degree as an attack on intellectuals and their upper class followers; in this respect it reassures Aristophanes' popular audience that his sympathies are not totally on the side of the knights and other upper class interests.[4] On the other hand the parabasis of the second *Clouds* tells us that Aristophanes regards the original play as *sophos* ("wise/clever"), itself a product of intellectualism and superior to the vulgarian comedy of the *Knights*. Aristophanes moreover finds fault with his audience for its inability to appreciate his play's intellectual subtlety, in which regard he comes to have a curious identification with the very intellectuals he satirizes. They are also misunderstood by the ignorant public, represented by the boorish rustic Strepsiades, who in turn becomes an object of satire. It is difficult to know whether this ambiguity of sympathies, both with and against the intellectuals and both with and against the common man, was also a feature of the original play; Aristophanes' remarks about its *sophia* and the fact of its having eluded popular favor suggest an affirmative answer. Seen in this light the *Clouds* exhibits a self-reflective complexity quite without equal even in Aristophanes' highly self-reflective work.

The failure of the first *Clouds* was a personal turning point for the young poet, accustomed as he was to success. He proceeded to adopt the pose of the offended and alienated reformer, not only in the parabasis of the second *Clouds*, but also in that of the *Wasps* (422 BC), his next play after the original *Clouds*. He presents himself in *Wasps* as a "purifier" of Comedy and of Athenian society, attempting to educate the public into better ways, but in this case not succeeding. The parabasis therefore highlights the significance of Aristophanes' self-identification with the young protagonist, Bdelycleon, the "Cleon hater," who tries to reform the political and social habits of his father Philocleon, the "Cleon-lover," with only partial success. In addition to being a generational conflict the opposition between Bdelycleon and Philocleon is also a class conflict between a cultured and socially ambitious gentleman and his poor, uneducated father who is a true speci-

---

4. On this function of the *Clouds* as an antiphonal counterweight to the *Knights*, see Robert 1967, 160–64.

men of the Athenian masses. Both are equally objects of humor in the play. The father-son allegory clearly mirrors the young poet's attempts to reform the ultimately incorrigible "Cleon-loving" public; he may succeed on the political side, as Aristophanes succeeds with plays like *Knights,* but he fails to educate the public on the cultural and intellectual side, as Aristophanes fails with the more intellectual *Clouds.* Aristophanes carefully deploys intertextual echoes of both plays in different parts of the *Wasps,* as I have shown, to delineate this self-referential structure.

With the *Peace* (421 BC), however, we see Aristophanes return to harmony with his public and the public returning to harmony with itself, bridging all political and class divisions. The panhellenic chorus joins together to celebrate the achievement of Trygaeus, whose name suggests Comedy, on the back of the dung beetle, symbolizing the devices of low humor. Through lowly means a great political goal is reached even as Aristophanes himself seems to take credit in the parabasis for the death of Cleon, which made peace possible. The play's emphasis is on festival reconciliation and reunion obtained through the expulsion of malignant forces. What differentiates the *Peace* from the four preceding plays is the more generic identity of its comic hero; although Aristophanes' personal role is still emphasized in the parabasis, Trygaeus is not a figure for Aristophanes personally, any more than the dung beetle is a figure for Cleon personally, but rather the generic spirit of Comedy. In its emphasis on communal action the Peace looks forward to Aristophanes' later plays.

The plays of Aristophanes' middle period (*Birds* through *Frogs,* 414 to 405 BC) do not feature parabases in which the poet defends himself, and also lack any sense of identification between the poet and protagonist. With his poetic identity well established before the public, Aristophanes dropped the "autobiographical" mode and explored the consequences of orchestrated group behavior instead, whether with the previously oppressed underclass of Birds or the women of *Lysistrata* and *Thesmophoriazusae.*[5] Even the quest of the *Frogs* is not an individual undertaking of Dionysus so much as a mission for the collective good of Athens. The comic heroes of these plays are in fact quite remote both from the poet and from our sympathies—the power-hungry sophist Peisthetaerus, the unemotional and impersonal Lysistrata, the bumbling and stupid in-law of Euripides, the god Dionysus (who is perhaps the closest to being a truly human character). In these plays characters

5. On the movement from "I" consciousness to "we" consciousness in these plays, see the interesting remarks of Seel 1960, 94–95.

are more important for their leadership or opposition in regard to the group than for their interest as individuals in their own right.

In spite of the parabasis being no longer autobiographical and despite its becoming more dramatically immanent in these plays, it is still key to each play's articulation of meaning. The parabases and choral odes of the *Birds* help us appreciate the relevance of sophistic doctrine to Peisthetaerus' overthrow of traditional religion and conquest of absolute Sovereignty for himself. The unique agonistic parabasis of the *Lysistrata* highlights both the male/female polarity and the militarist/anti-militarist arguments of the play, paralleling Lysistrata's agon with the Proboulos. The parabasis of the *Thesmophoriazusae* broadens the arguments for women's emancipation and role in city affairs, in many ways serving as an *apologia* for both the women's plays of 411. And the *Frogs* parabasis plays a crucial role in aligning the contest of the poets and its struggle between traditionalism and modernism with Athens' current political and military crisis.

In most of these plays what we see is a preoccupation with the ambiguities and intellectualist concerns of the *Clouds*, revised by Aristophanes around 417 BC. As we have shown, the *Birds* is an elaboration of many themes from the *Clouds*, with the master sophist Peisthetaerus acting as an unchallenged protagonist, in contrast with Socrates' antagonistic role in the *Clouds*. The sacrileges of 415 realized the *Clouds'* worst fears about the effects of sophistic teaching on upper class youth and their regard for traditional morality and piety, motivating Aristophanes here to dramatize the complete overthrow of the Olympian religion. The *Thesmophoriazusae* also reflects the structure of the *Clouds*, with the modernist poet Euripides taking the place of the modernist philosopher Socrates and the boorish in-law taking the place of the ignorant rustic Strepsiades. Like the *Clouds*, the *Thesmophoriazusae* is equally a satire on the intellectual (Euripides) and popular misunderstandings of the intellectual, and thus again instantiates the perennial conflict of Aristophanic comedy between intellectual refinement and lower-class farce. The same conflict pervades the structure of the *Frogs*, moving from a farcical first half to an intellectual debate in the second half of the play. And again we observe Aristophanes' sympathies on the fence between the modernism he presumes to hate (Euripides) and the archaism he presumes to revere, but which is equally an object of satire (Aeschylus). These tensions continue to be expressed even as late as the *Ecclesiazusae* of 392 BC.[6]

Who is the real Aristophanes? Is he the conservative traditionalist

6. See Appendix 5.

championing Marathon veterans or the "subtle-speaking Euripidaristophanizer" caricatured by Cratinus? Is he the critic of Socrates or the critic of Socrates' critics? Is he a reformer or a reactionary? Is he the friend of the common man or of the young knights? Is he a friend of women's emancipation or a purveyor of sexist jokes who should be banished from college reading lists because of his insensitivity? Is he a popular entertainer or a highbrow reformer of the comic art? Without being indecisive one can say that Aristophanes is all of these things. Behind the mask of Aristophanes one finds many masks, but this is not to say there is not at the same time also a real man there with real views and with all the complex contradictions which thoughtful and genuinely funny human beings possess.

Aristophanes and Callistratus

Much critical controversy has been devoted to the question of Aristophanes' relation to Callistratus as his producer. One school of thought, relying on Aristophanes' declarations in *Eq.* 512–45 and *Vesp.* 1018–22, believes that he was essentially unknown to the audience before the *Knights* and consequently that Cleon's "lawsuit" and all the self-references throughout the *Acharnians* pertain to Callistratus, who was publicly recognized as the producer (and for all most people knew, the author) of the play.[1] Others believe the production of the play was a mere formality, with everyone in the audience somehow knowing that it was actually written by Aristophanes and thus naturally attributing the "lawsuit" and the self-references to the author.[2] The scholia are of little help here; but Capps has demonstrated that the real poet's name as well as the producer's would be entered in the didascaliae with a formula like Ἀριστοφάνης ἐδίδασκε διὰ Καλλιστράτου.[3] The author's identity would certainly become a matter of public knowledge by the time of a play's publication and would probably be known all along by Athens' literary elite. It is therefore possible that at the time of his

---

1. Cf. Müller-Strübing 1873, 604–9; Gunning 1882, 71–84; Briel 1887, 22–37; Roemer 1902, 119–33; Rennie 1909, 11–21; Rostagni 1927, 293–302; MacDowell 1982, 24–25; Kraus 1985, 60–61.

2. This view has tended to predominate in recent criticism: cf. Fritzsche 1835 I, 301–16; Steinbrück 1865, 9–10; Leo 1878, 401–5; Hiller 1887, 361–80; Starkie 1909, 247–48; Steffen 1954, 7–21; Russo 1962, 59; Ste. Croix 1972, 363–64; Mastromarco 1979, 159–65; Halliwell 1980, 35–36; Sakhnenko 1983, 115–21; Perusino 1986, 54–57; Henderson 1990, 288.

3. Capps 1907, 187–93. Cf. Mastromarco 1979, 160–63. On the scholia, see chap. 3 n.18 above.

accusation Cleon knew Aristophanes to be the real author of the *Baby-lonians,* unless Aristophanes had asked Callistratus to present the play to the archon as his own work, as may be implied by *Vesp.* 1018–22.

On the other hand the general public is not likely to have known the author's name during the actual performance of this play; Callistra-tus' name was the only one publicly announced by the herald, judg-ing from the annunciatory formula of *Ach.* 11, εἴσαγ᾽ ὦ Θέογνι τὸν χορόν.[4] If his name had not in some way been concealed from the audience there is no point to Aristophanes' putting so much stress on the *Knights* as the first play in which he exposed his reputation to the vicissitudes of public favor (*Eq.* 512–45) and again calling attention to "secret plays" produced by others in *Nub.* 528–32 and *Vesp.* 1018–22. This must refer to more than merely someone else managing the production, since the *Wasps* was itself produced by Philonides (see chap. 6 n.1 above). Mastromarco and Halliwell have recently revived the theory first proposed by Leo that *Vesp.* 1018–22 refers to Aristoph-anes' assistance of other comic poets in writing plays prior to the *Banqueters.*[5] But MacDowell is clearly right in insisting on the parallels between this passage and *Eq.* 512–45 and on the strong probability of these passages both referring to the same event, which Aristophanes characterizes as a climactic turning point in his career (i.e. the shift from working undercover to producing plays openly under his own name).[6] It is clear that comic poets would often allow others to receive the public recognition for whole plays they had written; otherwise Eupolis' charge about having "written the *Knights* and given it to Ar-istophanes" (fr. 89 PCG) would lack even superficial plausibility, as would the information that Plato τὰς κωμῳδίας . . . αὐτὸς ποιῶν ἄλλοις ἐκδιδόναι διὰ πενίαν (Eustathius, *ad Il.* 302, 32–34). That Aristopha-nes also chose to use a producer for some of his later plays proves nothing about the extent to which his authorship of the first three plays was known or unknown to the public at the time of their production; quite possibly he might have chosen to keep his identity non-public in the first three plays while arranging a different relationship with Callis-tratus in the case of the *Birds* and *Lysistrata* and with Philonides in the case of the *Wasps* and *Frogs.* The *Proagon,* however, may have been another play in which Aristophanes wished for different reasons to keep his identity secret.[7]

Much of the controversy surrounding the self-references in the

4. Cf. Briel 1887, 14.
5. Leo 1878, 401 n.2; Mastromarco 1979, 166–73; Halliwell 1980, 37–41.
6. MacDowell 1982, 22–24. See also the criticisms of Perusino 1986, 47–53.
7. See p. 113–14 above.

Acharnians has to do with the use of the terms ποιητής (vv. 633, 641, 654) and διδάσκαλος (v. 628 "from the time when our chorus-master first presided over comic choruses . . ."). Those who read the parabasis with reference to Callistratus reinterpret *poiētes* to mean "director," and those who refer the passage to Aristophanes must interpret *didaskalos* as a metonymy for "comic poet."[8] The terms are sometimes used interchangeably, as in the parabasis of the *Knights* or *Peace,* yet it is important to underscore that Aristophanes was both poet and producer for those plays, whereas in the case of the *Acharnians* the poet and producer are two different people; using both terms in the course of the parabasis, evidently in regard to the same person, feeds the audience's impression that the publicly announced producer Callistratus was also the poet of the *Acharnians.*

What critics have not recognized about the parabasis of the *Acharnians* is that Aristophanes is putting us on, concealing beneath all the hyper-inflated overstatement a profoundly ironic understatement: the "poet" whose fame supposedly reaches all the way to the king of Persia is not actually the poet, while the real poet hides behind the mask of his producer and is virtually unknown. As throughout the *Acharnians* the play of identities must be deliberately meant to puzzle or mislead, especially if Kock and Schrader are right in contending that Cleon's charges were directed against both Callistratus and Aristophanes.[9]

Even if the charges were directed against Aristophanes alone, the general audience's deception concerning the poet's identity would not be any less; all we can be certain about is that Cleon's *eisaggelia,* if it was one, was not successful and that the case was never tried before a jury. The circle of those familiar with the case would thus have been fairly small, consisting mainly of last year's Boule and some of the poet's friends. Others may have heard some snippets of gossip about the case, but not enough to recognize with certainty that the author of the present play was not Callistratus: the statements of Dicaeopolis and the parabasis could be construed as a generic defense of comic poets' liberty.[10]

To be sure, some few members of the original audience would have

8. For the former view, cf. MacDowell 1982, 25. For the latter, cf. Hiller 1887, 362–64; Steffen 1954, 12–13; Halliwell 1980, 43–44; Perusino 1982a, 139–41.

9. Kock 1855, 22–26; Schrader 1877, 385–414.

10. Although the statements about Cleon's charges must have some historical reference, the audience need not construe them as an attack on this particular comic poet any more than the chorus' complaints about the choregus Antimachus (*Ach.* 1150–73) indicate that they were exactly the same choristers whom he had deprived of a banquet last year; their complaint, even though couched in the first person, is clearly a generic complaint on behalf of all comic choruses.

known with certainty that *Banqueters, Babylonians,* and *Acharnians* were all the work of Aristophanes, not Callistratus, under whose name they were publicly presented; that some of the poet's intimates were privy to his secret is made clear by *Eq.* 512–13, when they ask why he has not previously requested a chorus in his own name. As often in Aristophanes' work, full appreciation of his irony is possible only for the privileged *sophoi* who have enough knowledge of the details to "get" the joke, especially in cases where the joke is on the rest of the audience who fail to "get" it.

Ben Jonson and
the *Clouds* Parabasis

Although Aristophanic comedy naturally had its influence on Middle and New Comedy, as on Roman satire (see Horace, *Serm.* 1.4.1–2 *Eupolis atque Cratinus Aristophanesque poetae/atque alii quorum comoedia prisca virorum est . . .*), its topicality and allusiveness may have precluded its richness and vigor from being fully appreciated until the learned rediscovery of Greek literature in the European Renaissance, an age that truly paralleled the Athenian fifth century in its intellectual dynamism and social ferment. Aristophanes found his most resonant echo in the comedy of Ben Jonson, whose penchant for caustic social commentary and personal self-dramatization had little precedent either in Roman Comedy or previous Elizabethan drama but much in Attic Old Comedy.[1]

Given Jonson's interest in Aristophanes as a model and source of ideas, it should not surprise us that he was also fascinated by the uniquely Old Comic parabasis and its potential as a device for both social satire and the poet's public self-presentation. The lack of a conventional chorus in the Elizabethan theater made adoption of the actual parabatic form impossible for Jonson; yet he devised various

---

1. Jonson had received excellent training in Greek at Westminster and certainly knew Aristophanes' plays in the original. Aristophanic influence on Jonson's style of comedy has been widely acknowledged in Jonsonian criticism. For special studies, see Goldmark 1918, 24–29; Lord 1925, 157–61; Davison 1963, 151–57; Potter 1968, 290–99; Gum 1969; Dick 1974. On the knowledge of Greek comedy in sixteenth-century England generally, see Lever 1946, 169–74.

ways of translating the content and function of the parabasis into his own dramaturgical context—theoretical prologues and epilogues addressed by the poet to his audience and scenes of dramatic "induction" whose characters might reappear throughout the course of the play as a symbolic audience commenting upon events.[2]

I submit that Jonson's use of the parabasis went even further and molded his whole dramatic persona as an intellectual poet seeking to instruct his audience as well as to entertain it, but misunderstood and unappreciated by the vicissitudes of public favor.[3] Like Aristophanes Jonson adopted a quasi-autobiographical mode in some of his early "satiric" plays, identifying himself with alienated or undervalued characters in the play: Asper/Macilente in *Every Man Out of his Humour*, Crites in *Cynthia's Revels*, Horace in *The Poetaster*. And like Aristophanes he saw, or presumed to see, the failure of one of his plays as a personal rejection by his audience and a crisis or turning point in his career; in Jonson's case, however, the crisis occurred not once but repeatedly, such as after *The Poetaster*, after *Sejanus*, after *The Devil Is an Ass*, and after *The New Inn*.

It is from Aristophanes' reaction to the defeat of the *Clouds* that Jonson takes his stamp as a dramatic poet at perpetual war with his audience, often threatening to abandon the comic or tragic stage and often in fact doing so for other genres. The *Clouds* parabasis not only provides a general model for Jonson's relation to his audience but is a specific source for much of his literary theory and polemic. As we have observed in our discussion of this passage in chapter 5, its polemic is structured into three principal components: (1) Aristophanes' address to the elite among his audience rebuking them for their lack of loyalty (= *Nub.* 518–36), (2) his denial of having used cheap theatrical tricks (= *Nub.* 537–44), and (3) his criticism of theatrical rivals for reusing the same material (= *Nub.* 545–62). Obviously each of these topics becomes a major focal point of Jonson's dramatic theory.

(1). Perhaps the most fundamental tension in Jonson's poetics lies between serving the intellectual sophisticates in his audience (= Aristophanes' *sophoi* and *dexioi*) who properly seek moral instruction and playing to the inattentive, often uncomprehending mob that must be entertained.[4] While Jonson's preference is clearly for the more sophis-

2. On the specific influence of the parabasis on Jonson, see Lord 1925, 159; Potter 1968, 291; Gum 1969, 108–31; Dick 1974, 50–55.

3. On the centrality of the author-audience relationship in Jonson's work, see Sweeney 1985.

4. Cf. Dick 1974, 50; Sweeney 1985, 20. In reference to the audience of Elizabethan drama more broadly, see Harbage 1941, 92–157.

ticated audience, his relation even to this select group is far from unambiguous. In his earliest extant play (*The Case Is Altered*—c. 1598), the poetaster Antonio Balladino justifies using "stale stuff" to entertain the "common sort" rather than the "gentlemen" who need "every day new tricks" (I.2.40–74). Antonio is the negative image of a poet, perhaps modelled on Jonson's contemporary Anthony Munday,[5] and certainly an antitype of Jonson's own practice. But as we see later in the same play the "gentlemen" in the audience are hardly more attractive figures and are indeed quite hard to please:

> *Valentine:* Aye, ever, ever, and the people generally are very acceptive and apt to applaud any meritable work, but there are two sorts of persons that most commonly are infectious to a whole auditory. . . . one is the rude barbarous crew, a people that have no brains and yet grounded judgements; these will hiss anything that mounts above their grounded capacities. But the other are worth the observation, i' faith. . . . Faith, a few capricious gallants. . . . And they have taken such a habit of dislike in all things that they will approve nothing, be it never so conceited or elaborate, but sit dispersed, making faces and spitting, wagging their upright ears, and cry "filthy, filthy." Simply uttering their own condition, and using their wried countenances instead of a vice to turn the good aspects of all that shall sit near them, from what they behold.
>
> (*The Case Is Altered* 2.7.51–69)

A year later, in very similar terms, Asper, who clearly represents the "harsh" satirist Jonson himself, refers to self-styled critics in the audience:

> You can espy a gallant of this mark,
> Who, to be thought one of the judicious,
> Sits with his arms thus wreathed, his hat pulled here,
> Cries miaow, and nods, then shakes his empty head,
> Will show more several motions in his face
> Than the new London, Rome, or Nineveh,
> And, now and then, breaks a dry biscuit jest,
> Which, that it may more easily be chewed,
> He steeps in his own laughter. . . .
> How monstrous and detested is't, to see
> A fellow that has neither art nor brain
> Sit like an Aristarchus, or stark ass,
> Taking men's lines, with a tobacco face,
> In snuff, still spitting, using his wried looks

5. See Herford-Simpson 1950 IX, 308–9.

> (In nature of a vice) to wrest and turn
> The good aspect of those that shall sit near him,
> From what they do behold! Oh, 'tis most vile.
>   (*Every Man Out of his Humour* Induction 159–67, 177–84)

Asper contrasts with these apparent sophisticates the ideal audience
for which he produces the play:

> Attentive auditors,
> Such as will join their profit with their pleasure,
> And come to feed their understanding parts:
> For these, I'll prodigally spend myself,
> And speak away my spirit into air;
> For these, I'll melt my brain into invention,
> Coin new conceits, and hang my richest words
> As polished jewels in their bounteous ears.
>   (*Every Man Out of his Humour* Induction 201–8)

He concludes by telling the audience:

> We hope to make the circles of your eyes
> Flow with distilled laughter: if we fail,
> We must impute it to this only chance,
> "Art hath an enemy called Ignorance."
>   (*Every Man Out of his Humour* Induction 216–9)

Like Aristophanes Jonson attributes any dramatic failure necessarily to
a failure on the part of his audience, and particularly on the part of the
sophisticates in his audience, to live up to his ideal standards for them.[6]

In the induction to Jonson's next play, *Cynthia's Revels* (1600), the
pseudosophisticates are also derided for confusing sophistication in
clothing and appearance with literary taste and discernment (Induction 182–98). In the following prologue Jonson again contrasts these
critics with his ideal audience:

> If gracious silence, sweet attention,
> Quick sight, and quicker apprehension,
> (The lights of judgement's throne) shine anywhere;
> Our doubtful author hopes this is their sphere.
> And therefore opens he himself to those;

---

6. He expresses the same attitude in the final couplet of the Stage prologue to *The Staple of News* (1626): "If that not like you that he sends tonight, / 'Tis you have left to judge, not he to write" (Prologue 29–30).

> To other weaker beams his labours close:
> As loth to prostitute their virgin strain
> To every vulgar and adulterate brain.
> In this alone, his Muse her sweetness hath,
> She shuns the print of any beaten path;
> And proves new ways to come to learned ears:
> Pied ignorance she neither loves nor fears.
> Nor hunts she after popular applause,
> Or foamy praise that drops from common jaws:
> The garland that she wears, their hands must twine
> Who can both censure, understand, define
> What merit is: then cast those piercing rays,
> Round as a crown, instead of honored bays,
> About his poesy; which, he knows, affords
> Words above action: matter above words.
> (Cynthia's Revels Prologue)

The false sophisticates are little better than commoners. Jonson's self-proclaimed exclusiveness is particularly apt in opening *Cynthia's Revels,* of all his theatrical work the play apparently least suited to the world of public theater, being far more an allegorical masque in both form and intention, full of Greek names and mythological allusion.[7]

On the other hand Jonson's intentions were sometimes more democratic in scope, as apparent in the prologue to *Epicoene* (1609):

> Truth says, of old, the art of making plays
>   Was to content the people; and their praise
>   Was to the poet money, wine, and bays.
> But in this age, a sect of writers are
>   That only for particular likings care,
>   And will taste nothing that is popular.
> With such we mingle neither brains nor breasts;
>   Our wishes, like to those (make public feasts)
>   Are not to please the cook's tastes, but the guests' . . . .
> For to present all custard, or all tart,
>   And have no other meats to bear a part,
>   Or to want bread, and salt, were but coarse art.
> The poet prays you then, with better thought
>   To sit; and when his cates are all in brought,
>   Though there be none far fetched, there will dear-bought
> Be fit for ladies: some for lords, knights, squires,

---

7. The nature of this play may have been influenced by the reforms in boys' acting companies, such as the one that performed here, that took place in 1600, allowing evening audiences of a more selective character. See Miles 1986, 52–53.

> Some for your waiting wench, and city-wires,
> Some for your men, and daughters of Whitefriars.
> (*Epicoene* Prologue 1–9, 16–24)

As in the case of Aristophanes in the second and more popularized version of the *Clouds* Jonson here seems to have reconciled himself to a balanced mixture of intellectual profit and popular delight, containing bread and salt as well as custard and tarts, pleasing lords and ladies as well as Whitefriars ruffians.

Much later, in the induction of *The Magnetic Lady* (1632), Jonson again defends the idea of pleasing the "people" by citing the authority of antiquity (Induction 34–41), although this time defining the "people" in question more narrowly as "the venison side" as opposed to the "faeces, or grounds of your people, that sit in the oblique eaves and wedges of your house, your sinful sixpenny mechanics" (Induction 23–27).[8] In the same play, however, the chorus also criticizes sophisticates for their overclever penchant to overinterpret Jonson's plays by reading personal attacks into characters not intended as such (Act II, Chorus).[9]

Clearly the difference between the stance of Jonson and Aristophanes toward their audience lies in Jonson's sharp dichotomy of the upper class/lower class tension that is certainly present though more implicit in Aristophanes. Whereas Aristophanes appears to flatter, albeit ironically, his entire audience into believing they are among the select *sophoi* (*Nub.* 521–27; cf. *Vesp.* 1013–14) Jonson does not hesitate to abuse his audience for its vulgar tastes in the most unabashed terms.[10] Nevertheless we must recognize even in Jonson's most caustic insults to his audience a certain playfulness not unlike Aristophanes', as for instance in the contract he makes with the spectators in the induction of *Bartholomew Fair* (1614): they should all ("as well the curious and envious, as the favouring and judicious, as also the grounded judg-

8. Jonson also proclaims "delight" as his objective in the Court prologue to *The Staple of News* but again limits it to the delight of the better sort: "The rather being offered as a rite, / To scholars, that can judge, and fair report / The sense they hear, above the vulgar sort / Of nut-crackers, that only come for sight" (Prologue 5–8). As we shall see below, delight in stage spectacle and theatrics is denigrated as vulgar, in contrast with pleasure in the play's "sense" or moral import.

9. Jonson had earlier insisted on the same in his contract with the audience in the induction to *Bartholomew Fair* (Induction 119–30), demanding that they expel "any state-decypherer, or politic pick-lock of the scene so solemnly ridiculous, as to search out, who was meant by the gingerbread-woman, who by the hobby-horse man, who by the costard-monger. . . ." Both of these polemics go back to Aristophanes' joke in *Pax* 43–48 about the over-clever spectators who try to see the dung beetle as an allusion to Cleon (on which, see p. 141 above).

10. On the difference in the techniques of the two poets, see Dick 1974, 55.

ments and understandings") sit through the play with patience, and censure it only in proportion to the cost of their respective seats, the groundlings only sixpence worth, the better classes correspondingly more. Of all Jonson's plays *Bartholomew Fair* is the one in which the interaction and mingling of upper class and lower class characters is the most prominent; the trip to the sordid world of the fair is in a sense allegorical for visiting the theater itself. While Jonson's specific terms and formulation of the problem are somewhat different, the idea of discord between the refined comic poet and his uncomprehending audience is demonstrably Aristophanic.

(2). For both Aristophanes and Jonson the idea of catering to a vulgar audience was closely connected with the use of loud stage action and theatrical tricks. As early as *Every Man In his Humour* (1598) Jonson announces that he will not purchase popular favor by using such devices or by making radical shifts in time or place:

> Though need make many Poets, and some such
> As art and nature have not bettered much;
> Yet ours, for want, hath not so loved the stage,
> As he dares serve the ill customs of the age:
> Or purchase your delight at such a rate,
> As, for it, he himself must justly hate.
> To make a child, now swaddled, to proceed
> Man, and then shoot up, in one beard and weed,
> Past threescore years: or, with three rusty swords,
> And help of some few foot-and-half-foot words,
> Fight over York and Lancaster's long jars:
> And in the tiring-house bring wounds to scars.
> He rather prays you will be pleased to see
> One such, today, as other plays should be.
> Where neither Chorus wafts you o'er the seas;
> Nor creaking throne comes down, the boys to please;
> Nor nimble squib is seen, to make afeared
> The gentlewomen; nor rolled bullet heard
> To say it thunders; nor tempestuous drum
> Rumbles, to tell you when the storm doth come;
> But deeds, and language, such as men do use:
> And persons, such as Comedy would choose, . . .
>
> (*Every Man In his Humour* Prologue 1–22)

The language here is directly reminiscent of the *Clouds,* where Aristophanes abjures use of the phallus as a source of laughter for boys (*Nub.* 539), even as Jonson will not bring in a creaking throne "the boys to please." Instead of all these sensational bits of theater Jonson's drama relies on appropriate deeds, language, and persons; exactly so, Aristophanes announces at the end of his catalogue of rejected devices that his play "has come, trusting in herself and her words" (*Nub.* 544).

In the Prologue to *Volpone* (1605) Jonson gives us another catalogue of cheap stage tricks and crowd pleasers he has avoided:

> Yet, thus much I can give you, as a token
> > Of his play's worth, no eggs are broken;
> Nor quaking custards with fierce teeth affrighted,
> > Wherewith your rout are so delighted;
> Nor hales he in a gull, old ends reciting,
> > To stop gaps in his loose writing;
> With such a deal of monstrous and forced action
> > As might make Bedlam a faction:
> Nor made he his play, for jests, stolen from each table,
> > But makes jests, to fit his fable.
> And so presents quick comedy, refined,
> > As best critics have designed,
> The laws of time, place, persons he observeth,
> > From no needful rule he swerveth.
> All gall and copperas from his ink he draineth,
> > Only, a little salt remaineth;
> Wherewith he'll rub your cheeks, till red with laughter,
> > They shall look fresh, a week after.
> > > > > (*Volpone* Prologue 19–35)

The closing promise to send his audience away, cheeks refreshed with his "salt," reminds us of Aristophanes' promise at the end of the *Wasps* parabasis to send his auditors away with their garments smelling of "cleverness" (*dexiotēs, Vesp.* 1055–59).

In the induction to *Bartholomew Fair,* the Stage keeper complains about the absence of such props and spectacles from the play: "ne'er a sword and buckler-man . . . nor a little Davy, to take toll of the bawds there . . . nor a juggler with a well-educated ape. . . . Nor has he the canvas-cut in the night, for a hobby-horse man to creep into his she-neighbour, and take his leap there. Nothing! No: an some writer that I know had had but the penning o' this matter, he would have made you such a jig-a-jog in the booths, you should have thought an earthquake had been in the Fair!" (Induction 12–22). In contrast "master poets" like Jonson will have their own way rejecting such familiar devices as the old Stage keeper likes.

At the end of his career Jonson returns to this topos in the epilogue of *The New Inn* (1629) apologizing to the mob for not bringing the drunkards (Jug, Jordan, Barnaby, Tipto, Burst, Huffle, et al.) back onstage in the fifth act:

> He could have haled in
> The drunkards, and the noises of the Inn,
> In his last act, if he had thought it fit
> To vent you vapors in the place of wit:
> But better 'twas that they should sleep or spew
> Than in the scene to offend or him or you.
> *(The New Inn* Epilogue 13–18)

Similarly Jonson, after the first act of *The Magnetic Lady,* imagines the captious critic Damplay complaining that there has been no real action in the first act; to which the Boy of the house replies:

> *Boy:* But you would have all come together, it seems: the clock should strike five, at once, with the acts. . . . So, if a child could be born, in a play, and grow up to a man i' the first scene, before he went off the stage: and then after to come forth a squire, and be made a knight: and that knight to travel between the acts, and do wonders i' the Holy Land, or elsewhere; kill paynims, wild boars, dun cows, and other monsters; beget him a reputation, and marry an emperor's daughter for his mistress; convert her father's country; and at last come home, lame, and all-to-beladen with miracles.
>
> *Damplay:* These miracles would please, I assure you: and take the people! For there be of the people that will expect miracles, and more than miracles from this pen.
>
> *Boy:* Do they think this pen can juggle? I would we had Hocus Pocus for 'em then, your people; or Travitanto Tudesko.
> *(The Magnetic Lady* I. Chorus. 11–27)

Here more clearly than elsewhere Jonson associates the violation of dramaturgical principles and artistic standards with the desire of dramatists to please "the people." As we have seen in our discussion of the *Clouds* parabasis Aristophanes could hardly agree more.

(3). We observed in the *Volpone* prologue that Jonson condemned, along with violent stage action and violation of the three unities, the reuse of old jokes and dramatic material, such as the "gull, old ends reciting, / To stop loose gaps in his writing" or the "jests, stolen from each table." Of course, Jonson's very condemnation borrows from Aristophanes' polemic against his opponents in the *Clouds;* at least in

the context of Elizabethan/Jacobean drama Jonson was saying something new. We have noted also that Jonson, through the figure of
Antonio in *The Case Is Altered* (I.2.40–74), specifically associates poets'
tendency to reuse "stale stuff" with their desire to please the crowd as
opposed to the more elite and demanding members of the audience
who expect novelty.

It should not surprise us that Jonson's fullest attack on his opponents
for reusing and even plagiarizing old material (parallel to Aristophanes' attack on Eupolis, Hermippus, and others in *Nub.* 551–60) comes
in one of the two plays which form his contribution to the infamous
"War of the Theaters," *Cynthia's Revels* (1600):

> It is in the general behalf of this fair society here that I am to speak, at least
> the more judicious part of it, which seems much distasted with the im-
> modest and obscene writing of many in their plays. Besides, they could
> wish your poets would leave to be promoters of other men's jests, and to
> waylay all the stale apophthegms or old books they can hear of (in print,
> or otherwise) to farce their scenes withal. That they would not so penu-
> riously glean wit from every laundress or hackney-man, or derive their
> best grace, with servile imitation, from common stages, or observation of
> the company they converse with; as if their invention lived wholly upon
> another man's trencher. Again, that feeding their friends with nothing of
> their own but what they have twice or thrice cooked, they should not
> wantonly give out how soon they had dressed it; nor how many coaches
> came to carry away the broken meat, besides hobby-horses, and foot-cloth
> nags. (*Cynthia's Revels* Induction 158–72)

Again Jonson associates this lack of originality with catering to lower-
class elements of the audience who are most comfortable with the tried
and familiar. What Jonson goes on to say about the "ghosts" of old
plays walking around (Induction 177–81) certainly recalls what Aristophanes said about Eupolis and others rewriting the *Knights* and
calling it their own.

The Identity of the Chorus in the *Peace*

The chorus of the *Peace* enters in vv. 296–308 clearly identified as Panhellenes from both city and country, but appears elsewhere to be entirely Athenian (vv. 346–60) or entirely rural (vv. 556–59, 582–604, 1159–90). Many critics conclude that Aristophanes felt perfectly free about having his chorus change identity from scene to scene, but none have devoted much attention to the problem of costume.[1] Others have tried to rationalize the apparent inconsistencies by limiting the chorus to Attic farmers and by seeing the Panhellenes as either mute extras or imaginary members of the audience.[2] We can dismiss the belief of Stanger and Norwood[3] in the supposed inconsistencies deriving from clumsy contamination of two versions of the play.

In fact, the inconsistencies may not exist at all. Vv. 464–507 make it clear that the chorus consists of foreigners as well as Athenians, and vv. 508–11 make it clear that farmers were only part of the chorus; we need not imagine the Boeotians, Megarians, and nonfarmers as extras chased out of the orchestra, but merely as members of the chorus who dance and pull in a direction contrary to the others and move to the side from v. 508 until the parabasis. The choreography of this scene, like the staging of the *Peace* as a whole, was very complex, and there is no reason to believe the chorus could not break into semichoruses or

---

1. See Ehrenberg 1962, 55 n.1; Sifakis 1971b, 32; Dover 1972, 137–39; Zimmermann 1985 II, 263–65; Sommerstein 1985, xviii; Cassio 1985, 75–77.

2. On Panhellenes as extras see Rohdewald 1854, 10–11 n.6; Helmbold 1890, 17–18; Russo 1962, 223–25; Händel 1963, 145; Gelzer 1970, 1457; as imaginary audience: Arnoldt 1873, 55; Platnauer 1964, 95.

3. Stanger 1870, 31–34; Norwood 1931, 232–33.

even into several subgroups;[4] semichoruses were certainly used in the *Acharnians* and *Lysistrata*. Reference to individual members or components of a chorus is conventional from Alcman's *Partheneion* down to Aristophanes (cf. *Vesp.* 230–34, *Pax* 1142–55, or *Lys.* 254–356).

Nothing in the second parabasis limits its delivery to Attic farmers: τοὺς μὲν . . . ἡμῶν τοὺς δ᾽ . . . (*Pax* 1180, cf. v. 1185) rather suggests that some of the chorus are not farmers, even though complaint is being made on the farmers' behalf. Again it is quite conventional for an entire chorus to speak in the first person of paradigmatic personal experiences which could not be those of every chorus member but are representative experiences of some: we need not imagine that all the old women in the chorus of the *Lysistrata* filled every one of the special ritual offices listed in *Lys.* 641–47, or that all the old men were old enough to remember Cleomenes (*Lys.* 271–82). Similarly the Athenian allusions of *Pax* 346–60 need not suggest that the whole chorus is Athenian, any more than Hades' reference to Athens as πόλιν τὴν ἡμετέραν in *Ran.* 1501 means he is an Athenian: dramatic remarks addressed to an Athenian audience will necessarily allude to the Athenian context without implying anything concerning the identity of the speaker. A chorus consisting of some Athenians and some non-Athenians facing a primarily Athenian audience can speak collectively concerning experiences of its Athenian members without ceasing to be a Panhellenic chorus. Note the Athenian allusion of *Pax* 304 ("this Lamachus-hating [μισολάμαχος] day"), spoken at the very moment of the chorus' entrance as self-avowed Panhellenes (*Pax* 302). One of the principal aims of the *Peace* is to demonstrate the possibility of diverse and heterogeneous groups coming together—townsmen sympathizing with countrymen, Spartans with Athenians, and vice versa.

4. Platnauer (1964, xiv) evidently has a very low estimate of Aristophanes' dramaturgical imagination in declaring this "too elaborate for Aristophanes." The *Peace* is one of the plays Aristophanes chose to produce himself; perhaps with this in mind he experimented with special stage arrangements.

Political Allusions and the Chronology of the *Lysistrata* and *Thesmophoriazusae*

As we have observed in chapter 8, the most widely favored dating is to assign the *Lysistrata* to the Lenaea of 411 and the *Thesmophoriazusae* to the City Dionysia of the same year. Sommerstein has provided a thorough survey of the other options proposed by scholars and has convincingly refuted the assumptions behind all of these.[1] But the positive arguments he and others have advanced in favor of dating *Lysistrata* to the Lenaea and *Thesmophoriazusae* to the Dionysia are themselves open to equally forceful objections. As I understand it four principal arguments have been adduced, all based on political allusions within the plays:

(1) "*Lys.* 489–92 alludes to Peisander in a manner suggesting he is still considered a democrat and therefore the play must date to a period before his speeches had made it clear that he favored constitutional change in a less democratic direction."[2] Peisander left for Athens in December of 412, however, and Thucydides 8.53.1 suggests that he made his plans for constitutional change known in a public speech soon after arriving (i.e. sometime in January, before the Lenaea in early February);[3] even if we suppose that he spent several weeks in private maneuverings before making his speech, the city would still be full of rumors about his machinations by the time of the Lenaea. Moreover, nothing in *Lys.* 489–92 says Peisander is or ever was a friend of the *dēmos;* the lines say merely that he and the ambitious people

1. Sommerstein 1977a, 112–22.
2. This is my paraphrase of the argument as presented by *HCT* V, 189, and Henderson 1987, xxi–xxiii.
3. See *HCT* V, 117, 124, and Ostwald 1986, 353 n.66.

around him have always aimed at power in order to stir things up and enrich themselves at the public's expense.[4] Indeed the lines make much better sense on the assumption that Peisander has been much in the news lately and is now generally recognized as up to no good, making proposals inimical to the public. Aristophanes is saying that he has always been a troublemaker regardless of momentary ideology, not that he has always been a democrat. The passage implies that any apparent changes in Peisander's politics are merely opportunistic; his real motive has always been the lust for power and personal gain.[5]

Sommerstein adds a further refinement to this argument by suggesting that, because the political environment in Athens had become so dangerous by April of 411, it would be impossible for Aristophanes to criticize Peisander by name at the Dionysia without running a serious risk of assassination by the oligarchs.[6] I find it difficult to believe that Aristophanes would be so easily cowed, or that a comic poet who makes a three-line aside at the expense of Peisander and his friends would be considered a serious threat to them, like Androcles and other prominent democrats. Although the *Thesmophoriazusae* does not mention any of them by name, it contains several passages arguably even more unsympathetic to the oligarchs and their designs (see *Thesm.* 335–39, 356–67, 1143–44);[7] indeed, one could construe the *Lysistrata* to be a play rather favorable to installation of a new regime.[8] Accordingly, Aristophanes' fear of the oligarchs, assuming that he had any, does not provide a reliable basis for determining which play was presented at the Dionysia. Had he been truly afraid he would not have presented either play in the form we have it.

(2) The argument has also been made that the appeal to the Samian

4. Croiset (1909, 136–37) is right to interpret χοἰ ταῖς ἀρχαῖς ἐπέχοντες (*Lys.* 490) as members of the *hetairiai* or "political clubs," and thus as equivalent to the "knots of wool" which Lysistrata wants to comb out in her simile (*Lys.* 577–78). Under democracy they sought office for personal gain; now they are seeking political power and its advantages in another way.

5. Westlake (1980, 47–49) offers the correct interpretation of this passage, paraphrasing it thus: "Peisander may appear to be making a *volte face*, but in view of his record for conventional demagoguery it would be most unwise to trust him. His aim may well be, as it has been hitherto, to feather his own nest."

6. Sommerstein 1977a, 119–20. Against this view, see *HCT* V, 190–93, which believes the oligarchic campaign of terror did not begin until after the Dionysia.

7. Sommerstein (1977a, 125–26) is compelled to construe *Thesm.* 356–62 as having nothing to do with proposed constitutional changes. But within the context of the proposals that had unquestionably been advanced before the Dionysia of 411, this is how many in the audience would have understood the passage. If Aristophanes was truly terrified by the oligarchs he would not have said anything against "changing the laws," even if this merely refers to proposals for the recall of Alcibiades, as Sommerstein thinks.

8. This interpretation has in fact been advanced by Töttössy 1962, 273–82.

generals in *Lys.* 313 for help in suppressing the women's revolution would be impossible if anyone yet suspected them of complicity in oligarchic plans.[9] But what this line actually asks is *which* of the Samian generals could be relied upon to come and help. It may refer to dissension among the generals over the current plans,[10] or it could be a rhetorical question implying that none of the generals can really be relied upon to suppress a revolution (note the potential optative). In any event the generals' plans were probably evident already by the time of Peisander's activity in January. Hence this line is of no value for dating the play.

(3) "None of the many allusions to Persia (in the *Lysistrata*) reflect knowledge that a deal with Tissaphernes was in the making."[11] *Thesm.* 335–39 and 365–66 appear to reflect knowledge of such a deal and oppose it. On the other hand Lysistrata's admonition (*Lys.* 1133–34) suggests that the Athenians and Spartans should both be fighting the Persians rather than trying to ally themselves with the Persians against each other. Her admonitions would not apply equally to both sides unless the Athenians in fact were now seeking an alliance with Tissaphernes, as the Spartans had done for some time. Again the possibility of a deal with Persia was probably already in the air by the Lenaea of 411 and is equally deprecated in both plays anyway.

(4) The imprecations against "tyrants" in *Thesm.* 338–39 and 1143–44 are felt by some to be more serious and sincere than those of *Lys.* 616–19, 630–35, and thus to be more likely to reflect true anxiety over the possibility of an oligarchic coup.[12] This is a subjective impression based on the premise that we should take the Thesmophorian women and their paranoia about Euripides more seriously than we take the Old Men of the *Lysistrata* and their paranoia about the intentions of the Old Women. Nevertheless, as subjective impressions go, I incline to think it may be right.

In sum, arguments (1), (2), and (3) are of no value in determining the relative chronology of these two plays; (4) is subjective and may be right, but it is far from being provable with any rigor. I believe that it is correct to see the *Lysistrata* as prior to the *Thesmophoriazusae*, though more cogent reasons for holding this view are to be found in the intertextual relationship of the two plays, as I argue in chapter 8.

9. See Henderson 1987, xxiii.
10. See Croiset 1909, 135; Westlake 1980, 49–51. Σ*Lys.* 313 tells us that Didymus took the remark as an allusion to Phrynichus.
11. Henderson 1987, xxv.
12. Cf. Sommerstein 1977a, 122; Henderson 1987, xxiv.

APPENDIX 5

The Death of the Parabasis

The whole question of transition from Old Comedy to Middle Comedy is properly beyond the scope of this study;[1] to the extent, however, that one of its features was the total elimination of the parabasis, it merits some brief comment. It is wrong to regard the absence of the parabasis in Middle Comedy as the culmination of a long decline in the form, as some do,[2] since notions about the truncated and dramatically integrated parabases of *Birds* through *Frogs* as a "decline" from a rigid antecedent structure may be in error. As we have seen,[3] the parabases of these plays should be viewed as experiments with the form rather than as attempts to escape the form. The evidence of the comic fragments moreover suggests that parabases similar to those of *Acharnians* through *Peace* continued to be written even in the 410s and 400s.[4]

The loss of the parabasis must be seen rather as part of the general decline in the role of the chorus that we observe in the last two plays of Aristophanes and subsequent fourth-century comedy. Though the χοροῦ marks at *Eccl.* 729 and 876 are likely to have been inserted by Alexandrian scholars,[5] those in the *Plutus* may have greater authority in suggesting the "embolization" of the chorus, which is reduced to

1. For a fuller treatment of this issue, see Maidment 1935, 1–12, and Perusino 1986, 59–84.
2. See Barry 1942, 21–24; Strauss 1966, 272–73; Dearden 1976, 102.
3. See pp. 157–58 above.
4. Cf. Aristophanes, fr. 30–31, 58–59, 264–65, 347–48 PCG; Eupolis, fr. 89, 132 PCG; Metagenes, fr. 15 PCG; Plato, fr. 96, 99 PCG.
5. See Ussher 1973, xxvii–xxviii. However, the χοροῦ marks here are defended by Hunter 1979, 24–25, 28–31.

246

performing traditional set pieces not by the hand of the playwright.[6] The one developed choral element preserved in both plays is the parodos or entry of the chorus; this may confirm our thesis concerning the parodos (rather than the parabasis) as the original and primary medium of choral self-presentation in Attic comedy.[7]

Some have long assumed the role of the chorus to have been reduced either because of limited freedom for satire under oligarchic government[8] or because of economic constraints after Athens' defeat in the Peloponnesian War.[9] Others have pointed to the decline in standards of choral education and the influence of the New Music.[10] As Maidment has argued, however, the reduced role of choral elements probably has far more to do with changes in public taste.[11] In the more pessimistic and less flamboyant period after Athens' loss of empire the imperturbable self-confidence and loud self-assertion of the Old Comic chorus may have seemed jarringly discordant with the spirit of the times. Consequently Aristophanes turned instead toward a more ironic type of plot, one in which positive undertakings are defeated through their own internal contradictions.[12] As we have seen, Aris-

6. See Maidment 1935, 11–12; Handley 1953, 55–61; Koster 1957, 117–35; Sifakis 1971a, 416–17; Pöhlmann 1977, 69–81; Hunter 1979, 31–33; Perusino 1986, 66–69.

7. See pp. 26–27 above.

8. This theory, which has had many later proponents (see Kock 1856, 5–6; Hornung 1861, 25; Agthe 1866, 27–28), has its origins in Platonius, *De Diff. Com.* (= Test. I, 39–41 Koster), whose authority here has recently been defended by Perusino (1986, 76–79). See also Horace, *AP* 281–84. However, for strong arguments against it, see Maidment (1935, 6–7) and Barry (1942, 18), who point to many plays in the period after 405 that were wholly political. There is certainly no dearth of caustic allusion to political figures in the *Ecclesiazusae* (cf. Epicrates in v. 71, Agyrrhius in vv. 102–4, 184–88, Epigonus in v. 167, Aesimus in v. 208, Cephalus in vv. 248–53, Neocleides in vv. 254–55, 397–407, Amynon in v. 365, Antisthenes in v. 366), nor was the Athens of the early fourth century oppressively oligarchical; Aristophanes showed little hesitation in personal satire in the much more threatening environment of 411.

9. Again this thesis goes back to Platonius (= Test. I, 42–44 Koster) who is, however, clearly wrong in attributing the decline in choral songs to the discontinuance of *chorēgiai*. For relevant epigraphical evidence, see Maidment 1935, 5–6. Choruses were not necessarily much cheaper if they delivered set pieces as opposed to the poet's compositions. And despite the possibility of economic constraints having made extravagant costumes a thing of the past, this did not prevent choruses from performing at length, as we see with the "ragged" chorus of the *Frogs* (*Ran.* 405–10), although it may ultimately have made the chorus less interesting as an object of attention.

10. See Silk 1980, 148, and the detailed study of this problem in Nagy 1990, 404–10.

11. Maidment 1935, 7. Cf. Ferrari 1948, 183; Gelzer 1960, 266; Dover 1972, 195; Flashar 1975, 405–6.

12. On the profound pessimism of Aristophanes' last two plays, see the trenchant remarks of Auger 1979, 88–94. Aristophanes' ironic mode of plot construction has been well expounded by Newiger 1957, 173–76; Strauss 1966, 279–82, 295; Flashar 1975, 410–34; Maurach 1968, 1–24; Hertel 1969, 27–28; Heberlein 1981, 27–49; David 1984, 38–44.

tophanes had already had experience working with this type of plot in
the *Clouds* and *Birds,* in both of which plays the hero's quest is finally
revealed as something totally corrupt and unworthy of the audience's
sympathy. By the time of the *Ecclesiazusae* and *Plutus,* Aristophanes
may have determined that this plot form was sufficient in its own right
to generate the desired set of ideological tensions and associations
without need of extended parabatic focus or clarification.

What is striking about the *Ecclesiazusae* is that we nevertheless find
several traces of the parabasis, even with the form itself no longer
visible. Most conspicuous is the epirrheme of eight trochaic tetrameters we find as part of the choral exodos:[13]

> I wish to propose a small thing to the judges:
> To the clever, that they judge me remembering the clever things,   1155
> To those laughing gladly, that they judge me on account of
> > laughter;
> Then I ask nearly everyone to judge me clearly,
> And not let the allotment be a cause of anything to us,
> Since it has fallen as it has. Remembering all these things, it is right
> For you not to betray your oath, but always to judge choruses
> > correctly   1160
> And not liken your ways to naughty prostitutes,
> Who always remember only the things at the end.
>
> >   (*Eccl.* 1154–62)

Here we have the conventional appeal for audience favor, and more
particularly an appeal to the judges, as we sometimes find in parabasis epirrhemes.[14] Moreover we see again the dichotomy between
the clever, intellectual audience (v. 1155 τοῖς σοφοῖς μὲν τῶν σοφῶν
μεμνημένοις) and the common crowd, more interested in comic entertainment (v. 1156 τοῖς γελῶσι δ᾽ ἡδέως). But here, Aristophanes is
happy to accommodate both groups. Some critics are uncomfortable
with these lines, regarding them as a last-minute addition (after the
poet knew the order in which the plays would be presented) which
disrupts the promise of a μέλος μελλοδειπνικόν in v. 1153 and its
delivery in vv. 1166–67.[15] Even if they were added at the last minute,
the lines are not any the less deliberate and significant, suggesting as
they do that Aristophanes still found appeal in breaking the dramatic
illusion to confront his audience. As we have seen in the *Peace,* au-

---

13. On the "parabatic" nature of this passage, see Zielinski 1885, 182; Körte 1921,
1246; Händel 1963, 132; Perusino 1986, 64–65 n.20.

14. Cf. *Nub.* 1115–30, *Av.* 1102–17, and Pherecrates, fr. 102 PCG.

15. Cf. Wilamowitz 1903, 454; Robert 1922, 346–47; Russo 1962, 339.

dience involvement is altogether appropriate in the feast with which a comedy may conclude; this is particularly true here, because the communal dining instituted by the women includes by definition everyone in Athens.

The exodos is not the only place where the *Ecclesiazusae* breaks dramatic illusion in a manner reminiscent of the parabasis. We see the rupture also in vv. 888–89, apologetically introducing the agonistic duet between the young girl and the old hag for the favors of Epigenes: "even if this is a tedious annoyance (δι' ὄχλου)[16] for the spectators, all the same it presents some delight and comic entertainment." The ensuing battle for the young man is a scene that has been in fact δι' ὄχλου for many critics,[17] serving perhaps to prove the poet's wisdom in so prefacing it, much like the ironic deprecation of low-comic farcical elements in the revised *Clouds*. Again, as in the exodos, Aristophanes attempts to balance and conciliate the demands of his two audiences, the discriminating critics and the groundlings who want comic entertainment.

More important is the choral rupture of illusion we see leading into the agon between Praxagora and the menfolk, at a point almost exactly half way through the play, thus corresponding to the usual position of the parabasis:

> Now you must defend your friends, knowing how
> > To arouse a shrewd mind and philosophical thought.
> > For by common good fortune
> > The inventiveness of your tongue is going to delight
> > The citizen people   575
> With countless benefits of life. It is now time to reveal whatever you
> > can.
> Our city needs some clever discovery.
> > Only be sure to accomplish
> > Things never done nor said before,
> > Since they hate it, if they often see old things onstage.   580
> You must not hesitate, but take hold with high thoughts,
> As being swift wins the most favor among the spectators.
>
> (*Eccl.* 571–82)

In encouraging Praxagora's articulation of her new plans for the city, the chorus uses the vocabulary of philosophy and "New Thinking."

---

16. The phrase δι' ὄχλου also puns on the word's usual meaning of "crowd" or "mob," thus making allusion to the crowd of common theatergoers who are entertained by scenes such as this one.

17. Cf. Murray 1964, 196; Strauss 1966, 295.

Sophia is coupled with innovation, but with vv. 578–80, the perspective gradually shifts from the dramatic to the extradramatic, from Praxagora's innovative *sophia* and its effect on the Athens of the play to the play's innovative *sophia* and its effect on the theatrical audience. As in the earlier plays of Aristophanes, we see a parallel formed between the protagonist and the poet, the Athens of the play and the Athens sitting on the theater benches. This parallel between Athenians' insatiate desire for political novelty and that for theatrical novelty was the significant point of the *Knights'* parabasis.

The integration of the two realms is carried a step further when Praxagora opens the debate, not by turning to her male interlocutors, but by continuing the chorus' concern with the theatrical audience:

> *Prax.:* And indeed, I trust that I shall teach good things.
> If the spectators wish to start something new, and not
>   remain
> In their familiar and ancient customs—this is what I
>   especially fear.
> *Blep.:* Have no fear about starting something new. It is up to us
> To do this in preference to any other rule, and to disregard
>   ancient customs.
>
> (*Eccl.* 583–87)

It is only with Blepyrus' reply that we are drawn back into the dramatic context and the "audience" becomes the men of the play. The issue of the new ways and the old ways is highlighted here as one of the play's central paradoxes,[18] as often in the work of this "Euripidaristophanizing" poet. The chorus exhorts and encourages Praxagora to say something new, for both the sake of the dramatic city and the theatrical audience, and she in fact goes on to propose an extremely radical and new scheme of governance and social organization, the ultimate *reductio ad absurdum* of innovation-seeking democracy and absolute egalitarianism.[19] Still Praxagora introduces herself deprecatingly as wanting nothing new and hoping the spectators will keep to their usual customs. This pretense that the ultimate radicalism is actually the ultimate conservatism continues the themes of the prologue, in which Praxagora, also in her didactic mode (v. 215 διδάξω), argues that women are superior to men as governors because they alone do things "just as before" (vv. 221–28). In the parodos the women, like many Aristo-

18. On this paradox here, see Saïd 1979, 35.

19. On the relation of Praxagora's proposals to radical democratic ideas current in the depressed economic environment of the early fourth century, see David 1984, 24–25.

phanic choruses, glorify the frugality and self-sacrifice of earlier generations as opposed to the venality of the present day (vv. 303–10). The
paradox has its roots in the concept that family economy, as practiced
by women, is the most traditional form of social organization, predat-
ing the state and its laws. But just as in the *Birds,* we perceive this
utopian vision of a return to Nature turning into a dystopian totalitarianism of the worst sort, in which words come to mean their opposite, as
manipulated by the sophistic will to power.

Without the form of the parabasis we can still see Aristophanes
attempting to exploit brief ruptures of dramatic illusion to focus light
on the central paradoxes and tensions of his theatrical work.[20] This
testifies not to the weakness and obsolescence of the form, but to its
vital and continuing grip on the poet's imagination. The parabatic
impulse outlived the parabasis itself.

20. Note also the address to the audience in *Plutus* 760–64 inviting the audience to
share in the revelry accompanying the restoration of Plutus' eyesight. On the "parabatic"
nature of this passage, see Strauss 1966, 299.

Bibliography

Abel, L. 1963. *Metatheatre: A New View of Dramatic Form.* New York.

Agthe, C. 1866. *Die Parabase und die Zwischenakte der alt-attische Komödie.* Altona.

Albini, U. 1965. "Osservazioni sui Cavalieri di Aristofane." *Maia* 27: 19–29.

Albini, U. 1971. "La Pace di Aristofane una commedia minore?" *PP* 26: 14–25.

Allen, J. T. 1938. *On the Program of the City Dionysia during the Peloponnesian War* (= *UCPCP* 12.3). Berkeley, Calif.

Allison, R. H. 1983. "Amphibian Ambiguities: Aristophanes and His Frogs." *G&R* 30: 8–20.

Ambrosino, D. 1983. "Nuages et sens. Autour des Nuées d'Aristophane." *QS* 18: 3–60.

Apelt, O. 1912. *Platons Dialog Philebos.* Leipzig.

Arnoldt, R. 1873. *Die Chorpartien bei Aristophanes.* Leipzig.

Arnott, W. G. 1985. "Terence's Prologues." *Papers of the Liverpool Latin Seminar* 5: 1–7.

Arrowsmith, W. 1973. "Aristophanes' Birds: The Fantasy Politics of Eros." *Arion* ns 1: 119–67.

Auger, D. 1979. "Le théâtre d' Aristophane: Le myth, l'utopie et les femmes." In *Aristophane: Les femmes et la cité* (= *Cahiers de Fontenay* 17). Fontenay-aux-Roses.

Aurenche, O. 1974. *Les groupes d'Alcibiade, de Léogoras et de Teucros.* Paris.

Bailey, C. 1936. "Who Played Dicaeopolis?" In *Greek Poetry and Life: Essays Presented to Gilbert Murray.* Oxford.

Bain, D. 1977. *Actors and Audience: A Study of Asides and Related Conventions in Greek Drama.* Oxford.

Barchiesi, M. 1970. "Plauto e il 'metateatro' antico." *Il Verri* 31: 113–30.

Barry, E. 1942. "The Ecclesiazusae as a Political Satire." Diss. University of Chicago.

Bassett, S. 1923. "The Proems of the *Iliad* and *Odyssey*." *AJP* 44: 339–48.

Baudelaire, C. 1923. "De l'essence du rire." In *Oeuvres complètes*. Paris. I, 367–96.

Beck, G. 1965. "Beobachtungen zur Kirke-Episode in der Odyssee." *Philologus* 109: 1–29.

Beer, C. 1844. *Ueber die Zahl der Schauspieler bei Aristophanes*. Leipzig.

Benjamin, W. 1974. *Gesammelte Schriften*. Frankfurt a. M.

Bennett, L. J., and Tyrrell, W. B. 1990. "Making Sense of Aristophanes' *Knights*" *Arethusa* 23: 235–54.

Bergk, T. 1873. "Lösungen." *Philologus* 32: 122–39.

Bergler, E. 1956. *Laughter and the Sense of Humor*. New York.

Bergson, H. 1911. *Laughter: An Essay on the Meaning of the Comic*. Trans. C. Brereton and F. Rothwell. London.

Bertan, M. 1984. "Gli *Odysses* di Cratino e la testimonianza di Platonio." *Atene e Roma* ns 29: 171–78.

Bertram, C. H. 1865. *Der Sokrates des Xenophon und der des Aristophanes*. Magdeburg.

Bianchetti, S. 1979. "L'ostracismo di Iperbolo e la seconda redazione delle *Nuvole* di Aristofane." *SIFC* 51: 221–48.

Blum, R. 1977. *Kallimachos und die Literaturverzeichnis bei den Griechen*. Frankfurt a. M.

Bodson, L. 1973. "Gai, Gai! Sauvons-nous. Procédés et effets du comique dans *Lysistrata*." *AC* 42: 5–27.

Bonanno, M. G. 1972. *Studi su Cratete comico*. Padova.

Boruchowitsch, W. G. 1973. "Aristophanes als Herausgeber seiner Komödien." *AAntHung* 21: 89–95.

Bowie, A. M. 1982. "The Parabasis in Aristophanes: Prolegomena, *Acharnians*." *CQ* 32: 27–40.

Box, H. 1964. "Aristophanes, *Birds* 785–96, and *Thesmophoriazusae* 450–1." *CR* 78: 241–42.

Brelich, A. 1969. *Paides e Parthenoi*. Rome.

Brentano, E. W. H. 1871. *Untersuchungen über das griechische Drama, Erster Teil: Aristophanes*. Frankfurt a. M.

Briel, A. 1887. *De Callistrato et Philonide*. Berlin.

Brill, A. A. 1940. "The Mechanism of Wit and Humor in Normal and Psychopathic States." *Psychiatric Quarterly* 14: 731–49.

Brock, R. W. 1986. "The Double Plot in Aristophanes' *Knights*." *GRBS* 27: 15–27.

Brody, M. W. 1950. "The Meaning of Laughter." *Psychoanalytic Quarterly* 19: 192–201.

Bücheler, F. 1861. "Ueber Aristophanes Wolken." *NJbPP* 83: 657–89.

Buchheit, V. 1960. "Feigensymbolik im antiken Epigramm." *RhM* 103: 200–229.

Bugh, G. R. 1988. *The Horsemen of Athens*. Princeton, N.J.

Bundy, E. L. 1962. *Studia Pindarica* (= *UCPCP* 18). Berkeley, Calif.

Burkert, W. 1960. "Das Lied von Ares und Aphrodite: Zum Verhältnis von Odyssee und Ilias." *RhM* 103: 130–44.

Burkert, W. 1983. *Homo Necans: The Anthropology of Ancient Greek Sacrificial Ritual and Myth*. Trans. P. Bing. Berkeley, Calif.

Burkert, W. 1985. *Greek Religion*. Trans J. Raffan. Cambridge, Mass.

Burnett, A. 1989. "Performing Pindar's Odes." *CP* 84: 283–93.

Campbell, D. A. 1984. "The Frogs in the *Frogs*." *JHS* 104: 163–65.

Cantarella, R. 1962. "Le 'Rane' di Aristofane." *Dioniso* 36: 123–35.

Capps, E. 1907. "Epigraphical Problems in the History of Attic Comedy." *AJP* 28: 179–99.

Carey, C. 1989. "The Performance of the Victory Ode." *AJP* 110: 545–65.

Carrière, J. C. 1979. *Le Carnaval et la politique*. Paris.

Carter, L. B. 1986. *The Quiet Athenian*. Oxford.

Cassio, A. C. 1977. *Aristofane: Banchettanti*. Pisa.

Cassio, A. C. 1982. "Arte compositiva e politica in Aristofane: Il discorso di Ermete nella *Pace* (603–648)." *RFIC* 110: 22–44.

Cassio, A. C. 1985. *Commedia e partecipazione: La "Pace" di Aristofane*. Naples.

Catteruccia, L. M. 1961. *Premessa ad uno studio dei tipi scenici nelle commedie di Aristofane*. Rome.

Cavaignac, E. 1959. "Pythagore et Socrate." *RPh* 33: 246–48.

Ceadel, E. B. 1941. "Resolved Feet in the Trimeters of Euripides and the Chronology of the Plays." *CQ* 35: 66–89.

Chantraine, P. 1968–80. *Dictionnaire etymologique de la langue grecque*. Paris.

Chapman, G. A. H. 1983. "Some Notes on Dramatic Illusion in Aristophanes." *AJP* 104: 1–23.

Cole, T. 1967. *Democritus and the Sources of Greek Anthropology*. Cleveland, Ohio.

Connor, W. R. 1968. *Theopompus and Fifth-Century Athens*. Washington, D.C.

Connor, W. R. 1971. *The New Politicians of Fifth-Century Athens*. Princeton, N.J.

Cook, E. F. 1990. "Worlds in Apposition: Towards a Synoptic Interpretation of the Homeric Odyssey." Diss. University of California, Berkeley.

Cooper, L. 1922. *An Aristotelian Theory of Comedy*. New York.

Cornford, F. M. 1968. *The Origin of Attic Comedy*. 2d ed. Gloucester, Eng.

Croiset, M. 1909. *Aristophanes and the Political Parties at Athens*. Trans. J. Loeb. London.

Crotty, K. 1982. *Song and Action: The Victory Odes of Pindar*. Baltimore, Md.

Culler, J. 1981. *The Pursuit of Signs: Semiotics, Literature, Deconstruction*. Ithaca, N.Y.

Dale, A. M. 1969. *Collected Papers*. Cambridge, Mass.

Dalfen, J. 1975. "Politik und Utopie in den *Vögeln* des Aristophanes (Zu Ar., *Vögel* 451–638)." *Bollettino dell'Istituto di Filologia Greca* 2: 268–87.

David, E. 1984. *Aristophanes and Athenian Society of the Early Fourth Century* B.C. (= *Mnemosyne Suppl.* 81). Leiden.

Davison, P. H. 1963. "*Volpone* and the Old Comedy." *MLQ* 24: 151–57.

Dearden, C. W. 1976. *The Stage of Aristophanes*. London.

de Carli, E. 1971. *Aristofane e la sofistica*. Florence.

Defradas, J. 1969. "Le Chant des Grenouilles." *REA* 71: 23–37.

Degani, E. 1960. "Arifrade l'anassagoreo." *Maia* 12: 190–217.

de Man, P. 1969. "The Rhetoric of Temporality." In C. S. Singleton, ed., *Interpretation: Theory and Practice*. Baltimore.

Demand, N. 1970. "The Identity of the Frogs." *CP* 65: 83–87.

Denniston, J. D. 1927. "Technical Terms in Aristophanes." *CQ* 21: 113–21.

Denniston, J. D. 1934. *The Greek Particles*. 2d ed. Oxford.

Dessoir, M. 1970. *Aesthetics and Theory of Art*. Trans. S. A. Emery. Detroit.

Detienne, M. 1967. *Les maîtres de vérité dans la Grèce archaïque*. Paris.

Deubner, L. 1932. *Attische Feste*. Berlin.

Dick, A. L. 1974. *Paideia through Laughter: Jonson's Aristophanic Appeal to Human Intelligence*. The Hague.

Dihle, A. 1977. "Das Satyrspiel 'Sisyphos.'" *Hermes* 105: 28–42.

Dobrov, G. 1988. "The Dawn of Farce: Aristophanes." In J. Redmond, ed., *Themes in Drama 10: Farce*. Cambridge.

Dobrov, G. 1988. "Winged Words/Graphic Birds: The Aristophanic Comedy of Language." Diss. Cornell University.

Dodds, E. R. 1951. *The Greeks and the Irrational*. Berkeley, Calif.

Donlan, W. 1980. *The Aristocratic Ideal in Ancient Greece*. Lawrence, Kans.

Dooley, L. 1934. "A Note on Humor." *Psychoanalytic Review* 21: 50–57.

Dooley, L. 1941. "The Relation of Humor to Masochism." *Psychoanalytic Review* 28: 37–46.

Dörrie, H. 1956. "Aristophanes' Frösche 1433–1467." *Hermes* 84: 296–319.

Dover, K. J. 1959. "Aristophanes, *Knights* 11–20." *CR* 73: 196–99.

Dover, K. J. 1963. "Notes on Aristophanes' *Acharnians*." *Maia* 15: 6–25.

Dover, K. J. 1964. "The Poetry of Archilochus." In *Archiloque: Entretiens sur l'antiquité classique* 10. Vandoeuvres-Genève.

Dover, K. J. 1967. "Portrait-Masks in Aristophanes." In Westendorp Boerma 1967, 16–28.

Dover, K. J. 1968. *Aristophanes: Clouds*. Oxford.

Dover, K. J. 1972. *Aristophanic Comedy*. Berkeley, Calif.

Dover, K. J. 1978. *Greek Homosexuality*. Cambridge, Mass.

Dracoulides, N. N. 1967. *Psychanalyse d'Aristophane*. Paris.

Droysen, J. G. 1835–36. "Des Aristophanes Vögel und die Hermokopiden." *RhM* 3: 161–208, 4: 27–62.

Edmonds, J. M. 1957–61. *The Fragments of Attic Comedy*. Leiden.

Edmunds, L. 1980. "Aristophanes' *Acharnians*." *YCS* 26: 1–41.

Edmunds, L. 1987. "The Aristophanic Cleon's 'Disturbance' of Athens." *AJP* 108: 233–63.

Edmunds, L. 1987. *Cleon, Knights, and Aristophanes' Politics*. Lanham, Md.

Ehrenberg, V. 1962. *The People of Aristophanes*. 3d ed. New York.

Ehrhardt, G. 1890. *Interpolationen in des Aristophanes Wespen*. Görlitz.

Ehrman, R. K. 1985. "Terentian Prologues and the Parabases of Old Comedy." *Latomus* 44: 370–76.

Elderkin, G. W. 1940. "Aphrodite and Athena in the *Lysistrata* of Aristophanes." *CP* 35: 387–96.

Emerson, A. 1889. "On the Conception of Low Comedy in Aristophanes." *AJP* 10: 265–79.

Emonds, H. 1941. *Zweite Auflage im Altertum*. Leipzig.

Enger, R. 1853. *Ueber die Parabase der Wolken des Aristophanes.* Ostrowo.

Enger, R. 1856. "Zu Aristophanes: Wer recitierte das Epirrhema?." *RhM* 10: 119–20.

Erbse, H. 1954. "Sokrates im Schatten der aristophanischen Wolken." *Hermes* 82: 385–420.

Erbse, H. 1975. "Dionysos' Schiedspruch in den 'Fröschen' des Aristophanes." In K. Vourveris & A. Skiadas, eds., Δώρημα *Hans Diller zum 70. Geburtstag: Dauer und Überleben des antiken Geistes.* Athens.

Erbse, H. 1982. "Über das politische Ziel der aristophanischen Komödie." In *Studi in onore di Aristide Colonna.* Perugia.

Fabrini, P. 1975. "La rappresentabilità delle Nuvole di Aristofane." *ASNP* ser. 3, 5.1: 1–16.

Ferrari, C. 1948. "Il frammento del papiro berlinese 11771 e la trasformazione del coro da Aristofane a Menandro." *Dioniso* 11: 177–87.

Fisher, R. K. 1984. *Aristophanes' Clouds: Purpose and Technique.* Amsterdam.

Flashar, H. 1975. "Zur Eigenart des aristophanischen Spätwerks." In Newiger 1975, 405–34.

Foley, H. P. 1982. "The 'Female Intruder' Reconsidered: Women in Aristophanes' *Lysistrata* and *Ecclesiazusae.*" *CP* 77: 1–21.

Foley, H. P. 1988. "Tragedy and Politics in Aristophanes' *Acharnians.*" *JHS* 108: 33–47.

Fornara, C. W. 1973. "Cleon's Attack against the Cavalry." *CQ* 23: 24.

Forrest, W. G. 1975. "Aristophanes and the Athenian Empire." In B. Levick, ed., *The Ancient Historian and His Materials.* Farnborough, Eng.

Forrest, W. G. 1975. "An Athenian Generation Gap." *YCS* 24: 37–52.

Fraenkel, E. 1962. *Beobachtungen zu Aristophanes.* Rome.

François, G. 1977. "L'encodage stylistique dans les *Cavaliers* d'Aristophane." *LÉC* 45: 3–30.

Freud, S. 1928. "Humour." *International Journal of Psychoanalysis* 9: 1–6.

Freud, S. 1938. *Basic Writings.* Trans. A. A. Brill. New York.

Frye, N. 1949. "The Argument of Comedy." In D. A. Robertson, ed., *English Institute Essays 1948.* New York.

Frye, N. 1957. *The Anatomy of Criticism.* Princeton, N.J.

Geissler, P. 1925. *Chronologie der Altattischen Komödie.* Berlin.

Gelzer, T. 1956. "Aristophanes und sein Sokrates." *MH* 13: 65–93.

Gelzer, T. 1959. "Tradition und Neuschöpfung in der Dramaturgie des Aristophanes." *A&A* 8: 15–31.

Gelzer, T. 1960. *Der epirrhematische Agon bei Aristophanes.* Munich.

Gelzer, T. 1970. "Aristophanes." *RE Suppl.* 12: 1392–1569.

Gelzer, T. 1972. "Alte Komödie und hohe Lyrik: Bermerkungen zu den Oden in Pap. Oxy. 2737." *MH* 29: 141–52.

Gentili, B. 1988. *Poetry and Its Public in Ancient Greece.* Trans. A. T. Cole. Baltimore.

Genz, H. 1865. "De parabasi." Diss. Berlin.

Ghiron-Bistagne, P. 1973. "Un calembour méconnu d'Aristophane: *Acharniens* 400, *Oiseaux* 787." *RÉG* 86: 285–91.

Giangrande, G. 1963. "The Origin of Attic Comedy." *Eranos* 61: 1–24.

Gigante, M. 1948. "La città dei giusti in Esiodo e gli 'Uccelli' di Aristofane."
    Dioniso 11: 17–25.
Gilbert, G. 1877. *Beiträge zur inneren Geschichte Athens.* Leipzig.
Giner, C., and J. de Hoz. 1979. "Aristófanes, Aves 737–800." In C. Codoñer,
    ed., *El commentario de textos griegos y latinos.* Madrid.
Goldmark, R. I. 1918. *Studies on the Influence of the Classics on English Literature.*
    New York.
Gomme, A. W. 1975. "Aristophanes and Politics." In Newiger 1975, 75–98.
Gomme, A. W., A. Andrewes, and K. J. Dover. 1945–81. *A Historical Commen-
    tary on Thucydides.* Oxford.
Gooch, P. W. 1987. "Socratic Irony and Aristotle's *Eiron:* Some Puzzles." *Phoe-
    nix* 41: 95–104.
Goodwin, W. W. 1890. *Syntax of the Moods and Tenses of the Greek Verb.* 2d ed.
    Boston.
Goody, J., and I. Watt. 1968. "The Consequences of Literacy." In J. Goody, ed.,
    Literacy in Traditional Societies. Cambridge.
Goossens, R. 1946. "Autour de l'expédition de Sicile." *AC* 15: 43–60.
Göttling, E. W. 1856. "Über die Redaction der Wolken des Aristophanes."
    *Berichte über die Verhandlung der königlichen sächsischen Gesellschaft der Wissen-
    schaften zu Leipzig, Philol.-hist. Classe* 8: 15–32.
Gröbl, J. N. 1889–90. *Die ältesten Hypotheseis zu Aristophanes.* Dillingen.
Grote, G. 1862. *A History of Greece.* 2d ed. London.
Gum, C. 1969. *The Aristophanic Comedies of Ben Jonson.* The Hague.
Gundert, H. 1935. *Pindar und sein Dichterberuf.* Frankfurt a. M.
Gunning, J. H. 1882. *De Babyloniis Aristophanis Fabula.* Traiecti ad Rhenum.
Guthrie, W. K. C. 1961–81. *A History of Greek Philosophy.* Cambridge.
Hackforth, R. 1972. *Plato's Philebus.* Cambridge.
Halbertsma, T. 1856. *Specimen literarium continens priorem partem prosopographiae
    Aristophaneae.* Leiden.
Haldane, J. A. 1965. "A Scene in the Thesmophoriazusae (295–371)." *Phi-
    lologus* 109: 39–46.
Halliwell, S. 1980. "Aristophanes' Apprenticeship." *CQ* 30: 33–45.
Halliwell, S. 1982. "Notes on Some Aristophanic Jokes (*Ach.* 854–9; *Kn.* 608–
    10; *Peace* 695–9; *Thesm.* 605; *Frogs* 1039)." *LCM* 7: 153–54.
Halliwell, S. 1984. "Ancient Interpretations of ὀνομαστὶ κωμῳδεῖν in Aris-
    tophanes." *CQ* 34: 83–88.
Hamaker, H. G. 1854. "Aanteekeningen op de Wespen van Aristophanes."
    Mnemosyne 3: 241–60.
Hamilton, R. 1985. "The Well-Equipped Traveller: *Birds* 42." *GRBS* 26: 235–
    39.
Händel, P. 1963. *Formen und Darstellungsweisen der aristophanischen Komödie.*
    Heidelberg.
Handley, E. W. 1953. "XOPOY in the *Plutus.*" *CQ* 3: 55–61.
Handley, E. W. 1982. "Aristophanes' Rivals." *PCA* 79: 23–25.
Handley, E. W., and J. Rea. 1957. *The Telephus of Euripides* (= *BICS Suppl.* 5).
    London.

Hansen, H. 1976. "Aristophanes' Thesmophoriazusae: Theme, Structure, Production." *Philologus* 120: 165–85.

Harbage, A. 1941. *Shakespeare's Audience*. New York.

Harman, E. G. 1920. *The Birds of Aristophanes Considered in Relation to Athenian Politics*. London.

Harriott, R. M. 1986. *Aristophanes: Poet and Dramatist*. Baltimore.

Harsh, P. W. 1934. "The Position of the Parabasis in the Plays of Aristophanes." *TAPA* 65: 178–97.

Harvey, F. D. 1971. "Sick Humour: Aristophanic Parody of a Euripidean Motif?" *Mnemosyne* 24: 362–65.

Havelock, E. A. 1957. *The Liberal Temper in Greek Politics*. London.

Havelock, E. A. 1972. "The Socratic Self as It Is Parodied in Aristophanes' *Clouds*." *YCS* 22: 1–18.

Havelock, E. A. 1982. *The Literate Revolution in Greece and Its Cultural Consequences*. Princeton, N.J.

Hazlitt, W. 1903. *Collected Works*. London.

Heath, M. 1987. *Political Comedy in Aristophanes*. Göttingen.

Heberlein, F. 1981. "Zur Ironie im 'Plutos' des Aristophanes." *WJA* ns 7: 27–49.

Hegel, G. W. F. 1920. *The Philosophy of Fine Arts*. Trans. F. P. B. Osmaston. London.

Heidhues, B. 1897. *Über die Wolken des Aristophanes*. Cologne.

Heinimann, F. 1945. *Nomos und Physis: Herkunft und Bedeutung einer Antithese im griechischen Denken des 5. Jahrhundert*. Basel.

Helmbold, H. 1890. *Aristophanis Pax superstes utrum prior sit an retractata*. Jena.

Henderson, J. 1972. "The Lekythos and *Frogs* 1200–1248." *HSCP* 76: 133–44.

Henderson, J. 1975. *The Maculate Muse: Obscene Language in Attic Comedy*. New Haven, Conn.

Henderson, J. 1980. "'Lysistrate': The Play and Its Themes." *YCS* 26: 153–218.

Henderson, J. 1987. *Aristophanes: Lysistrata*. Oxford.

Henderson, J. 1990. "The *Dēmos* and the Comic Competition." In Winkler and Zeitlin 1990, 271–313.

Henrichs, A. 1976. "The Atheism of Prodicus." *Cronache Ercolanesi* 6: 15–21.

Herford, C. H., and P. and E. Simpson. 1925–52. *Ben Jonson*. Oxford.

Herington, C. J. 1963. "A Study in the *Prometheia*, Part II: *Birds* and *Prometheia*." *Phoenix* 17: 236–43.

Hermann, G. 1799. *Aristophanis Nubes cum scholiis*. Leipzig.

Hertel, G. 1969. *Die Allegorie von Reichtum und Armut*. Nürnberg.

Herter, H. 1947. *Vom dionysischen Tanz zum komischen Spiel*. Iserlohn.

Higgens, W. E. 1977. "A Passage to Hades: The Frogs of Aristophanes." *Ramus* 6: 60–81.

Hiller, E. 1887. Rev. Briel 1887. *Philologischer Anzeiger* 17: 361–80.

Hobbes, T. 1839–45. *English Works*. London.

Hofmann, H. 1970. "Ein Kommentar zum 'Anagyros' des Aristophanes (P. Oxy. 2737)." *ZPE* 5: 1–10.

Hofmann, H. 1976. *Mythos und Komödie: Untersuchungen zu den Vögeln des Aristophanes.* Hildesheim.

Hooker, G. T. W. 1960. "The Topography of the *Frogs.*" *JHS* 80: 112–17.

Hooker, J. T. 1980. "The Composition of the Frogs." *Hermes* 108: 169–82.

Horn, W. 1970. *Gebet und Gebetsparodie in den Komödien des Aristophanes.* Nürnberg.

Hornung, H. T. 1861. "Commentationis de partibus comoediarum Graecarum particula." Diss. Berlin.

Howald, E. 1922. "ΑΕΝΑΟΙ ΝΕΦΕΛΑΙ," *Sokrates* 47: 23–42.

Hubbard, T. K. 1985. *The Pindaric Mind: A Study of Logical Structure in Early Greek Poetry* (= *Mnemosyne Suppl.* 85). Leiden.

Hubbard, T. K. 1986a. "Parabatic Self-Criticism and the Two Versions of Aristophanes' *Clouds.*" *CA* 5: 182–97.

Hubbard, T. K. 1986b. "Pegasus' Bridle and the Poetics of Pindar's *Thirteenth Olympian.*" *HSCP* 90: 27–48.

Hubbard, T. K. 1986c. "The Subject/Object-Relation in Pindar's *Second Pythian* and *Seventh Nemean.*" *QUCC* ns 22: 53–72.

Hubbard, T. K. 1987. "Pindar and the Aeginetan Chorus: *Nemean* 3.9–13." *Phoenix* 41: 1–9.

Hubbard, T. K. 1989. "Old Men in the Youthful Plays of Aristophanes." In T. M. Falkner and J. de Luce, eds., *Old Age in Greek and Latin Literature.* Albany, N.Y.

Hubbard, T. K. 1990. "The Knights' Eleven Oars (Aristophanes, *Eq.* 546–47)." *CJ* 85: 115–18.

Hubbard, T. K. 1991. "Remaking Myth and Rewriting History: Cult-Tradition in Pindar's *Ninth Nemean.*" *HSCP* 94: (forthcoming).

Hulton, A. O. 1972. "The Women on the Acropolis: A Note on the Structure of the *Lysistrata.*" *G&R* 19: 32–36.

Hunter, R. L. 1979. "The Comic Chorus in the Fourth Century." *ZPE* 36: 23–38.

Hurst, A. 1971. "Aeschylus or Euripides? Aristophanes: Frogs 1413 and 1434." *Hermes* 99: 227–40.

Jacoby, F. 1959. *Diagoras Ὁ Ἄθεος* = (*Abhandlungen der deutschen Akademie der Wissenschaften zu Berlin, Klasse für Sprachen, Literatur und Kunst* 1959.3). Berlin.

Janko, R. 1984. *Aristotle on Comedy: Towards a Reconstruction of Poetics II.* Berkeley, Calif.

Kagan, D. 1981. *The Peace of Nicias and the Sicilian Expedition.* Ithaca.

Kagan, D. 1987. *The Fall of the Athenian Empire.* Ithaca.

Kahn, C. H. 1960. *Anaximander and the Origins of Greek Cosmogony.* New York.

Kakridis, T. J. 1970. "Phrynicheisches in den Vögeln des Aristophanes." *WS* ns 4: 38–51.

Kannicht, R. 1983. "Dikaiopolis: Von der Schwierigkeit, ein rechter Bürger zu sein." In W. Barner et al., eds., *Literatur in der Demokratie: Für Walter Jens zum 60. Geburtstag.* Munich.

Kant, I. 1951. *Critique of Judgment.* Trans. J. H. Bernard. New York.

Kassel, R., and C. Austin. 1983–. *Poetae Comici Graeci.* Berlin.

Katz, B. 1976. "The *Birds* of Aristophanes and Politics." *Athenaeum* 54: 353–81.

Kent, R. G. 1905. "The Date of Aristophanes' Birth." *CR* 19: 153–55.

Kerferd, G. B. 1981. *The Sophistic Movement.* Cambridge.

Ketterer, R. C. 1980. "Stripping in the Parabasis of the *Acharnians.*" *GRBS* 21: 217–21.

Keyssner, K. 1932. *Gottesvorstellung und Lebensauffassung im griechischen Hymnus.* Stuttgart.

Kierkegaard, S. A. 1965. *The Concept of Irony, with Constant Reference to Socrates.* Trans. L. M. Capel. New York.

Kleinknecht, H. 1937. *Die Gebetsparodie in der Antike.* Stuttgart.

Kock, C. 1856. *De parabasi, antiquae comoediae Atticae interludio.* Progr. Anclam.

Kock, F. G. K. T. 1855. *De Philonide et Callistrato.* Guben.

Kock, T. 1882. *Ausgewählte Komödien des Aristophanes: II, Die Ritter.* 3d ed. Berlin.

Kock, T. 1894. *Ausgewählte Komödien des Aristophanes: I, Die Wolken.* 4th ed. Berlin.

Kock, T. 1898. *Ausgewählte Komödien des Aristophanes: III, Die Frösche.* 4th ed. Berlin.

Koechly, H. 1859. *Akademische Vorträge und Reden.* Zürich.

Koelb, C. 1984. *The Incredulous Reader: Literature and the Function of Disbelief.* Ithaca.

Koester, H. 1835. *Commentatio de Graecae comoediae parabasi.* Stralsund.

Koestler, A. 1964. *The Act of Creation.* New York.

Köhnken, A. 1971. *Die Funktion des Mythos bei Pindar.* Berlin.

Kolb, F. 1979. "Polis und Theater." In G. A. Seeck, ed., *Das griechische Drama.* Darmstadt.

Kolster, W. H. 1829. *De parabasi, veteris comoediae atticae parte antiquissima.* Altona.

Konstan, D. 1985. "The Politics of Aristophanes' *Wasps.*" *TAPA* 115: 27–46.

Konstan, D. 1986. "Poésie, politique et rituel dans les *Grenouilles* d'Aristophane." *Metis* 1: 291–308.

Konstan, D. 1990. "A City in the Air: Aristophanes' *Birds.*" *Arethusa* 23: 183–207.

Kopff, E. C. 1977. "*Nubes* 1493ff.: Was Socrates Murdered?" *GRBS* 18: 113–22.

Körte, A. 1921. "Komödie (attische)." *RE* 11: 1226–56.

Koster, W. J. W. 1957. *Autour d'un manuscrit d'Aristophane écrit par Démétrius Triclinius.* Groningen.

Kowzan, T. 1983. "Les comédies d' Aristophane, véhicule de la critique dramatique." *Dioniso* 54: 83–100.

Kranz, W. 1949. "Parabasis." *RE* 18: 1124–26.

Kraus, W. 1985. *Aristophanes' Politische Komödien: Die Acharner/Die Ritter.* Vienna.

Kris, E. 1952. *Psychoanalytic Explorations in Art.* New York.

Laín Entralgo, P. 1970. *The Therapy of the Word in Classical Antiquity.* Trans. L. J. Rather and J. M. Sharp. New Haven, Conn.

Landfester, M. 1967. *Die Ritter des Aristophanes.* Amsterdam.

Landfester, M. 1977. *Handlungsverlauf und Komik in den frühen Komödien des Aristophanes.* Berlin.

Lapalus, E. 1934. "Le Dionysos et l'Héraclès des *Grenouilles.*" *RÉG* 47: 1–20.

Lefkowitz, M. R. 1981. *The Lives of the Greek Poets*. Baltimore.

Lefkowitz, M. R. 1988. "Who Sang Pindar's Victory Odes?" *AJP* 109: 1–11.

Lenz, L. 1980. "Komik und Kritik in Aristophanes' 'Wespen.'" *Hermes* 108: 15–44.

Leo, F. 1878. "Bemerkungen zur attischen Komödie." *RhM* 33: 400–417.

Lever, K. 1946. "Greek Comedy on the Sixteenth Century English Stage." *CJ* 42: 169–74.

Lever, K. 1956. *The Art of Greek Comedy*. London.

Lewis, D. M. 1955. "Notes on Attic Inscriptions (II)." *BSA* 50: 1–36.

Lind, H. 1985. "Neues aus Kydathen: Beobachtungen zum Hintergrund der 'Daitales' und der 'Ritter' des Aristophanes." *MH* 42: 249–61.

Littlefield, D. J. 1968. "Metaphor and Myth: The Unity of Aristophanes' *Knights*." *Studies in Philology* 65: 1–22.

Long, T. 1976. "The Parodos of Aristophanes' *Wasps*." *ICS* 1: 15–21.

Loraux, N. 1980–81. "L'acropole comique." *Ancient Society* 11/12: 119–50.

Lord, L. E. 1925. *Aristophanes: His Plays and His Influence*. Boston.

Lübke, H. 1883. *Observationes criticae in historiam veteris Graecorum comoediae*. Berlin.

Luppe, W. 1971. "Der 'Anagyros'-Kommentar Pap. Oxy. 2737." *APF* 21: 93–110.

Luppe, W. 1973. "'Anagyros'—oder nicht? Zur Identifizierung von Pap. Oxy. 2737." *ZPE* 11: 275–88.

MacDowell, D. M. 1959. "Aristophanes, *Frogs* 1407–67." *CQ* 9: 261–68.

MacDowell, D. M. 1971. *Aristophanes: Wasps*. Oxford.

MacDowell, D. M. 1982. "Aristophanes and Kallistratos." *CQ* 32: 21–26.

MacDowell, D. M. 1983. "The Nature of Aristophanes' *Akharnians*." *G&R* 30: 143–62.

Maidment, K. J. 1935. "The Later Comic Chorus." *CQ* 29: 1–24.

Marr, J. L. 1970. "Who Said What about Alcibiades? *Frogs* 1422–34." *CQ* 20: 53–55.

Mastromarco, G. 1974. *Storia di una commedia di Atene*. Florence.

Mastromarco, G. 1979. "L'esordio 'segreto' di Aristofane." *QS* 10: 153–92.

Mastromarco, G. 1988. "Trame allusive e memoria del pubblico (Acarn. 300–301 ~ Caval. 314)." In S. Boldrini et al., eds., *Filologia e forme letterarie: Studi offerti a Francesco Della Corte*, vol. I. Urbino.

Mattingly, H. B. 1977. "Poets and Politicians in Fifth-Century Greece." In K. H. Kinzl, ed., *Greece and the Eastern Mediterranean in Ancient History and Prehistory*. Berlin.

Maurach, G. 1968. "Interpretationen zur attischen Komödie." *Acta Classica* 11: 1–24.

Mauron, C. 1964. *Psychocritique du genre comique*. Paris.

Maxwell-Stuart, P. G. 1973. "The Dramatic Poets and the Expedition to Sicily." *Historia* 22: 397–404.

Mazon, P. 1904. *Essai sur la composition des Comédies d'Aristophane*. Paris.

Meineke, A. 1839. *Fragmenta Poetarum Comoediae Antiquae*. Berlin.

Merry, W. W. 1880. *Aristophanes: The Acharnians*. Oxford.

Merry, W. W. 1893. *Aristophanes: The Wasps.* Oxford.

Meyer, H. 1933. *Hymnische Stilelemente in der frühgriechischen Dichtung.* Cologne.

Miles, R. 1986. *Ben Jonson: His Life and Work.* London.

Miller, A. M. 1982. "*Phthonos* and *Parphasis:* The Argument of *Nemean* 8.19–34." *GRBS* 23: 111–20.

Miller, H. W. 1947. "On the Parabasis of the *Thesmophoriazusae* of Aristophanes." *CP* 42: 180–81.

Miller, H. W. 1948. "Euripides' *Telephus* and the *Thesmophoriazusae* of Aristophanes." *CP* 43: 174–83.

Milobenski, E. 1964. *Der Neid in der griechischen Philosophie.* Wiesbaden.

Miralles, C., and J. Portulas. 1983. *Archilochus and the Iambic Poetry.* Rome.

Mitchell, T. 1835. *The Acharnians of Aristophanes.* London.

Montuori, M. 1966. "Socrate tra Nuvole prime e Nuvole seconde." *Accademia Nazionale di Scienze Morali e Politiche, Napoli* 77: 151–205.

Moorton, R. F. Jr. 1988. "Aristophanes on Alcibiades." *GRBS* 29: 345–59.

Moulton, C. 1981. *Aristophanic Poetry.* Göttingen.

Moutsopoulos, E. 1964. "La philosophie de la musique et le théâtre d'Aristophane." In Χάρις: Κωνσταντίνῳ Ι. Βουρβέρῃ 'Αφιέρωμα. Athens.

Muecke, F. 1977. "Playing with the Play: Theatrical Self-Consciousness in Aristophanes." *Antichthon* 11: 52–67.

Muff, C. 1872. *Ueber den Vortrag der chorischen Partieen bei Aristophanes* Halle.

Müller, A. 1863. *Aristophanis Acharnenses.* Hannover.

Müller-Strübing, H. 1873. *Aristophanes und die historische Kritik.* Leipzig.

Murphy, C. T. 1972. "Popular Comedy in Aristophanes." *AJP* 93: 169–89.

Murray, G. 1964. *Aristophanes: A Study.* 2d ed. New York.

Murray, R. D. Jr. 1958. *The Motif of Io in Aeschylus' Suppliants.* Princeton, N.J.

Naber, S. A. 1883. "De Aristophanis Nubibus." *Mnemosyne* ser. 2, 11: 161–89, 303–22.

Nagy, G. 1979. *The Best of the Achaeans.* Baltimore.

Nagy, G. 1990. *Pindar's Homer: The Lyric Possession of an Epic Past.* Baltimore.

Neil, R. A. 1901. *The Knights of Aristophanes.* Cambridge.

Nestle, W. 1936. "Die Horen des Prodikos." *Hermes* 71: 151–70.

Newiger, H.-J. 1957. *Metapher und Allegorie: Studien zu Aristophanes.* Munich.

Newiger, H.-J., ed., 1975. *Aristophanes und die alte Komödie.* Darmstadt.

Newiger, H.-J. 1980. "War and Peace in the Comedy of Aristophanes." *YCS* 26: 219–37.

Newiger, H.-J. 1983. "Gedanken zu Aristophanes' 'Vögeln.'" In C. K. Soile, ed., "'Αρετῆς μνήμη:" 'Αφιέρωμα "εἰς μνήμην" τοῦ Κωνσταντίνου Ι. Βουρβέρη. Athens.

Nicole, J. 1884. "Le poète tragique Carcinus et ses fils dans la parabase de la Paix d' Aristophane." In *Mélanges Graux.* Paris.

Norwood, G. 1930. "The *Babylonians* of Aristophanes." *CP* 25: 1–10.

Norwood, G. 1931. *Greek Comedy.* London.

Nussbaum, M. 1980. "Aristophanes and Socrates on Learning Practical Wisdom." *YCS* 26: 43–97.

Ober, J. 1989. *Mass and Elite in Democratic Athens.* Princeton, N.J.

Ober, J., and B. Strauss. 1990. "Drama, Political Rhetoric, and the Discourse of Athenian Democracy." In Winkler and Zeitlin 1990, 237–70.

Olson, E. 1968. *The Theory of Comedy*. Bloomington, Ind.

Ostwald, M. 1986. *From Popular Sovereignty to the Sovereignty of Law*. Berkeley, Calif.

Paduano, G. 1973. "La città degli Uccelli e le ambivalenze del nuovo sistema etico-politico." *SCO* 22: 115–44.

Paduano, G. 1974. *Il giudice giudicato: Le funzioni del comico nelle "Vespe" di Aristofane*. Bologna.

Paduano, G. 1982. "Le *Tesmoforiazuse*: ambiguità del fare teatro." *QUCC* 40: 103–27.

Page, D. L. 1970. *Select Papyri III: Literary Papyri*. London.

Parke, H. W. 1977. *Festivals of the Athenians*. Ithaca.

Parker, R. 1983. *Miasma: Pollution and Purification in Early Greek Religion*. Oxford.

Penniston, J. K. 1983. "Aspects of Death in Classical Comedy." Diss. University of Minnesota.

Perusino, F. 1981. "Aristofane e il *Maricante* di Eupoli." *RFIC* 109: 407–13.

Perusino, F. 1982a. "Aristofane poeta e didascolo." *Corolla Londinensis* 2: 137–45.

Perusino, F. 1982b. "Cratino, la *Kline* e la Lira: Una Metafora ambivalente nei *Cavalieri* di Aristofane." *Corolla Londinensis* 2: 147–59.

Perusino, F. 1986. *Dalla commedia antica alla commedia di mezzo: Tre studi su Aristofane*. Urbino.

Petersen, E. 1862. "Dichter und Chorlehrer." *NJbPP* 85: 649–73.

Phillipson, R. 1932. "Sokrates' Dialektik in Aristophanes' Wolken." *RhM* 81: 30–38.

Pickard-Cambridge, A. W. 1953. *The Dramatic Festivals of Athens*. Oxford.

Pickard-Cambridge, A. W. 1962. *Dithyramb, Tragedy and Comedy*. 2d ed. Oxford.

Pieters, J. T. M. F. 1946. *Cratinus: Bijdrage tot de Geschiedenis der vroeg-Attische Comedie*. Leiden.

Platnauer, M. 1949. "Three Notes on Aristophanes' *Wasps*." *CR* 63: 6–7.

Platnauer, M. 1964. *Aristophanes: Peace*. Oxford.

Pohlenz, M. 1912. "Eupolis und Aristophanes." *Hermes* 47: 314–17.

Pohlenz, M. 1952. "Aristophanes' Ritter." *Nachrichten der Akademie der Wissenschaften in Göttingen, Philologisch-historische Klasse* 95–128.

Pohlenz, M. 1953. "Nomos und Physis." *Hermes* 81: 418–38.

Pöhlmann, E. 1977. "Der Überlieferungswert der χοροῦ-Vermerke in Papyri und Handschriften." *WJA* ns 3: 69–81.

Pollard, J. R. T. 1948. "The *Birds* of Aristophanes—A Source Book for Old Beliefs." *AJP* 69: 353–76.

Poppelreuter, J. 1893. *De comoediae atticae primordiis*. Berlin.

Potter, J. M. 1968. "Old Comedy in 'Bartholomew Fair.'" *Criticism* 10: 290–99.

Pucci, P. 1960. "Saggio sulle Nuvole." *Maia* 12: 3–42, 106–29.

Pucci, P. 1987. *Odysseus Polutropos: Intertextual Readings in the Odyssey and the Iliad*. Ithaca.

Radermacher, L. 1954. *Aristophanes' "Frösche."* 2d ed. Vienna.

Raines, J. M. 1935. "Literary Criticism in the Writings of the Poets of Old Greek Comedy." Diss. Cornell University.

Ranke, K. F. 1846. *De Aristophanis Vita Commentatio.* Leipzig.

Rau, P. 1967. *Paratragodia: Untersuchungen zu einer komischen Form des Aristophanes.* Munich.

Reckford, K. J. 1967. "Aristophanes' Ever-flowing Clouds." *Emory University Quarterly* 22: 222–35.

Reckford, K. J. 1974. "Desire with Hope: Aristophanes and the Comic Catharsis." *Ramus* 3: 41–69.

Reckford, K. J. 1977. "Catharsis and Dream-Interpretation in Aristophanes' *Wasps.*" *TAPA* 107: 283–312.

Reckford, K. J. 1979. "'Let Them Eat Cakes'—Three Food Notes to Aristophanes' *Peace.*" In G. W. Bowersock et al., eds., *Arktouros: Hellenic Studies presented to Bernard M. W. Knox.* Berlin.

Reckford, K. J. 1987. *Aristophanes' Old-and-New Comedy, Vol. I: Six Essays in Perspective.* Chapel Hill, N.C.

Redard, G. 1949. *Les noms grecs en -της, -τις.* Paris.

Redfield, J. 1963. "Die 'Frösche' des Aristophanes: Komödie und Tragödie als Spiegel der Politik." *Antaios* 4: 422–39.

Redfield, J. 1990. "Drama and Community: Aristophanes and Some of His Rivals." In Winkler and Zeitlin 1990, 314–35.

Rehdantz, C. 1862. *De parabasi in Aristophanis Acharnensibus commentatio.* Magdeburg.

Reinhardt, K. 1960. *Vermächtnis der Antike.* Göttingen.

Reinhold, M. 1976. "The Generation Gap in Antiquity." In S. Bertman, ed. *The Conflict of Generations in Ancient Greece and Rome.* Amsterdam.

Rennie, W. 1909. *The Acharnians of Aristophanes.* London.

Rhodes, P. J. 1972. *The Athenian Boule.* Oxford.

Ribbeck, W. 1884. *Die Acharner des Aristophanes.* Leipzig.

Robert, C. 1922. "Aphoristische Bemerkungen zu den Ekklesiazusen des Aristophanes." *Hermes* 57: 321–56.

Robert, F. 1967. "Sur le contraste entre les *Nuées* et les *Cavaliers.*" *RÉG* 80: 160–64.

Rodríguez Alfageme, I. 1985. "Aristófanes, *Acharn.* 652–4. El poeta y Egina." *Estudios Clásicos* 89: 61–65.

Roemer, A. 1902. *Studien zu Aristophanes und den alten Erklärern derselben.* Leipzig.

Rogers, B. B. 1904. *The Thesmophoriazusae of Aristophanes.* London.

Rogers, B. B. 1910. *The Acharnians of Aristophanes.* London.

Rohdewald, W. 1854. *Ueber die Comödie des Aristophanes: der Frieden.* Detmold.

Romilly, J. de. 1973. "Gorgias et le pouvoir de la poésie." *JHS* 93: 155–62.

Rosellini, M. 1979. "*Lysistrata:* Une mise en scène de la féminité." In *Aristophane: Les femmes et la cité* (= *Cahiers de Fontenay* 17). Fontenay-aux-Roses.

Rosen, R. M. 1983. "Old Comedy and the Iambographic Tradition." Diss. Harvard University.

Rosen, R. M. 1988. *Old Comedy and the Iambographic Tradition.* Atlanta.

Rosenmeyer, T. G. 1972. "Notes on Aristophanes' *Birds.*" *AJP* 93: 223–38.

Rostagni, A. 1925–27. "I primordii di Aristofane." *RFIC* 53: 161–85, 465–93;
55: 289–330.

Roussel, P. 1951. "Étude sur le principe de l'ancienneté dans le monde hellé-
nique du Ve siècle av. J.-C. à l'époque romaine." *Mémoires de l'Institut National
de France, Académie des Inscriptions et Belles-Lettres* 43.2: 123–227.

Ruck, C. 1975. "Euripides' Mother: Vegetables and the Phallos in Aristophanes." *Arion* ns 2: 13–57.

Russo, C. F. 1962. *Aristofane, autore di teatro.* Florence.

Rusten, J. S. 1977. "*Wasps* 1360–1369: Philokleon's τωθασμός." *HSCP* 81:
157–61.

Saïd, S. 1979. "*L'Assemblée des Femmes:* Les femmes, l'économie et la politique."
In *Aristophane: Les femmes et la cité* (= *Cahiers de Fontenay* 17). Fontenay-aux-
Roses.

Ste. Croix, G. E. M. de. 1972. *The Origins of the Peloponnesian War.* Ithaca.

Sakhnenko, L. A. 1983. "Аристофан и Каллистрат." *Vestnik Drevnei Istorii* 165:
115–21.

Sandbach, F. H. 1977. *The Comic Theater of Greece and Rome.* New York.

Sartori, F. 1957. *Le Eterie nella vita politica Ateniese del VI e V secolo A. C.* Rome.

Sartori, F. 1974. "Riflessi di vita politica ateniese nelle 'Rane' di Aristofane." In
L. Barbesi, ed., *Scritti in onore di Caterina Vassalini.* Verona.

Schein, S. L. 1979. *The Iambic Trimeter in Aeschylus and Sophocles: A Study in
Metrical Form.* Leiden.

Schlegel, A. W. von. 1846. *Course of Lectures on Dramatic Art and Literature.*
Trans. J. Black. London.

Schmid, W. 1948. "Das Sokratesbild der Wolken." *Philologus* 97: 209–28.

Schopenhauer, A. 1958. *The World as Will and Representation.* Trans. E. F. J.
Payne. Indian Hills, Ky.

Schrader, H. 1877. "Kleon und Aristophanes' Babylonier." *Philologus* 36: 385–
414.

Schwandke, G. 1898. *De Aristophanis Nubibus Prioribus.* Halle.

Schwarze, J. 1971. *Die Beurteilung des Perikles durch die attische Komödie und ihre
historische und historiographische Bedeutung.* Munich.

Schwinge, E.-R. 1975. "Kritik und Komik: Gedanken zu Aristophanes' Wespen." In J. Cobet et al., eds., *Dialogos: Für Harald Patzer zum 65. Geburtstag.*
Wiesbaden.

Schwinge, E.-R. 1975. "Zur Ästhetik der Aristophanischen Komödie am Bei-
spiel der Ritter." *Maia* 27: 177–99.

Schwyzer, E., and A. Debrunner. 1966. *Griechische Grammatik.* Munich.

Scodel, R. 1980. *The Trojan Trilogy of Euripides.* Göttingen.

Scodel, R. 1987. "The Ode and Antode in the Parabasis of *Clouds.*" *CP* 82: 334–
35.

Seel, O. 1960. *Aristophanes oder Versuch über Komödie.* Stuttgart.

Segal, C. P. 1961. "The Character and Cults of Dionysus and the Unity of the
Frogs." *HSCP* 65: 207–42.

Segal, C. P. 1962. "Gorgias and the Psychology of the Logos." *HSCP* 66: 99–155.

Segal, C. P. 1969. "Aristophanes' Cloud-Chorus." *Arethusa* 2: 143–61.

Seidensticker, B. 1972. "Beziehungen zwischen den beiden Oidipusdramen des Sophokles." *Hermes* 100: 255–74.

Seidensticker, B. 1978. "Archilochus and Odysseus." *GRBS* 19: 5–22.

Seidensticker, B. 1982. *Palintonos Harmonia: Studien zu komischen Elementen in der griechischen Tragödie.* Göttingen.

Sicking, C. M. J. 1967. "Aristophanes Laetus?." In Westendorp Boerma 1967, 115–24.

Sifakis, G. M. 1971. "Aristotle, *E. N.* IV, 2, 1123a19–24, and the Comic Chorus in the Fourth Century." *AJP* 92: 410–32.

Sifakis, G. M. 1971. *Parabasis and Animal Choruses.* London.

Silk, M. 1980. "Aristophanes as a Lyric Poet." *YCS* 26: 99–151.

Simon, E. 1983. *Festivals of Attica: An Archaeological Commentary.* Madison, Wis.

Slater, N. W. 1985. *Plautus in Performance: The Theatre of the Mind.* Princeton, N.J.

Slater, W. J. 1969. "Futures in Pindar." *CQ* 19: 86–94.

Sodano, A. R. 1961. "La parodos parabatica dei 'Plutoi' di Cratino. Metrica e struttura." *Rendiconti della Accademia di Archeologia, Lettere e Belle Arti, Napoli* ns 36: 37–54.

Solomos, A. 1974. *The Living Aristophanes.* Trans. M. Felheim. Ann Arbor, Mich.

Sommerstein, A. H. 1974. "Aristophanes, *Frogs* 1463–5." *CQ* 24: 24–27.

Sommerstein, A. H. 1977a. "Aristophanes and the Events of 411." *JHS* 97: 112–26.

Sommerstein, A. H. 1977b. "Notes on Aristophanes' *Wasps.*" *CQ* 27: 261–77.

Sommerstein, A. H. 1980a. *The Comedies of Aristophanes, Vol. I: Acharnians.* Warminster.

Sommerstein, A. H. 1980b. "Notes on Aristophanes' *Knights.*" *CQ* 30: 46–56.

Sommerstein, A. H. 1981. *The Comedies of Aristophanes, Vol. II: Knights.* Warminster.

Sommerstein, A. H. 1983. *The Comedies of Aristophanes, Vol. IV: Wasps.* Warminster.

Sommerstein, A. H. 1985. *The Comedies of Aristophanes, Vol. V: Peace.* Warminster.

Sommerstein, A. H. 1986. "The Decree of Syrakosios." *CQ* 36: 101–8.

Sommerstein, A. H. 1987. *The Comedies of Aristophanes, Vol. VI: Birds.* Warminster.

Sourvinou, C. 1971. "Aristophanes, *Lysistrata* 641–647." *CQ* 21: 339–42.

Spatz, L. S. 1972. "Metrical Motifs in Aristophanes' 'Clouds.'" *QUCC* 13: 62–82.

Spencer, H. 1859–60. "The Physiology of Laughter." *Macmillan's Magazine* 1: 395–402.

Spyropoulos, E. S. 1975. "Μάγνης ὁ κωμικὸς καὶ ἡ θέση του στὴν ἱστορία τῆς ἀρχαίας ἀττικῆς κωμῳδίας." *Hellenika* 28: 247–74.

Stanford, W. B. 1963. *Aristophanes: The Frogs.* 2d ed. London.

Stanger, J. 1870. *Ueber Umarbeitung einiger Aristophanischen Komödien.* Leipzig.

Stark, R. 1953. "Sokratisches in den 'Vögeln' des Aristophanes." *RhM* 96: 77–89.

Starkie, W. J. M. 1897. *The Wasps of Aristophanes.* London.

Starkie, W. J. M. 1909. *The Acharnians of Aristophanes.* London.

Steffen, V. 1954. "De Aristophane a Cleone in ius vocato." *Eos* 57: 7–21.

Steinbrück, F. 1865. *Aristophanis Acharnensium parabasin commentario critico atque exegetico illustravit.* Stargard.

Stinton, T. C. W. 1976. "Iphigeneia and the Bears of Brauron." *CQ* 26: 11–13.

Stone, I. F. 1988. *The Trial of Socrates.* Boston.

Stone, L. M. 1981. *Costume in Aristophanic Comedy.* New York.

Stow, H. L. 1936. "The Violation of the Dramatic Illusion in the Comedies of Aristophanes." Diss. University of Chicago.

Strauss, L. 1966. *Socrates and Aristophanes.* Chicago.

Sutton, D. F. 1980. *Self and Society in Aristophanes.* Washington, D.C.

Süvern, J. W. 1835. *Essay on "The Birds" of Aristophanes.* Trans. W. R. Hamilton. London.

Süvern, J. W. 1836. *Two Essays on "The Clouds" and on "The ΓΗΡΑΣ" of Aristophanes.* Trans. W. R. Hamilton. London.

Svenbro, J. 1976. "La parole et le marbre: Aux origines de la poétique grecque." Diss. Lund University.

Sweeney, J. G. III. 1985. *Jonson and the Psychology of Public Theater.* Princeton, N.J.

Taillardat, J. 1962. *Les Images d'Aristophane.* Paris.

Taplin, O. 1983. "Tragedy and Trugedy." *CQ* 331–33.

Taplin, O. 1987. "Phallology, *Phlyakes,* Iconography and Aristophanes." *PCPS* 213: 92–104.

Taylor, A. E. 1911. *Varia Socratica.* Oxford.

Teuffel, W. 1852. "Zu Aristophanes' Wolken." *Philologus* 7: 325–53.

Thompson, W. E. 1966. "The Functions of the Emergency Coinages of the Peloponnesian War." *Mnemosyne* 19: 337–43.

Tierney, M. 1935. "The Parodos in Aristophanes' *Frogs.*" *Proceedings of the Royal Irish Academy* 42: 199–202.

Todd, O. J. 1915. "Quo modo Aristophanis rem temporalem in fabulis suis tractaverit." *HSCP* 26: 1–71.

Tomin, J. 1978. "Socratic Gymnasium in the *Clouds.*" *SO* 62: 25–32.

Torrance, R. M. 1978. *The Comic Hero.* Cambridge, Mass.

Töttössy, C. 1962. "Lysistrate and the Oligarchic Coup d' Etat." *AAntHung* 10: 273–82.

Trotzky, J. 1926. "La Parabase." In *Recueil Gébélev.* Leiningrad.

Tschiedel, H.-J. 1984. "Aristophanes und Euripides: Zu Herkunft und Absicht der Weiberkomödien." *GB* 11: 29–49.

Tucker, T. G. 1906. *The Frogs of Aristophanes.* London.

Turato, F. 1971–72. "Le leggi non scritte negli 'Uccelli' di Aristofane." *Atti e Memorie dell' Accademia Patavina di Scienze, Lettere, ed Arti* 84.3: 113–43.

Turato, F. 1972. *Il problema storico delle "Nuvole" di Aristofane.* Padua.

Untersteiner, M. 1954. *The Sophists*. Trans. K. Freeman. New York.

Ussher, R. G. 1973. *Aristophanes: Ecclesiazusae*. Oxford.

Ussher, R. G. 1977. "Old Comedy and 'Character': Some Comments." *G&R* 24: 71–79.

Vaio, J. 1971. "Aristophanes' *Wasps:* The Relevance of the Final Scenes." *GRBS* 12: 335–51.

Vaio, J. 1973. "The Manipulation of Theme and Action in Aristophanes' *Lysistrata.*" *GRBS* 14: 369–80.

van Daele, H. 1923. *Aristophane*. Paris.

van der Valk, M. 1967. "Observations in Connection with Aristophanes." In Westendorp Boerma 1967, 125–44.

van der Valk, M. 1981–82. "A Few Observations on the *Ranae* of Aristophanes." *Humanitas* 33/34: 95–126.

van Leeuwen, J. 1893. *Aristophanis Vespae*. Leiden.

van Leeuwen, J. 1896. *Aristophanis Ranae*. Leiden.

van Leeuwen, J. 1901. *Aristophanis Acharnenses*. Leiden.

van Leeuwen, J. 1904. *Aristophanis Thesmophoriazusae*. Leiden.

van Leeuwen, J. 1908. *Prolegomena ad Aristophanem*. Leiden.

van Looy, H. 1975. "Les 'Oiseaux' d'Aristophane: Essai d'interprétation." In J. Bingen et al., eds., *Le monde grec: Hommages à Claire Préaux*. Brussels.

Vickers, M. 1989. "Alcibiades on Stage: *Thesmophoriazusae* and *Helen.*" *Historia* 38: 41–65.

Vlastos, G. 1987. "Socratic Irony." *CQ* 37: 79–96.

Von der Mühll, P. 1964. "Weitere pindarische Notizen." *MH* 21: 168–72.

Walsh, G. B. 1984. *The Varieties of Enchantment*. Chapel Hill, N.C.

Welsh, D. 1983. "The Chorus of Aristophanes' *Babylonians.*" *GRBS* 24: 137–50.

Werner, J. 1969. "Aristophanische Sprachkunst in den 'Fröschen' (V. 1–30)." *Philologus* 113: 10–23.

West, M. L. 1974. *Studies in Greek Elegy and Iambus*. Berlin.

West, M. L. 1983. *The Orphic Poems*. Oxford.

West, S. 1988–. *A Commentary on Homer's Odyssey*. Oxford.

Westendorp Boerma, R. E. H., ed. 1967. *ΚΩΜΩΙΔΟΤΡΑΓΗΜΑΤΑ: Studia Aristophanea Viri Aristophanei W. J. W. Koster in Honorem*. Amsterdam.

Westlake, H. D. 1980. "The *Lysistrata* and the War." *Phoenix* 34: 38–54.

Whitman, C. H. 1964. *Aristophanes and the Comic Hero*. Cambridge, Mass.

Whitman, C. H. 1969. "ΛΗΚΥΘΙΟΝ ΑΠΩΛΕΣΕΝ." *HSCP* 73: 109–12.

Whittaker, M. 1935. "The Comic Fragments in Their Relation to the Structure of Old Attic Comedy." *CQ* 29: 181–91.

Wilamowitz-Moellendorff, U. von. 1870. *Observationes criticae in comoediam graecam selectae*. Berlin.

Wilamowitz-Moellendorff, U. von. 1880. "Von des attischen Reiches herlichkeit." *Philologische Untersuchungen* 1: 1–96.

Wilamowitz-Moellendorff, U. von. 1893. *Aristoteles und Athen*. Berlin.

Wilamowitz-Moellendorff, U. von. 1903. "Der Schluss der Ekklesiazusen des Aristophanes." *SPAW:* 450–55.

Wilamowitz-Moellendorff, U. von. 1908. "Pindars siebentes nemeisches Gedicht." *SPAW:* 328–52.

Wilamowitz-Moellendorff, U. von. 1919. "Lesefrüchte." *Hermes* 54: 54–57.

Wilamowitz-Moellendorff, U. von. 1927. *Aristophanes: Lysistrate*. Berlin.

Wilamowitz-Moellendorff, U. von. 1935. *Kleine Schriften*. Berlin.

Williams, T. 1964. "The Sausage Seller's Vision." *WS* 77: 52–60.

Wills, G. 1969. "Aeschylus' Victory in *The Frogs*." *AJP* 90: 48–57.

Wills, G. 1969. "Why Are the Frogs in the *Frogs?*." *Hermes* 97: 306–17.

Wilson, A. M. 1974. "A Eupolidean Precedent for the Rowing Scene in Aristophanes' *Frogs?*" *CQ* 24: 250–52.

Wilson, N. 1982. "Two Observations on Aristophanes' *Lysistrata*." *GRBS* 23: 157–63.

Winiarczyk, M. 1987. "Nochmals das Satyrspiel 'Sisyphos.'" *WS* 100: 35–45.

Winkler, J. J., and F. I. Zeitlin, eds. 1990. *Nothing to Do with Dionysos? Athenian Drama in Its Social Context*. Princeton, N.J.

Winterstein, A. 1984. "Contributions to the Problem of Humor." *Psychoanalytic Quarterly* 3: 303–16.

Witten, F. 1877. *De Nubium fabula ab Aristophane retractata*. Erfurt.

Wolfring, W. 1979. "Jugend- und Erziehungsprobleme bei Aristophanes." *Wiener humanistische Blätter* 21: 17–24.

Woodbury, L. 1965. "The Date and Atheism of Diagoras of Melos." *Phoenix* 19: 178–211.

Woodbury, L. 1976. "Aristophanes' *Frogs* and Athenian Literacy: *Ran.* 52–53, 1114." *TAPA* 106: 349–57.

Worthington, I. 1987. "Aristophanes' *Knights* and the Abortive Peace Proposals of 425 B.C." *AC* 56: 56–67.

Zannini Quirini, B. 1987. *Nephelokokkygia: La prospettiva mitica degli "Uccelli" di Aristofane*. Rome.

Zawadzka, I. 1964. "Τόλμα jako motyw tragiczny u Sofoklesa." *Eos* 54: 44–55.

Zeitlin, F. I. 1981. "Travesties of gender and genre in Aristophanes' *Thesmophoriazusae*." In H. P. Foley, ed., *Reflections of Women in Antiquity*. New York.

Zelle, H. A. W. 1892. *De comoediarum graecarum saeculo quinto ante Christum natum actarum temporibus definiendis*. Halle.

Zielinski, T. 1885. *Die Gliederung der altattischen Komödie*. Leipzig.

Zimmermann, B. 1984–85. *Untersuchungen zur Form und dramatischen Technik der Aristophanischen Komödie*. Königstein.

Zwerling, I. 1955. "The Favorite Joke in Diagnostic and Therapeutic Interviewing." *Psychoanalytic Quarterly* 24: 104–14.

General Index

Acharnians, 7, 11, 19–20, 22, 29–30, 32,
35, 40, 41–60, 63, 70–71, 89 n.6, 94
n.17, 95 n.22, 95 n.24, 100 n.40, 114
n.3, 117, 123–26, 136–37, 146 n.17,
148 n.23, 151 n.35, 156, 186 n.85, 187
n.87, 193–94, 195 n.108, 209 n.140,
221, 227–30, 242
Acharnians, chorus of, 7, 11, 42–47, 53–
58, 123–24, 127, 192–93, 221
Achilles, 75, 212
Aegina, 52
Aeolosicon, 24, 100 n.40
Aeschinades, 156
Aeschines, 41 n.1
Aeschylus, 25, 147 n.16, 210–18, 224;
Agamemnon, 63 n.8, 214 n.150; *Eleu-
sinioi,* 40; *Libation Bearers,* 212; *Prome-
theus Bound,* 40, 167; *Psychostasia,* 213;
Seven Against Thebes, 40, 63 n.8; *Sup-
pliants,* 40, 63 n.8
Aesop, 35 n.85, 75, 135, 150, 194
Aether, 107
Agamemnon, 36
Agathon, 31
Agon, 23, 25–26, 132, 189, 196, 224, 249
Agoracritus, 70, 72
Agroikos, 4–5 n.8
Alazōn, 2–8, 13, 15, 71, 150
Alcibiades, 159–60, 162, 177 n.55, 179,
187 n.88, 202 n.128, 208, 214–15, 244
n.7
Alcman, 26, 242
Ameipsias, 105 n.52, 160
Amphiaraus, 87 n.68, 157 n.1

Amphipolis, 148 n.23
Amynias, 138
Anagyros, 86 n.64, 105, 157 n.1, 194 n.104
Anapests. *See under* Parabasis
Anaxagoras, 85 n.58, 88
Anaximander, 166
Andocides, 160 nn.11–12, 162 n.16, 177
nn.54–55, 178 n.58
Androcles, 244
Andromeda, 185
Anthesteria, 58
Antimachus, 42
Antode. *See under* Parabasis
Aphrodite, 38
Apollo, 167
Apragmosynē, 137, 159–61, 221 n.2
Archedemus, 205, 208 n.135
Archilochus, 24 n.42, 63 n.8, 72
Arginusae, 210
Ariphrades, 84–85, 87, 138–39, 154
Aristides, 18 n.9, 200
Aristogeiton, 193
Aristomache, 198
Aristotle, 2, 4–5, 13, 23–24, 43 n.10, 44,
52 n.31, 71, 74, 146 n.16
Artemis, 84
Ascondas, 135
Assemblywomen, 34, 216, 224, 246–51
Astrateia, 82–83, 86
Athena, 81, 107, 183–84, 191
Athenaeus, 41 n.1, 74 n.34, 162 n.16
Audience, 13–15, 32 n.72, 41–42, 44–47,
73–77, 88, 94, 102, 116–18, 155–56
n.52, 219, 227–30, 248–50

Index of Passages Discussed

AESCHINES, **I.173:** 162 n.18; **3.76:** 41 n.1
AESCHYLUS
Agamemnon, **717–36:** 214 n.150; **1399:**
63 n.8
Prometheus Bound, **547–49:** 167
Seven Against Thebes, **612:** 63 n.8
Suppliant Maidens, **203:** 63 n.8
AESOP, *Vita* (Perry), **G, W:** 75 n.36
AMEIPSIAS (K), **fr. 9:** 105 n.52
ANDOCIDES, **I.15:** 160 n.11; **I.27:** 160
n.12, 177 n.54, 178 n.58; **I.35:** 162
n.16; **I.36:** 160 n.12, 178 n.58; **I.37–42:**
177 n.55; **I.43:** 160 n.12, 178 n.58;
I.44: 160 n.11; **I.49:** 160 n.11; **I.52:** 160
n.11; **I.55:** 160 n.11; **I.59:** 160 n.11;
I.63: 162 n.16; **I.65–66:** 177 n.55
ANTIPHON, **6.35:** 199 n.114; **6.50:** 199
n.114
ARCHILOCHUS (W), **fr. 5:** 72; **fr. 96.4:** 63
n.8; **fr. 252:** 72; **fr. 295(a):** 72
ARISTIDES, **49.47:** 18 n.9
ARISTOPHANES
Acharnians, **Hyp. I:** 42–43 n.7; **1–16:** 27
n.58; **5–8:** 35, 41; **9–12:** 42; **11:** 228;
13–14: 42; **15–16:** 42; **20:** 41; **63:** 2
n.2; **87:** 2 n.2; **98–125:** 52; **104:** 51;
106: 51; **109:** 2 n.2; **135:** 2 n.2; **142–
44:** 50; **237–79:** 23 n.35; **241–79:** 43;
299–302: 53 n.35; **300–301:** 34, 40,
151 n.35; **311–12:** 63; **325–57:** 187
n.87; **353–57:** 44; **369–74:** 51; **372–73:**
47; **373:** 2 n.2; **374:** 46; **377–82:** 53
n.35; **377–84:** 46, 114 n.3; **380:** 46
n.18; **410–13:** 31 n.64; **440–44:** 47;
475–78: 35, 65 n.13, 209 n.140; **485–
87:** 44; **488–89:** 63; **496–507:** 43 n.8;
496–508: 114 n.3; **497–507:** 45; **499–
500:** 44 n.15; **502:** 46 n.18; **502–7:** 53
n.35; **557–58:** 63; **558:** 63; **563:** 63;
572–625: 56, 58; **578:** 63; **595–619:**
42; **607–17:** 44; **626:** 50 n.25, 77; **626–
27:** 18; **626–64:** 47–53; **626–718:** 94
n.17; **627:** 28, 48; **628:** 95 n.22, 228–
29; **628–29:** 19; **630:** 46 n.18; **632:** 77;
633: 50 n.26, 228–29; **634:** 55; **635:**
55; **636–40:** 50 n.27; **641:** 50 n.26,
228–29; **642–43:** 51 n.30; **644–45:** 61;
645: 45; **652–655:** 20; **654:** 52 n.31,
228–29; **655:** 45; **659–62:** 53 n.36;
659–64: 19 n.11, 20, 53 n.34; **661:** 45;
664: 55; **665–66:** 21; **665–718:** 53–56;
676–91: 124; **688:** 56 n.40; **692–700:**
123; **692–702:** 21; **713–18:** 195 n. 108;
725–26: 55 n.37, 56; **729–835:** 146
n.17; **801–2:** 69 n.21; **825:** 2 n.2; **836–
59:** 56; **848–53:** 42; **880–94:** 194; **900–
58:** 55 n.37; **904–28:** 56; **971–99:** 23,
56–58; **978–87:** 21 n.26; **979–87:** 56
n.42; **983:** 2 n.2; **990–99:** 21 n.26, 56
n.42; **993:** 58 n.43; **1016:** 2 n.2; **1018–
36:** 70–71; **1028:** 71 n.26; **1059–68:**
70–71; **1071–1142:** 58; **1150:** 42;
1150–57: 229 n.10; **1154–55:** 42;
1156–61: 42; **1164–73:** 42; **1173:** 42
n.6; **1190–1227:** 58; **1198–1231:** 43;
1224–34: 58; **1227:** 58; **1228:** 58; **1231:**
58; **1233:** 58
Assemblywomen, **215:** 250; **215–28:** 216
n.155; **221–28:** 250; **303–10:** 250–51;
311–71: 101 n.43; **571–82:** 249–50;

Library of Congress Cataloging-in-Publication Data

Hubbard, Thomas K.
  The mask of comedy: Aristophanes and the intertextual parabasis /
Thomas K. Hubbard.
     p.   cm.— (Cornell studies in classical philology; v. 51)
  Includes bibliographical references and index.
  ISBN 0-8014-2564-6 (cloth)
  1. Aristophanes—Political and social views. 2. Athens (Greece)—Social conditions.
3. Literature and society—Greece. 4. Social problems in literature. 5. Drama—Chorus
(Greek drama) 6. Intertextuality. 7. Comedy. I. Title. II. Series.
PA3879.H77 1991
882'.01—dc20
                                                                        91-11953